MODERN
CURRICULUM
FOR GIFTED AND ADVANCED
ACADEMIC STUDENTS

MODERN
CURRICULUM
FOR GIFTED AND ADVANCED
ACADEMIC STUDENTS

EDITED BY
TODD KETTLER, PH.D.

A COPUBLICATION OF THE

NATIONAL ASSOCIATION FOR
Gifted Children

Routledge
Taylor & Francis Group

NEW YORK AND LONDON

Library of Congress Cataloging-in-Publication Data

Modern curriculum for gifted and advanced academic students / edited by Todd Kettler, Ph.D.
  1 online resource.
Description based on print version record and CIP data provided by publisher; resource not viewed.
ISBN 978-1-61821-474-4 (ebook) – ISBN 978-1-61821-475-1 (epub) – ISBN 978-1-61821-473-7
(pbk.)
1. Gifted children--Education--Curricula--United States. 2. Curriculum planning--United States. I.
Kettler, Todd
LC3993.9
371.95--dc23
                        2015028451

First published in 2016 by Prufrock Press Inc.

Published in 2021 by Routledge
605 Third Avenue, New York, NY 10017
2 Park Square, Milton Park, Abingdon, Oxon OX14 4RN

Routledge is an imprint of the Taylor & Francis Group, an informa business

Copyright © 2016 Taylor & Francis Group

Cover and layout design by Raquel Trevino

ISBN: 9781032144818 (hbk)
ISBN: 9781618214737 (pbk)

DOI: 10.4324/9781003236696

TABLE OF CONTENTS

SECTION 3: DEVELOPING DOMAIN EXPERTISE THROUGH RIGOROUS CURRICULUM DESIGN

BOLD VISION FOR DEVELOPING TALENT IN AN AGE OF STANDARDS

INTRODUCTION TO MODERN CURRICULUM FOR GIFTED AND ADVANCED ACADEMIC STUDENTS

TODD KETTLER

Gifted education hovers anxiously on the periphery of educational policy, practice, and priority. There are no federal mandates for gifted education programs and services. Only about half of the states at any given time have policies requiring gifted education, and in many of those, there are no evaluation and accountability mechanisms to incent quality. I have been a participant observer to this phenomenon as I spent 12 years as a director of gifted and advanced academic programs. At an administrative retreat, I once told my good friends and colleagues who were directors of language arts and mathematics that our jobs were very different. I pointed out that each day they come to work with the assumption that everyone supports curriculum and instruction efforts in language arts and mathematics. Sure, they had disagreements in the ranks, but no one questioned why students learn math, reading, and writing. I, on the other hand, dedicated half of my work to advocating to sustain existing efforts in gifted education with little time left for developing better and broader visions. Each staffing and budget meeting held the possibility of reductions to gifted education, even in a state that mandated we provide services.

Surely, the reasons for gifted education's peripheral role are complex. As a field, we do not systematically build a research base of curriculum and instructional interventions that demonstrate effectiveness as we ought to. But even that likely agreed-upon statement leads to further complexities. We debate the definitions of giftedness and suffer the consequences of inequities. We struggle to measure meaningful outcomes, and in many cases our program evaluations, if they exist at all, focus on what the adults are doing rather than how the students are achieving. Once I asked a superintendent of a very successful school district how he measured the quality of the gifted program, and in a joking manner, he replied, "The number of parent complaints." While we both laughed a little, we also knew there was a sad truth to the statement.

What is a modern curriculum for gifted and advanced academic students, and why do we need it? It seems that gifted education is searching for a curriculum identity. I make this suggestion based on the following observations and experiences. First, I believe we have taken on a parasitic role in curriculum, and this may be linked to the emergence of differentiation movements in the 1980s. Policies and practices at that time led to increasingly diverse classrooms and a reduction in ability grouping in the wake of de-tracking. Gifted education seemed to carry the torch of differentiated instruction. Many of the field's best thinkers proposed strategies and techniques on how educators of gifted students could differentiate the standard school curriculum to meet the needs of gifted learners. In spite of some evidence that differentiation was far more discussed than actually implemented, this became the primary approach of many school districts to provide gifted education services. The evolution of differentiated instruction went beyond ability-based modifications to include increasingly suspect learning-style modifications and student choices in activities. By the end of the 20th century, it seemed differentiated instruction had become the instructional approach for all students and its biggest organizational advocate was the Association for Supervision and Curriculum Development (ASCD), rather than the National Association for Gifted Children (NAGC). Perhaps the present culmination of this parasitic status is the emergence of the Common Core State Standards (CCSS). Again, gifted education's role has been to articulate how to differentiate the standards for gifted learners. While we may not be satisfied with that role, it was better than the alternative, which was to succumb to those who said the CCSS standards may have eliminated the need for gifted education at all.

Second, we seem indecisive and apprehensive about the most popular advanced academic programs to have emerged in the last two decades. I have attended multiple College Board conferences and heard the statement that the Advanced Placement (AP) program is not gifted education. I have attended multiple International Baccalaureate (IB) conferences and heard the same statement about IB. Furthermore, I have been at gifted and talented conferences and heard advocates for gifted education say the same thing—AP and IB are not gifted education. At the same time, I consult in and work with many school districts, some of which are among the most successful in their states. When I gather data on what the gifted students are doing in those middle and high schools, I find that they are for the most part participating in AP and IB programs. In a similar way, the third program that has grown tremendously is dual/concurrent enrollment in college courses. Again, many gifted education administrators claim it is not a gifted education program, but many gifted students seem to participate in early college enrollment in high schools of all sizes and locales. All three of these programs have grown tremendously in the last 20 years, and some researchers in gifted education have advocated for their merits with gifted students. However, these initiatives largely remain the purview of general education, not gifted education.

Third, reform efforts under the headings of 21st-century education have gathered significant attention in educational practice and reform movements. These include inquiry models such as Project- and Problem-Based Learning (PBL); online and blended learning models; flipped classrooms; science, technology, engineering, and mathematics (STEM) initiatives; career and technology academies; and service learning initiatives merged with the core curriculum. Again, curriculum innovation seems more likely to emerge from general education rather than gifted education in each of these areas. I recently visited a high school mathematics and science academy that required students to score above the 90th percentile on SAT for admission, and approximately 50% of the graduates were National Merit Finalists or Scholars. They described themselves as an advanced math and science program, but intentionally minimized their use of the term *gifted* when describing either their students or their curriculum. I visited another high school academy devoted to a collection of career academies including medicine, robotics, law and policy, culinary arts, and digital arts. Alhough I observed amazing career-focused achievement and advanced curriculum, gifted education or gifted students were never mentioned. These issues were not limited to high schools. In the last 3 years, I have made multiple visits to three highly successful STEM elementary schools. One of them offered the STEM program bilingually in a balance of Spanish and English. When I asked about the gifted and talented students, they described how their needs were met through the open-ended project nature of the curriculum. In fact, the GT specialist at one school said the entire program was GT curriculum and parents of GT students were eager to get their kids into the program.

Those three trends may indicate that we need to rethink gifted curriculum. How can we move beyond the limitations of differentiating core curriculum to engaging ways of developing exceptional talent in a broad spectrum of fields and disciplines? I propose that a modern approach to gifted curriculum should focus on advanced conceptual understandings. Advanced conceptual understandings form the foundation for creative thinking, critical thinking, and problem solving within and across disciplines. To a large degree, modern gifted curriculum should include an inquiry focus within a constructivist learning paradigm. The goal of gifted curriculum includes the following: (1) developing increasing independence as a learner, (2) fostering active intellectual engagement with classical and contemporary ideas and issues, and (3) developing advanced products and performances reflecting conceptual insight and complex thinking.

Additionally, we need to think about both the microcurriculum as a set of learning and assessment tasks, as well as the macrocurriculum as an advanced course of study for gifted and advanced students. This approach to macrocurriculum may yield more fruitful avenues for accommodating the purposes and values of AP, IB, and dual/concurrent enrollment options. The macro approach to gifted curriculum should explore how the goals of gifted education can effectively merge with some 21st-century models, especially STEM programs, advanced career academies, and online/blending learning opportunities. In many ways, technological innovations have opened a brave new world of opportunities for gifted education. Modern curriculum for gifted and advanced learners is not intended to offer a panacea or an ultimate solution. It is designed to further the conversation about how we make sense of giftedness, talent development, and educational innovation.

Modern Curriculum for Gifted and Advanced Academic Students is arranged in three sections moving from big ideas to the application of those ideas. The first section includes chapters to generate future-focused thinking. How do we make sense of ubiquitous technology and the capacity to access seemingly limitless information? What can we learn from the history of the idea of differentiation to help us forge a bold future for gifted education? This first section also address the foundations of two emergent paradigms that have offered alternatives to traditional ways of thinking about gifted education. Specifically, in what ways do the talent development paradigm and the differentiation paradigm inform our thinking about learning design for gifted and advanced academic students? To close the first section, we consider the nature of curriculum design in the age of standards. Most importantly, how might or should the Common Core State Standards (CCSS) and Next Generation Science

Standards (NGSS) impact innovative work in gifted education curriculum and instruction?

The second section of *Modern Curriculum for Gifted and Advanced Academic Students* explores curriculum elements necessary to focus on advanced conceptual understandings, develop independent learners, foster intellectual engagement, and create advanced products and performances reflecting conceptual insight and complexing thinking. This section includes chapters on developing critical thinking and creative thinking across all subject areas and all grade-levels. How can we design inquiry-based curriculum for gifted and advanced learners, including detailed recommendations for implementing Project-Based Learning models? What role do independent research and personalization of learning play in learning designs for gifted and advanced students? How do we define appropriate learning outcomes for advanced products and performances? Perhaps more importantly, what tools might we use to measure those outcomes systematically? Finally, what possibilities remain untapped in gifted education curriculum innovation through the use of blended learning approaches to emphasize advanced talent development and personalization?

The final section of *Modern Curriculum for Gifted and Advanced Academic Students* includes examples of how to innovate learning design in the four core curriculum areas of language arts, mathematics, science, and social studies. There are two chapters for each discipline. One chapter focuses on learning design from a talent development perspective, and one chapter focuses on learning design from a differentiation perspective. Much debate in our field has centered on these theoretical models, but in many ways, the day-to-day operations of gifted curriculum and instruction from either the talent development or differentiation approach are vaguely understood at best. These models are intended to both bring some specificity to the approaches within the modern curriculum framework and to expand our understanding of a new era of curriculum possibilities.

Each chapter includes discussion questions and implications for research. The discussion questions could be used as part of a course in gifted education curriculum and instruction or in professional learning designs in school systems. The implications for research are intended to generate ideas and possibilities for those actively engaged in gifted education research.

Ideally, *Modern Curriculum for Gifted and Advanced Academic Students* helps us think in ways that are both careful and innovative about the role of gifted education, and specifically, learning designs in gifted education. May the discourse that emerges imagine the role of leadership and advocacy, the need for specific and quality school-based intervention research, and the hope for bold visions projecting gifted education and advanced academics into a relevant and viable future. I do not believe that our communities and boards of education oppose exceptional achievement and the development of gifted students. I do believe they await a clear and consistent vision of how that could be accomplished. In what ways might our field reach in and reach out to lead a new wave of excellence that does not forsake equity? What role might gifted education play in educational reforms including, but not restricted to, school choice, magnet schools, academies, and STEM and STEAM innovations? Gifted and advanced students crave more than underground programs with periphery importance. Perhaps *Modern Curriculum for Gifted and Advanced Academic Students* helps to start that conversation.

SECTION 1

MODERN APPROACHES TO GIFTED EDUCATION CURRICULUM

CHAPTER 1

CURRICULUM DESIGN IN AN ERA OF UBIQUITOUS INFORMATION AND TECHNOLOGY
NEW POSSIBILITIES FOR GIFTED EDUCATION

TODD KETTLER

"Good gifted curriculum, where it exists, should set the standards for learning at world-class levels."—Joyce VanTassel-Baska (1994, p. 397)

I recently spoke to a group of educational administrators on the topic of leadership in gifted education. They were mostly directors and coordinators of gifted and advanced academic programs; some were assistant superintendents or chief academic officers. I posed the following question of support for gifted education programs, "How many of you enjoy almost unrestricted support for gifted education in your school districts?" Two or three hands eased into the air, but silently they retreated as hesitantly as they were raised. The gravity of unrestricted support sinks in slowly. I would have followed up with "Why not?", but I can generally predict those responses as we have voiced them as a field for years, decades even. Instead, I offered a story from my own experiences as the director of advanced academic and gifted education programs at two large school districts in Texas. I was appointed to serve on interview teams for many school positions during my school leadership work. I distinctly remember interviewing several candidates for head football coach, which falls just below the superintendent in school hierarchy in many places, and I also

DOI: 10.4324/9781003236696-2

remember interviewing a number of candidates to direct fine arts programs. In those interviews, we knew much of the information about the candidates from document review, references, and preliminary meetings. There were two distinct features of the interviews that bore the gravity of the decision making: vision and leadership. Our team wanted to be sold on a vision for excellence in athletics or fine arts, and we needed to assess whether the candidate possessed the leadership skills to make that vision a reality for the kids in our schools.

The potential coaches and fine arts directors talked about outstanding performance and achievement in their respective areas. They talked about systematic opportunities to involve as many kids as possible and train and develop those who have the desire and motivation to push toward our highest levels of performance. They talked about the benefits to the school and community when we compete for state championships and elite performance awards in the arts. They painted a vision of our most elite performers rising through the system and being sought after by the best colleges in the nation. They sold us on a world-class vision of performance and achievement in football, performance arts, and visual arts. Our selection team made our decisions, and for years, I watched the football coaches and fine arts directors garner near unrestricted support for their programs.

Then I looked my audience in the eye and asked, "When was the last time you vividly painted a picture of world-class gifted education in your school?" After a brief pause, I repeated the question, clarifying that world-class is bolder than great; it's systematically excellent. World-class changes kids lives in ways unimaginable; world-class is the conduit to dreams and genius. Then I suggested what I believe to be true. Most do not know how to paint the vision of world-class gifted education. Some in that room likely even questioned their own leadership to build such a vision into reality. I asked them why athletics and fine arts develop gifted athletes, artists, and performers with near unrestricted support, while we try to develop gifted mathematicians, scientists, and writers and often remain tangential to the entire enterprise. That is an amazingly complex, yet important, question—one whose answer, I think, involves vision, equity, and capacity. Do we as educators of the most advanced students present a clear vision of excellence, make it equitably available to all students, and demonstrate the capacity to develop elite academic performances at world-class levels?

Never did a candidate for head football coach or director of fine arts sit at the head of the interview table and explain how he or she was going to meet the needs of our athletes, artists, and performers. They did meet and even exceed the needs of many students, but need-meeting does not a bold vision make.

Did they differentiate in a way to take the best students to heights seemingly unimagined? Of course they did; the cellists who wanted to attend Julliard did not have the same practice and instruction as those seeking to make the all-state orchestra, who did not have the same instruction as those wanting to play a few songs with the holiday ensemble. But differentiated instruction does not a bold vision make; it is simply a means to an end. It is time we think boldly about gifted education and learning designs capable of turning those bold visions into viable opportunities for students.

In 1986, the National Association for Gifted Children (NAGC) published a special issue of *Gifted Child Quarterly* devoted to theory and research on curriculum in gifted education (Volume 30, Issue 4). It was arguably one of the most significant collections of scholarship on the topic of gifted education curriculum in the history of the field. Joyce VanTassel-Baska and Harry Passow served as guest editors for the special issue. Passow (1986) contributed a paper on gifted education curriculum at the secondary level, but I think the most significant ideas from that manuscript were not even specific to secondary gifted education. Passow argued that lack of a clear concept of the goals of gifted education was to blame for undermining curriculum efforts. He stated, "...curriculum planning must begin with clear goals and objectives if curricular efforts are to be meaningful. Without a clear concept of what it is we expect the gifted and talented students to achieve, what it is we want them 'to become,' our curriculum efforts will be directionless" (p. 186).

Roughly 30 years later, Passow's cautionary statements about a lack of clear goals seem as relevant as they were in 1986. Renzulli (2012) offered a similar sentiment suggesting that without theory, practices in gifted education are fragmented and loosely connected. Specifically, fragmentation undermines clarity and consistency of goals, services, and evaluation. In their articulate description of three competing paradigms in gifted education, Dai and Chen (2014) also offered compelling evidence that the field is fragmented, contested by multiple theories, and searching for direction (Ambrose, VanTassel-Baska, Coleman, & Cross, 2010). Thus, I argue that Passow was absolutely correct about the vital relationship between goals and curriculum. Without clear goals, recommendations for curriculum and learning designs are meaningless.

Bold Goals for World-Class Gifted Education

Finding statements of the goal of gifted education in the field's literature is surprisingly difficult. Subotnik, Olszewski-Kubilius, and Worrell (2011) suggested that goals in the field generally fall into two categories, self-actualization or development of eminence, and they made a talent development argument that eminence ought to be the goal of gifted education. Subotnik and Rickoff (2010) similarly made an argument for eminence as the goal of gifted education, and they suggested that curriculum in the field of gifted education actually may be discouraging pursuits of eminence as a goal. However, developing eminence as a goal of gifted education has its critics; the October 2012 issue of *Gifted Child Quarterly* (Volume 56, Issue 4) featured several critical responses to eminence as a goal for gifted education. It may be fair to characterize the field of gifted education as in a dilemma. Curriculum experts know that curriculum development without goals is problematic at best and meaningless at worst; however, the field seems mired in theoretical debates about what the goal ought to be.

There is a pragmatic axiom that asserts the meaning of a thought can be found in the actions it produces. The pragmatist is less concerned with ultimate truth of an idea and more concerned with whether the idea produces actions and habits that are judged useful or productive (e.g., Peirce, 1878/1992). Subotnik et al. (2011) hinted at the pragmatic axiom and claimed that the ". . . goal [of gifted education] is to develop the talents of children and youth at the upper ends of the distribution in all fields of endeavor to maximize those individuals' lifetime contributions to society" (p. 23). Eminence as a goal for gifted education leads to socially valuable ends (contributions to society). Furthermore, it leads to useful and productive program design and curriculum development (domain specific talent development). Eminence ought to be the grand goal of gifted education, not because we may develop eminence by the time students reach high school graduation, but because we seek to increase the number of individuals capable of achieving eminence in adulthood.

To understand an orchestrated approach to elite talent development leading to potential eminence, I have been engaged in a 3-year, ethnographic case study of an elite youth baseball program (Kettler, 2015). The baseball program works with children and youth ages 8 to 18 with the explicit goal of transitioning players to college and professional baseball. It is estimated that only 6.8% of high school baseball players will play at the college or professional level (National Collegiate Athletics Association, 2013). The baseball club has been operating for 25 years. Teams in the club have won 15 national championships and more than 150 players have received scholarships to play college baseball. Twenty-six players from the club have been drafted into professional baseball, and in 2014, both the American League and National League Cy Young award winners were alumni of the baseball club. It is a good example of systematically developing elite talent in a specific domain projecting young men on a trajectory that may lead to eminence. One goal of the study was to compare baseball talent development with the athletic talent development studies in Bloom's work (Kalinowski, 1985a, 1985b; Monsaas, 1985) and the Subotnik et al. (2011) model for talent development. Additionally, I wanted to understand the nuances of the process of developing elite talent in athletics in order to apply those principles to the work of developing mathematical talent, writing talent, or computer science talent. The following seven principles have emerged from the study (Kettler, 2015):

- » The goal of the program is clear and explicitly stated.
- » The goal of the program is bold—elite performance leading to the highest level of achievement and recognition in the domain.
- » The goal fundamentally drives the work of the teams and the players.
- » Players are required to try out to be invited to participate in the club, and even if they are accepted, participation is annual, with new tryouts each year.
- » Not all players will achieve the goal of college or professional baseball, but all are treated as though they will.
- » Achieving the goal requires discipline, commitment, and practice combined with focused instruction, mentorship, and participation on the most competitive stages in the domain.
- » To potentially achieve the goal, players prioritize work in their talent area and minimize distraction in other areas.

When we view gifted education as a talent development process, we assimilate principles of learning and design from highly successful talent development models, including athletic talent. Eminence should be the goal propelling gifted education into productive 21st-century relevance, but eminence alone is too broad. The baseball talent development program successfully prepares young men for a career trajectory that may lead to eminence, but their operational goals focused on performance by the end of high school. In order to develop world-class gifted education, we must translate the possibility of eminence into discipline specific goals that are bold, clear, and explicitly stated. These operational goals should focus on elite performances by the end of high school. For instance, learning from the baseball model, the following examples of goal statements would be influential to guide practice in a school district and research for those studying gifted education:

» The gifted STEM program develops elite talent in mathematics, science, engineering, and technology in order to place students in prestigious colleges and universities to pursue degrees and careers in STEM fields.

» The gifted writing program develops elite talent in literary and journalistic writing in order to place students in prestigious liberal arts programs to pursue degrees and careers in media and communications.

» The gifted leadership program develops elite talent in law, policy, and business in order to place students in elite colleges and universities to pursue degrees and careers in fields of business, law, and leadership.

» The gifted social sciences program develops elite talent in psychology, education, and sociology in order to place students in elite colleges and universities to pursue degrees and careers in the social science disciplines.

The pursuit of clarity does not stop with those goal statements. The next step is to establish empirical indicators to verify that students are performing at elite levels in those areas. What are the exemplars of elite performance in science and mathematics in high school, middle school, and elementary school? What external validations confirm elite writing talent in high school, middle school, and elementary school? In the baseball case study, I found that players at the high school level are very familiar with the metrics of elite performance. Position players knew how fast they needed to run, how they would be expected to demonstrate arm strength and accuracy, and how to demonstrate batting skills against the most talented pitching. Pitchers knew the velocities associated with elite performance; they knew the metrics of earned run averages, WHIP (walks and hits allowed per inning pitched), and strikeout ratios based on batters faced. The players learned these metrics because the coaches and directors of the club teach them specifically and they measure them often. What are the equivalent metrics for elite performances in social sciences, journalism, visual arts, or computer science? What are the metrics of elite performance in mathematics, biology, or business? Those are the questions schools need to ask, and the field of gifted education needs to study.

Curriculum and Learning Design
in Gifted Education

Once we establish bold goals that are both relevant and compelling, we face the daunting task of building curriculum pathways to make those attainable. Gifted education curriculum reflects the process of developing elite talent projecting toward eminent levels of adult achievement.

Designing and implementing advanced curriculum is arguably the most important task of those working in the field of gifted education (Borland, 1989; VanTassel-Baska & Brown, 2007). Gifted education is built upon the principle of individual differences, that some learners demonstrate outstanding performance or are capable of elite levels of performance compared to their peers. Moreover, these differences require modified approaches commensurate with ability and aligned with goals of superior performance (Renzulli, 2012). Models and theories of curriculum development abound in gifted education, and national standards for gifted education include standards for curriculum and instruction (National Association for Gifted Children [NAGC], 2010). In spite of the scholarship and the recommendations associated with advanced curriculum in gifted education, questions and challenges remain. The field struggles to bridge the gaps between research and practice, and gifted education often falls on or even beyond the margins of educational reform efforts both local and national. The challenge to shake images of elitism and segregation looms like a timeless albatross. In the face of these challenges, calls to rethink (Subotnik et al., 2011), reexamine (Renzulli, 2012), and go beyond gifted education (Peters, Matthews, McBee, & McCoach, 2014) highlight what has been called a fractured, porous, and contested enterprise (Ambrose et al., 2010)

There were times when innovations in curriculum and instruction oped in gifted education and later flowed into the mainstream practices eral education. Gifted education embraced critical thinking, constr and self-directed independent research in the 1950s (Passow, 1958) ative productivity and problem-based and project-based learning i (Renzulli, 1977, 1982). Curriculum and instruction to develop cr ing was widely adopted in gifted education in the 1970s and 198 1979, 1981), and creative problem solving was a staple of gifted before problem solving became a focus of 21st-century ed & Treffinger, 1985; Treffinger, 1986). Gifted education use omy to emphasize higher order thinking skills before it wa Enrichment through depth and complexity and differentia as gifted education practices before wider adoption into general education at the end of the 20th century.

Despite the field's history of innovation in curriculum theory and learning design, we might be hard pressed to assemble evidence that curriculum and instructional innovations are emerging from gifted education to influence general education today. In fact, the opposite may be true. Differentiation strategies have dominated gifted education, creating a parasitic relationship in which gifted education is seen largely as an add-on or a reaction to general education curriculum. The emergence of the Common Core State Standards and Next Generation Science Standards may be the culmination of gifted education's unintentional retreat to supporting role. Are we content for gifted education to be seen as the toolbox of differentiation strategies to modify the real curriculum, an occasional tweak here and there nebulously adding layers of rigor?

I am not advocating abandoning differentiation strategies or systemic approaches to modifying core curricula. However, I do believe we need to forge new visions of innovation in curriculum and learning design in gifted educa- . Dai and Chen (2014) painted an accurate picture of our competing para- of research and practice. Distinct differences separate the historic gifted radigm from the emerging differentiation and talent development par- These theoretical differences have significant consequences for the day- actice of gifted education including defining and identifying gifted stablishing programs and services, and developing curriculum. We ead their critique as a story of harmless intellectual divergence or as a field in search of direction and innovation.

riculum in an Age of Innovation

a vision for world-class education, Stewart (2012) argued, changing, technology is changing, and our understanding of r—but schools have remained the same" (p. 141). Some might education has similarly remained the same. To further exam- n that gifted education curriculum has largely remained the hree well-regarded texts on gifted education curriculum in Gallagher's *Teaching the Gifted Child* (2nd ed.) from 1975, ka's *Comprehensive Curriculum for Gifted Learners* (2nd une Maker and Aleene Nielson's *Curriculum Development for Gifted Learners* (2nd ed.) from 1995. These books by eminent scholars in the field provide insights into curriculum thinking roughly 40 and 20 years ago respectively.

In the textual analysis, I came across an interesting idea influencing the development of curriculum for gifted learners: "There has been the tremendous explosion of knowledge in the area of science and a new emphasis on creativity" (Gallagher, 1975, p. 74). Forty years later, one could write a textbook or journal article on the topic of gifted education curriculum beginning with the exact same sentence. Gallagher's text focused on content modifications for gifted curriculum in the four core disciplines of mathematics, science, social studies, and language arts. Gallagher further argued that knowledge is continually changing and that learning experiences for gifted students should focus on inquiry and problem solving, independent investigations, and idea production. The text offers specific examples of problem-based learning in each discipline and specific chapters on developing curriculum to include an emphasis on creativity and problem-solving strategies.

VanTassel-Baska (1994) emphasized content modifications when developing curriculum for gifted learners. She advocated close examination of the existing curriculum matched against the needs of gifted and advanced learners. VanTassel-Baska repeatedly called for serious attention to advanced content matched to appropriate instructional strategies. "We must attend to issues of world-class standards for curriculum for the gifted and the means by which those standards can be set and documented" (VanTassel-Baska, 1994, p. 13). Her curriculum text includes explanations of curriculum modifications across content, process, and product dimensions; developing scope and sequence for gifted curriculum; and conceptual units of instruction. Examples of application of these curriculum modifications are presented in specific chapters on mathematics, science, social studies, and language arts.

Maker and Nielson (1995) defended the idea that curriculum for gifted learners should be qualitatively different than the typical curriculum. Their qualitatively different curriculum was learner-centered and constructivist. Maker and Nielson focused less on content modification and more on learner-directed divergence in a fluid curriculum. They focused on curriculum complexity achieved through interdisciplinary design and teaching for thinking and feeling. Although their text included specific chapters on learning environments, content, process, and products, it did not include specific chapters on the core curriculum areas.

In many ways, curriculum thinking through the first decades of the 21st century varies little from the thinking during the final three decades of the 20th century. We have populated the gifted education landscape with curriculum models offering various interpretations on how to modify curriculum content, processes, and products (VanTassel-Baska & Brown, 2007). We still emphasize creative thinking, problem solving, inquiry, and independent learning and authentic research. What has changed is the vision for general education. Zhao (2012) described a world-class school as a "community of learners engaged in creating meaningful products located on a global campus" (p. 242). Statements like that might have described gifted education at one time, but today they characterize curriculum evolution in general education (e.g., Collins & Halverson, 2009; Fullan, 2013; Thomas & Brown, 2011).

It is a good time to think differently about curriculum in gifted education, not because our previous thinking was not sufficient. In fact, curriculum thinkers in our field have displayed remarkable vision bringing innovation to curriculum and instruction for decades. We need to think differently because we are more explicitly focusing on developing eminence and elite levels of talent in an era of ubiquitous information and technology. We need bold visions of world-class gifted education that apply principles of elite talent development to STEM, writing and communication, leadership studies, humanities, social sciences, and the arts. Modern curriculum for gifted and advanced learners may still include emphases on creativity, problem solving, inquiry, and independent research, but those are mere components supporting the development of domain-specific talents on elite trajectories.

Curriculum for Elite Talent Development

I recently interviewed an exceptionally talented high school student who plans to study biochemical engineering upon graduation. She told me that her favorite subject is chemistry, and she looks forward to a career in that area. I replied that she must have taken a number of courses in chemistry, and she looked puzzled. She said, "I've only taken one chemistry course." I replied that I supposed she had been doing some independent research in chemistry-related topics. Again, she looked puzzled: "No, I have not done any independent research in chemistry." "Why not?" I asked, "Isn't it your favorite subject in which you aspire to pursue a highly technical career?" She replied that it is her passion, and she wished she had more time to study it. I suggested that time is a constant and how each of us spends time is a matter of priority, and I asked where her time is being allocated if it is not to her primary area of interest. She said she spends all of her time studying for Advanced Placement (AP) courses in English and U.S. History. At this point, I looked puzzled. I asked why she had made those choices. She said her school only offered one chemistry course, and gifted students were expected to take AP courses in English and social studies.

In 3 years of the ethnographic case study of elite talent development in baseball, I had never encountered a baseball player who lamented that he had been advised to take some time off of baseball to take part in some sports in which he had little talent and less interest. In fact, the opposite was true. Those athletes had given up most if not all other pursuits in order to focus on developing their talents in baseball. The high school student I was interviewing had participated in a typical high school gifted education program. She took honors classes with modified curriculum in all core curriculum areas. She was mildly accelerated in mathematics and completed a total of six AP courses and examinations. However, her curriculum did not suggest a trajectory toward elite talent development.

Contrast her experience to the opportunities at another high school with which I have worked (Innovative High School) that looked at gifted education differently. This large high school offered 23 AP courses and an International Baccalaureate Diploma Programme. It had an extensive partnership with a local college articulating more than 90 college courses that could be taken concurrently by advanced high school students. Perhaps most importantly, this high school had options for creating focused areas of study through flexible schedules and credit acquisition. All students had the option to take mastery exams throughout the year to accelerate with credit-by-exam policies. The school had also developed an approved list of online course vendors through which students could earn high school credits in all core curriculum areas. Students at Innovative High could earn up to 10 of the required 24 high school credits though online courses, and the school offered schedule release time for students who were taking online courses.

The gifted student with a passion for chemistry at Innovative High School could take language arts and social studies courses online and complete them in less than half of the time required in traditional face-to-face courses. She could take honors chemistry as a freshman, followed by AP Chemistry as a sophomore. Then during her junior and senior year, she could take four college-level chemistry courses through the articulated agreement with the local college. Specifically, they had approved college-level Introduction to Chemistry I and II followed by Organic Chemistry I and II. These options would easily be part of the student's schedule because she could have completed her graduation requirements in social studies by the end of her second year in high school using online courses approved by Innovative High School. Additionally, at

Innovative High School, the student could select an elective known as scientific research, in which she would have a faculty mentor work with her on developing authentic research projects to be entered in regional, state, and national science fairs. At Innovative High School, these options for advanced specialization exist for chemistry, biology, physics, mathematics, literature, writing, and social studies. They also had specialized career field options for advanced students in computer science and health sciences.

The second high school in this comparison approaches gifted education as a process of elite talent development in the age of technology. Technology is used to leverage time and compact curriculum. Acceleration has traditionally been thought of as something one does only in a field of strength or interest. Innovative High School used acceleration in curriculum areas in which the student was not particularly interested. This compacting of the course requirements in some areas allowed for focused and intensive study in an area of interest. Using the recommendations for bold goals made above, Innovative High School adopted a goal of preparing elite levels of STEM talent in order place students in prestigious colleges and universities to pursue STEM careers. Students completing two high school courses and four college courses in biology, chemistry, physics, mathematics, or programming are exceptionally prepared in those areas compared to even the gifted high school student who took one or perhaps two courses in a subject in high school, even if the curriculum had been enriched for gifted or advanced learners.

Technology and widely available information should be seen as game-changers for developing elite talents and exceptional students. The example above included relatively simple technologies associated with online courses from third parties. Many universities offer online learning opportunities, open courseware, and MOOCs (Massive Open Online Courses). One of the most prominent reasons for resistance to acceleration in areas of strength has been lack of courses available. Schools every year hold students back from needed acceleration because the students will run out of courses before the senior year. That problem has been absolutely erased with the technologies associated with online learning. Acceleration, flexible schedules, and customized learning pathways ought to take center stage in developing elite levels of talent.

Curriculum Innovations

Curriculum can be understood on four different levels (see Table 1.1). At the macro level, curriculum is the required course of study—specific courses

TABLE 1.1

Four Levels of Curriculum

Level	Description
Curriculum as Course of Study	» Sequence of required courses such as graduation plans (e.g., four math credits, four language arts credits, four science credits, etc.) » Available courses of study to supplement or replace the required courses of study (e.g., AP courses, dual enrollment college courses)
Curriculum as Standards	» Scope and sequences of learning outcomes in specific disciplines » Common Core State Standards for Mathematics and English/Language Arts » State standards in multiple disciplines » College Board or International Baccalaureate standards and learning outcomes
Curriculum as Learning Design	» Learning experiences developed by teachers as a way to teach standards and achieve specified outcomes » Units of study developed by schools or school district curriculum writers » Commercially available units of study (e.g., William & Mary Units, Engineering Is Elementary, etc.) » Influenced by models of curriculum (e.g., Integrated Curriculum Model, Enrichment Triad Model, Understanding by Design)
Curriculum as Authentic Engagement	» Participation in authentic tasks in extracurricular areas » Participation in authentic tasks in cocurricular areas, courses designed for authentic engagement or independent study » Learning with a mentor, tutor, or expert in a field of study

that students must take. This includes graduation requirements, although in some cases graduation requirements include menus of course options. At the micro level, curriculum is learning design. Learning design includes the lesson plans of teachers, curriculum units developed by curriculum writing teams, any commercially purchased curriculum, and adaptations to commercially purchased curriculum. Most curriculum models and differentiation strategies apply to the learning design level of curriculum (e.g., depth and complexity, differentiation menus, curriculum compacting, enrichment opportunities). The bridge between the macro, course of study, curriculum and the micro, learning design, curriculum, is the middle level: curriculum as standards and learning outcomes. Standards and learning outcomes provide tangible guidance to increase the consistency and specificity of learning design. Government bodies, including state boards of education, generally develop and adopt standards and learning outcomes to which schools in those jurisdictions adhere. The fourth level of curriculum is the curriculum of authentic engagement. Authentic engagement includes planned experiences in which the student learns from tutors, mentors, and experts in the field. Authentic engagement may include participation in communities of other students developing elite talent, and these communities may be face-to-face or virtual. Previous studies have documented that these experiences have played a role in talent development historically (Lubinski & Benbow, 2006; Olszewski-Kubilius, 1998; Sternberg, 2001; Subotnik et al., 2011), and conceiving of authentic engagement as a facet of curriculum makes the school more accountable for facilitating the opportunities.

Curriculum for elite talent development requires that we intentionally modify and align the curriculum at each of the four levels to help students achieve the domain-specific metrics of elite performances. At the course of study level, we modify the curriculum so that students focus on developing talent with minimal distractions. We seek ways to leverage technology to compact curriculum as well as to provide advanced learning opportunities. At the standards level, we employ techniques of differentiation to modify students' learning experiences to match areas of strength and focus. Beginning with Common Core State Standards, Next Generation Science Standards, or even state-specific standards, we seek to add depth and complexity, rigorous thinking, and advanced product/performance expectations. At the learning design level, we focus on inquiry learning and problem-based and project-based designs. We design learning to emphasize domain-specific emphases on creative thinking, critical thinking, and innovation. We employ those curriculum models in our field that have demonstrated evidence of effectiveness at building expertise and achieving advanced outcomes. We design units of instruction to include independent studies and authentic research.

The following recommendations are intended to guide our curriculum thinking toward bold visions and world-class outcomes:

- » Start with explicit goals defining elite levels of performance in the domains in which gifted education applies.
- » Identify the metrics that will be measured regularly as indicators of elite levels of student achievement in the domains in which gifted education applies.
- » Modify curriculum at all four levels to craft customized, domain-specific opportunities for students to achieve at elite levels.
- » Embrace information and technology as tools that redefine our capacity to develop elite talents and place students on trajectories of excellence and potential eminence.

Moving Past Fracture and Contest

Talent development is not mysterious. In fact, we have decades of evidence on how it develops and which factors matter most in the process. Historically, we may have acted as though talent development is largely limited to what occurs outside of school. Although it is true that out-of-school opportunities have played important roles in the process, it is also true that we should be seeking greater overlap between school and those opportunities. Collins and Halverson (2009) predicted, "As learning moves out of school, our conception of learning will begin to broaden, and we will see more hybrid experiences that begin in the classroom and move into other contexts" (p. 129). Therefore, our conception of learning must broaden, and the curriculum of gifted education ought to systematically incorporate all we know about developing talent in mathematics, science, social studies, language arts, humanities, and the arts. Collins and Halverson also warned that if we keep imposing outdated conceptions of learning and curriculum in schools, ". . . technologies will leech critical learning resources, such as student motivation, attention, and resources out of the educational system" (p. 131). World-class gifted education should not be limited to talent development centers and elite academies like the Indiana Academy for Science, Mathematics, and Humanities or the Texas Academy of Math and Science. Equity alone demands that we think bigger, and changing conceptions of curriculum and opportunity are the vehicles to drive this innovation.

In their concluding remarks regarding the fractured, porous, and contested nature of the field, Ambrose et al. (2010) suggested that gifted education may never attain the unity that sounds so alluring. They encourage broad analyses of the field seeking to find and develop a few productive frameworks and selectively abandon others. Perhaps we abandon the idea that a curriculum for gifted students exists. Although the idea has ambitious appeal, it may be better replaced with conceptions of curriculum connected to specific purposes. Let us imagine curriculum for developing elite mathematical talent, elite science talent, or elite writing talent. Let us imagine a humanities approach to curriculum that does not seek to develop a narrow talent at all, but rather to nurture wisdom, morality, and virtue. Harry Passow (1986) warned that without a clear conception of the goal for gifted education, curriculum efforts would be meaningless. Experience tells us that Passow statement was and is true.

Implications for Research

As we innovate curriculum and learning opportunities, so too must we focus systematic inquiry into these efforts. For starters, we need more research on the appropriate domain-specific metrics characterizing elite performances. As I learned in the study of baseball talent development, the metrics are clearly established in the domain and the students and the coaches/teachers absolutely know what those metrics include. How might we study STEM talent development so that we can clearly articulate metrics for high school performances in those fields of study? How might we clearly communicate to the aspiring writer what elite writing performance looks like in late adolescence? Without clear goals or viable measures of performance, it becomes difficult to coax students into the required levels of motivation, discipline, and practice needed to achieve at elite levels.

Talent development in specific domains may be very nuanced and subtle, making it difficult or impossible to study with large control group studies. We need well-designed case studies with transparent methodologies and valid analytics to study the processes of talent development in young people. What types of learning experiences are helpful at building a romance or love for a discipline? Which environments or communities of learning support and sustain uncommon commitment and long-term motivation? How can we design learning experiences that will help students identify areas of intense interest that may inform postsecondary education and career choices?

We also need research on administrative arrangements conducive to talent development. For instance, how can schools develop policies to flexibly award credits and modify the timelines to speed up some learning while extending other learning? How can schools systematically embrace technologies associated with open courseware, MOOCs, and informal online learning communities as valid aspects of talent development and the course of study curriculum? We currently have students who learn to develop apps for mobile devices through YouTube videos and free online mini-courses, but the school cannot award them credit. At the same time, other students complete the curriculum for electives in computer science without successfully developing or publishing any software, and they do earn credits. Learning has already moved out of school, but our policies for awarding credit are well behind the innovations in learning. It is a good time to think differently or find ourselves increasingly obsolete in the area of advanced learning technologies.

Discussion Questions

1. Why is it so difficult to find agreement on the goals of gifted education?
2. What would you expect to be included in world-class gifted education?
3. In what ways will technology and information change the way we think about curriculum in gifted education and advanced academics?
4. How might the emphasis on standards both help and also hinder gifted education curriculum developers?
5. How has the emphasis on differentiation impacted approaches to developing advanced curriculum for talent development?

References

Ambrose, D., VanTassel-Baska, J., Coleman, L. J., & Cross, T. L. (2010). Unified, insular, firmly policed, or fractured, porous, contested, gifted education? *Journal for the Education of the Gifted, 33*, 453–478.

Borland, J. H. (1989). *Planning and implementing programs for the gifted.* New York, NY: Teachers College Press.

Collins, A., & Halverson, R. (2009). *Rethinking education in the age of technology: The digital revolution in America.* New York, NY: Teachers College Press.

Dai, D. Y., & Chen, F. (2014). *Paradigms of gifted education: A guide to theory-based, practice-focused research.* Waco, TX: Prufrock Press.

Fullan, M. (2013). *Stratosphere: Integrating technology, pedagogy, and change knowledge.* Toronto, Ontario, Canada: Pearson.

Gallagher, J. J. (1975). *Teaching the gifted child* (2nd ed.). Boston, MA: Allyn & Bacon.

Isaksen, S., & Treffinger, D. J. (1985). *Creative problem solving: The basic course.* Buffalo, NY: Bearly Limited.

Kalinowski, A. G. (1985a). The development of Olympic swimmers. In B. S. Bloom (Ed.), *Developing talent in young people* (pp. 139–192), New York, NY: Ballantine Books.

Kalinowski, A. G. (1985b). One Olympic swimmer. In B. S. Bloom (Ed.), *Developing talent in young people* (pp. 193–210), New York, NY: Ballantine Books.

Kettler, T. (2015). [Developing athletic talent: A case study in elite baseball]. Unpublished raw data.

Lubinski, D., & Benbow, C. P. (2006). Study of mathematically precocious youth after 35 years: Uncovering antecedents for the development of math-science expertise. *Perspectives on Psychological Science, 1,* 316–345.

Maker, C. J., & Nielson, A. B. (1995). *Curriculum development and teaching strategies for gifted learners* (2nd ed.). Austin, TX: Pro-Ed Publisher.

Monsaas, J. A. (1985). Learning to be a world-class tennis player. In B. S. Bloom (Ed.), *Developing talent in young people* (pp. 211–269), New York, NY: Ballantine Books.

National Association for Gifted Children. (2010). *NAGC pre-K–grade 12 gifted programming Standards: A blueprint for quality gifted education programs.* Retrieved from http://www.nagc.org/sites/default/files/standards/K-12%20programming%20standards.pdf

National Collegiate Athletics Association. (2013). *Estimated probability of competing in athletics beyond the high school interscholastic level.* Retrieved from https://www.ncaa.org/sites/default/files/Probability-of-going-pro-methodology_Update2013.pdf

Olszewski-Kubilius, P. (1998). Research evidence regarding the validity and effects of talent search educational programs. *Journal of Secondary Gifted Education, 9,* 106–114.

Passow, A. H. (1958). Enrichment of education for the gifted. In N. B. Henry (Ed.), *Education for the gifted* (pp. 193–221). Chicago, IL: University of Chicago Press.

Passow, A. H. (1986). Curriculum for the gifted and talented at the secondary level. *Gifted Child Quarterly, 30,* 186–191. doi:10.1177/001698628603000409

Peirce, C. S. (1878/1992). How to make our ideas clear. In N. Houser & C. Kloesel (Eds.), *The essential Peirce* (Vol. 1, pp. 124–141). Bloomington IN: Indiana University Press.

Peters, S. J., Matthews, M. S., McBee, M. T., & McCoach, D. B. (2014). *Beyond gifted education: Designing and implementing advanced academic programs.* Waco, TX: Prufrock Press.

Renzulli, J. S. (1977). *The enrichment triad model: A guide for developing defensible programs for the gifted and talented.* Mansfield Center, CT: Creative Learning Press.

Renzulli, J. S. (1982). What makes a problem real: Stalking the illusive meaning of qualitative differences in gifted education. *Gifted Child Quarterly, 26,* 147–156. doi:10.1177/001698628202600401

Renzulli, J. S. (2012). Reexamining the role of gifted education and talent development for the 21st century: A four-part theoretical approach. *Gifted Child Quarterly, 56,* 150–159. doi:10.1177/0016986212444901

Stewart, V. (2012). *A world-class education: Learning from international models of excellence and innovation.* Alexandria, VA: Association for Supervision and Curriculum Development.

Sternberg, R. J. (2001). Giftedness as developing expertise: A theory of the interface between high abilities and achieved knowledge. *High Ability Studies, 12,* 159–179. doi:10.1080/13598130120084311

Subotnik, R. F., & Rickoff, R. (2010). Should eminence based on outstanding innovation be the goal of gifted education and talent development? Implications for policy and research. *Learning and Individual Differences, 20,* 358–364. doi:10.1016/j.lindif.2009.12.005

Subotnik, R. F., Olszewski-Kubilius, P., & Worrell, F. C. (2011). Rethinking giftedness and gifted education: A proposed direction forward based on psychological science. *Psychological Science in the Public Interest, 12*(1), 3–54. doi:10.1177/1529100611418056

Thomas, D., & Brown, J. S. (2011). *A new culture of learning: Cultivating the imagination for world of constant change.* Lexington, KY: CreateSpace.

Torrance, E. P. (1979). An instructional model for enhancing incubation. *Journal of Creative Behavior, 13,* 23–35.

Torrance, E. P. (1981). Predicting the creativity of elementary school children (1958–80) and the teacher who "made a difference." *Gifted Child Quarterly, 25,* 55–62.

Treffinger, D. J. (1986). Research on creativity. *Gifted Child Quarterly, 30,* 15–19.

VanTassel-Baska, J. (1994). *Comprehensive curriculum for gifted learners* (2nd ed.). Boston, MA: Allyn & Bacon.

VanTassel-Baska, J., & Brown, E. F. (2007). Toward best practice: An analysis of the efficacy of curriculum models in gifted education. *Gifted Child Quarterly, 51,* 342–358. doi:10.1177/0016986207306323

Zhao, Y. (2012). *World class learners: Educating creative and entrepreneurial students.* Thousand Oaks, CA: Corwin.

CHAPTER 2

DIFFERENTIATED CURRICULUM
LEARNING FROM THE PAST AND EXPLORING THE FUTURE

JENNIFER L. JOLLY

". . . it is by no means improbable that the educational methods best adapted to gifted children will be found to have wide applicability in the training of all children. Normal pedagogy has certainly benefited from the pedagogy of defectives; it has far more to learn from the pedagogy of the gifted." (Terman, 1924, p. viii)

Over the past several decades, *differentiation* has become part of the lexicon of mainstream education and has also been identified as the panacea to meet the learning needs of the majority of American school children. A concept initially introduced by the gifted education community more than 50 years ago, school districts across the country now promote the practice in their vision statements or as part of their districtwide instructional practices. For example, Oakland Unified School District (n.d.) promotes that, "Our teachers are focused on meeting every student exactly where s/he is at and moving each child forward through a repertoire of differentiated learning" (n.d., para. 2), while St. Louis Public Schools (2013) advances to its teaching core that, "The St. Louis Public Schools has identified differentiation as the instructional core. Differentiation is customized instruction based on the students' needs" (p. 3).

DOI: 10.4324/9781003236696-3

These statements serve as evidence of the varied interpretations regarding the practice of differentiation from what gifted education intended as a curricular intervention for gifted learners. These versions are exacerbated by the failure to understand the original tenets of the practice and their intention. Yet, there exists an expectation that teachers will be skilled implementers of the practice, and that all children will benefit equally from this type of specialized instruction—even in the face of limited empirical support and uneven operationalization. With the annexation of differentiation from gifted education by the larger education community, what does the practice mean for gifted and advanced learners, especially when implementation is often in name only (Westberg, Archambault, Dobyns, & Salvin, 1993).

This chapter explores how curriculum has moved from different to differentiated in attempting to meet the learning needs of gifted students in both heterogeneous and homogenous classroom environments. This includes the various interpretations and operationalizations of differentiation and the subsequent impact and consequences for gifted learners.

Qualitatively Different Education

As the formalized study of gifted learners was established, curriculum considerations became a natural point of research, inquiry, and practice. Until the early part of the 20th century, acceleration or the grouping of learners by ability was the most commonly practiced curricular adjustment made for advanced learners. However, these practices were not widespread or systematically implemented (Jolly, 2004). As the field evolved and gifted children were studied in laboratory school settings, curricular changes in addition to acceleration were applied and analyzed. Initial research settings grouped gifted children homogenously, which differed from the common organization of gifted students in schools who were typically educated in regular education classrooms. Lulu Stedman in California and Leta Hollingworth in New York focused on moving away from the typical teaching methods that dominated classrooms in the early 20th century, such as drill and recitation and providing a more individualized approach to learning that better matched students' abilities. These investigations were the first empirical studies regarding the curricular needs of gifted learners (Hollingworth, 1926; Jolly, 2004; Stedman, 1924).

Lulu Stedman

Lulu Stedman, who could best be described in today's vernacular as an assistant professor of professional practice, carried out her investigations at the University of California, Southern Branch (present-day UCLA) in the early decades of the 20th century. Her tenure also overlapped with Lewis Terman's brief tenure at Southern Branch and one could only assume he influenced her interest in gifted students (Jolly, 2006; Terman, 1930). He would later serve as editor of Stedman's *Education of Gifted Children* (Stedman, 1924).

In *Education of Gifted Children*, Stedman (1924) began to explore the idea of individualized and flexible instruction for gifted learners. She noted, "To plan any but a flexible curriculum for gifted curriculum for gifted children would be analogous to putting a saddle and bridle on Pegasus" (p. 11). She described a structure that incorporated both individual instruction and group discussion and "regardless of interest or ability, each individual, whether working alone or in a group, must have his own assignment" (p. 9). Stedman also advocated for each student being able to move through the curriculum at his or her own pace so that "no time is squandered through children waiting for slower members of the class" (p. 10). Assignments were to be problem-based rather than focused on drill and memorization and to consist of research components, and each student was to be assigned individual study plans tailored to his or her learning needs. Recitation was completely discarded in the "opportunity rooms" that Stedman organized. Opportunity rooms were precursors to today's self-contained classrooms where gifted students are grouped homogeneously. Class discussion of individual projects was also encouraged in order for students to clarify their own thinking and to challenge the thinking of their classmates. She also felt that, "Much of the drill, explanation, and development necessary in teaching average children can be eliminated from the course of study for gifted children" (p. 11), which could free up time to move on to more "abstract material and complicated problems" (p. 11), which resemble elements of contemporary curriculum compacting methods.

Stedman (1924) supported the use of acceleration but also valued the implementation of "qualitative enrichment" (p. 11). She provided 19 distinct examples of how this enrichment might be achieved—some of which resemble current differentiation practices. A sampling of these include (a) a reduction in time spent on certain subjects in comparison to average students, (b) the decrease or total elimination of drill and recitation, (c) the development of independently study skills, and (d) the flexible grouping of children based on ability and/or interest (Stedman, 1924).

Leta Hollingworth

As a professor of educational psychology at Teachers College, Leta Hollingworth conducted her research in New York City public schools during the 1920s and 1930s. Her initial work with gifted children at P.S. 165 laid the groundwork for what would become *Gifted Children: Their Nature and Nurture*, the first widely regarded textbook about gifted children. Hollingworth also used "opportunity rooms" to provide special classes for gifted children. Rather than treat gifted children as a homogeneous group, she further distinguished among gifted children based on ranges of IQ scores—one class made up of children with IQs above 155 and the other of IQs between 134 and 155 (Jolly, 2004). Curriculum would be based on the learning needs commensurate with these ranges.

She advocated for an adjustment in the rate and depth of gifted children's learning and a balance between acceleration and enrichment. Hollingworth's experimental classrooms, like Stedman's, would also be devoid of recitation. She advocated for project-based learning and wanted to capitalize on the "incidental learning" that naturally occurred when gifted children went beyond the curriculum led by their natural curiosity (Hollingworth, 1926, p. 309). Hollingworth's "Evolution of Common Things" curriculum developed at Speyer School/P.S. 500 focused on student-centered, problem-based activities that were developed with the teacher acting as a facilitator of learning rather than the leader and provider of information and learning activities (Klein, 2002).

What each of these researchers proposed and practiced was markedly different in what and how children were taught in the early part of the 20th century. Curriculum and instruction was child-centered—matched to children's academic needs rather than children having to regulate themselves to narrow and rigid curricula and instructional strategies monopolized by the teacher.

Administrative Arrangements

For a substantial part of the 1940s and 1950s, limited progress was made in the field of gifted education. Other priorities overshadowed what little work was being done on behalf of gifted children. Administrative arrangements including special schools, independent study, out-of-school programs, and special in-school programs were narrowly explored as ways to meet the needs of gifted learners (Robins, 2010). Acceleration continued to be instituted but qualitatively different practices for gifted children were restricted (Robins, 2010). In some instances, nontraditional approaches such as learning contracts and flexible grouping were initiated. Considered a form of acceleration, contracts were limited to a finite period of time, allowing students to work "at their own rate" (Krueger, Allen, Ebeling, & Roberts, 1951, p. 264). The content included in the contract expanded upon skills or content already being taught in class and allowed the gifted students to move beyond their peers. However, teachers expressed concerns regarding the basic preparation of the contract materials,

> Contracts must be continually revised to fit changing content and the changing needs of different groups. The actual typing, mimeographing . . . is expensive and time consuming, perhaps, in some instances, out of proportion to the values to be achieved . . . . most important of all is the motivation of each student's endeavor to carry out his own purposes and achieve worthy outcomes; he will not do so through contract assignments, prepared and assigned by adults. (Krueger et al., 1951, p. 264)

Flexible grouping was another strategy proposed to address the varying ability levels of learners in American classrooms. Carleton Washburne, the longtime superintendent of the Winnetka School System just outside of Chicago, IL, described flexible grouping, which allowed each child to progress at his or her own rate in subjects such as mathematics or reading. This grouping still focused on a common curriculum for the entire class regardless of ability, "Arithmetic will inevitably come in—those who can solve the harder problems that come up in connection with a discussion or a project will do; the simpler problems will be solved by the ones on the earlier steps of the ladder" (Washburne, 1953, p. 147). Despite these attempts to provide gifted learners a different type of learning experience that took their advanced learning rates into account, special provisions were capricious at best.

Different Transitions to Differentiation

The launch of the Soviet Union's Sputnik I in 1957 and subsequent passage of the United States' National Defense Education Act of 1958 refocused an interest on the learning needs of gifted students and, with that, the revitalization of the field of gifted education (Jolly, 2009). A reconceptualization of what gifted children would need to study and why soon became the focal point for scholars, hoping to eventually influence practitioners. The concept of differentiated curricula was to become part of a larger compilation of services and programming for gifted learners.

The teaching efforts of mid-20th century American teachers found many focused on students of average ability or those who were in the middle range with few allowances for those students who were behind or ahead of the set curriculum (Hartman, 2008). What researchers and educators knew about gifted children was not being reflected in the models or strategies of teaching (Ward, 1961). Ward (1961) noted, "We appear to be more sufficient in knowledge about the gifted person than in the knowledge of the nature of instructional processes appropriate to the qualities, which distinguished him from the generality of his fellows" (p. 533).

Ward (1961, 1980) envisioned both individualized instruction and modifying curriculum in conjunction with acceleration and at the time the ever increasingly popular Advanced Placement Program as ways to meet the learning needs of gifted students. He also proposed including practices that should be deliberate and match the behavioral characteristics of gifted children, which distinguished them from other children (Ward, 1961). He outlined criteria that distinguished gifted students from traditional students. These criteria included: (a) greater capacity for learning, (b) greater capacity for thought, (c) motivation or drive, and (d) broad rather than narrow understanding or skills. Furthermore, he queried how these criteria or factors impacted the educative process. Ward referred to this as "a differential theory of education or of educational experience" (Ward, 1961, p. 534). Previous research also indicated that these childhood differences carried over into adulthood and subsequent careers that included leadership roles and social responsibility. Curriculum for the gifted in schools would need to reflect these behavioral differences and prepare students for their future roles in society. Ward offered,

> that an adequate theory integrate (a) a conception of pedagogical and curricular processes, (b) a view of the cultural content available for educational purposes and how proper selections can be made from it, and (c) an understanding of the perceptual, conceptual, and rational capacities of the intellectually superior as a special group. (1961, p. 535)

Intended for use with gifted students in homogeneous settings, Ward had the opportunity to implement his model of "differential education" at the Governor's School of North Carolina, a summer residential program, which opened in 1963 to approximately 400 gifted high school students (Ward, 1979). However, Ward intended these axiomatic ideas for use with gifted students in homogenous settings, never as a nostrum to meet the learning needs of all students (Gubbins, 1994).

The Proliferation of Differentiation

The Marland Report (Marland, 1972) provided the first federal definition of giftedness, which included a declaration about the type of schooling that was required: "these are children who require differentiated education programs and/or services beyond those normally provided by the regular school program in order to recognize their contribution to society and self" (p. 2). The report did not explicate the details of what these differentiated education programs would entail, but nonetheless the language included suggests that gifted children required something beyond the average. Similar to Ward, other gifted educators suggested that a differentiated education would demand a complex compendium of services. Harry Passow and Abe Tannenbaum (1978) described a systematic approach to educating gifted and talented children,

> A differentiated curriculum for gifted and talented must be considered in the context of a comprehensive program for such students. A definition of the gifted and talented provides direction for the selection and use of identification and for the design of educational opportunities or curriculum. Identification is related to curriculum and instruction both in terms of diagnosing the particular needs of a student population, in indicating necessary learning objectives and contributing to curricular differentiation. All of the elements of a comprehensive program are interrelated. (p. 14)

After the release of the *Marland Report* and successive federal and state funding, a number of models and frameworks for gifted programming propagated that included differentiated curriculum and instruction as keystones to meet the needs of gifted learners. Two representative examples include the work of Sandra Kaplan and Abe Tannenbaum.

Kaplan (1975) identified a number of methods to differentiate activities for gifted students. These included (a) accelerated content, (b) more complex content, (c) exploration of content beyond the normal curriculum, (d) curriculum choices based on student interest, (e) investigation of abstract concepts, (f) availability and use of multiple and varied advanced-level resources, (g) allowances for extended time for greater depth in learning, (h) problem solving or new ideas, (i) compacting of lesson stages to account for faster learning rates, (j) opportunities to generate new ideas or problem solve, (k) connection of knowledge and skills across disciplines, and (l) cultivation of higher-level research skills. Kaplan continued to emphasize the connection between how a student exhibited his or her giftedness and the curriculum and instruction provided (Passow & Tannenbaum, 1978).

The Tannenbaum Model for Differentiating Education for the Gifted built off the core subjects taught in school with content and process adjustments. These included telescoping, expansion of basic skills, programming changes by augmenting the curriculum "laterally," out-of-school opportunities for students to interact with experts in fields in which they had special affinity or interest, social-emotional adjustments, and adjustments to the cognitive processes (Passow & Tannenbaum, 1978, p. 31).

Both of these examples focused on amplifying, enhancing, and extending the regular curricula based on the learning needs of gifted children. The agreement or parallel nature between how a student was gifted and the type of curriculum and programming provided was the key to both of these models.

Differentiation Gone Awry

The momentum and progress afforded by the Marland Report and subsequent funding was stalled in part by the Educational Consolidation and Improvement Act (ECIA). The ECIA allowed states to decide how to disperse federal aid (New York State Department of Education, 2006). In many instances, services for gifted children were eliminated altogether or collapsed into the regular classroom. Specialized services (e.g., pull-out programs or self-contained classrooms) and the instruction and curricula provided in these environments would now be the expectation of regular classroom teachers. In theory, a differentiated education would be offered in the regular classroom and is often described by adapting the curriculum through changing product, process, or content to meet learners' needs. This appeared to be a cost-effective measure rather than abandoning their learning needs altogether (Hertberg-Davis, 2009). However, this arrangement proved deleterious for gifted students' learning needs. Few curricular or instructional modifications were made for gifted learners in regular classrooms (Archambault et al., 1993; Westberg et al., 1993).

Eventually differentiation lost its signature "elements which distinguish[ed] it from being suitable for education" for gifted and talented children (Kaplan, 1975, p. 100), and moved to being a strategy ascribed to all children (Kaplan, 2007). Differentiation has been diluted and overpromised as a strategy by mainstream education to serve all students in regular classrooms (Kaplan, 2007). Competing notions as to what differentiation is and is not have also exacerbated the situation. The National Association for Gifted Children (2014) described contemporary differentiated learning experiences as (a) the design and/or selection of curriculum; (b) the selection and use of instructional practices, including grouping strategies, varied resources, and variations to the pacing of instruction; and (c) the assessment of learning, all of which rely on assessment evidence demonstrating learner differences (para 1).

Additional obstacles to the fidelity of the implementation of differentiation both curricular and instructional include an absence of rigorous professional development, the lack of preservice instruction that includes differential education, and the absence of support for teachers by school administrators for the implementation of differentiated curriculum and instruction (Center for Talented Development, 2006; Tomlinson, 2014).

Recent educational climates have also invoked mixed messages. These environments have relied heavily on prescribed and scripted curriculum and high-stakes testing, which run counter to differentiation. The era of No Child Left Behind has been a particularly low point for gifted children. Teachers focused their efforts on struggling learners and those students who had already evidenced mastery of the curriculum were not provided any differentiated curriculum and left to fend for themselves (Jolly & Makel, 2010).

A new juncture for differentiation has begun with the introduction of the Common Core State Standards (CCSS) in 2011–2012 and full implementation of the standards expected by 2015–2016 from participating states. The differentiation of curriculum and instruction applied to these new standards appears necessary. Kaplan (2011) has suggested that, "new considerations of what differentiation is and what differentiation is not will be needed when the new standards are fully implemented" (p. 60).

Conclusion

Nearly a century of research and practice has informed a consensus regarding gifted learners' requirements for a qualitatively different learning experience. Much of what is practiced today in the field of gifted education has foundations in the prior work done by the earlier pioneers in the field and these early curricular adjustments have remained or have vestiges in the way differentiation is practiced today. The concept of differentiation introduced by Ward in the 1960s has been reinvented to meet the learning needs of all students. Finn (2012) noted, this "false belief . . . would magically enable every teacher to succeed with every kid in a mixed classroom" (para. 3). This reinvention has been to the detriment of gifted students. The nuances and specialized practice of differentiating content and skills in concert with students' abilities, interest, and aptitude have failed to translate to high-quality learning experiences for gifted learners. Instead a reductionist rendition of differentiation has emerged that sometimes consists of presenting a series of activities for students to choose from a predetermined menu far removed from a curriculum matched to the behaviors exhibited by gifted students that Ward and Kaplan describe in their work. Perhaps differentiation finds itself at a crossroads in need of yet another reconceptualization, which would be guided by a larger corpus of evidence to support its use, greater fidelity of development and implementation, and stronger support for use in schools.

Future of Differentiation

The hyperbole surrounding contemporary differentiation, which promises elixir-like qualities in terms of meeting the needs of all students, has instead failed to meet the needs of the very students differentiation had been developed to meet—the gifted. Should gifted education reclaim differentiation or abandon the practice altogether for a reconceptualized pedagogy and curriculum for the gifted? As gifted students continue to spend the majority of their school days in regular education classrooms, identifying ways to meet their academic and social and emotional needs continues to challenge educators. What is apparent is that differentiation has not proven to be the panacea to this educational dilemma (Finn, 2012).

Implications for Research

The research on differentiation is underdeveloped, especially for a practice that is so widely discussed and promoted in schools. First and foremost, there is little understanding of the impact differentiation has on student achievement and academic growth. In fact, some of the common differentiated practices such as menus of activities and student choice likely result in negligible or no academic effects. Additional points of inquiry include barriers to differentiation, teachers' understanding of differentiation, and administrators' support of differentiation in schools. At present, most of the studies examining differentiated practice have been conducted in elementary school settings. We know even less about differentiated curriculum and instruction at secondary levels. Lastly, if the field of gifted education does indeed look for a new pedagogy and curriculum for gifted, what are those possibilities and how do they account for the deficiencies of the differentiated curriculum approach?

Discussion Question

1. How would you characterize the changing of differentiation over time?
2. What are some of the most powerful barriers that prevent differentiated practices from being effectively implemented?
3. Imagine if you rank-ordered various types of differentiated practices from the least disruptive to the most disruptive, what would that ranked list look like? Furthermore, is there a relationship between how disruptive the practice is and how effective it is in terms of student achievement growth?
4. Which seems to be a more fruitful path, solving the barriers preventing effective differentiation or establishing a new approach to pedagogy and curriculum for gifted education?

References

Archambault, F. X., Westberg, K. L., Brown, S., Hallmark, B. W., Zhang, W., & Emmons, C. L. (1993). Classroom practices used with gifted third and fourth grade students. *Journal for the Education of the Gifted, 16,* 103–119.

Center for Talent Development. (2006). *Differentiation in the classroom.* Retrieved from http://www.ctd.northwestern.edu/resources/display/ Article/?id=134&pf=1

Gubbins, E. J. (1994). *When "differentiated" becomes disconnected from curriculum.* Retrieved from http://www.gifted.uconn.edu/nrcgt/newsletter/ winter94/wintr941.html

Finn, C. E. (2012). Gifted students have 'special needs' too. *The Atlantic.* Retrieved from http://www.theatlantic.com/national/archive/2012/12/ gifted-students-have-special-needs-too/266544/

Hartman, A. (2008). *Education and the Cold War: The battle for the American school.* New York, NY: Palgrave Macmillan.

Hertberg-Davis, H. (2009). Myth 7: Differentiation in the regular classroom is equivalent to gifted programs and is sufficient: Classroom teachers have the time, the skill, and the will to differentiate adequately. *Gifted Child Quarterly, 53,* 251–253.

Hollingworth, L. S. (1926). *Gifted children: Their nature and nurture.* New York, NY: The Macmillan Company.

Jolly, J. L. (2004). *A conceptual history of gifted education: 1910–1940.* Retrieved from ProQuest Database. (3136863)

Jolly, J. L. (2006). Lulu Stedman's contributions to gifted education. *Gifted Child Today, 29*(1), 49–53.

Jolly, J. L. (2009). A resuscitation of gifted education. *American Educational History Journal, 36*(1), 37–52.

Jolly, J. L., & Makel, M. (2010). No Child Left Behind: The inadvertent costs for high-achieving and gifted students. *Childhood Education, 87,* 35–40.

Kaplan, S. N. (1975). *Providing programs for the gifted and talented: A handbook.* Reston, VA: The Council for Exceptional Children.

Kaplan, S. N. (2007). Differentiation: Asset or liability for gifted education? *Gifted Child Today, 30*(3), 23–24.

Kaplan, S. N. (2011). Differentiating the differentiated curriculum. *Gifted Child Today, 34*(3), 59–60.

Klein, A. G. (2002). *A forgotten voice: A biography of Leta Stetter Hollingworth.* Scottsdale, AZ: Great Potential Press.

Krueger, L., Allen, W. P., Ebeling, E., & Roberts, R. H. (1951). Administrative problems in educating gifted children. In P. Witty (Ed.), *The gifted child* (pp. 257–266). Boston, MA: D.C. Heath and Company.

Marland, S. P., Jr. (1972). *Education of the gifted and talented: Report to the Congress of the United States by the U.S. Commissioner of Education and background papers submitted to the U.S. Office of Education.* Washington, DC: U.S. Government Printing Office.

National Association for Gifted Children. (2014). *Differentiation of curriculum and instruction: Position paper.* Retrieved from http://www.nagc.org/sites/default/files/Position%20Statement/Differentiating%20Curriculum%20and%20Instruction.pdf

New York State Education Department. (2006). *Federal education policy and the states, 1945–2009: A brief synopsis.* Albany, NY: Author.

Oakland Unified School District. (n.d.). *Context and vision.* Retrieved from http://siteplan.ousd.k12.ca.us/SitePlanVision.aspx?SelectedYear=2013&SiteCode=106

Passow, A. H., & Tannenbaum, A. J. (1978). *Differentiated curriculum for the gifted and talented: A conceptual model.* Rockville, MD: Office of Projects for the Gifted and Talented Montgomery County Public Schools.

Robins, J. H. (2010). *An explanatory history of gifted education: 1940–1960.* Retrieved from ProQuest Database. (3407826)

Stedman, L. M. (1924). *Education of gifted children.* Yonders-on-Hudson, NY: World Book Co.

St. Louis Public Schools. (2013). *District-wide professional development.* Retrieved from http://www.slps.org/cms/lib03/MO01001157/Centricity/Domain/343/August%206-7%20District-PD%202013%20%202014.pdf

Terman, L. M. (1924). Editor's introduction. For *Education of gifted children.* Yonkers-on-Hudson, NY: World Book Co.

Terman, L. M. (1930). Autobiography of Lewis M. Terman. In C. Murchison (Ed.), *History of psychology in autobiography* (Vol. 2, pp. 293–331). Worcester, MA: Clark University Press.

Tomlinson, C. A. (2014). Differentiated instruction. In J. A. Plucker & C. M. Callahan (Eds.), *Critical issues and practices in gifted education: What the research says* (2nd ed., pp. 197–210). Waco, TX: Prufrock Press.

Ward, V. S. (1961). The function of theory in program for the gifted. *Teacher College Record, 62,* 532–539.

Ward, V. S. (1979). Governor's School of North Carolina. In A. H. Passow (Ed.). *The gifted and the talented: Their education and development.* The sev-

enty-eighth Yearbook of the National Society for the Study of Education (pp. 209–217). Chicago, IL: The University of Chicago Press.

Ward, V. S. (1980). *Differential education for the gifted.* Ventura, CA: Ventura Country Superintendent of Schools Office.

Washburne, C. W. (1953). Adjusting the program to the child. *Educational Leadership, 11,* 138–147.

Westberg, K. L., Archambault, F. X., Dobyns, S. M., & Salvin, T. J. (1993). The classroom practices observation study. *The Journal for the Education of the Gifted, 15,* 120–146.

CHAPTER 3

IMPLICATIONS OF THE TALENT DEVELOPMENT FRAMEWORK FOR CURRICULUM DESIGN

PAULA OLSZEWSKI-KUBILIUS
AND ERIC CALVERT

Talent development as a framework for understanding giftedness and advancing gifted education services has gained momentum fueled in part by recent publications, discussions (Dai, 2010, 2011; Dai & Chen, 2014; Subotnik, Olszewski-Kubilius, & Worrell, 2011), and dissatisfaction with the efficacy and sustainability of traditional approaches in contemporary schools.

However, the basic tenets underlying the talent development framework are not new and were apparent in the writings of many distinguished individuals in gifted education in the late 1980s and 1990s including Don Treffinger, John Feldhusen, Carolyn Callahan, Joe Renzulli, and others (see Schroth, Collins, & Treffinger 2011). These leaders in the field wanted the focus of gifted education more on "recognizing and nurturing students' talents than on identifying and labeling children as 'gifted'" (Schroth et al., 2011, p. 39). Collectively, these early views on talent development advocated for a broader conception of intelligence and ability beyond IQ, a recognition of the role of noncognitive traits in exceptional achievement, and a greater focus on serving a broader range of gifted students with varied program models and services—especially underidentified students who are socioeconomically disadvantaged.

DOI: 10.4324/9781003236696-4

Talent development is gaining traction because it is consistent with research from psychology (Subotnik et al., 2011) on the development of intelligence and abilities, specifically the importance of domain specific abilities and the malleability of intelligence (Dweck, 2012; Ericsson, Nandagopal, & Roring, 2005). Talent development is also consistent with research on the effect of noncognitive and psychological factors on school achievement (Farrington et al., 2012) and research on the factors that influence the attainment of eminence within specific domains of talent (Subotnik et al., 2011). Talent development is attractive to practitioners because it puts a greater focus on the development of emergent talent and potential, which offers more opportunity and direction within gifted education to address the needs of a wider range of children, especially low-income and culturally and linguistically diverse gifted students.

Finally, the talent development framework is compatible with networked views of learning (e.g., Siemens, 2005), problem solving, and creativity. These perspectives acknowledge that factors extrinsic to the individual can powerfully limit or extend ability (Clark, 2008), and that problem solving and creative production in practice are often activities of organizations or communities rather than individuals acting in isolation. If, ultimately, creative and productive activity occur in contexts, not vacuums, then learning and talent development must be viewed as contextualized activities (Barab & Plucker, 2002). Thus, important goals in a curriculum focused on talent development include developing an individual's capacity to recognize affordances in natural, social, and technological environments that may multiply individual abilities, and to skillfully and ethically engage with (and add value to) these extended cognitive resources.

Critical Features of the Talent Development Framework and the Implications for Curriculum

Greater Focus on Domain-Specific Abilities

In the traditional gifted child framework, high general intellectual ability defines giftedness, usually in the form of high scores on IQ tests or other cognitive ability tests. In the talent development framework, general ability is considered foundational to the development of more specific, domain-relevant abilities such as mathematical, verbal, or spatial abilities (Olszewski-Kubilius

& Thomson, 2015; Subotnik et al., 2011). Research supports the importance and predictive validity of domain-specific abilities for achievement. Studies have shown, for example, that verbal versus quantitative tilt in abilities (i.e., high scores on tests of verbal versus mathematical reasoning ability) in middle school students is related to differences in domains of adult accomplishment. Typically, verbal tilt increases the probability of accomplishments in the humanities and quantitative tilt increases the probability of accomplishments in science, technology, engineering, and mathematics (STEM) fields (Park, Lubinski, & Benbow 2007; Wai, Lubinski, & Benbow, 2009). Not only do domain specific abilities matter, but the *pattern* of abilities is useful in determining future educational and career paths for students. For example, high mathematical ability along with high spatial ability is associated with success in STEM fields, particularly engineering and physics (Wai, Lubinski, & Benbow, 2009). From the talent development perspective, general ability is a better indicator of talent and academic potential in young children and in the early stages of talent development; however, domain-specific academic abilities become increasingly important as abilities naturally differentiate with development, particularly by middle and high school.

Curricular implications of a focus on domain-specific abilities include: (1) greater tolerance for early specialization among gifted children, (2) greater tolerance for unevenness in achievement across academic domains rather than a focus on well-rounded academic development, and (3) deliberate focus on integrating learning experiences that provide opportunities for students to connect with and learn the cultures and technologies of communities and fields outside the school that can further develop their talents and provide potential pathways to adult achievement.

It should be noted that, within the field of gifted education, the talent development approach is often framed and critiqued as an alternative to traditional models of gifted education. However, in the broader educational context, it may also be viewed as a challenger to the current dominant paradigm in American education reform that implicitly assumes the best path for improving educational outcomes across the board involves increasing efforts to diagnose and remediate deficits. Although the focus of talent development in the gifted education context is to create pathways to potential eminence in a talent domain, the talent development model is philosophically compatible with emerging alternatives to the dominant deficit remediation paradigm. This includes asset-based instruction approaches advocated by some school leaders and scholars focused on low-income populations (Paek, 2008) and strength-based approaches to improving learning outcomes for at-risk students (Maton,

Schellenbach, Leadbetter, & Solarz, 2004) and students with disabilities (Montgomery County Public Schools, 2004). This philosophical concordance presents a new opportunity for gifted educators embracing the talent development model (particularly in culturally and economically diverse schools) to build coalitions with educators and advocates who have historically been indifferent or hostile to traditional gifted education programs. These bridges to other educators will help to ensure the sustainability of talent development programs that are more compatible and consonant with the culture of the school or district.

Giftedness as Developmental and Domain-Specific Trajectories

In the traditional gifted child approach, exceptional ability and/or high intelligence are viewed as all-or-none traits of an individual—you have it or you don't (Dai, 2010; Dai & Chen, 2014). In the talent development perspective, ability is viewed as malleable and changing over time. In its earliest form, typically in very young children, talent is best described as potential for future achievement. As children develop and grow—and with nurturance, opportunity, effort, study, and practice—potential is further developed into competence and expertise that is increasingly demonstrated in exceptional levels of achievement and high motivation for a field or domain. The last stage of talent development, typically achieved in adulthood, is creative productivity, artistry, and/or even eminence (Olszewski-Kubilius & Thomson, 2015; Subotnik et al., 2011).

Children can vary in the timing or their progress through these stages as a result of the presence or absence of opportunities and poverty. For example, some children start school having had considerable exposure to books, music, math, and science. They are ready to start with an advanced curriculum and accelerated placement in school. Other students, particularly those from poverty, may have exceptional learning potential that is not obvious or demonstrated through above grade-level knowledge or achievement because of a lack of early stimulation and exposure. These children can benefit from early enriched instruction and curricula to both nurture and obviate their potential, followed by subsequent opportunities to access high-level courses and/or accelerated placements (Olszewski-Kubilius & Thomson, 2015).

Because of its emphasis on domain-specific abilities, the talent development framework acknowledges that various academic fields have unique trajectories (Subotnik et al., 2011). For example, some academic domains, like mathematics, lend themselves to early precocity and children can begin formal study at the start of school or even earlier. Other areas, such as psychology or history, require a longer period of building foundational knowledge and skills, including analytical writing and critical reading, such that serious study can only begin much later, for example, at secondary school or college (Olszewski-Kubilius & Thomson, 2015; Subotnik et al. 2011). Of course, access to certain subjects is controlled by the structure of current schooling, which typically and unnecessarily limits students' access to subjects like philosophy or engineering until college. These unique trajectories influence when identification should occur and when programming might begin for different academic subjects.

Deliberate Cultivation of Noncognitive and Psychosocial Skills Related to Domains

Psychosocial skills are those that enable a person to deliberately, ethically, and productively marshal environmental, social, and technological resources in the service of one's goals. Under the talent development framework, psychosocial skills are considered essential to the fruition of ability and potential into creative productivity in adulthood—as critical and necessary as cognitive skills. Additionally, these are viewed as skills that can be learned and coached, with particular skills being more important at particular stages of talent development and perhaps also for different fields of study and practice (Olszewski-Kubilius, 2015).

Research has shown that growth mindsets and psychosocial skills, such as self-regulation and selecting self-efficacious behaviors, become increasingly critical determiners of whether students can progress to higher levels of talent development and that these skills can be taught and developed by teachers and other adults (Subotnik et al., 2011; Subotnik, Pillmeier, & Jarvin, 2009). However, the particular psychosocial skills that need attention and cultivation vary with the stage of talent development. For example, growth mindsets that emphasize the role of effort and practice to achievement, and teachability, which involves being open to instruction and feedback, are critical when children are learning the foundational techniques and knowledge of their talent field. However, independent thinking, confidence to challenge and question instructors, and knowing one's strengths and weaknesses becomes important when individuals are move advanced in their fields (Subotnik & Jarvin, 2005). The talent development framework emphasizes the deliberate cultivation of psychosocial skills that support high achievement, rather than leaving these to chance.

Gifted education specialists and others can help children acquire these psychosocial skills by building their development into programming and curricula and their interactions with students (Farrington et al., 2012). For example, teachers can make sure they convey, through their verbal messages to children and feedback on projects and assignments, the importance of effort, study, and practice, as well as ability. Dweck (2008) made some recommendations for the kinds of praise that promote malleable, as opposed to fixed, mindsets in children. Educators can provide opportunities for children to take intellectual risks, such as projects that are difficult and require them to work on the edges of their current competency level, or ones that allow them to put novel ideas forward in a supportive context. Educators can provide emotional support to gifted children at critical transition points, such as when they move to more challenging and competitive academic environments, and assist parents in learning how to support their child at home during these times. It is also key that educators model resiliency and strategies for coping productively with perceived failures, setbacks, and threats to self-esteem and confidence (Olszewski-Kubilius & Thomson, 2015).

As in traditional gifted education models, the talent development framework encourages gifted educators to create curricula involving the use of biographies, films, or successful adults from the community to discuss the potential stresses and strains of giftedness such as peer rejection, isolation, feeling different, or even bullying (Hébert, 2009). Educating other school personnel about the psychological aspects of giftedness and enlisting the aid of school psychologists and social workers to work with gifted children who are being victimized, are extremely isolated, or suffer from debilitating anxiety, shyness, or perfectionism are other necessary strategies (Olszewski-Kubilius & Thomson, 2015).

However, the talent development framework challenges traditional thinking about affective curricula just as it challenges a deficit-focused approach to curriculum design and school improvement. The framework encourages educators and researchers to explore adaptations of approaches drawn from positive psychology and performance psychology. Gifted educators and school leaders may also find that pedagogy and coaching techniques used by athletic coaches, bandleaders, and theater instructors can be adapted and applied in other contexts. Academic talent development research mirrors sports performance psychology in recognizing that the ability to engage in ongoing deliberate practice in low-stakes situations and the ability to self-regulate mental focus and emotional arousal in high-stakes situations are critical for long-term success and peak performance. Explicitly drawing these connections for students and teaching concepts (e.g., mindfulness) that are transferrable across multiple talent domains (e.g., athletics, music, and academics) may be effective strategies for increasing academic achievement and improving performance in other areas.

Learning and Creative Development Occur Inside and Outside of School

The development of academic talent requires early programming including both enrichment and accelerative opportunities. From the talent development perspective, the nature of the opportunities offered should be matched to the domain of talent and the stage of talent development (Olszewski-Kubilius & Thomson, 2015). In order to capture late bloomers, the provision of these opportunities should be dependent on a child's level of developed talent rather than chronological age or grade. Early exposure through enrichment is important for young children to bring out and develop potential and interest. Enrichment, faster-paced instruction, and all forms of acceleration are important for children who are developing skills and acquiring knowledge within their talent areas and are ready to move ahead at a faster pace. Special programs for older students should enable them to do work that mirrors the actual activities of professionals within the field, have significant interactions with adult professionals, and through these gain some initial exposure to the norms and culture of the talent field (Olszewski-Kubilius, 2015; Olszewski-Kubilius & Thomson, 2015).

Because the nature of talent changes over time, optimal programming must also. For younger children, enrichment that exposes them to varied domains of talent and is challenging will ferret out interests and passion and cultivate motivation, as well as help parents and educators discern emerging abilities. For elementary and middle school children, programming that focuses on developing content knowledge and technique through all forms of acceleration and enrichment, thereby extending and deepening students' understanding of a subject area or domain, is appropriate. Early entrance to school, fast-paced classes, subject or grade acceleration, enrichment classes and clubs, contests, and competitions are all options at this stage (Olszewski-Kubilius & Thomson, 2015).

Secondary students require programming that continues skill development through advanced courses such as Advanced Placement (AP) and International Baccalaureate (IB); however, they also need opportunities to pursue special interests through independent projects, especially if these can focus on more authentic work in a domain alongside adult professionals. Enrichment at this stage could include exposing students earlier to some subject areas that are typically not studied until college such as sociology, philosophy, or engineering and to different types of careers and professional paths (Olszewski-Kubilius & Thomson, 2015).

Other program options include internships and mentorships focused on conducting research or real-world applications within a field. At all stages of talent development, in-school opportunities should be combined with outside-of-school programs offered through community-based organizations, universities, or cultural institutions. Schools may also offer some of these through extracurricular programs and opportunities, but educators can also help by directing gifted students and their families to other outside-of-school and supplemental opportunities. Research has indicated that participation in a high and varied dose of precollege educational STEM activities both inside and outside-of-school is related to a higher rate of notable STEM accomplishments in adulthood (Wai, Lubinski, Benbow, & Steiger, 2010).

It is critical that programming for gifted and talented learners be in place continuously from kindergarten through high school and beyond. Currently, research shows that there are significant gaps in programming in most school districts (National Association for Gifted Children & Council of State Directors of Programs for the Gifted, 2011). Gifted programming might be available in some subject areas only (typically mathematics or language arts) or only at a few grade levels. Formal gifted programming rarely begins in the early primary grades, thereby missing many important years to cultivate talent and ability in younger children and prepare low-income children for later advanced coursework. Similarly, programming for secondary gifted students often consists only of AP or IB classes when a much richer diet of opportunities is needed for talent development (Olszewski-Kubilius & Thomson, 2015). One of the implications of the talent development framework is that teachers with deeper content expertise and mentors will be needed, especially at the secondary level where the curriculum should include a broader range of courses, as well as more advanced and cross-disciplinary content. This may require employing individuals with advanced degrees or significant professional experience in the domain as instructors or pairing them with classroom teachers to codesign curricula and provide coaching and guidance on professional paths and careers to students.

Not only do talent domains have unique trajectories, so do gifted children. Although talent development programs capitalize on the motivation and interest that students demonstrate, they can engender and cultivate these as well. Some children enter school already having had a great deal of exposure to varied talent domains by parents, extended family members, and through participation in district and community programs. They are ready to move ahead with instruction focused on further skill and knowledge acquisition. Other children, particularly low-income children, start school having had fewer opportunities to learn and ability and interest that is less evident and less developed. Schools, districts, and specifically gifted specialists need to see their roles as crafting talent-developing opportunities for all students that match their particular stages of development. This can consist of all types of enrichment programs for students whose talents, motivation, and interests are just emerging while simultaneously having accelerative programs for students with ability that is already demonstrated in high achievement and motivation (Olszewski-Kubilius & Thomson, 2015). Table 3.1 describes a framework for a talent development curriculum scope and sequence.

Technology Plays a Growing Role in Talent Development

The talent development framework recognizes that formal learning, or learning that takes place through experiences with designed curriculum, represents only a subset of all learning. Particularly for students with intense interests in a topic or domain, self-directed learning can, and typically does, play a powerful role in the talent development process. In the Internet era, this is particularly true when high interest is coupled with access to a facility with relevant technology tools.

Much attention has been given to the use of the Internet by adolescents and young adults for social purposes. Recent research on the behavior of youth online has found that most students also engage in learning and behavior focused on talent development online. For example, research conducted as part of the Digital Youth Project (Ito et al., 2012) found that although the vast majority of students participate in online social networks for friendship-driven purposes, many also engage in online interest-driven networking to connect with others in their talent domains. Further, the authors suggested that the opportunity to lurk at the fringes of a community of people with greater expertise plays a valuable role in allowing novices who may lack local mentors to learn about the culture, vocabulary, and structure of a domain. Finally, the authors described a level of online engagement they termed "geeking out," in which Internet users are not merely consuming media related to their interests,

TABLE 3.1

Talent Development Across Grade Bands

Early Grades	Middle Grades	High School and Transition to Adulthood
Students are afforded opportunities for exploration.	Enrichment begins to shift focus from breadth to depth within students' areas of interest and strength, but opportunities to explore new domains continue.	Enrichment focuses on providing opportunities for advanced learning in areas of strength and interest.
Enrichment focuses on exposing students to a variety of topics, domains, and experiences.	Cocurricular, extracurricular, and community-based experiences related to the talent domain tap into rising importance of social interaction, begin to build experience learning outside the home and school.	Cocurricular, extracurricular, community-based, and informal learning are high priorities.
Cultivating positive risk-taking, intrepidness, and social skills are important goals.		Opportunities for career exploration, including extended authentic learning experiences, are core components of the curriculum.
Students who show early indicators of ability and interest around a topic or domain are afforded opportunities for deeper exploration.	Students receive early exposure to higher education and career opportunities in the talent domain.	Long-range academic planning is a core component of the curriculum.
Exposing students to authentic vocabulary in these fields is a priority.		Capacity for self-directed learning is cultivated through significant online learning experiences and guided independent study.
Capacity for self-directed learning is cultivated through center-based learning and choice-based differentiation.	Student capacity for self-directed learning is cultivated through short-term project-based and problem-based learning.	Facilitating students' early entry into domains of talent is a top priority, especially for students from populations underrepresented in those domains.
		Students are explicitly taught how to navigate cultures of fields related to their domains and are supported in building networks of peers and mentors.

but are actively sharing their own work, engaging in cycles of peer-to-peer feedback, and, in some cases, engaging in creative collaboration.

Given the obvious potential of the Web as a platform for developing talent, while open-ended, self-directed learning is, by nature, not designed, schools can play a vital role in supporting this behavior and equipping students with the skills required to connect with online communities that can support the development of their talents safely, ethically, and effectively. Core technology skills and multimedia and transmedia literacy are becoming essential for all students. However, gifted students, particularly those with specialized interests or abilities that exceed those of local peers, can particularly benefit from opportunities to connect with communities of peers, mentors, and critics with common interests in online communities. Therefore, curricula focused on developing technology and media literacies should be differentiated for gifted students emphasizing knowledge, skills, and behaviors required to successfully enter, participate in, and benefit from online communities and audiences related to their talent areas.

Formal learning experiences in more structured online environments can also play valuable roles in talent development. First, because online classes can potentially draw students from a much larger pool than can neighborhood schools, they offer potential for bringing together critical masses of students with highly specialized interests. When properly designed to take advantage of the affordances of the online format, courses can be more individualized and differentiated than is often possible in traditional school settings (Thomson, 2010). Although many students participating in online gifted education programs do so on their own outside of a traditional school, a growing number of schools, especially those with limited local course offerings, are recognizing the potential of online programs to expand options for their gifted students (Setzer & Lewis, 2005). This trend is particularly strong among rural schools and high-poverty schools, which more frequently cite providing opportunities for students to accelerate as an important reason for offering distance education courses to local students (Queen & Lewis, 2011).

Fully realizing the potential of online learning to support talent development may require educational institutions to adopt more flexible thinking with respect to policies governing use of social media, filtering of online content, and approaches to teaching online safety. Responsible parents and educators are right to consider the safety and privacy of students. However, school leaders and educators must consider the opportunity cost of any restrictions they impose on students and school networks with respect to online activity, balancing potential risks against potential opportunities and benefits. Although many schools pay lip service to the idea of digital citizenship, instruction in this area often focuses almost exclusively on preventing undesirable behaviors such as bullying and plagiarism. Fundamentally, citizenship is not just about complying with laws and norms, but active participation and contribution. One goal of education focused on talent development is to develop students' ability to engage in creative productivity and leadership; thus, educators should explore ways to leverage the Web to provide spaces for students to share their work with increasingly wider and more authentic audiences (Ito et al., 2013). Additionally, educators can help students create peer and mentor networks that can support the development of their talent, particularly through key transitions from primary to secondary education and from college to career entry. Additionally, structural changes may be needed for schools to take advantage of the potential of online learning to support more differentiated instruction and flexible pacing. For example, the National Educational Technology Plan (U.S. Department of Education, 2010) calls for reconsidering structures and practices deeply entrenched in formal K–12 education such as rigid age-based grouping, lockstep curriculum pacing, and seat-time based credit. Structural changes that increase access to optimally challenging and engaging curricula and increase opportunities for students to form connections with peers, collaborators, and mentors would likely be conducive to talent development.

Goal of Gifted Education Is Creative Productivity in Adulthood

A key distinction between the traditional gifted child approach and the talent development framework is the intended outcome or goal of gifted programming. In the gifted child approach, providing educational programs that are a better match to students' learning abilities is the immediate goal, and the long-term goal is often unspecified. Also, short- and long-term outcomes vary greatly by school or district or type of program model employed (Dai, 2010).

In the talent development framework, the immediate goal is to help children acquire both the cognitive and psychosocial skills needed to move to the next stage of talent development—to move from potential to competency to expertise—and to keep students on that path. The long-term goal is to enable more gifted individuals to become creative producers in adulthood and achieve at eminent levels (Subotnik et al., 2011). However, given that the path from childhood to adulthood is long, filled with chance events and affected by choices and opportunities, it is not expected that all or even many gifted children will reach eminence. The goal of talent development is to prepare children with the knowledge and psychosocial skills and provide the support they need to be able to function at the highest levels they desire in their chosen fields. Individuals may decide not to proceed on a path toward eminence, but the choice should be based on personal values and preferences rather than poor psychosocial skills, inadequate preparation, or lack of appropriate opportunities (Olszewski-Kubilius & Thomson, 2015). By having the highest levels of achievement and creativity as the long-term goal of programming, it is hoped that many more gifted children will be put onto paths toward levels of excellence in their chosen areas of interest and talent.

Implications for Research

Although talent development models have been the subject of research for decades, there remain implications for research for the talent development approach to gifted education. Implications for research range from teacher competencies to nuances of talent development trajectories to the leveraging of technology to redistribute time and opportunity. Dai and Chen (2014) suggested that there is a gap between the vision of talent development and current educational systems, and that gifted education policies and practices may lead to frustration when mixing competing paradigms. Thus, for starters, more research is needed on the relationship between identification for services and the development of talent. Research is also needed to better understand the nature of talent and achievement in domains including emergent domains that remain ill-defined involving innovation and technology.

More research is needed to understand the knowledge and skill competencies required for teachers to become coaches and mentors in talent development, especially in high school where domain-specificity and participation in fields of practice are becoming highly specialized. For instance, what types of mathematical problem-solving skills and advanced mathematical application skills are needed for high school mathematics teachers? What types of writing skills and experiences must language arts and social studies teachers have in order to develop advanced creative and expository writers in literature, history, and political science? These research opportunities must also lead to more informed practices of teacher development and recruitment for talent development approaches to gifted education.

Research in academic talent development still lags behind research in sports and fine arts talent development. Sports fields like baseball, soccer, and hockey have well-developed systems of developing the talents of young athletes from childhood to early adulthood. Highly specialized sports clubs and coaches recruit, motivate, and teach young athletes and mentor them into elite performance and eminence in those fields. Academic talent domains such as mathematics, science, and writing could continue to learn from the systematic talent development models in sports and fine arts. More research is needed on how to bring those talent development models into existing school structures. Moreover, knowledge of those processes needs to be deeply embedded in the practices of teachers.

Discussion Questions

1. In what ways does the talent development approach to gifted education differ from more traditional approaches to gifted education?
2. When thinking of curriculum as a broadly defined set of learning experiences, how might schools intentionally design ways to develop academic talent leading to elite levels of performance and achievement?
3. How can technology be leveraged to create more opportunities to develop academic talent areas?
4. In what ways might a talent development approach to schooling differ from more typical well-rounded approaches to schooling? What might be the strengths and weaknesses of both approaches to gifted education?

References

Barab, S. A., & Plucker, J. A. (2002). Smart people or smart contexts? Cognition, ability, and talent development in an age of situated approaches to knowing and learning. *Educational Psychologist, 37*, 165–182.

Clark, A. (2008). *Supersizing the mind: Embodiment, action, and cognitive extension*. New York, NY: Oxford University Press.

Dai, D. Y. (2010). *The nature and nurture of giftedness: A new framework for understanding gifted education*. New York, NY: Teachers College Press.

Dai, D. Y. (2011). Hopeless anarchy or saving pluralism? Reflections on our field in response to Ambrose, VanTassel-Baska, Coleman, and Cross. *Journal for the Education of the Gifted, 34,* 705–731.

Dai, D. Y., & Chen, F. (2014). *Paradigms of gifted education.* Waco, TX: Prufrock Press.

Dweck, C. S. (2008). *Mindsets. The new psychology of success.* New York, NY: Ballantine.

Dweck, C. S. (2012). Mindsets and malleable minds: Implications for giftedness and talent. In R. F. Subotnik, A. Robinson, C. M. Callahan, & P. Johnson (Eds.), *Malleable minds: Translating insights from psychology and neuroscience to gifted education* (pp. 7–18). Storrs: University of Connecticut, The National Research Center on the Gifted and Talented .

Ericsson, K. A., Nandagopal, K., & Roring, R. W. (2005). Giftedness viewed from the expert-performance perspective. *Journal for the Education of the Gifted, 28,* 287–311.

Farrington, C. A., Roderick, M., Allensworth, E., Nagaoka, J., Keyes, T. S., Johnson, D. W., & Beechum, N. O. (2012). *Teaching adolescents to become learners. The role of noncognitive factors in shaping school performance: A critical literature review.* Chicago, IL: University of Chicago Consortium on Chicago School Research.

Hébert, T. P. (2009). Guiding gifted teenagers to self-understanding through biography. In J. L. VanTassel-Baska, T. L. Cross, & F. R. Olenchak (Eds.), *Social-emotional curriculum with gifted and talented students* (pp. 259–287). Waco, TX: Prufrock Press

Ito, M., Gutierrez, K., Livingstone, S., Penual, B., Rhodes, J., Salen, K., . . . Watkins, S. C. (2013). *Connected learning: An agenda for research and design.* Irvine, CA: Digital Media and Learning Research Hub.

Maton, K. I., Schellenbach, C. J., Leadbetter, B. J., & Solarz, A. L. (Eds.). (2004). *Investing in children, youth, families, and communities: Strength-based research and policy.* Washington, DC: American Psychological Association.

Montgomery County Public Schools, Office of Strategic Technologies and Accountability. (2004). *A guidebook for twice exceptional students: Supporting the achievement of gifted students with special needs.* Rockville, MD: Montgomery County Public Schools Department of Curriculum and Instruction.

National Association for Gifted Children, & Council of State Directors of Programs for the Gifted. (2011). *State of the states in gifted education 2010– 2011.* Washington, DC: Authors.

Olszewski-Kubilius, P. (2015). The role of outside of school programs in talent development for secondary students. In S. Moon & F. Dixon (Eds.), *Handbook of secondary gifted education* (2nd ed., pp. 261–281). Waco, TX: Prufrock Press.

Olszewski-Kubilius, P., & Thomson, D. T. (2015). Talent development as a framework for gifted education. *Gifted Child Today, 38*(1), 49–59.

Paek, P. L. (2008). Asset-based instruction: Boston Public Schools. In P. L. Paek, *Practices worthy of attention: Local innovations in strengthening secondary mathematics* (pp. 4–7). Austin, TX: Charles A. Dana Center at The University of Texas at Austin.

Park, G., Lubinski, D., & Benbow, C. P. (2007). Contrasting intellectual patterns predict creativity in the arts and sciences: tracking intellectually precocious youth over 25 years. *Psychological Science, 18,* 948–952. doi:10.1111/j.1467-9280.2007.02007.x

Queen, B., & Lewis, L. (2011). *Distance education courses for public elementary and secondary school students: 2009–10* (NCES 2012-008). Washington, DC: U.S. Department of Education, National Center for Education Statistics.

Schroth, S. T., Collins, C. L., & Treffinger, D. J. (2011). Talent development: from theoretical conceptions to practical applications. In T. L. Cross & J. R. Cross (Eds.), *Handbook of counselors serving students with gifts and talents* (pp. 39–52). Waco, TX: Prufrock Press.

Setzer, J. C., & Lewis, L. (2005). *Distance education courses for public elementary and secondary school students: 2002–03* (NCED 2005-010). Washington, DC: U.S. Department of Education, National Center for Education Statistics. Retrieved from http://nced.ed.gov/pubs2005/2005010.pdf

Siemens, G. (2005). Connectivism: A learning theory for the digital age. *International Journal of Instructional Technology and Distance Learning, 2*(1), 3–10.

Subotnik, R. F., & Jarvin, L. (2005). Beyond expertise: Conceptions of giftedness as great performance. In R. J. Sternberg & J. E. Davidson (Eds.), *Conceptions of giftedness* (2nd ed., pp. 343–357). New York, NY: Cambridge University Press.

Subotnik, R. F., Olszewski-Kubilius, P., & Worrell, F. C. (2011). Rethinking giftedness and gifted education: A proposed direction forward based on psychological science. *Psychological Science in the Public Interest, 12*(1), 3–54. doi:10.1177/1529100611418056

Subotnik. R. F., Pillmeier, E., & Jarvin, L. (2009). The psychosocial dimensions of creativity in mathematics. In R. Leikin, A. Berman, & B. Koichu (Eds.),

Creativity in mathematics and the education of gifted students (pp. 165–179). Rotterdam, Netherlands: Sense Publishers.

Thomson, D. L. (2010). Beyond the classroom walls: Teachers' and students' perspectives on how online learning can meet the needs of gifted students. *Journal of Advanced Academics, 21,* 662–712.

U.S. Department of Education, Office of Educational Technology. (2010). *Learning powered by technology: The National Educational Technology Plan.* Retrieved from https://www.ed.gov/sites/default/files/netp2010.pdf

Wai, J., Lubinski, D., & Benbow, C. P. (2009). Spatial ability for STEM domains: Aligning over 50 years of cumulative psychological knowledge solidifies its importance. *Journal of Educational Psychology, 101,* 817–835.

Wai, J., Lubinski, D., Benbow, C. P., & Steiger, J. H. (2010) Accomplishment in science, technology, engineering, and mathematics (STEM) and its relation to STEM educational dose: A 25-year longitudinal study. *Journal of Educational Psychology, 102,* 860–871. doi:10.1037/a0019454

CHAPTER 4

AN ADVANCED ACADEMICS APPROACH TO CURRICULUM BUILDING

SCOTT J. PETERS AND MICHAEL S. MATTHEWS

What Are the Specific Goals of Gifted Education, and What Type of Curriculum Design Best Supports Students and Educators Working Toward Those Goals?

In this chapter, we choose to use the term *advanced academics* in place of *gifted and talented* for many reasons that will become clear later in this chapter. However, first we want to make a few points before we discuss this approach. We believe that the goals of gifted and talented education are the same as those of any advanced academics program: to assure that all students learn, are appropriately challenged, and have their academic needs met in school. Of course, not all references to "giftedness" deal with K–12 schools. This is the first major difference between the differentiation paradigm and the talent development paradigm, and is part of the reason why we have chosen to avoid the term *gifted*. The advanced academic model is concerned solely with the education of students in schools. It is not focused on adult learners, talent in other

DOI: 10.4324/9781003236696-5

areas of the lifespan, or those individuals who are gifted or otherwise advanced in areas not addressed in schools (e.g., gifted welders or potters, unless those areas of study are part of the academic curriculum of a school, in which case these domains would fall under the advanced academic model). Furthermore, although affective needs are undeniably important and can influence students' academic outcomes, these needs are not directly a focus of the advanced academics model.

Because of its narrow focus on academic skills taught in the schools (that is, as chosen by the schools), there are aspects of the advanced academics model with which many gifted education proponents might disagree. For example, our model is only interested in whether a student is formally categorized as "gifted" if that characteristic or status means she is not being effectively challenged in school and therefore needs some special intervention. If a student has an IQ of 145 but is otherwise happy and being appropriately challenged in her regular education placement, then she would require no specialized program or intervention. Our job then, as gifted or advanced academic professionals, is simply to stay out of the way until our support or intervention is needed. In this way the advanced academic model shares many similarities to the "Gifted education without gifted children" approach proposed by James Borland (2005).

Our stated purpose requires some further unpacking. A major tenet of the advanced academic model is that as many students as possible should be academically challenged as often as possible while engaged in compulsory education. Readers familiar with educational psychology might recognize this as an attempt to assure that students are working within their Zone of Proximal Development (ZPD) as often as possible while at school. On one hand, making sure students are challenged is a fairly straightforward task. Any attempt at teaching someone a new skill starts with the teacher figuring out what the student already knows. However, in practice, this type of needs-based education is far less common than it should be.

A study by Engel, Claessens, and Finch (2013) using data from the Early Childhood Longitudinal Study found that 95% of kindergarteners entered school having mastered concepts such as identifying some one-digit numbers, recognizing geometric shapes, and counting up to 10. Despite this widespread proficiency, their teachers reported spending more than 13 days per month reteaching this content. The end result was a net negative effect on student learning. To us, this represents a stunning level of mismatch between curriculum and student need that almost certainly reflects a lack of appropriate challenge in mathematics for large numbers of students. Such a mismatch goes far beyond gifted education programming or the students traditionally served therein.

The goal of advanced academic programs and services is to try to bring all students' academic needs into line with the curriculum and instruction they are receiving in school. Advanced academic need, we suggest, can best be conceptualized in terms of readiness to learn content that is more advanced than what is being taught in the grade-level classroom. Because of their lack of connection to immediate educational need, concepts and comparisons such as cut scores or national norms are not relevant.

When there is a mismatch between need and instruction, specialized advanced academic programing is needed. In this fashion, the advanced academic model is very similar to special education services—especially as implemented within a Response to Intervention framework. When there is alignment between student need and instruction, even if a particular student is light-years ahead of her classroom peers, specialized programming is not needed because the student is being challenged effectively in the current setting. In essence, *advanced academics can be seen as setting out to alleviate academic need at the advanced end of the performance spectrum for any domain taught in schools*. In our view, any program focused on advanced or gifted learners should have this alleviation of unmet need at its core.

Luckily, much of this perspective is aligned with best practices in traditional gifted education models. For example, academic needs cannot be met except through domain-specific programming. In a similar fashion, gifted education scholars long have advocated for a continuum of services that is aligned both with the content area of a student's talent domain(s), and with his or her level of need (Gentry, 2009; Subotnik, Olszewski-Kubilius, & Worrell, 2011). Where these perspectives differ is in the belief that the concept or identification of "the gifted" or "giftedness" is needed in order to achieve the goal of challenging advanced learners in the classroom setting (see Peters, Kaufman, Matthews, McBee, & McCoach, 2014).

Three Necessary Pieces of Information

This brings us to the question, what kinds of curriculum are best suited to meet student needs and to assure that students remain challenged consistently? In order to determine which students are or are not having their needs met, a concerned teacher or administrator needs to know three things: (1) the student's current level of mastery in the domain being considered, (2) the material being taught in the student's current educational placement or classroom, and (3) the ability of the student's teacher to differentiate instruction in order to effectively address the student's demonstrated need. We have listed these three items in order according to the ease with which the information can be gathered or, in some cases, how likely it is to already exist in the schools.

An upside to the extensive testing that takes place in today's schools is that it offers a treasure-trove of data; some of it is potentially helpful, while other parts are less so. We suggest that these data provide a wealth of information regarding what students currently know and can do with regard to the subjects that are tested. These data, with the addition of self-report measures regarding student interest, classroom preassessments, and computer-based data systems (which often include past grades and behavior data), allow an interested teacher or administrator a comprehensive look at a student's current level of mastery in a given content area. It's certainly not perfect, but it offers a much wider range of information than we believe is often appreciated.

Compared to the other two pieces of information, it is relatively easy to determine what students already know. This will become even more true in the coming years for those states that implement the Smarter Balanced Assessment system or that already use the Measures of Academic Progress® (MAP®), since these adaptive tests with high ceilings also provide much closer to real-time access to student performance results. This information can provide teachers with a student's current level of need almost immediately. However, knowing what students already know is necessary but not sufficient in order to establish whether a student needs an advanced academic intervention. This is where we believe traditional gifted education falters. Schools also need to know if a need is already or could potentially be met by the "regular" education classroom and curriculum. That's where the next two pieces of data come into play. Student-level information is not enough; schools also need information about the educational context into which the student will be placed.

The second piece of data needed to determine who is being challenged and who might need an advanced academic intervention involves what is taught, as well as where, and when. This information can come from several sources. First, the Common Core State Standards, Next Generation Science Standards, and the National Curriculum Standards for Social Studies all include general guidelines based on grade level. State-level content standards can further narrow down what is "typically" taught at a given grade level, as can examination of curricula, textbooks, thematic lessons, etc. All of this information can be used to create a curriculum map in order to better understand what a student in a given classroom or grade level is "supposed" to learn. This is not a perfect system, but it offers a good place to start. There is also another, even easier way to determine what will be covered in a given class—ask the teacher. If he or she doesn't know what will be taught in the class or can't articulate that information, then the school has a larger issue at hand. Using the data gathered in step one, teachers can look at those students who are farthest from "average" or "grade level" and then compare those students' scores (and what content they represent mastery of) against their own instructional plans for the upcoming class. Some students will be fine given the content to be taught—because it meets their instructional needs. These are students who are relatively close in their readiness to the content that will be taught in the class, and as such the teacher can reach them through differentiation (see next step). There will also be a few students who are far behind and for whom the teacher will need remediation or special education support, possibly from another teacher whose role is as a dedicated classroom support specialist. Crucially, there will also be some who score at levels that indicate the curriculum that teacher has planned will be insufficiently challenging. These are the students in need of advanced academic programming. We believe that the teachers in the Engel et al. (2013) study likely were unaware that so many of their students already knew the content they were teaching. If they were, surely they would have spent fewer than 13 days per month reviewing material their students already had mastered.

So far, the concerned teacher has identified the level of mastery of his or her students (Step 1) and compared it to the curriculum he or she was planning to teach (Step 2). For those students for whom these two pieces of information are perfectly aligned, we can assume they will be effectively challenged (further assuming that teachers are following general best practices regarding differentiation for different interests, learning styles, etc.). The only remaining issue is this: How far is too far from the average for a teacher to effectively differentiate to meet a student's need? How far can a teacher differentiate or, putting it another way, how far from average should one teacher be expected to differentiate?

This is by far the hardest question to answer, for a variety of reasons. First, some teachers are better able to differentiate than others, and this doesn't necessarily correlate with experience. Peters, Matthews, McBee, and McCoach (2014) reported that nationally the middle two-thirds of eighth-grade readers ranged in scores from fourth-grade level proficiency to college-level proficiency. Can one teacher be expected to reach all of these learners? Could that teacher reach the other one-third of students who are even farther behind or farther ahead? These are difficult if not impossible questions to answer.

What makes this issue even more complicated is that some content areas are easier to differentiate within than others. Perhaps it's easier to differentiate for a wide range of reading needs than it is for a similar range of math needs, though this is difficult to nail down with any precision. Again, this is where the classroom teacher can become involved in the process. He or she can look at the range of students who will enter his or her class in the coming fall and decide which ones fall outside of his or her ability to differentiate. Teachers may ask themselves, "Which students will I not be able to reach even if I apply my best differentiation skills?" Those, then, are the students who on the remedial end need additional support interventions and who on the advanced end will benefit from an advanced academic intervention.

This process, if followed closely, will accomplish the goal of assuring that all students will be in a classroom or receive a supplementary service that is well-aligned with what they already know and can do. An added benefit is that we have achieved it without the need for the term gifted at all. This is not to suggest that this process is easy. But if it can be accomplished, "gifted" identification can be significantly downplayed. We are not saying that "gifted" individuals do not exist. Instead, we only suggest that the concept of giftedness is not necessary if our goal is to assure all students are appropriately challenged. If in a particular school the term gifted or the process of gifted identification is necessary to achieve that goal, as for example when funding needs to be allocated, this is fine. But if it's not, we can all save the time, money, energy, and controversy that goes along with gifted identification (cf. Matthews, Ritchotte, & Jolly, 2014) and focus on making sure all students are challenged.

What Does Gifted Education Look Like in Language Arts, Mathematics, Science, and Social Studies?

The simplest answer to this question is that "gifted education" or advanced academic programming in language arts, math, science, and social studies can and should look different for every school or district based on the current level of need and understanding of the students enrolled. Put another way: *There is no such thing as gifted-specific programs or services.* The question posed above assumes that language arts, math, science, and social studies have been adopted as content areas that are to be taught in schools. If this is the case (which of course it nearly always is), then it is the school's responsibility to assure an appropriately challenging education to all students enrolled in these particular domains. Although this may seem obvious, we point this out because a given school could just as easily adopt visual arts, business, or dance as the "academic" areas in which it would then need to provide an appropriately challenging curriculum. Not every domain of human endeavor can or should be addressed by school-based programming. What "counts" is up to states, school boards, and local communities. Individuals have expressed concern over the idea of advanced academics as being too narrow in focus—too focused on typical academic areas of math and reading (Delisle, 2014). But nothing in our model says that only math and reading should be addressed. Rather, we believe it is up to the local school, district, and community to decide what areas should be addressed or "counted" under the academics in advanced academics (see Peters, Matthews et al., 2014, for a discussion of what this process might look like).

A hallmark of the advanced academic model is that we do not seek to prescribe any particular curriculum. Instead, we believe that the program to be provided should be based on whatever content is not currently being provided elsewhere in the areas the school and its various stakeholders have decided to serve.

Unlike traditional gifted education practices, we see gifted-specific programs—meaning those that are good by their very nature only for students identified as gifted—as a misnomer. Because the advanced academic model has no need for the label of "giftedness," there is similarly no need for a *gifted* curriculum. Those with experience in gifted education might wonder what role this leaves for enrichment programs such as Destination Imagination or Creative Problem Solving. This brings us to the defining characteristic of advanced academic programming: a program is only appropriate for an advanced learner if it is *directly related to his or her identified need*. Further, a program should only be restricted to identified advanced learners if it would be appropriate *only* for advanced learners and not for other students. In other words, if a program would be good for all students—or at least for some population broader than just those deemed advanced in any particular content area—then it should be left open to a wider range of students. This is not a new idea, of course; it has been stated in other terms at least as far back as the writings of Harry Passow. We acknowledge that enrichment programs are often very positive learning experiences—but there is little evidence that they are positive *only* for gifted or advanced learners.

So what does this mean "gifted education" should look like in language arts, math, science, or social studies? It means the curriculum should look like whatever it is that comes next in the advanced student's learning progression. This again returns to the idea of a need-based educational model, in which what a student should be taught is based on what he or she already knows. Such a model has gained attention in recent years with the Personalized Learning approach advocated by the United States Department of Education. Such models require the loosening of traditional school structures and policies such as fixed age-based grades and classrooms and requirements for a certain number of hours or days in a given grade level, and instead adopt a proficiency-based promotion system.

How Should Educators Design Learning Experiences to Develop Advanced Talents in an Era of Standards, Specializations, and Ubiquitous Technology?

There are several education initiatives that on initial inspection would appear to impede efforts to challenge advanced learners. However, some of these same initiatives also offer opportunities. The renewed focus by U.S. schools on standards is perhaps the greatest challenge. With the widespread adoption of the Common Core State Standards, there is even more pressure for all students to be doing the same things at the same time—regardless of their level of prior knowledge—which is completely antithetical to the advanced academic or Response to Intervention (RtI) models. However, at the same time many states and districts are adopting educator effectiveness or teacher evaluation systems that focus heavily on student growth as not only a goal, but also as a means through which instructional staff will be evaluated or even compensated.

These two initiatives highlight the conflicted nature of the American educational system. On one hand, there is a desire to be able to say that all students, regardless of family background or prior educational circumstances, will learn the same thing in schools regardless of where they live or what they already know. This has obvious logistical appeal, as it would greatly standardize the process of teaching and make it more efficient (and thereby also less costly). The downside is that demonstrating growth in an educational system based solely on age is very difficult, as demonstrated by roughly 40 years of stagnant NAEP scores (see National Center for Educational Statistics, 2013).

Despite the challenges inherent in the contemporary standards movement, the renewed attention on student growth offers a clear opportunity for advocates of advanced learners. If the goal is growth for all students, then all students need appropriately challenging curriculum that is based on what they already know. If they are simply retaught what they already know (as was the case in the Engel et al. 2013 article cited earlier), then no growth is likely to happen. This brings up the question of who hasn't been challenged in schools and/or growing for the last decade and what, as a system, we will need to do to challenge these students as we move forward. In our minds, this is the question every school principal and district superintendent should be asking him- or herself every year in the weeks before the semester starts.

Despite this opportunity, there are two challenges related to growth for advanced learners: getting it and showing it. By "getting it" we mean providing a sufficiently challenging education to all learners so that they actually learn more (or more deeply). Much of this we have already discussed. However, what makes some growth especially challenging is that the content necessary to show it has, in the past, never been taught in K–12 schools. For example, a student who exhausts all math courses by the time she is a high school freshman (i.e., by completing AP Calculus BC) would need some additional advanced math courses in order to grow. But what else is there? It's unlikely that anything other than college-level material will challenge this student. Although this clearly is a challenge for K–12 schools, it also represents a catalyst for improving collaboration and articulation between K–12 schools and institutions of higher education. Luckily, many states have already been breaking down the K–12/K–16 barrier in order to broaden access to college courses for high school students.

Although getting growth out of students is certainly challenging, an even larger unknown is how teachers and schools can show growth in advanced learners. McCoach, Rambo, and Welsh (2013) outlined some of the major challenges with measuring growth in advanced learners, as well as some of the key requirements for such systems. One seemingly obvious issue is that any instrument used to measure the growth of a particular student must have sufficient range—a high enough test ceiling—in order to do so. If a school has provided the student described in the previous paragraph with the advanced calculus that she needs in order to grow (getting growth), then the next step becomes how to show or measure that growth for educator effectiveness systems. The traditional tests measuring accomplishment in high school mathematics content will be unable to measure this student's continued academic growth in this area. In fact, if she is forced to repeat the traditional state achievement tests, it is likely that her performance may decline over time due to regression to the mean and to the greater elapsed time between the testing date and the time when the tested skills last were practiced. Something else must be used to measure these types of desirable, but not easily measurable, outcomes.

If the content the student is learning will not be accounted for by a standard, grade-level achievement test, then there are two primary options. Warne (2014) discussed using out-of-level or above-level tests in order to have a valid measure of the student's growth. In this fashion, a student in eighth grade might be given a 10th-grade test because the questions on that test better measure the student's level of mastery. The major hurdle with this approach is that many states forbid this practice with regard to state achievement testing. These states require that students take the "grade-level" achievement test even if that test has no chance of being a valid measure of the student's current level of mastery. Such is the challenge of showing growth in advanced learners.

The second option for showing growth in advanced learners is to use a computer adaptive test (CAT). Examples of such tests include the Graduate Record Examination (GRE), the Northwest Evaluation Association's Measures of Academic Progress®, and the Smarter Balanced Assessment Consortium's summative assessment. What characterizes these tests is that they have no "grade level" per se. Instead, they adapt based on student responses. If a student gets a question right, the test gives him or her a harder question. Likewise if the student gets a question wrong, he or she gets an easier question. In this fashion, a single computerized "test" is able to assess a far wider range of content, and usually in a much shorter time, than any paper-pencil test. Of course, some test ceiling still exists and many advanced students can still hit the ceilings on such tests, but for the most part they are far better suited to the assessment of growth at the high end of the scale than nonadaptive measures. In other cases, the classroom teacher might need to use classroom-level assessment in order to document growth as part of a student learning objective (SLO), but this does not help when the goal is to show student growth for broader accountability purposes.

What Is the New Frontier in Curriculum Design for Gifted and Advanced Students?

Although it's certainly far from an exciting new innovation, we believe the new frontier in curriculum for advanced students is to better align advanced academic programs and interventions with the general education curriculum. Initiatives such as Response to Intervention are ideal for such alignment, as illustrated in Figure 4.1.

In our experience, RtI has been an effective vehicle for inserting consideration of advanced learners into general education discussions—from classroom-level differentiation to full-grade acceleration. The RtI model presented in Figure 4.1 helps individuals see that advanced academic services are simply meeting student needs in the same way that remedial Tier III programs do. The more extreme the student's need is, the more intense the responding intervention becomes.

A second new frontier is the expansion of available programs historically seen as being "for the gifted" to a wider group of learners. For example, early enrichment programs should be open to all students who are interested so that students can explore content areas and develop their passions and talents. This in turn may lead to tensions between quality and quantity, and may create a need for different methods of assessing student readiness, such as trial placement. Peters and his colleagues (2014) provide greater depth of discussion on these issues, which space precludes addressing in this chapter. What is most clear to us is that any new frontier in "gifted" or advanced academic education must be closely tied to other educational innovations and reforms such as teacher evaluation, standards, and Response to Intervention. We believe many of the challenges of the past regarding gifted education have stemmed from programs and services being reserved for a particular class of people, "the gifted," as opposed to being seen as part of a larger continuum of needs-based interventions that are available based on transparent and especially achievable criteria. The more that gifted education advocates argue that what they want provided for advanced learners is the same thing that should be provided to all students, the more successful they are likely to be in meeting the instructional needs of all learners, including those identified as gifted.

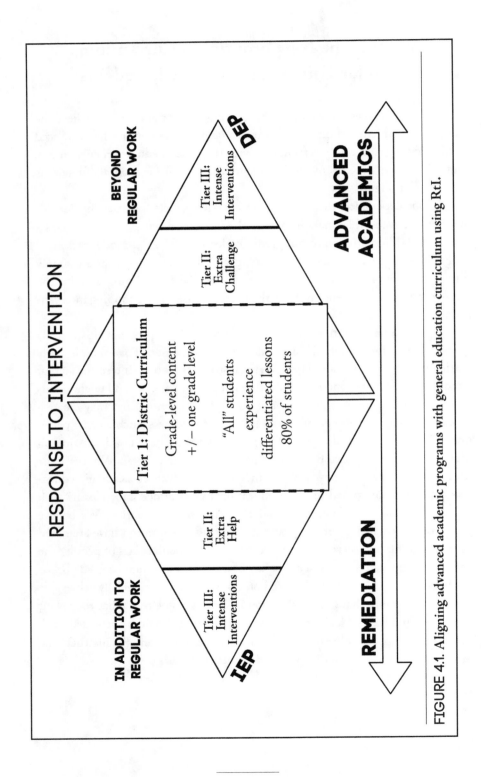

FIGURE 4.1. Aligning advanced academic programs with general education curriculum using RtI.

Implications for Research

Gifted is a vague label to communicate a nebulous construct. Thus, it is difficult or impossible to conduct research on "the gifted" as if they were all one homogenous group. Furthermore, it may be difficult or impossible to study curriculum effectiveness in gifted education considering the diverse nature of the gifted population. Perhaps more fruitful avenues of research include studies of interventions designed to alleviate academic need fostered by the mismatch between student ability and the curriculum.

We need to realize there is no such thing as a generic "gifted" program. In order for a program to result in any positive outcomes, it must be domain-specific and targeted at a student's area of need. Because of this we should avoid researching the effects of "gifted" programs where "giftedness" is the predictor variable. At the very least, we should be far more systematic in defining the populations who participate in research studies related to advanced academics.

Finally, we need well-designed research studies to examine the effects of Response to Intervention approaches to gifted education. This approach has become more common (cf. Coleman & Johnsen, 2013), and at the present time, use of the model outpaces research on the model. We need studies to examine associations between specific interventions across all three tiers and student achievement within the academic areas served.

Discussion Questions

1. Is "giftedness" as a concept necessary in your school or district in order to assure that all students are adequately challenged by the curriculum?
2. What barriers might impede implementing an advanced academics approach in school districts?
3. What would be the consequences of opening the vast majority of traditionally gifted programs to all learners? For example, what would be the downside of allowing all students to enroll in a particular enrichment program if they were interested?
4. What types of interventions would you classify into the three tiers of an RtI model for gifted education?

References

Borland, J. (2005). Gifted education without gifted children: The case for no conception of giftedness. In R. J. Sternberg & J. E. Davidson (Eds.), *Conceptions of giftedness* (pp. 1–19). New York, NY: Cambridge University Press.

Coleman, M. R., & Johnsen, S. K. (Eds.). (2013). *Implementing RtI with gifted students: Service models, trends, and issues.* Waco, TX: Prufrock Press.

Delisle, J. (2014, May 7). 'Gifted' label is crucial to ensure access to much-needed services [Letter to the editor]. *Education Week, 33*(30), 34.

Engel, M., Claessens, A., & Finch, M. A. (2013). Teaching students what they already know? The (mis)alignment between mathematics instructional content and student knowledge in kindergarten. *Educational Evaluation and Policy Analysis, 35,* 157–178.

Gentry, M. (2009). Myth 11: A comprehensive continuum of gifted education and talent development services. *Gifted Child Quarterly, 53,* 262–265.

Matthews, M. S., Ritchotte, J. A., & Jolly, J. (2014). What's wrong with giftedness? Parents' perceptions of the gifted label. *International Studies in Sociology of Education, 24,* 372–393. doi:10.1080/09620214.2014.990225

McCoach, D. B., Rambo, K. E., & Welsh, M. (2013). Assessing the growth of gifted students. *Gifted Child Quarterly, 57,* 56–67.

National Center for Educational Statistics. (2013). *The nation's report card: Trends in academic progress 2012.* Retrieved from http://nces.ed.gov/nationsreportcard/pubs/main2012/2013456.aspx

Peters, S. J., Kaufman, S. B., Matthews, M., McBee, M. T., & McCoach, D. B. (2014, April 16). Gifted ed. is crucial, but the label isn't. *Education Week, 33*(28), 40, 34.

Peters, S. J., Matthews, M. S., McBee, M. T., & McCoach, D. B. (2014). *Beyond gifted education: Designing and implementing advanced academic programs.* Waco, TX: Prufrock Press.

Subotnik, R. F., Olszewski-Kubilius, P., & Worrell, F. C. (2011). Rethinking giftedness and gifted education: A proposed direction forward based on psychological science. *Psychological Science in the Public Interest, 12,* 3–54. doi:10.1177/1529100611418056

Warne, R. T. (2014). Using above-level testing to track growth in academic achievement in gifted students. *Gifted Child Quarterly, 58,* 3–23.

CHAPTER 5

GIFTED EDUCATION IN THE AGE OF CONTENT STANDARDS

JOYCE VANTASSEL-BASKA

Gifted education has always coexisted alongside general curriculum and the standards that have governed its use in schools. Even as early as the 1920s, the Speyer School in New York City used a modified curriculum developed by Leta Hollingworth (1926) that extended the regular curriculum standards, added to them, and deleted those areas not necessary for gifted students. As has been noted, this curriculum was an excellent model for thinking about differentiation of the core curriculum even today, as it employed the techniques of acceleration, complexity, depth, and creativity. It also used the core curriculum standards as the basis for differentiation. Just as standards framed differentiation in one of our pioneer programs, today we also find ourselves awash in a new standards environment that requires us to find ways to reconcile differentiation for the gifted with core curriculum for all. This chapter will delineate the nature of the current standards environment and what might be our best response to it.

DOI: 10.4324/9781003236696-6

What Are the Common Core State Standards?

The Common Core State Standards (CCSS) are K–12 content standards, developed in English language arts (ELA) and mathematics, to illustrate the curriculum emphases needed for students to develop the skills and concepts required for the 21st century. Adopted by 45 states to date, the CCSS are organized into key content strands and articulated across all years of schooling and, in most cases, replace the existing state content standards. The Next Generation Science Standards have now been released as well, and they have similarly been adopted by many states to replace or supplement existing standards. The initiative has been state-based and coordinated by the National Governors Association (NGA) and the Council of Chief State School Officers (CCSSO). Designed by teachers, administrators, and content experts, the CCSS and NGSS are intended to prepare K–12 students for college and the workplace (Council of Chief State School Officers, 2011).

The new CCSS are evidence based, aligned with expectations for success in college and the workplace, and informed by the successes and failures of the current standards and international competition demands. The new standards stress rigor, depth, clarity, and coherence, drawing from the National Assessment of Educational Progress (NAEP) Frameworks in Reading and Writing and the Trends in International Mathematics and Science Study (TIMSS). They provide a framework for curriculum development work in which states are currently engaged, working within and across local districts to design relevant curriculum and to align current practice to the new standards (Council of Chief State School Officers, 2011).

Issues in Implementing the New CCSS

The introduction of the CCSS has demonstrated how difficult it is to implement sweeping curriculum reform in the absence of sufficient time, funding, and foresight. These new standards in both ELA and mathematics hold great promise for elevating the level of learning in American schools, yet suffer from the same lack of focused attention to implementation that many other reform projects have encountered. Moreover, the problems of implementation are not just in the educational aspects of the standards. They also extend to the political rhetoric surrounding their adoption.

There are many myths perpetuated about these new standards, argued on the nightly news, radio talk shows, and in town halls. These myths pose a real danger to the careful thinking and design work that has preceded the standards' roll-out in schools. One of the most dangerous myths is that the standards represent a federal takeover of education that will lead to a national curriculum rather than our current state-based models. Although it is true that the CCSS attempts to standardize what needs to be learned by American students at given stages of development in these core subject areas, it does not represent an attempt to dictate to schools or teachers as to how to go about ensuring that learning has occurred.

Moreover, the impetus for the CCSS came from a coalition of the National Governor's Association and the Council of Chief State School Officers who have been concerned for some time about the level of U.S. student performance on international tests like PISA (Program for International Student Assessment) and TIMSS (Trends in International Mathematics and Science Study). In the most recent PISA testing, for example, 34 of 65 countries and school systems had a higher percentage of 15-year-olds scoring at the advanced levels in mathematics than the United States did (Organisation for Economic Co-operation and Development, 2014). Several European countries had at least twice the proportion and many Asian countries had far more. Evidence over several years of testing reveals two disturbing facts. One, the United States has shown little to no progress in its position in these core subject areas. Two, older American students lag behind their international counterparts to a greater extent than younger American students, suggesting a lack of rigor in the U.S. curriculum as they progress through school.

Another concern surrounding the CCSS is that many groups attack it, seemingly for opposite reasons. Conservatives have attacked it because of its strong emphases on standardization that might be perceived as federally controlled. Liberals, however, have also attacked it, using the same standardization argument, but on the basis that it may contribute to less individual attention for students. Adding to the groups that are openly hostile are more localized issues related to teacher and administrator capacity to implement. There are numerous arguments about CCSS emphases within the teaching of both math and ELA. In ELA, some groups are concerned that students will be less exposed to great literature because of the standards' emphasis on nonfiction reading. Other groups worry that students will not learn sufficiently the operations of mathematics while focusing too much attention on the processes that undergird problem solving.

Finally, there are and continue to be strong debates over the efficacy of the new assessments that have been proposed. Although most educators would acknowledge that 50 separate state assessments is an inefficient way to assess the learning level of students within the United States, there is less agreement on a viable alternative. The CCSS assessment models clearly represent a step in the direction of more performance-based types of items that are more open-ended and require greater effort on the part of the student to complete. However, it is not clear that U.S. students will perform well under these new testing formats and online conditions, a legitimate concern voiced by several states.

Assumptions About Giftedness and Talent Development

Just as there are general myths about the CCSS that need debunking, so too, the gifted community must be careful to assert in a proactive way the need for modification in the common core for gifted students. Often there persists the myth that the interpretation of these advanced standards at the classroom level will be sufficiently challenging to accommodate even our top learners. Yet as we have examined the fundamental issues of educating gifted learners, it appears that this belief is false.

A set of underlying assumptions about the constructs of giftedness and talent development has driven the thinking behind the efforts of the gifted community to align the work of the CCSS to gifted education (Hughes, Kettler, Shaughnessy-Dedrick, & VanTassel-Baska, 2014; Johnsen, Ryser, & Assouline, 2014; Johnsen & Sheffield, 2013; VanTassel-Baska, 2013). These assumptions are:

» Giftedness is developed over time through the interaction of potential with nurturing environmental conditions. Thus the process is developmental, dynamic, and malleable.

» Many learners show preferences for particular subject matter early and continue to select learning opportunities that match their predispositions if they are provided with opportunities to do so. For children of poverty, it is primarily the schools that must provide relevant opportunities to develop their domain-specific potential. However, for many children, the markers of talent development emerge from work done in school but also outside of school in cocurricular or extracurricular contexts.

» Aptitudes may emerge as a result of exposure to high-level, challenging activities in an area of interest. Thus teachers should consider using advanced learning activities and techniques as a stimulus for all learners.

» In the talent development process, there is an interaction effect between affect and cognition, leading to heightened intrinsic motivation of the individual and focus on the enjoyable tasks associated with the talent area. This dynamic tension catalyzes movement to the next level of advanced work in the area.

» Intellectual, cultural, and learning diversity among learners may account for different rates of learning, different areas of aptitude, different cognitive styles, and different experiential backgrounds. Working with such diversity in the classroom requires teachers to differentiate and customize curriculum and instruction, always working to provide an optimal match between the learner and her readiness to encounter the next level of challenge.

Rationale for the Common Core in Gifted Education

The adoption of the CCSS in almost every state is cause for gifted education as a field to reflect on its role in appropriately supporting gifted and high-potential learners in the content areas. As a field, we have not always differentiated systematically in the core domains of learning, but rather focused on interdisciplinary concepts, higher level skills, and problem solving, typically across domains. With the new CCSS, it becomes critical for us to show how we are differentiating for gifted learners within a set of standards that are reasonably rigorous in each subject area.

It has been stated by some educators that the CCSS core does not require any special differentiation for the gifted and may obviate the need for gifted education services because the standards are already written at an advanced level. Unfortunately, although the standards are strong, they are not sufficiently advanced to accommodate the needs of most gifted learners. As the CCSS developers have noted, some students will traverse the standards before the end of high school, which will require educators to provide advanced content for them. Beyond accelerative methods, however, there is also a need to enrich the standards by ensuring that there are open-ended opportunities to meet the standards through multiple pathways, more complex thinking applications, and real world, problem-solving contexts. This requires a deliberate strategy among gifted educators to ensure that the CCSS are translated in a way that allows for differentiated practices to be employed with gifted and high-potential students.

As with all standards, new assessments likely will drive the instructional process. As a field, we must be aware of the need to differentiate new assessments that align with the CCSS as well. Gifted learners will need to be assessed through performance-based and portfolio techniques that are based on higher level learning outcomes than the new CCSS may employ (VanTassel-Baska, 2008, 2013).

Although the new CCSS are a positive movement for all of education, it is important to be mindful of the ongoing need to differentiate appropriately for our top learners within these standards. As a field, it is also critical that we agree on the need to align with this work so our voices are at the table as the CCSS become more important as foundational curricula, along with the newly revised InTASC Model Core Teacher Standards, for elevating teacher quality and student learning nationwide.

Aligning Common Core With Gifted Education Programming Standards

All differentiation is based on an understanding of the characteristics of gifted and high-potential students *and* the content standards within a domain. The emergence of the CCSS will require the field of gifted education to examine its own practices and align them more fully to the NAGC Pre-K–Grade 12 Gifted Programming Standards for curriculum, instruction, and assessment (Johnsen, 2012). Because the gifted programming standards in curriculum require us to engage in two major tasks in curriculum planning—alignment to standards in the content areas and the development of a scope and sequence— using the CCSS is a natural point of departure. The effort must occur in vertical planning teams within districts and states in order to ensure consistency and coherence in the process. There are three major strategies that may be employed to accomplish the task for gifted education:

1. *Provide pathways to accelerate the CCSS for gifted learners.* Some of the CCSS address higher level skills and concepts that should receive focus throughout the years of schooling, such as a major emphasis on the skills of argument. However, there are also more discrete skills that may be clustered across grade levels and compressed around higher level skills and concepts for more efficient mastery by gifted students. This accelerative approach needs to be a first step in the differentiation process for both the language arts and the mathematics standards at each stage of development.

    Additionally, diagnostic assessment tools need to be developed to learn where individual gifted students fall on the continuum of reading skills, writing proficiency, and research-based project work in order to assure proper placement within English language arts (ELA). In mathematics, there is a need to ensure that the level of problem solving is sufficiently challenging for gifted learners. Again, as in the case of ELA, diagnostic tools geared to the mathematics standards are required to ensure appropriate beginning points for curriculum use with the gifted.

2. *Provide examples of differentiated task demands to address specific standards.* Standards like the research standard in ELA lend themselves to differentiated interpretation through demonstrating what a typical learner in grade level might be able to do at a given stage of development versus what a gifted learner might be able to do. The differentiated examples should show greater complexity and creativity, using a more advanced curriculum base. In ELA, while typical learners might learn the parts of speech and practice their application across grades K–8, gifted learners might instead explore the relationship of these parts of speech and their function in different sentence patterns at an earlier stage of development. Other degrees of differentiation may take place by adding complexity to the task and using enrichment techniques that address student needs and district demographics.

    Choice of materials also demonstrates the extent to which differentiation has been considered. In language arts, the choice of picture books conveys this distinction well. The difference between *Where's Waldo* and *Anno's Journey* illustrates the difference between the use of a simple idea of finding a small boy in a series of changing pictures versus the complexity of a changing environment encountered by an unknown traveler on each page, made more complex as the reader continues the journey. In mathematics, the use of materials that promote open-ended nonalgorithmic math problems versus close-ended problems with a set response characterize the deliberate choice of differentiated materials that respond well to the new standards at an appropriate level.

3. *Create interdisciplinary product demands to elevate learning for gifted students and to efficiently address multiple standards at once.* Because ELA and mathematics standards can be grouped together in application, much of the project work that gifted educators might already use could be revised to connect to the new CCSS and show how multiple standards could be addressed across content areas. For example, research projects could be designed that address the research standard in ELA and the data representation standard in mathematics by delineating a product demand for research on an issue, asking researchable questions, using multiple sources to answer them, and then representing findings in tables, graphs, and other visual displays that are explained in text and presented to an audience with implications for a plan of action. Such a project might be possible for the gifted learner at an earlier grade than for a typical learner. Ensuring that such interdisciplinary projects address the core elements of the new standards is central to their efficacy.

One way to ensure that is to craft follow-up questions for gifted students to respond to after they have completed their project. For example:

» What new skills of analysis have you learned from this project?

» What ideas have you explored that were new to you in this project?

» How are math and language arts connected as disciplines? What examples of these ideas did you learn through the project?

» What new questions do you have about what you studied, based on the research done?

Differentiated Task Demands for Gifted and Advanced Learners in ELA

Although the processes for differentiation noted above need to be enacted in both ELA and mathematics, as well as the new science standards (Adams, Cotabish, & Ricci, 2014), the following set of examples focus on the reading standards within CCSS-ELA in order to provide an explicit example of the process to be enacted with target standards. Both math and science guidebooks have also been developed to aid gifted educators in negotiating this differentiation process (see Adams et al., 2014; Johnsen et al., 2014)

Review of Research on Differentiation for the Gifted in Language Arts

Current research on differentiation of the language arts curriculum for gifted learners has centered on the importance of an integrated approach that attends to both accelerative and enriched approaches. Research-based curriculum materials have been developed to provide models for school districts to employ in implementation of the new common core standards that stress the importance of higher level thinking and problem solving.

Research studies have demonstrated that differentiated curriculum for the gifted in language arts enhances critical thinking in the subject area, including analysis of text and other critical reading behaviors (VanTassel-Baska, 2010; VanTassel-Baska, Zuo, Avery, & Little, 2002). Studies have also documented that growth gains in literary analysis and persuasive writing have consistently resulted from the use of differentiated materials that feature advanced reading selections in multiple genres (Feng, VanTassel-Baska, Queck, Bai, & O'Neill, 2005; VanTassel-Baska, Avery, Little, & Hughes, 2000; VanTassel-Baska, Johnson, Hughes, & Boyce, 1996). The achievement of low-income students in the subject area has also been studied, suggesting that the use of advanced strategies in language arts demonstrates longitudinal growth for these students, as well as growth in both reading comprehension and critical thinking (VanTassel-Baska, Bracken, Feng, & Brown, 2009; VanTassel-Baska & Stambaugh, 2006). Other studies have also documented enhanced fluency as a lower level outcome of strategy differentiation (Reis, Eckert, McCoach, Jacobs, & Coyne, 2008). In a study of gifted student preferences for differentiation, Kanevsky (2011) found that students enjoy challenging and efficient learning opportunities that demonstrate real learning, suggesting the need for strategies that focus on real-world issues and themes.

Accelerated Reading and the Provision for Off-Level Materials

A necessary differentiation in the CCSS-ELA is the judicious selection and use of off-level reading material for the gifted at all stages of development (see Standard 10). In general, all text selections should be considered for their Lexile level of one or more grade levels above the designated grade-level band and/or their level of complexity of language and thought. An excellent resource that has consistently been used in the gifted community to locate such texts is *Some of My Best Friends Are Books* (Halsted, 2009).

Furthermore, it is important to ensure that in the informational text standards, there is stronger attention to primary source documents than to those that are secondary. The use of original speeches, seminal documents, and artifacts such as diaries and letters is encouraged and should be reflected in the examples provided for advanced learners. For instance, teachers can use both excerpts and full text opinions from landmark Supreme Court cases (see http://www.streetlaw.org), milestone documents as diverse as the Treaty of Paris to Jefferson's secret message to Congress regarding Lewis and Clark's expedition (see http://www.ourdocuments.gov), famous speeches in American history, and full texts of every inaugural address delivered by Presidents of the United States.

In the literary text standards, the use of classical texts is favored over the use of children's and adolescent literature that may have little lasting value. The use of varied genres encourages the scope of reading so the employment of poetry, myth, fable, and short story contribute to exposure and appreciation of multiple forms of literature. Moreover, the use of genres that favor short selections encourages the depth of reading required for sufficient analytical work by students, even those who are advanced readers.

Consideration for the interest of advanced readers for certain genres, authors, and specific works should also be given in the selection of texts. Activity archetypes may be held constant while making more individualized reading selections. Independent reading of advanced learners should focus on their interest levels, but be balanced with challenging choices that provide a broad scope of reading materials.

Proficiency in reading for the gifted may best be judged through an assessment of reading comprehension and critical reading behaviors, not fluency, as many of these readers come to school already fluent beyond current age and grade placements. Consequently, the use of silent reading time, mandated in many school settings, should be targeted toward these skills through the use of center-based activities, book discussion groups, and reflective writing based on a recent reading.

Once ELA Standard 10 has been addressed for gifted learners, then the translation of the CCSS may be differentiated further through adding greater complexity, depth, and creativity to any given task demand through attending to the explicit translation of other reading standards.

Task demands can be constructed around those texts that integrate the other CCSS-ELA standards of language, writing, and speaking and listening. In the informational text strand, choices of text may be made in order to enhance interdisciplinary reading in the history and science content areas. In order to demonstrate this interdisciplinary integration, each set of task demands may have multiple parts that address multiple standards—Part I is typically a reading and discussion of the text selection; Part II is a writing assignment, linked to the selected reading in some way; Part III constitutes a project assignment and/or an in-class presentation related to the example text. Thus the reading standards are aligned to both writing and speaking standards within the CCSS-ELA framework in a deliberate way.

However, not all of the CCSS-ELA standards are equal in their need for differentiation beyond text selection. Because there is a parallelism between information text and literature standards, differentiation may be accomplished across selected corresponding standards in each strand.

Important standards that do deserve attention for the differentiation process in the ELA curriculum are those that address the key components of (a) citing the main idea and providing supporting evidence from text sources, (b) describing the importance of time sequence in understanding text, (c) the use of words and phrases to establish text meaning, and (d) engaging in the comparative analysis of texts with respect to key elements. These standards ought to be analyzed for how they become more complex as students mature from primary to intermediate to middle school and high school levels in order to build an integrated and coherent scope and sequence of task demands. The questions and process in Figure 5.1 illustrate the thinking processes to guide appropriate differentiation of task demands.

Figure 5.2 presents an example using CCSS-ELA Reading Literature Standard 9. This example illustrates the differentiation process put to work,

What reading selections (literature and informational text) will illustrate appropriate advanced-level text for gifted learners to use as the standards are addressed?

Process to be followed:
- » Locate advanced texts that match the demands of the standards.
- » Deconstruct the text through questions and activities.
- » Design corresponding writing and speaking and listening activities.

What level and type of complexity needs to be added to ensure challenge for the gifted?

Process to be followed:
- » Focus on higher order skill sets (e.g., analysis, synthesis, evaluation, and creation).
- » Add variables to study.
- » Design corresponding writing and speaking and listening activities.

What aspects of creativity can be designed into the task demands that provide open-endedness in product modality and/or response?

Process to be followed:
- » Provide choice in activity sets, products to be developed, and questions to be answered.
- » Ask students to design a real-world model and articulate how it works visually and verbally.
- » Design corresponding writing and speaking and listening activities.

What approach to the task demand will ensure depth of thinking and understanding of important concepts and ideas?

Process to be followed:
- » Focus questions and activities on an abstract concept or theme found in the selected texts.
- » Ensure that questions probe connections of the concept to other texts and stimuli.
- » Design corresponding writing and speaking and listening activities.

FIGURE 5.1. Questions to ask in the learning design process.

CCSS-ELA Standard: RL. 9-10.9 Analyze how an author draws on and transforms source material in a specific work (e.g., how Shakespeare treats a theme or topic from Ovid or the Bible or how a later author draws on a play by Shakespeare). (Grade 9)

Part I

1. Have students read the myth of Daedalus and Icarus, translated by Ovid, from an online source.
2. Discuss the myth, using the following questions:
   a. What purpose did this myth serve for ancient Greeks and Romans?
   b. What was its moral?
   c. What pattern does the myth follow?
   d. What aspects of human behavior does the myth demonstrate?
   e. Icarus tries out the wings that his father Daedalus created that eventually are responsible for his demise. What aspects of being creative or innovative are being explored here? What lessons are learned?
   f. What lessons are revealed about fathers and sons?
   g. How does Ovid's style as a writer contribute to the telling of the myth?

Part II

1. Now ask students to read the William Carlos Williams poem from the 20th century called "Icarus."
2. Discuss the following questions, based on the poem:
   a. What words are important in conveying the tone of the poem?
   b. What images that Williams uses are the most powerful? Why?
   c. What is the theme of this poem?
   d. How do you react to it?
   e. What structural devices does Williams use to heighten the impact of his poem?

FIGURE 5.2. Example of differentiated lesson design in language arts. *Note.* Adapted from *Indiana High Ability Project (HAP) in English Language Arts (ELA)* by Indiana Department of Instruction, 2013, Indianapolis, IN: Author, and *A Teacher's Guide to Using the Common Core State Standards for Gifted and Advanced Learners in the English Language Arts* (pp. 79–80) by C. Hughes, T. Kettler, E. Shaughnessy-Dedrick, and J. VanTassel-Baska, 2014, Waco, TX: Prufrock Press. Copyright 2013 by Indiana Department of Instruction and 2014 by National Association for Gifted Children. Adapted with permission.

Part III

1. Now project the image of the Bruegel painting of Icarus on an LCD screen and ask students to study it as a visual depiction of the event.
2. Regarding the comparison of myth, picture, and poem, ask students:
   a. How do Williams and Bruegel each interpret the myth? Are there distinctions in their interpretation that reflects the different time periods in which they worked?
   b. How does each artist extend the myth for the audience of his time?
   c. Both the writer and the painter were working in innovative forms in their art when they did these works. What aspects of creativity do you see in each product?
   d. Read about Bruegel and Williams in respect to their work. Analyze the similarities and differences in artist and author style.

Part IV

1. Have students select a Roman myth of their choice and create a poem and illustration that depicts that myth, using a modern form of poetry. Have them write an artist's statement about key aspects of interpretation (i.e., theme, vocabulary, structure, images and symbols).

Implementation

This task demand may be implemented using small groups for the discussion within a class period. A second period will be needed to engage dyads in the project work. Teachers may want to ensure that students are successfully analyzing the three art forms via the class discussion by using question probes as follow-up for some questions.

Assessment

Student products should be judged according to the following criteria:
» interpretation of the myth selected in both words and images,
» quality of the products,
» use of creative and innovative ideas,
» use of effective images in both the poem and the illustration,
» effective discussion of artistic elements employed, and
» command of language mechanics (i.e., spelling, grammar, and usage)

FIGURE 5.2. Continued.

highlighting the use of advanced text, complexity, creativity, and in-depth questions and activities. It further illustrates how writing and speaking and listening standards are addressed in an integrative way. Ideas for implementation and assessment are also included.

Issues of Implementation

As noted earlier in this chapter, a number of issues cloud our thinking about the concept of the CCSS as well as its effective implementation. In the 4 years since gifted programs have been engaging in the differentiation process related to implementation of the CCSS, the following issues have emerged as primary within and across school districts and states. These issues, while still unresolved totally, provide a picture of the nature and extent of the struggles with making this latest reform initiative work well for our best learners.

Professional Development

Any reform initiative requires a strong emphasis on professional development that is conducted systematically and continuously in order for the effort to be institutionalized (Learning Forward, 2011; National Governors Association Center for Best Practices & CCSSO, 2010). Many states and districts to date have not mandated such training, nor have they focused on the need to differentiate the CCSS for gifted learners, leaving such details up to classroom teachers and gifted specialists. The result of this oversight is a fragmented and incoherent implementation of the CCSS for top students within schools and districts, with parental concerns over the level of rigor afforded by the new standards.

Scope and Sequence of Curriculum

In the area of mathematics, in particular, there is a real concern that the new standards are driving out the traditional precalculus sequence that currently enables gifted students to accelerate their mathematics learning in a predictable way. Where districts have not discussed and worked out a viable scope and sequence for top learners that integrates accelerative opportunities within the CCSS, confusion and frustration result on the part of students and parents. In both CCSS subjects, discussion and articulation of offerings at each level of instruction needs to occur (Johnsen & Sheffield, 2013; Johnsen et al., 2014).

Teacher Preparation

Just as professional development is necessary for CCSS implementation, so too must teachers be trained in the processes of differentiation for the gifted if the translations noted in this chapter are likely to occur. Currently, many teachers working with the gifted have no such systematic training (VanTassel-Baska, 2008). Nor do they have a sufficient background in curriculum development per se to prepare them for the nature of the tasks required. In the absence of shifting our focus in differentiation to the CCSS and its requirements, we as a field risk extinction through fragmented efforts and underprepared personnel.

Administrative Support

The CCSS reform will be only as successful for gifted learners as building principals allow it to be by providing important instructional leadership for the work outlined in this chapter. Research suggests that principals must show visible support, be actively involved in the process, and monitor the outcomes if a reform is to work successfully (Cotabish & Robinson, 2012; VanTassel-Baska & Little, 2011). CCSS implementation for gifted learners is no exception. Awareness is not enough; engagement in organizing collaborative vertical teams of teachers in both ELA and mathematics is essential to ensuring that implementation moves forward in an organized and productive way at the building level.

Alignment

Often arguments have been made that differentiation of core curriculum creates a fragmentation in the scope and sequence of curricular offerings in the key areas of language arts and mathematics. In truth, without careful attention to alignment issues, such results may continue to occur. However, the gifted education community has been careful to ensure that differentiated work with the CCSS has been aligned with both gifted and general curriculum documents.

The resources designed around the CCSS for use by teachers with gifted learners were developed in alignment with the NAGC programing standards in key areas (Johnsen, 2012), the NAGC-CEC teacher education standards (National Association for Gifted Children & Council for Exceptional Children, 2013), and also the 21st-century skill sets. Thus, the work is connected and integrated in important ways to multiple professional communities, within gifted education, but also across general education.

Implications for Research

Numerous curriculum models in gifted education have been developed and implemented. Fewer have been subjected to valid and rigorous research (VanTassel-Baska & Brown, 2007). Curriculum design and implementation for gifted and advanced learners in the present age of content standards requires careful delineation of the standards at both a general education level and a gifted and advanced level. Curriculum designers and researchers must work in conjunction to develop and field test differentiated curricula in a way that validates differentiated outcomes. The field of gifted education needs field-based studies to document gifted students' performance in relation to the CCSS. We may make assumptions that gifted students will perform at more advanced levels of the standards, but research evidence is necessary to substantiate those assumptions. Researchers may look for ways to document the effect of differentiated learning experiences as a result of curriculum modification within the CCSS. In what ways does increasing the complexity of the standards in reading and writing lead to advanced-level products and performances in reading and writing? Additionally, given the challenges of implementation discussed above, field-based studies may be designed to measure the effects of professional development on the implementation of CCSS at multiple levels of complexity to account for individual differences between gifted and typical learners.

Conclusion

The CCSS in English language arts and mathematics presents a daunting challenge to our schools at a time when they may be least prepared to take it on, especially given lack of funding for teacher salaries, declining morale, and competing agendas. Yet it also offers the best hope for coherent high-level schooling for our students. The gifted education community must join this effort and transform our work to demonstrate to all that high-level standards need high-level translations in the classroom if all students are to fulfill their learning potential. For gifted learners, that requires differentiation of the CCSS in a comprehensive, articulated way.

Discussion Questions

1. What distinguishes a gifted curriculum from the regular curriculum?
2. In what ways has the emergence of content standards changed curriculum design and specifically curriculum design in gifted education?
3. How might curriculum designers in gifted education create high-quality assessments to document differentiated outcomes commensurate with increased complexity of the standards?
4. What support can be designed to help curriculum designers, teachers, and administrators successful integrate the CCSS in gifted education settings?

References

Adams, C., Cotabish, A., & Ricci, M. K. (2014). *Using the next generation science standards with gifted and advanced learners.* Waco, TX: Prufrock Press.

Cotabish, A., & Robinson, A. (2012). The effects of peer coaching on the evaluation knowledge, skills of gifted program administrators. *Gifted Child Quarterly, 56,* 160–170. doi:10.1177/0016986212446861

Council of Chief State School Officers. (2011). *InTASC model core teaching standards: A resource for state dialogue.* Retrieved from http://

www.ccsso.org/resources/programs/interstate_teacher_assessment_consortium_%28intasc%29.html

Feng, A. X., VanTassel-Baska, J., Quek, C., Bai, W., & O'Neill, B. (2005). A longitudinal assessment of gifted students' learning using the Integrated Curriculum Model (ICM): Impacts and perceptions of the William & Mary Language Arts and Science Curriculum. *Roeper Review, 27,* 78–83.

Halsted, J. W. (2009). *Some of my best friends are books: Guiding gifted readers* (3rd ed.). Tucson, AZ: Great Potential Press.

Hollingworth, L. S. (1926). *Gifted children: Their nature and nurture.* New York, NY: The Macmillan Company.

Hughes, C., Kettler, T., Shaughnessy-Dedrick, E., & VanTassel-Baska, J. (2014). *A teacher's guide to using the Common Core State Standards for gifted and advanced learners in the English language arts.* Waco, TX: Prufrock Press.

Indiana Department of Public Instruction. (2013). *Indiana high ability project (HAP) in English language arts (ELA).* Indianapolis, IN: Author.

Johnsen, S. K. (Ed.). (2012). *NAGC Pre-K–grade 12 gifted education programming standards: A guide to planning and implementing high-quality services.* Waco, TX: Prufrock Press.

Johnsen, S. K., Ryser, G. R., & Assouline, S. G. (2014). *A teacher's guide to using the Common Core State Standards with mathematically gifted and advanced learners.* Waco, TX: Prufrock Press.

Johnsen, S. K., & Sheffield, L. J. (Eds.). (2013). *Using the Common Core State Standards for mathematics with gifted and advanced learners.* Waco, TX: Prufrock Press.

Kanevsky, L. (2011). Deferential differentiation: What types of differentiation do students want? *Gifted Child Quarterly, 55,* 279–299.

Learning Forward. (2011). *Standards for professional learning: Learning communities.* Retrieved from http://www.learningforward.org/standards/learningcommunities/index.cfm

National Association for Gifted Children, & Council for Exceptional Children. (2013). *NAGC-CEC teacher knowledge and skills for gifted and talented education.* Retrieved from http://www.nagc.org/sites/default/files/standards/NAGC-%20CEC%20CAEP%20standards%20(2013%20final).pdf

National Governors Association Center for Best Practices, & Council of Chief State School Officers. (2010). *Common Core State Standards for English language arts.* Washington, DC: Author. Retrieved from http://www.corestandards.org/the-standards

Organisation for Economic Co-operation and Development. (2014). *PISA 2012 results in focus: What 15-year-olds know and what they can do with what they know.* Retrieved from http://www.oecd.org/pisa/keyfindings/pisa-2012-results-overview.pdf

Reis, S. M., Eckert, R. D., McCoach, D. B., Jacobs, J. K., & Coyne, M. (2008). Using enrichment reading practices to increase reading fluency, comprehension, and attitudes. *Journal of Educational Research, 101,* 299–314.

VanTassel-Baska, J. (Ed.). (2008). *Alternative assessments with gifted students.* Waco, TX: Prufrock Press.

VanTassel-Baska, J. (2010). *Patterns and profiles of promising learners from poverty.* Waco, TX: Prufrock Press.

VanTassel-Baska, J. (Ed.). (2013). *Using the Common Core State Standards for English language arts with gifted and advanced learners.* Waco, TX: Prufrock Press.

VanTassel-Baska, J., Avery, L. D., Little, C., & Hughes, C. (2000). An evaluation of the implementation of curriculum innovation: The impact of the William & Mary units on schools. *Journal for the Education of the Gifted, 23,* 244–272.

VanTassel-Baska, J., Bracken, B., Feng, A., & Brown, E. (2009). A longitudinal study of reading comprehension and reasoning ability of students in elementary Title I schools. *Journal for the Education of the Gifted, 33*(1), 7–37.

VanTassel-Baska, J., & Brown, E. (2007). Towards best practice: An analysis of the efficacy of curriculum models in gifted education. *Gifted Child Quarterly, 51,* 342–358.

VanTassel-Baska, J., Johnson, D. T., Hughes, C. E., & Boyce, L. N. (1996). A study of language arts curriculum effectiveness with gifted learners. *Journal for the Education of the Gifted, 19,* 461–480.

VanTassel-Baska, J., & Little, C. A. (Eds.). (2011). *Content-based curriculum for gifted learners* (2nd ed.). Waco, TX: Prufrock Press.

VanTassel-Baska, J., & Stambaugh, T. (2006). Project Athena: A pathway to advanced literacy development for children of poverty. *Gifted Child Today, 29*(2), 58–65.

VanTassel-Baska, J., Zuo, L., Avery, L., & Little, C. A. (2002). A curriculum study of gifted-student learning in the language arts. *Gifted Child Quarterly, 46,* 30–43.

SECTION 2

COMPONENTS OF MODERN GIFTED EDUCATION CURRICULUM

CHAPTER 6

A DIFFERENTIATED APPROACH TO CRITICAL THINKING IN CURRICULUM DESIGN

TODD KETTLER

The development of critical thinking skills is arguably the most consistent component of curriculum models in gifted education (see Jacobs & Borland, 1986; Passow, 1986; Tannenbaum, 1983; VanTassel-Baska, 1986; VanTassel-Baska & Little, 2011; Ward, 1961). Additionally, critical thinking is widely lauded as an increasingly important skill for 21st-century learning, including accessing and transforming prolific streams of information (Trilling & Fadel, 2009). For instance, the *Harvard Education Letter* recently listed critical thinking as the most important skill for the 21st century (Walser, 2008). The Partnership for 21st Century Skills (2004), one of the leading education advocacy organizations with business and state departments of education, has repeatedly called for the integration of critical thinking, problem solving, and communication skills across all areas of the curriculum.

From the middle to the later years of the 20th century, critical thinking may have been viewed as a differentiated learning goal for gifted students. It was differentiated in the sense that although it was clearly identified as an outcome for gifted students, critical thinking was not widely considered an outcome for general education. However, in the present educational climate, critical thinking has become a learning goal for all students. This shift may be evidenced by

DOI: 10.4324/9781003236696-8

the emphasis on argumentation in the Common Core State Standards (CCSS) for English Language Arts (National Governors Association Center for Best Practices & Council of Chief State School Officers, 2010) and the new frameworks focused on critical thinking in College Board's Advanced Placement program. This emphasis on critical thinking may also explain increasing use of inquiry teaching methods such as problem-based learning in classrooms at all levels. Thus, gifted education should no longer look at curriculum designed to foster critical thinking as qualitative differentiation. Curriculum standards to develop critical thinking are currently in place for all students across all core-content areas. Instead, I argue that curriculum designers in gifted education ought to consider critical thinking as a developed skill of which gifted students may have advanced levels compared to their general education peers (Kettler, 2014). Like other areas where gifted students typically display advanced skills, such as reading and mathematics, gifted curriculum should articulate a differentiated approach to teaching critical thinking that responds to characteristics of gifted learners.

What Is Critical Thinking?

Definitions of critical thinking abound, and any attempt to articulate curriculum theory involving critical thinking can be hampered by loosely agreed upon descriptions of what it means to think critically. Ennis (1996) defined critical thinking as reasonable and reflective thinking that is focused on making decisions about what to do or what to believe. Black (2007) defined it as analytical thinking that underlies rational discourse including analyzing, evaluating, and constructing arguments. Facione (1990) defined it as purposeful, self-regulatory judgment including interpretation, analysis, and evaluation of the context in which the judgment is based.

After exploring numerous delineations of thinking and evaluating educational standards for critical thinking, I recommend the following definition: Critical thinking is reflective thinking using principles of reason, logic, and evidence to analyze, evaluate, and construct consistent and coherent arguments, understandings, and judgments.

Critical thinking is not only a skill used to develop outcomes of learning, but also a component of the process of learning. As students construct meaning and understandings of new ideas, they ought to be using the skills of analysis and evaluation concurrent with concept formation. Gone is the era of an authoritative curriculum in which students are expected to acquire the commodity of knowledge. Instead, today's students encounter a curriculum of prolific information and competing perspectives. Critical thinking skills characterize the epistemology of the 21st-century learning environment. Students must use principles of reason, logic, and evidence to create consistent and productive understandings. Thus, the curriculum designer no longer assumes the role of knowledge organizer, one who packages and sequences facts, details, concepts, and theories into a course of study. Rather, the curriculum designer creates learning experiences in which students confront information and experiences and through reflection, analysis, and evaluation make meaningful understandings and judgments about the way things are and why it matters.

Although the Common Core State Standards do not offer an explicit definition of critical thinking, there are specific strands within those documents that provide educators with a standards-based understanding of what critical thinking looks like in the general education curriculum. The CCSS for language arts is the most formal articulation of critical thinking in the core curriculum, and within the language arts standards, critical thinking skills have also been articulated for literacy in history/social studies, as well as science and technical subjects. The CCSS for mathematics includes critical thinking in its standards of mathematical practice, but the skills are not clearly articulated across grade-level standards.

Critical thinking requirements are specified in the college and career readiness anchor standards for language arts. All students are expected to use logic, reason, and evidence to evaluate written and oral texts and construct arguments analyzing substantive topics (see Table 6.1). College and career readiness reading anchor standard 8 is considered the primary critical thinking standard for reading. Students begin in the primary years identifying reasons to support authors' points in texts. During the middle and late elementary years, students identify and explain logic, reason, and textual evidence. In middle school, all students recognize and evaluate the effectiveness of arguments in text based on principles of rationality and evidentiary support. By high school, all students should be analyzing complex arguments and fallacious reasoning in lengthy texts including seminal works in United States history, such as political documents (see Table 6.2).

All students in middle school and high school are expected to use critical thinking skills while reading in core content areas as well. The CCSS for language arts specify critical thinking skills for literacy in history/social studies as well as science and technical subjects (see Tables 6.3 and 6.4). Students distin-

TABLE 6.1

Critical Thinking in the Common Core State Standards for Language Arts

(National Governors Association Center for Best Practices & Council of Chief State School Officers, 2010)

Domain	Critical Thinking Standard
Reading	**College/Career Readiness Anchor: Reading Standard 1** Read closely to determine what the text says explicitly and make logical inferences from it; cite specific textual evidence when writing or speaking to support conclusions.
	College/Career Readiness Anchor: Reading Standard 8 Delineate and evaluate the argument and specific claims in a text, including the validity of the reasoning as well as the relevance and sufficiency of the evidence.
Writing	**College/Career Readiness Anchor: Writing Standard 1** Write arguments to support claims in an analysis of substantive topics or texts using valid reasoning and relevant and sufficient evidence.
	College/Career Readiness Anchor: Writing Standard 9 Draw evidence from literary or informational texts to support analysis, reflection, and research.
Speaking and Listening	**College/Career Readiness Anchor: Speaking/Listening Standard 3** Evaluate a speaker's point of view, reasoning, and use of evidence and rhetoric.
	College/Career Readiness Anchor: Speaking/Listening Standard 4 Present information, findings, and supporting evidence such that listeners can follow the line of reasoning.

guish between fact and opinion and evaluate authors' claims based on evidence and principles of reason in the social studies disciplines. Similarly, in science and technical subjects all students are expected to recognize arguments, distinguish fact from opinion, and analyze data as evidentiary support for claims and hypotheses.

Critical thinking is not limited to reading standards. All students are expected to construct arguments reflecting logic, reason, and evidentiary support not only in language arts, but also in the history/social studies and science/technical subjects disciplines. The college and career readiness anchor standard 1 for writing delineates a sequence of skills for constructing arguments in language arts. Additionally, argumentative writing standards are specified for writing across the curriculum in history/social studies and science/

TABLE 6.2

Critical Thinking Scope and Sequence for Reading Informational Text

Grade	Standard (Anchor Standard 8)
K	With prompting and support, identify the reasons an author gives to support points in a text.
1	Identify the reasons an author gives to support points in a text.
2	Describe how reasons support specific points the author makes in a text.
3	Describe the logical connection between particular sentences and paragraphs in a text (e.g., comparison, cause/effect, first/second/third in a sequence).
4	Explain how an author uses reasons and evidence to support particular points in a text.
5	Explain how an author uses reasons and evidence to support particular points in a text, identifying which reasons and evidence support which points.
6	Trace and evaluate the argument and specific claims in a text, distinguish claims that are supported by reasons and evidence from claims that are not.
7	Trace and evaluate the argument and specific claims in a text, assessing whether the reasoning is sound and evidence is relevant and sufficient to support the claims.
8	Delineate and evaluate the argument and specific claims in a text, assessing whether the reasoning is sound and the evidence is relevant and sufficient; recognize when irrelevant evidence is introduced.
9–10	Delineate and evaluate the argument and specific claims in a text, assessing whether the reasoning is sound and the evidence is relevant and sufficient; identify false statements and fallacious reasoning.
11–12	Delineate and evaluate the reasoning in seminal U.S. texts, including the application of constitutional principles and use of legal reasoning (e.g., in U.S. Supreme Court majority opinions and dissents) and the premises, purposes, and arguments in works of public advocacy (e.g., The Federalist, presidential addresses).

technical subjects (see Table 6.5). Students in all subjects are expected to introduce claims relative to the disciplinary content and support those claims using logic, reason, and evidence. Furthermore, all students are expected to anticipate counterclaims and analyze strengths and weaknesses of those counterclaims based on standards of reason.

TABLE 6.3

Critical Thinking Standards for History and Social Studies

Grades	Literacy in History/Social Studies Standard 8
6–8	Distinguish among fact, opinion, and reasoned judgment in text.
9–10	Assess the extent to which the reasoning and evidence in a text support the author's claims.
11–12	Evaluate the author's premises, claims, and evidence by corroborating or challenging them with other evidence.

TABLE 6.4

Critical Thinking Standards for Science and Technical Subjects

Grades	Literacy in Science and Technical Subjects Standard 8
6–8	Distinguish among facts, reasoned judgment based on research findings, and speculation in text.
9–10	Assess the extent to which the reasoning and evidence in a text support the author's claim or a recommendation for solving a scientific or technical problem.
11–12	Evaluate the hypotheses, data, analysis, and conclusions in a science or technical text, verifying the data when possible and corroborating or challenging conclusions with other sources of information.

The critical thinking expectations in the CCSS for language arts are perhaps the most clearly articulated critical thinking standards in the curriculum history of critical thinking emphases. This scope and sequence covers all grades from kindergarten through high school, and it includes literacy across the curriculum. Most importantly, these are the curriculum standards for critical thinking expectations for all students. How are we to understand curriculum development for critical thinking with gifted and advanced learners relative to the CCSS scope and sequence? What evidence-based practices inform the development of critical thinking curriculum and instruction?

TABLE 6.5

Critical Thinking Writing Standards for Social Studies and Science

Grades	Standard 1: Writing arguments focused on discipline-specific content.
6–8	a. Introduce claims about a topic or issue, acknowledge and distinguish the claims from alternate or opposing claims, and organize the reasons and evidence logically.
	b. Support claims with logical reasoning and relevant, accurate data and evidence that demonstrate an understanding of the topic or text, using credible sources.
	c. Use words, phrases, and clauses to create cohesion and clarifying the relationships among claims, counterclaims, reasons, and evidence.
9–10	a. Introduce precise claims, distinguish the claims from alternate or opposing claims, and create an organization that establishes clear relationships among the claims, counterclaims, reasons, and evidence.
	b. Develop claims and counterclaims fairly, supplying data and evidence for each while pointing out the strengths and limitations of both claims and counterclaims in a discipline-appropriate form and in a manner that anticipates the audience's knowledge level and concerns.
	c. Use words, phrases, and clauses to link the major sections of the text, create cohesion, and clarify the relationships between claims and reasons, between reasons and evidence, and between claims and counterclaims.
11–12	a. Introduce precise, knowledgeable claims, establish the significance of the claims, distinguish the claims from alternative or opposing claims, and create an organization that logically sequences the claims, counterclaims, reasons, and evidence.
	b. Develop claims and counterclaims fairly and thoroughly, supplying the most relevant data and evidence for each while pointing out the strengths and limitations of both claims and counterclaims in a discipline-appropriate form that anticipates the audience's knowledge level, concerns, values, and possible biases.
	c. Use words, phrases, and clauses as well as varied syntax to link the major sections of the text, create cohesion, and clarify the relationships between claims and reasons, between reasons and evidence, and between claims and counterclaims.

Teaching Critical Thinking

When intentionally trying to improve students' critical thinking skills, teaching approaches and curriculum matter (Abrami et al., 2008). Specifically, the most effective method for designing curriculum to teach critical thinking is known as the mixed-method approach (Ennis, 1989). In the mixed-method approach, an independent scope and sequence of critical thinking skills is taught (general method) combined with the infusion of critical thinking goals and learning experiences in course content (infusion method; McCarthy-Tucker, 1998). When designing a critical thinking curriculum using the mixed-methods approach, a direct instruction in critical thinking skills component is included. This direct instruction could be a separate course in critical thinking or a strand of curriculum within an existing course. For instance, a school might decide to include a critical thinking curriculum strand as part of its language arts program so that critical thinking is directly taught on a determined schedule across all grade levels. In addition to the direct instruction in critical thinking, specific critical thinking objectives are built into the curriculum of other course content. Thus, critical thinking objectives are added to the social studies or science content to coordinate with the skills that are taught in the direct instruction curriculum. Curriculum designers should make critical thinking requirements clear, and the largest student gains have been found where critical thinking skills were developed separately and then applied directly to learning tasks within content specific instruction. The least effective approach to teaching critical thinking is the immersion approach, where students are expected to develop critical thinking skills as a by-product of high-quality subject-matter instruction (Abrami et al., 2008). Despite lack of evidence of effectiveness, this immersion approach remains popular in many schools and classrooms.

Professional learning in how to teach critical thinking skills is also an important component of implementing an effective critical thinking curriculum (Feuerstein, 1999; VanTassel-Baska, Zuo, Avery, & Little, 2002). Abrami et al. (2008) found that published studies where teachers had specific training revealed more student growth in critical thinking than studies where teachers had no specific training. Teachers and administrators need to learn exactly what is and is not considered critical thinking. They need to know what the learner objectives include, and what it looks like as both direct instruction and infusion into course content. Teachers need specific examples of how they can teach and assess critical thinking in their content area. Furthermore, in studies where the administrators monitored lesson plans for inclusion of critical thinking and observed classrooms specifically looking for critical thinking, teachers were more consistent in implementation and students showed larger gains in critical thinking skills.

Some instructional strategies are more effective than others at developing critical thinking skills and dispositions. Opportunities for dialogue/discussion have shown evidence of improving students' critical thinking skills, especially when the teacher poses quality questions to the whole class or to small groups of students. Additionally, having students engage in authentic or situated problems where problem-solving expectations are present improves critical thinking skills. Some evidence also supports role-playing methods as effective at developing critical thinking skills. Examples from the research include nurse and patient role-playing in nursing education and policy debates in which students play designated roles in social studies classes (Abrami et al., 2014).

In summary, students' critical thinking skills do not tend to develop by accident or mere time spent in school. Instead, improved student thinking performance is associated with an intentional approach that combines direct instruction in discrete critical thinking skills and a curriculum that requires students to apply those critical thinking skills to the learning of concepts, issues, and ideas in specific content curricula. Furthermore, teachers need both initial and ongoing professional learning in critical thinking, and administrators need training and tools to support the fidelity of the instructional program.

A Differentiated Approach to Teaching Critical Thinking

Previous research has provided evidence that as early as fourth grade, there is a moderate to strong relationship between cognitive ability and developed critical thinking skills (Kettler, 2014). Gifted students tend to perform significantly higher on standardized assessments of critical thinking than their general education peers. It is possible, or even likely that this difference could be found earlier than fourth grade, but standardized measures of critical thinking for younger children are not available. Therefore, as in the teaching of reading skills or math skills, when teaching critical thinking skills, one-size instruction does not fit all students. Thus, a differentiated approach to critical thinking curriculum and instruction is needed.

A differentiated approach to critical thinking curriculum and instruction modifies the depth, breadth, and pace at which gifted or advanced students practice and learn critical thinking skills. A differentiated approach starts with the assumption that all students will be developing skills as critical thinkers, but some students, namely those with advanced cognitive abilities, will master skills earlier and learn faster than other students. A differentiated approach includes the following elements: (a) explicit goals and objectives related to advanced critical thinking, (b) articulation of an advanced taxonomy of critical thinking skills, (c) mechanisms to accelerate students' progress through the standard critical thinking curriculum, (d) content modification to increase the complexity of critical thinking tasks, and (e) authentic assessment rubrics capable of measuring advanced levels of critical thinking across content areas.

Critical Thinking Goals

Begin with the end in mind. Establish a clear goal for the emphasis on critical thinking development in the gifted education program. Harry Passow (1986) argued that, "Without a clear concept of what it is we expect the gifted and talented to achieve, what it is we want them 'to become,' our curriculum efforts will be directionless" (p. 186). Clearly stated goals not only give curriculum developers direction, but they also allow them some direction on measurement to determine the effectiveness of the curriculum and instructional design. I recommend something like the following:

Students participating in the gifted and talented program will develop advanced critical thinking skills as evidenced by the development of products and performances reflecting critical analysis and evaluation, clear and coherent arguments, and the formation of well-reasoned judgments and decisions.

This broad goal for developing gifted students' critical thinking skills can be further broken into subject-specific gifted program objectives, such as the following:

> » In the gifted and talented program in language arts, students will develop advanced critical thinking skills as evidenced by the develop-

ment of clear and coherent argumentative papers analyzing and evaluating the reasoning in classic and contemporary texts.

» In the gifted and talented program in social studies, students will develop advanced critical thinking skills as evidenced by the introduction and development of claims that represent innovative ideas and insightful commentary on issues of government, politics, geography, and economics.

» In the gifted and talented program in science, students will develop advanced critical thinking skills as evidenced by the development of scientifically supported claims that corroborate or challenge myths, ideas, and theories.

The goals and objectives ought to connect the standards of critical thinking and the specificity of the content being studied. The goals and objectives should also point toward a systematic measurement of whether and to what extent the goals have been achieved at the individual student level as well as the program level.

Advanced Taxonomy of Critical Thinking Skills

The CCSS for language arts have provided a thoughtful articulation of critical thinking in language arts with connections to other disciplines. Other specific critical thinking taxonomies have been developed (see Black, 2008; Facione, 1990). Perhaps the most current and researched critical thinking taxonomy is the one developed by Cambridge Assessment (Black, 2008, 2009). The Cambridge taxonomy was developed as an intermediate step in the development of Cambridge Assessment's new test of critical thinking among secondary students, Critical Thinking AS/A. The role of the advanced taxonomy of critical thinking skills is to provide designers of gifted or advanced curriculum with an articulated set of skills that are more complex and demanding than those skills in the foundational curriculum.

We can assume the CCSS for language arts sequence of critical thinking skills in reading and writing form the grade-level expectations for all students (see Table 6.2). Based on evidence suggesting that gifted students may be more proficient at critical thinking than their grade-level peers, the need to differentiate learning experiences and expectations is likely to arise. A taxonomy of critical thinking skills (Table 6.6) serves as a tool for curriculum designers and teachers to make modification to the learning experiences of gifted students in a systematic way. The advanced taxonomy can serve as a tool for teachers making instructional modifications at the individual classroom level, and it can also serve as a tool for curriculum designers engaged in developing a set of specific skills to be taught as part of the gifted and talented curriculum.

At the deepest level of critical thinking curriculum development, the design team would use the advanced taxonomy to articulate a grade-level scope and sequence of the skills in the taxonomy. Then clear expectations and sample lessons would be developed for integrating that scope and sequence of skills in the core content curriculum for gifted and advanced learners. This advanced scope and sequence of critical thinking skills does not replace the scope and sequence presented in the CCSS-ELA. Instead it becomes the foundation for a differentiated approach to meeting the stated program goal of developing advanced critical thinking skills. Ideally, the scope and sequence of advanced critical thinking skills also includes required and recommended advanced-level products and performances and accompanying rubrics to measure student performance and document growth and achievement.

Mechanisms to Accelerate

Acceleration is perhaps the mostly widely supported evidence-based practice in gifted education (Colangelo, Assouline, & Gross, 2004; Southern & Jones, 1991; Swiatek & Benbow, 1991). Essentially, there are two ways of thinking about acceleration. In the first way, acceleration involves acceleration of the student to the curriculum (grade-skipping, early entrance, credit by examination). In the second way, acceleration involves acceleration of the curriculum to the student (curriculum compacting, content acceleration, tiered objectives). A differentiated approach to teaching critical thinking involves the second type of acceleration, moving students through articulated standards or taxonomy of skills at a faster rate than would be expected.

For example, a typical fourth-grade student is expected to be able to explain how an author uses reasons and evidences to support particular points in a text (see Table 6.2). Through preassessment and observation, the teacher may realize that gifted or advanced students master this skill quickly, well before the other students. Thus, rather than continuing to practice the same already-mas-

TABLE 6.6

Cambridge Assessment Taxonomy of Critical Thinking Skills and Processes

Skill	Processes
1. Analysis	1A. Recognizing and using the basic terminology of reasoning
	1B. Recognizing arguments and explanations
	1C. Recognizing different types of reasoning
	1D. Dissecting an argument
	1E. Categorizing the component parts of an argument and identifying its structure
	1F. Identifying unstated assumptions
	1G. Clarifying meaning
2. Evaluation	2A. Judging relevance
	2B. Judging sufficiency
	2C. Judging significance
	2D. Assessing credibility
	2E. Assessing plausibility
	2F. Assessing analogies
	2G. Detecting errors in reasoning
	2H. Assessing the soundness of reasoning within an argument
	2I. Considering the impact of further evidence upon an argument
3. Inference	3A. Considering the implications of claims, points of view, principles, and suppositions
	3B. Drawing appropriate conclusions based on reason and/or evidence
4. Construction	4A. Selecting material relevant to an argument
	4B. Constructing a coherent and relevant argument or counter-argument
	4C. Taking arguments further
	4D. Forming well-reasoned judgments
	4E. Responding to dilemmas
	4F. Making and justifying rational decisions
5. Self-Reflection	5A. Questioning one's own preconceptions
	5B. Careful and persistent evaluation of one's own reasoning

Note. Adapted from *Critical Thinking—A Definition and Taxonomy for Cambridge Assessment: Supporting Validity Arguments About Critical Thinking Assessments Administered by Cambridge Assessment* (pp. 9–10) by B. Black, retrieved from http://www.cambridgeassessment.org.uk/Images/126340-critical-thinking-a-definition-and-taxonomy.pdf.

tered skill, the teacher may differentiate the critical thinking expectation by accelerating the objective. Thus, the differentiated task reflects the fifth-grade standard (which asks students to explain how an author uses reasons and evidences to support particular points in a text, identifying which reasons and evidences support which points). Perhaps after a few repetitions, the gifted or advanced students master the skill of connecting the reasons and the evidences supporting each point. Further acceleration may include differentiated learning tasks at the sixth- or seventh-grade level of the standard.

This content standard acceleration exemplifies relatively simple instructional differentiation. The instructional strategy results in a tiered instructional approach where the most advanced tier of students is working on a differentiated task informed by advanced levels of the same standard that the on-level students are practicing. To effectively implement this differentiated approach, teachers need to understand the flow of the standards across grade levels such as the standard flow chart presented in Table 6.2. Thus, in the differentiated approach to critical thinking, curriculum and instruction are interconnected so that teachers are provided not only the sequence of the objectives, but perhaps even curriculum examples of how to teach the standard at above-grade levels.

Content Modification for Complexity

In addition to the mechanisms to accelerate, the differentiated approach to teaching critical thinking includes content modifications for complexity. Complexity maintains the same grade-level standard, but differentiates the learning experience though modifications to the content or product demands. For instance, in the example above, a fourth-grade student is expected to explain how an author uses reasons and evidences to support particular points in a text. Whereas the acceleration approach increased the demands of the thinking process using the same informational text, the modification for complexity keeps the grade-level thinking process but differentiates the complexity of the text. One way to differentiate text complexity is to use primary documents with advanced vocabulary and more sophisticated reasoning. Thus, where the typical fourth-grade assignment may involve reading a news editorial provided in the school curriculum, the gifted or advanced critical thinking task might require the student to read the Declaration of Independence and identify how the author used reasons and evidences to support particular points in the text.

In some cases where students are particularly advanced, the teacher may combine the mechanism for acceleration and content modification and have students read the more advanced text and perform the above-grade-level standard.

A teacher or curriculum designer might make content modifications for complexity within critical thinking tasks by invoking strategies to increase depth and complexity (Kaplan, 2009). For instance, in the fourth-grade example, the student may be expected to explain how the author uses reasons and evidences to support particular points, then also consider how those same reasons and evidences may be alternately considered from a different point of view. The task may also be differentiated for complexity by requiring the student to identify a parallel or analogous relationship where that author might make a different claim using the same reasons and evidences. Further, the task demand could be differentiated for complexity by requiring the student to point out fallacies or incongruities in the author's argument.

The advanced taxonomy of critical thinking could also be used to support modifications for complexity. In the fourth-grade task where the student is to read a news editorial and explain how the author uses reason and evidences to support his points, the teacher could increase the complexity of the task demand by judging the sufficiency of the author's evidence or assessing the plausibility of the author's recommendations (see Table 6.6). By using the advanced taxonomy of critical thinking skills, the teacher or curriculum designer is able to differentiate the thinking process skills required to complete the task.

Authentic Assessments of Critical Thinking

The final component of the differentiated approach to teaching critical thinking is authentic assessment of advanced task demands using rubrics to delineate levels of critical thinking proficiency. The recommended goal stated that students will develop advanced critical thinking skills as evidenced by the development of products and performances reflecting critical analysis and evaluation, clear and coherent arguments, and the formation of well-reasoned judgments and decisions. Ultimately those products and performances must be evaluated, and the evaluation may be a combination of content mastery and critical thinking skill proficiency.

In order to assess advanced critical thinking skills, teachers and curriculum designers will need to develop and use rubrics that have high performance ceilings. In other words, differentiated task demands dictate the use of differentiated rubrics to assess performance. Assessment of advanced critical thinking ought to focus on the two big ideas in critical thinking standards: argument analysis and argument construction. Quality indicators of both analysis and construction include coherent use of reasoning and evidence, depth of analysis, recognition of complexity, honest consideration of multiple perspectives, consistency, and avoidance of fallacies and contradictions.

Advanced-level products may include construction of coherent arguments to support claims and ideas in core content areas. These constructions may include traditional and innovative products such as formal papers and multimedia documentaries. Performances may include oratories, debates, and active participation in discussion seminars. Consideration should be given to what constitutes an advanced product or performance. In some cases, all students create the same product or performance and the distinction of advanced is a qualitative difference. In other cases, gifted and advanced students may create products and performances that are unique or unlike those developed by typical learners. Ideally, through the process of curriculum construction, clear descriptions of advanced products and performances are developed across grade levels and core subject areas. Furthermore, quality rubrics with high performance ceilings would accompany those product/performance descriptions.

Conclusion and Implications for Research

Developing critical thinking skills has been a consistent goal for gifted education for decades, but in the present age of instant information and ubiquitous technology, developing critical thinking for all students is widely regarded as an important educational outcome. Evidence suggests gifted and advanced students will demonstrate more advanced levels of critical thinking than typical grade-level peers. Thus, it is recommended that educational systems consider both typical and differentiated approaches to critical thinking skill development. Curriculum designers focusing on gifted and advanced students are in a position to articulate advanced critical thinking outcomes and create learning experiences that develop advanced critical thinking skills. This approach conceives of thinking skill development similar to literacy and numeracy skill development. Individual differences in the learners' abilities require differentiated curriculum and instruction to meet appropriate advanced performance goals.

Although the field of gifted education has long advocated development of critical thinking skills, our documented evidence of actually accomplishing that goal is limited. Our field seems to be moving into a new era where all students are taught to think critically, and gifted students are expected to develop advanced levels of proficiency. There are a few implications for needed research. First, we have no research at this time to document how gifted students are performing on the critical thinking standards within the CCSS language arts. Although evidence suggests gifted students will be advanced compared to grade-level peers, we do not know if they will be advanced with regard to the standards. Second, we need to design advanced critical thinking curricula in language arts, social studies, and science and develop scalable authentic assessments to measure the efficacy of those curricula. Third, we need systematic development and validation of high-quality assessment protocols that reliably measure growth and achievement in domain-specific critical thinking products and performances. Fourth, we know that successful implementation of critical thinking curriculum and instructional strategies require professional learning and implementation accountability. To that end, we need studies designed to measure the types of training that are most effective at equipping teachers to integrate advanced critical thinking into their content specific curricula.

More than 75 years ago, John Dewey (1925) and Edward Glaser (1941) expressed concern that education in the United States was mediocre or worse at developing a thinking citizenry willing and capable to critically evaluate public and privately held beliefs. Contemporary analysis by Susan Jacoby (2008) suggested little progress has been made since Dewey and Glaser made those pleas for a critical thinking curriculum. The future is an open book of possibility for taking seriously the charge to teach our most advanced students to claim reason, clarity, and consistency as their hallmarks.

Discussion Questions

1. What evidence suggests that creating and implementing a critical thinking approach to learning is not universally accepted as an educational goal?
2. In what ways is critical thinking more of a general set of skills and in what ways is it more of a domain-specific set of skills?

3. What are challenges or barriers to making critical thinking a clearly recognizable feature of core content curricula?
4. What types of professional learning might be necessary to prepare teachers and administrators to fully implement a differentiated approach to critical thinking?

References

Abrami, P. C., Bernard, R. M., Borokhovski, E., Waddington, D. I., Wade, C. A., Persson, T. (2014). Strategies for teaching students to think critically: A meta-analysis. *Review of Educational Research.* Advance online publication. doi:10.3102/0034654314551063

Abrami, P. C., Bernard, R. M., Borokhovski, E., Wade, A., Surkes, M. A., Tamim, R., & Zhang, D. (2008). Instructional interventions affecting critical thinking skills and dispositions: A state 1 meta-analysis. *Review of Educational Research, 78,* 1102–1134.

Black, B. (2007). Critical thinking: A tangible construct? *Research Matters: A Cambridge Assessment Publication, 2,* 2–4.

Black, B. (2008). *Critical thinking—a definition and taxonomy for Cambridge Assessment: Supporting validity arguments about critical thinking assessments administered by Cambridge Assessment.* Retrieved from http://www.cambridgeassessment.org.uk/Images/126340-critical-thinking-a-definition-and-taxonomy.pdf

Black, B. (2009). *Introducing a new subject and its assessment in schools: The challenges of introducing Critical Thinking AS/S level in the U.K.* Retrieved from http://www.cambridgeassessment.org.uk/Images/126122-introducing-a-new-subject-and-its-assessment-in-schools-the-challenges-of-introducing-critical-thinking-as-a-level-in-the-uk.pdf

Colangelo, N., Assouline, S. G., & Gross, M. U. M. (2004). *A nation deceived: How schools hold back America's brightest students.* Iowa City: University of Iowa, The Connie Belin and Jacqueline N. Blank International Center for Gifted Education and Talent Development.

Dewey, J. (1925). *Experience and nature.* Chicago, IL: Open Court.

Ennis, R. H. (1989). Critical thinking and subject specificity: Clarification and needed research. *Educational Researcher, 18*(3), 4–10.

Ennis, R. H. (1996). *Critical thinking.* New York, NY: Prentice Hall.

Facione, P. A. (1990). *Critical thinking: A statement of expert consensus for purposes of educational assessment and instruction. Research findings and recommendations.* Newark, DE: American Philosophical Association. (ERIC Document Reproduction Services No. ED315423)

Feuerstein, M. (1999). Media literacy in support of critical thinking. *Journal of Educational Media, 24*(1), 43–54.

Glaser, E. M. (1941). *An experiment in the development of critical thinking.* New York, NY: Teachers College, Columbia University.

Jacobs, H. H., & Borland, J. H. (1986). The interdisciplinary concept model: Theory and Practice. *Gifted Child Quarterly, 30,* 159–163. doi:10.1177/001698628603000403

Jacoby, S. (2008). *The age of American unreason.* New York, NY: Pantheon Books.

Kaplan, S. K. (2009). Layering differentiated curricula for the gifted and talented. In F. A. Karnes, & S. M. Bean (Eds.), *Methods and materials for teaching the gifted* (3rd ed., pp. 107–135). Waco, TX: Prufrock Press.

Kettler, T. (2014). Critical thinking skills among elementary school students: Comparing identified gifted and general education student performance. *Gifted Child Quarterly, 58,* 127–136. doi:10.1177/0016986214522508

McCarthy-Tucker, T. S. N. (1998). Teaching logic to adolescents to improve thinking skills. *Korean Journal of Thinking and Problem Solving, 8*(1), 45–66.

National Governors Association Center for Best Practices, & Council of Chief State School Officers. (2010). *Common Core State Standards for English language arts.* Washington, DC: Author.

Partnership for 21st Century Skills. (2004). *Moving education forward.* Retrieved from http://www.21stCenturyskills.org

Passow, A. H. (1986). Curriculum for the gifted and talented at the secondary level. *Gifted Child Quarterly, 30,* 186–191. doi:10.1177/001698628603000409

Southern, T., & Jones, E. (Eds.). (1991). *The academic acceleration of gifted students.* New York, NY: Teachers College Press.

Swiatek, M. A., & Benbow, C. P. (1991). Ten-year longitudinal follow-up of ability matched accelerated and unaccelerated gifted students. *Journal of Educational Psychology, 83,* 528–538.

Tannenbaum, A. J. (1983). *Gifted children: Psychological and educational perspectives.* New York, NY: Macmillan.

Trilling, B., & Fadel, C. (2009). *21st century skills: Learning for life in our times.* San Francisco, CA: Jossey-Bass.

VanTassel-Baska, J. (1986). Effective curriculum and instructional models for talented students. *Gifted Child Quarterly, 30,* 164–169. doi:10.1177/001698628603000404

VanTassel-Baska, J., & Little, C. A. (Eds.). (2011). *Content-based curriculum for high ability learners* (2nd ed.). Waco, TX: Prufrock Press.

VanTassel-Baska, J., Zuo, L., Avery, L. D., & C. A. Little. (2002). A curriculum study of gifted student learning in language arts. *Gifted Child Quarterly, 46,* 30–44.

Walser, N. (2008). Teaching 21st century skills. *Harvard Education Letter, 24*(5), 1–3.

Ward, V. (1961). *Educating the gifted: An axiomatic approach.* Columbus, OH: Charles Merrill Company.

CHAPTER 7

LEARNING AS A CREATIVE ACT

RONALD A. BEGHETTO

Learning is creation, not consumption—Meier (2000)

It has been said that learning is a creative act. Indeed some of the earliest creativity researchers have acknowledged the central role that creativity plays in academic learning (Barron, 1969; Guilford, 1950; Torrance, 1959; Vygotsky, 1967/2004; Warnock, 1978). Curriculum designers, however, sometimes view creativity and academic learning as important, but separate curricular goals (Beghetto & Kaufman, 2009). Why might this be the case? What is at the heart of this inconsistency? Can we really say that learning is a creative act? If so, what would the implications be for the design of modern curricula?

The purpose of this chapter is to address these questions. More specifically, I will discuss why creativity and academic learning are sometimes viewed as incompatible goals. I will then attempt to illustrate how creativity serves as an act of learning and how learning can become a creative act. I will close by providing suggestions for how these insights might be used to guide the design of creative learning experiences and highlight implications for research.

DOI: 10.4324/9781003236696-9

Valued But Separate Goals

Teachers who value creativity and subject matter learning may feel caught between two seemingly incompatible curricular goals (Beghetto, 2007). They want to incorporate creativity into their curriculum, but worry that doing so might lead to curricular chaos. Similarly, they recognize the importance of developing their students' academic competence, but worry that focusing too much on standardized curricula will crush their students' (and their own) creativity. One way to resolve this tension is to view creativity as an add-on or separate goal. As any educator knows, however, there is always more to cover than time to cover it. Consequently, teachers may feel that they need to choose between creativity and academic work.

An example of how teachers make such a choice comes from a study I conducted a few years ago (Beghetto, 2008). I explored whether college students interested in becoming teachers (but who have not yet taught), believed that creativity and academic subject matter were compatible (both/and) or separate (either/or) goals. More than two thirds of prospective teachers (68.5%, $N = 176$) indicated that they believed there was a specific grade level when teachers should emphasize memorizing academic facts rather than focus on encouraging students' creative imagination. The prospective teachers disproportionately nominated the elementary grades as the grade level when teachers should focus on memorization (at the expense of cultivating the creative imagination).

Prospective teachers' rationale for separating creativity and academic learning represented two types of beliefs: (1) a memorization-as-foundation belief and (2) a memorization-as-time-to-get-serious belief. The first refers to a belief that students need a foundation of facts prior to being able to think creatively. This is somewhat understandable, but still problematic in that it does not recognize that learning facts can be aided by imaginative or creative thought. The second is a bit more fatalistic and refers to the belief that creativity is frivolous and, at some point, students need to get down to the serious business of memorizing academic facts so they are ready for the rigors of later schooling and the world of work. Importantly, not all prospective teachers believed creativity should be separated from academic learning, but the majority did.

In the context of the present discussion, the key take-away from the above study is the fact that these respondents were prospective teachers. This suggests that these beliefs developed, at least in part, from their own prior experiences as K–12 students. Moreover, the majority of these prospective teachers seemed to believe that, at some point, they as teachers would need to choose between creativity and academic learning. This is an example of how narrow beliefs about creativity can carry over from one's prior schooling experiences and influence educators' instructional beliefs.

The simple truth is, unless creativity is meaningfully embedded in the curriculum, then there is little chance that teachers will be able to make room for it. Establishing some sort of extra "creativity time" is not feasible. Even if it were, separating creativity from academic learning would do little by way of developing students' creative competence. Indeed, creative competence does not develop in a vacuum (Guilford, 1950). It requires a domain (Baer, 2012). In the context of the classroom, the academic subject areas serve as the domain in which students' creative competence can be nurtured.

Fortunately, there are curricula that include creativity. Many of these curricula are aimed at the most advanced students. This focus on providing specialized curricula for "gifted" students is likely an upshot of Marland's 1972 landmark report on educating advanced students. In his report, Marland specified "creative and productive thinking" as one of six possible indicators of talent and giftedness. Importantly, however, Marland referred to creative expression as separate from academic learning. In the years following his report, it is therefore not surprising that curricula based on his indicators of giftedness tend to also separate creative expression from academic learning.

Consider, for example, the "academic" and "innovative" paths described in the *Child-Responsive Model of Giftedness* (Callahan & Miller, 2005) or "schoolhouse" and "creative-productive" giftedness presented in the *Three-Ring Conception of Giftedness* (Renzulli, 2005). Although these curricula have done much to increase recognition that creativity and academic learning can be compatible curricular goals, conceptualizing them as different paths or different types of giftedness can preclude the recognition on the part of educators that creativity is an act of learning.

Why are creativity and academic learning often conceptualized as separate curricular goals or paths? One reason is because many of us have inherited an overly narrow view of academic learning that does not reward or include creative expression. Indeed, much of modern schooling is based on an *acquisition-reproduction* view of the educated mind (Beghetto, 2013). According to this view, the most highly educated individuals are those who have amassed "a great deal of the most important knowledge" (Egan & Gajdamaschko, 2003, p. 84) and can rapidly and accurately reproduce it.

On the basis of this view, the academic curriculum represents a catalogue of ready-made curricula that teachers can easily deliver to students for quick acquisition and accurate reproduction (Beghetto, 2013; Hatano, 1993; Sawyer,

2010). In fact, the prototypical teaching meme that gets passed on from one generation of teachers to the next is: Teachers ask known-answer questions, students provide a response, and then teachers immediately assess whether that response matches what was expected. Mehan (1979) has described this as the Initiate, Respond, and Evaluate (IRE) pattern of talk.

Cazden (2001) has called IRE the default pattern of school talk. IRE is so widespread that it can be readily observed in children playing school. As a result, students quickly learn that when teachers ask questions the correct response is typically the expected response (Beghetto, 2007; Black & Wiliam, 1998). Consequently, by the time students leave school, it is likely that they have learned that classroom success is less about providing their own creative ideas and more about figuring out the quickest and most direct route to produce *what* their teacher expects to hear and *how* their teacher expects to hear it (see Beghetto, 2010a).

School success therefore becomes more of a guessing game (i.e., guess what your teacher wants) than an opportunity to share and receive feedback on one's own ideas and insights. Successful students—who later go on to become teachers—may hold a very narrow conception of what it means to "understand" something in a classroom setting. This restricted view of understanding can be represented in the following notation:

$$U_s = W_e \times H_e$$

The U_s represents student understanding, W_e represents *what* is expected (i.e., the answer or outcome) and H_e represents *how* it is expected (i.e., the method or approach used to arrive at that answer). The key aspect of this formulation is that U_s represents a multiplicative relationship between W_e and H_e. Consequently, student understanding requires matching both what the teacher expects and how the teacher expects it. Below is an example I frequently use to illustrate how this formulation guides instructional practice.

Imagine a teacher who has taught her second-grade students how to use the concept of "borrowing" when performing double-column subtraction. In the case of the problem, 26 – 17, the teacher would expect that students arrived at the answer of 9 (i.e., W_e). Moreover, when asked how they arrived at that answer, the teacher would expect an explanation (i.e., H_e) that matches the previously taught approach (i.e., "borrow 10 from 20, add it to 6, that would be 16, subtract from 7, and that would be 9").

Understanding in this case requires the student to provide the expected answer (i.e., "9") *and* the expected method for arriving at that answer (i.e., use of the borrowing strategy). On first blush, this may seem completely reasonable (particularly in the context of something as straight forward as math), but the problem with this view of understanding is that it leaves no room for original or creative expression. Indeed, keeping with the notation, originality would be represented as:

$$O = (1 - W_e) \times (1 - H_e)$$

Originality would be anything different from what is expected and how it is expected. Originality is a key aspect of creativity, but many people (mistakenly) equate creativity with originality (Beghetto, 2010b). In fact, most thesauruses and dictionaries list originality as a synonym for creativity. This, in turn, results in creative expression being viewed as antithetical to student understanding:

$$C = O \neq U_s$$

In the context of this math example, it is true that there is little room for creativity in the answer (W_e). There is no getting around the fact that the answer to 26 − 17 is 9 (not "butterflies" or "pizza"). There is, however, room for creativity in the method of arriving at that answer (H_e).

Imagine a student, Gary, who explained that he arrived at "9" by ". . . adding 3 back to 6." Although Gary has provided the expected answer (W_e), his explanation is by most accounts quite surprising ($1 - H_e$). In such a case, a seemingly reasonable response from a teacher might involve gently dismissing Gary—saying something like, "Gary, that's not what I was looking for. Why don't you think about that some more and I'll call on someone else?" Recall the prototypical teacher-talk meme results in teachers immediately evaluating a student response (based on what the teacher expects to hear). Doing so, however, can result in missed opportunities to recognize and develop students' creative potential (as will be discussed below).

Creativity in a Classroom Context

When creativity is viewed as unconstrained originality, it is easy to understand how inviting creativity into the classroom would be viewed as blindly jumping down a curricular rabbit hole. Fortunately, creativity is more than originality. Researchers are in general agreement that creativity refers to anything that is both original and task-appropriate as defined within a particular context (Beghetto, 2013; Plucker, Beghetto, & Dow, 2004). This definition can be illustrated in the following notation (adapted from Beghetto & Kaufman, 2014; Simonton, 2012):

$$[C = O \times TA]_{context}$$

The C represents creativity, the O represents originality, and the TA represents task appropriateness. All three are defined by a particular social, cultural, and historical context. If an original expression of an idea, behavior, or product is not viewed as appropriate for a particular task, then it cannot be said to be creative. Similarly, if that expression is task appropriate, but not viewed as original for that particular context then it is simply conforming to expectation (and not creative). Creativity requires both O *and* TA and context matters when it comes to making judgments about creativity.

A student's short story, for example, might be viewed as creative in one context (e.g., ninth-grade English class), but not in another context (e.g., a submission to *New Yorker* magazine). In this way, creativity can be thought of as constrained originality (Keller & Keller, 1996). In the context of the classroom, originality is constrained by the learning task. Let's return to the double column subtraction example (26 − 17 = 9) to illustrate.

Gary explained that he arrived at "9" by "... adding 6 back on to 3." Although he provided the expected answer, his explanation was very surprising. At this point, it is impossible to know whether Gary is confused, being silly, or has a creative idea that needs to be more clearly articulated. Immediately evaluating this explanation as incorrect because it is different from what was expected does little by way of knowing whether there is something more going on and also does little to help Gary. In this situation, a teacher simply needs to take a moment to remind Gary of the task constraints and explore the unusual explanation (rather than immediately evaluate his response as incorrect), with statements like, "Helps us understand this Gary. I'm not seeing how adding 6 and 3 fits with the problem we are trying to solve. . . . Can you explain how it fits?"

Because they are still learning a domain, students often need support in articulating their ideas. Many times, their first attempts at articulating their ideas will be rough, unpolished, and seemingly confused. When teachers take the time to draw out students' ideas, they often discover that students have an underlying conception that is new and meaningful to them and can thereby still be considered creative (at least at a subjective level; see Beghetto &

Kaufman, 2007; Runco, 1996; Stein, 1953). Of course, subjective (or mini-c) experiences of creativity do not always rise to the level of more objective (or larger C) judgments of creativity (i.e., viewed as creative in the eyes of others). Importantly, however, subjective experiences of creativity serve as the genesis of more objective forms of creative expression (Kaufman & Beghetto, 2009). Moreover, teachers can support the development from subjective (mini-c) to more objective (little-c) forms of creativity through feedback (Beghetto & Kaufman, 2014).

If Gary's teacher invites him to further explain his surprising response, then she may help him articulate a conception that refines his understanding. Doing so may even benefit the learning of others. When this happens, even the teacher has an opportunity to learn. Imagine if Gary's teacher asked him to explain his response $(26 - 17 = 9)$ and he provided the following explanation[1]: "First you take off 10 from 20 and that would be 10 ... take off 7 more and now you have 3 ... add the 6 back on and that would be 9."

In this case, Gary has a very original approach. The approach, however, is more than simply original. It's mathematically accurate and, thereby, creative. This example illustrates how creativity serves as an act of learning and, in some cases, how learning can serve as a creative act. This assertion requires a bit more clarification.

Creativity as an Act of Learning

The acquisition-reproduction view of learning (discussed earlier) is at odds with contemporary views of learning. The acquisition-reproduction view represents a belief that learners' conceptions should directly correspond with their teachers' conceptions. This is problematic on many levels, not the least of which is the fact that students who share similar social, cultural, and historical backgrounds with their teachers will be privileged in such an arrangement. Indeed, they are more likely to be able to guess what their teacher wants to hear and how their teacher wants to hear it. The more diverse—and potentially creative—the students' interpretation or insight, the more likely it will be dismissed.

---

1   The initial part of the scenario and initial student response is fictionalized, but the student's approach to solving the problem is adapted from videotaped footage of an actual second-grade student (Kamii, 2000).

Fortunately, contemporary learning theorists recognize that students enter the classroom with robust conceptions about subject matter, which are largely influenced by their unique sociocultural experiences (Donovan & Bransford, 2005). Accordingly, learning can be said to result from a process of interpreting new experiences in light of our prior knowledge. Given that no two people have exactly the same experience, the assumption that learners' conceptions can ever directly correspond with their teacher's expectations and conceptions is untenable. Most teachers, of course, do not take such an extremist position (i.e., learners must match exactly what is expected). Still, the acquisition-reproduction view of learning is so pervasive that even those with a more moderate position may privilege students who can most quickly converge on their expectations. When this happens, teachers may view anything that doesn't easily fit into what they expect as irrelevant, surplus knowledge. This surplus, however, is filled with creative potential (Beghetto, 2013). Allowing students an opportunity to combine their unique personal insights with the subject matter being presented can, as was the case with Gary, result in new and meaningful insights.

Creativity researchers have long argued that at the heart of much creativity are diverse conceptual combinations (Ward, Smith, & Vaid, 1997). Indeed, some of the most creative insights and innovations have resulted from such combinations (combining diverse and, even seemingly irrelevant concepts, ideas, and objects). Consider the iPhone, for instance. The combination of cell phone, portable music player, and handheld computer has resulted in a revolutionary technological innovation.

A view of learning that privileges quick convergence on the teachers' fixed expectations undermines the development of students' creative and academic competence. Moreover, according to some learning theorists, the attempt to arrive at a "shared understanding" is not even possible. Von Glasersfeld (1995) for example, has argued that because we can never really know anything beyond our own subjective interpretations, a more feasible goal would be to strive for compatible (rather than shared) conceptions with each other.

How does this relate to the assertion that creativity is an act of learning? One key way it relates is in the recognition from contemporary learning theorists (particularly those espousing a constructivist view) that learning results from a constructive or combinatorial process. Students construct their understanding of what is being taught by combining what they already know with what they newly experience. This combinatorial process is a creative process. The combination of elements changes those elements into something new. In the case of learning, the combination of prior knowledge with new experience results in a change in personal knowledge. In this way, change serves as a common link between learning and creativity.

When students develop a new understanding, they have engaged in a mini-c creative process. This process involves interpreting experiences, actions, and events in a new and personally meaningful way (Beghetto & Kaufman, 2007). The student interprets the experience, act, or event through the lens of his or her prior knowledge and experiences. This interpretation combines prior knowledge with the new experience, resulting in a new and personally meaningful understanding. The resulting understanding may or may not be compatible with the teacher's (or some other socially agreed upon) understanding. The student, however, has still engaged in a (mini-c) creative act of learning.

In order for a students' personal understanding to rise to a socially compatible understanding, he or she needs to share and receive feedback on the new understanding. With patient support and feedback from their teachers (or some skilled other), students may arrive at a compatible understanding. Importantly, this is not a one-way process. Sometimes this will require students to modify their personal understanding. Other times, teachers will need to adjust their expectations. Still other times, teachers *and* students will need to modify what they expect and understand. Depending on the particular situation, compatible conceptions will result from slight modifications. This can be something as simple as a teacher taking a moment to ask a student to repeat an idea and then working with the student so the idea is more clearly articulated and understood.

In some cases, more radical modifications will be needed. This can take several iterations over a much longer time span. It can also require students and teachers to abandon their prior conceptions in light of more viable conceptions. In other cases, compatibility may not be achieved. Even in those cases, however, engaging in this process is valuable (both for students and teachers). Incompatible conceptions may result in reinitiating the process (during that interaction or at some later time).

In sum, striving for a socially compatible understanding requires that teachers carefully listen to and help their students develop their mini-c insights into little-c contributions (Beghetto, 2013). Also, by dint of students sharing and receiving feedback on their personal understanding, they may contribute to the learning and understanding of others (including teachers). When this happens, learning can be said to be a creative act. It is in this way that creativity is an act of learning and, in turn, can result in learning being a creative act.

Recommendations for Curricular Design and Implementation

How might these ideas be applied in curriculum design and implementation? In this section, I recommend several design and implementation principles that current and new generations of educators can use in when writing and applying academic curricula in support of creativity.

Take a "Both/And" Approach

Start with the assumption that creativity and academic learning are compatible curricular goals. Doing so will allow you to break from the "either/or" paradox of valuing creativity and academic learning, but feeling as though one comes at the expense of the other. By endorsing a "both/and" approach, it is much easier to simply ask the question of, "What if . . ." and develop creative combinations and connections in the curriculum that would otherwise go unnoticed. A simple heuristic would be finding ways to invite students to share their interests and then blend those interests with academic subject matter. This can result in microprojects that individual students or small groups of students can work on to add a meaningful context to the academic subject matter being learned. A student's interest in becoming a hairstylist could be combined with teaching the concept of ratio and result in a lesson on *mullet math*[2]. A mullet is a hairstyle popularized in the 1980s (cut short on top and grown-out long in the back). In this example, students can derive a formula for calculating a "mullet ratio" (ratio of short hair in front and long hair in back) and then use ratio to assess and design different styles of mullets. Beyond being a somewhat humorous example of how math can be put in the service of everyday learning and life, such a lesson also provides an opportunity for students to develop a deeper and more meaningful understanding of mathematics.

---

2   For an example of how an actual teacher developed a mullet ratio for teaching mathematics, see http://mrvaudrey.com/2013/12/21/mullet-ratio-2013/. Similarly, Jay Breslow, one of my doctoral students at the University of Oregon, has developed a model of creative collaboration—called the Community Creativity Collective, 3-C model—which expands on this idea by involving members of the community in lesson design and delivery.

Expect and Assess Creativity

Including a creativity requirement in assessments is perhaps one of the best ways to include creativity in the curriculum. One of the best ways to signal the importance of something is to assess it. Fortunately, creativity can be assessed alongside academic learning. Creativity rubrics can be developed and used to assess creativity (see Beghetto, 2013; Brookhart, 2013). One of the easiest ways, however, is to simply require students to put their own unique twist on the work they are doing. When students re-present content in their own way, they not only have an opportunity to express their creativity but also to deepen and demonstrate their understanding.

Aim for Disciplined Originality

Classroom creativity can, and often must, thrive in curricular constraints. Rather than attempt to remove constraints, think about how the curriculum can be designed to encourage originality within those constraints. If creativity (C) is the combination of originality (O) and task appropriateness (TA) in a particular context, then think of curriculum design as an opportunity to invite original student responses (O) into the academic conventions and constraints (TA) of the particular subject area (context). One way to do so is to first identify all the points of engagement in the curriculum. Points of engagement include activities, thinking prompts, assessments, or any part of the curriculum that attempts to engage student thinking. Once those have been identified, modify the prompt so that it encourages both originality and adherence to the task constraints. Any number of creative thinking prompts can be used to generate novelty in the context of task constraints. Creative thinking prompts refer to anything that encourages students to put their own unique spin on the academic content (e.g., *Imagine what would happen if . . . ; Suppose that . . . ; How many unique ways can you . . . ; What's a new way of . . .*). A standard math story problem could, for example, be modified to encourage students to not only arrive at the correct answer [TA] but to try to come up with as many unique ways of solving the problem as they can [O]. Here's a simple formulation that illustrates how this principle serves as an overlay for the two core elements of creativity and can be used for curricular design and implementation:

$$\frac{[Creative\ Thinking\ Prompt]}{Originality} \quad x \quad \frac{[Academic\ Learning\ Goal]}{Task\ Appropriate}$$

Approach Curricula as a Means to Some Other End

Often, educators and curriculum designers treat academic subject matter as an end in itself. Conversely, when it comes to designing and delivering more engaging learning experiences a key design principle is what can be called the "means to another end" (MAE) principle (Beghetto, Kaufman, & Baer, 2014). This principle uses creativity and subject matter learning as a means to some other instructional end (or goal). Curricula and instructional techniques that use this approach include cases, scenarios, problems, inquiry, and design projects as vehicles for putting students' (and even teachers') learning and creativity to work. Importantly, no technique, on its own, guarantees creative learning. Educators and curriculum designers need to ensure that the techniques and curricula they design and implement maximize the chances that students will have a meaningful learning experience. The following guidelines (adapted from Schmidt, van der Molen, te Winkel, & Wijnen 2009) can be helpful when designing and implementing learning tasks: (1) design and use problems or issues of inquiry that students can relate to and will spark (and sustain) their interest while learning; (2) design positive and structured interactions amongst students that require them to draw on and share their prior (emerging) knowledge with each other; (3) actively and frequently engage students in conversations to check understanding and provide necessary supportive feedback; and (4) plan enough time and content-based materials necessary to support, structure, and check students' self-directed learning.

Approach Design and Implementation Creatively

How can we expect our students to take creative risks in their learning if we are not willing to do the same in how we design and deliver our curriculum? Accomplished creators are sensible risk-takers who are open to new experiences (Feist, 1998; Sternberg & Lubart, 1995). Students will benefit from curricular experiences that encourage the expression of these traits and from educators who model these traits. Curriculum designers would therefore do well to make sure that the curricula they develop provide numerous opportunities for students to explore academic content in new and multiple ways. An academic curriculum that values creativity should be so saturated with opportunities for creative expression that creativity can be recognized in even the smallest of curricular content activities. Students must also feel that it is worth the risk to share their ideas and participate in new learning experiences. One of the best ways to support creative risk taking is to establish a creativity-supportive classroom environment (Beghetto & Kaufman, 2014). This includes helping students develop the self-knowledge and situational awareness so that they can understand when and what type of creative expression is most appropriate for the task at hand (Kaufman & Beghetto, 2013). When creativity becomes a normal part of the curriculum, students and teachers will be in a better position to recognize how learning is a creative act and how creative expression can be in service of everyday acts of learning.

Implications for Research

Although the theoretical link between creativity and learning has long been asserted, the empirical work is still in its infancy. The old saw "more research is needed" certainly holds true for this line of inquiry. The research that exists is sparse and somewhat inconclusive. Researchers who have explored the link between creativity and academic achievement have yielded mixed results. Some researchers have demonstrated stronger relationships, others more modest relationships, and yet others no or conflicting relationships (see Kaufman, Beghetto, & Dilly, in press, for a review). Mixed results, such as these, are symptomatic of a program of research that is not well defined. Also, it is no surprise when different results emerge from the use of different types of methods and measures of creativity (e.g., self-reports, divergent thinking measures, product assessments) and learning (e.g., grade point averages, achievement tests, teacher ratings, students' academic beliefs). There are also many factors that can influence the relationship between creativity and learning and thereby need to be taken into consideration when designing studies, including: type of curriculum and instructional strategies used (Schacter, Thum, & Zifkin, 2006); beliefs and attitudes of students and teachers (Beghetto, 2010b); type of domain (e.g., Baer, 2012), and the sociocultural context (Amabile & Pillemer, 2012; Niu, 2007). Consequently, the implications for research are manifold in this area, including the need for:

» better specified theoretical models of learning and creativity that offer the theoretical assertions conducive to various forms of empirical study (e.g., qualitative, quantitative, single-subject, and microgenetic);

» research designs that use multiple measures of creativity and learning and examine the development of creativity and learning over time and within and across varied domains and contexts; and

» combining of efforts amongst researchers across domains and cultural contexts.

I recognize that these recommendations are ambitious and, at this point, serve more as aspirational (than immediately attainable) goals. Current and new generations of researchers, however, can make great strides toward these goals by taking small and steady steps aimed at establishing clear and collaborative programs of research. In this way, the theoretical and conceptual links between creativity and learning can be tested, refined, and more clearly understood.

Discussion Questions

1. How might creativity be better represented in the design and delivery of academic curricula?
2. What kinds of instructional and curricular support do teachers need to integrate creativity into the design and delivery of their everyday lessons?
3. What role can and should educational leaders play in supporting awareness about the relationship between creativity and academic learning?
4. What other barriers might get in the way of viewing creativity as an act of learning? What will it take to overcome these barriers?
5. How might educators continue to develop their understanding of creativity and the role it plays in the academic curriculum?
6. What lingering questions remain regarding the role that creativity plays in academic learning?

References

Amabile, T. M., & Pillemer, J. (2012). Perspectives on the social psychology of creativity. *The Journal of Creative Behavior, 46,* 3–15.

Baer, J. (2012). Domain specificity and the limits of creativity theory. *Journal of Creative Behavior, 46,* 16–29.

Barron, F. (1969). *Creative person and creative process.* New York, NY: Holt, Rinehart, & Winston.

Beghetto, R. A. (2007). Ideational code-switching: Walking the talk about supporting student creativity in the classroom. *Roeper Review, 29,* 265–270.

Beghetto, R. A. (2008). Prospective teachers' beliefs about imaginative thinking in K–12 schooling. *Thinking Skills and Creativity, 3,* 134–142.

Beghetto, R. A. (2010a). Prospective teachers' prior experiences with creativity suppression. *International Journal of Creativity and Problem Solving, 20,* 29–36.

Beghetto, R. A. (2010b). Creativity in the classroom. In J. C. Kaufman & R. J. Sternberg (Eds.), *Cambridge handbook of creativity* (pp. 447–463). New York, NY: Cambridge University Press.

Beghetto, R. A. (2013). *Killing ideas softly? The promise and perils of creativity in the classroom.* Charlotte, NC: Information Age Press.

Beghetto, R. A., & Kaufman, J. C. (2007). Toward a broader conception of creativity: A case for "mini-c" creativity. *Psychology of Aesthetics, Creativity, and the Arts, 1,* 73–79.

Beghetto, R. A., & Kaufman, J. C. (2009). Intellectual estuaries: Connecting learning and creativity in programs of advanced academics. *Journal of Advanced Academics, 20,* 296–324.

Beghetto, R. A., & Kaufman, J. C. (2014). Classroom contexts for creativity. *High Ability Studies, 25,* 53–69. doi:10.1080/13598139.2014.905247

Beghetto, R. A., Kaufman, J. C., & Baer, J. (2014). *Teaching for creativity in the common core.* New York: Teachers College Press.

Black, P., & Wiliam, D. (1998). Inside the black box: Raising standards through classroom assessment. *Phi Delta Kappan, 80,* 139–148.

Brookhart, S. M. (2013). Assessing creativity. *Educational Leadership, 70,* 28–34.

Callahan, C. M., & Miller, E. M. (2005). A child-responsive model of giftedness. In R. J. Sternberg & J. E. Davidson (Eds.), *Conceptions of giftedness* (2nd ed., pp. 38–50). Cambridge, England: Cambridge University Press.

Cazden, C. B. (2001). Classroom discourse: The language of teaching and learning (2nd ed.). Portsmouth, NH: Heinemann.

Donovan, S. M., & Bransford, J. D. (Eds.). (2005). *How students learn: History, mathematics, and science in the classroom.* Washington, DC: The National Academies Press.

Egan, K., & Gajdamaschko, N. (2003). Some cognitive tools of literacy. In A. Kozulin, B. Gindis, V. S. Ageyev, & S. M. Miller (Eds.), *Vygotsky's educational theory in cultural context* (pp. 83–98). Cambridge, England: Cambridge University Press.

Feist, G. J. (1998). A meta-analysis of personality in scientific and artistic creativity. *Personality and Social Psychology Review, 2*, 290–309.

Guilford, J. P. (1950). Creativity. *American Psychologist, 5*, 444–454.

Hatano, G. (1993). Time to merge Vygotskian and constructivist conceptions of knowledge acquisition. In E. A. Forman, N. Minick, & C. A. Stone (Eds.), *Contexts for learning: Sociocultural dynamics in children's development* (pp. 153–166). New York, NY: Oxford University Press.

Kamii, C. (2000). *Double-column addition: A teacher uses Piaget's theory* [VHS Tape]. New York, NY: Teachers College.

Kaufman, J. C., & Beghetto, R. A. (2009). Beyond big and little: The four C model of creativity. *Review of General Psychology, 13*, 1–12.

Kaufman, J. C., & Beghetto, R. A. (2013). In praise of Clark Kent: Creative metacognition and the importance of teaching kids when (not) to be creative. *Roeper Review, 35*, 155–165.

Kaufman, J. C., Beghetto, R. A., & Dilley, A. E. (in press). Understanding creativity in the schools. In A. Lipnevich, F. Preckel, & R. D. Roberts (Eds.), *Psychosocial skills and school systems in the 21st century: Theory, research, and applications.* New York: Springer Science.

Keller, C. M., & Keller, J. D. (1996). *Cognition and tool use: The blacksmith at work.* New York, NY: Cambridge University Press

Marland, S. P. (1972). Education of the gifted and talented: Report to the Congress of the United States by the U.S. Commissioner of Education. Washington, DC: Department of Health, Education and Welfare.

Mehan, H. (1979). *Learning lessons: Social organization in the classroom.* Cambridge, MA: Harvard University Press.

Meier, D. (2000). *The accelerated learning handbook.* New York, NY: McGraw-Hill.

Niu, W. (2007). Individual and environmental influences on Chinese student creativity. *The Journal of Creative Behavior, 41*, 151–175.

Plucker, J., Beghetto, R. A., & Dow, G. (2004). Why isn't creativity more important to educational psychologists? Potential, pitfalls, and future directions in creativity research. *Educational Psychologist, 39*, 83–96.

Renzulli, J. S. (2005). The three-ring conception of giftedness: A developmental model for promoting creative productivity. In R. J. Sternberg & J. E. Davidson (Eds.), *Conceptions of giftedness* (2nd ed., pp. 217–245). Cambridge, England: Cambridge University Press.

Runco, M. A. (1996). Personal creativity: Definition and developmental issues. *New Directions in Child Development, 72*, 3–30

Sawyer, R. K. (2010). Learning for creativity. In R. A. Beghetto & J. C. Kaufman (Eds.), *Nurturing creativity in the classroom* (pp. 172–190). New York, NY: Cambridge University Press.

Schacter, J., Thum, Y. M., & Zifkin, D. (2006). How much does creative teaching enhance elementary school students' achievement? *The Journal of Creative Behavior, 40,* 47–72.

Schmidt, H. G., van der Molen, H. T., te Winkel, W. W. R, & Wijnen, W. H. F. W (2009). Constructivist, problem-based learning does work: A meta-analysis of curricular comparisons involving a single medical school. *Educational Psychologist, 44,* 227–249.

Simonton, D. K. (2012). Taking the US patent office criteria seriously: A quantitative three- criterion creativity definition and its implications. *Creativity Research Journal, 24,* 97–106.

Stein, M. I. (1953). Creativity and culture. *The Journal of Psychology, 36,* 311–322.

Sternberg, R. J., & Lubart, T. I. (1995). *Defying the crowd: Cultivating creativity in a culture of conformity.* New York, NY: Free Press.

Torrance, E. P. (1959). Current research on the nature of creative talent. *Journal of Counseling Psychology, 6,* 309–316.

von Glasersfeld, E. (1995). *Radical constructivism: A way of knowing and learning.* London, England: Falmer.

Vygotsky, L. S. (2004). Imagination and creativity in childhood (M. E. Sharpe, Inc., Trans.). *Journal of Russian and East European Psychology, 42,* 7–97. (Original work published 1967)

Ward, T. B., Smith, S. M., & Vaid, J. (1997). *Creative thought: An investigation of conceptual structures and processes.* Washington, DC: American Psychological Association.

Warnock, M. (1978). *Imagination.* Berkeley: University of California Press.

CHAPTER 8

INQUIRY LEARNING MODELS AND GIFTED EDUCATION

A CURRICULUM OF INNOVATION AND POSSIBILITY

SHANNON BUERK

Prevailing thought on thriving in the 21st century converges on a fairly succinct set of outcomes for learners—outcomes that have long been considered higher order thinking skills and cornerstones for curriculum in gifted education. The new emphasis on these skills in the age of innovation and technology moves beyond beneficial to necessary. Calling them "survival skills," Wagner (2010) included the following: adaptability and agility, leading by influence and collaboration across networks, critical thinking and problem solving, effective oral and written communication, accessing and analyzing information, curiosity and imagination, and initiative and entrepreneurship. Pink (2006) suggested that abilities we once thought frivolous "increasingly will determine who flourishes and who flounders" (p. 3). Others argue persuasively for a similar set of ethical, creative, and entrepreneurial skills as a foundation for individual success and societal viability (Gardner, 2009; Robinson, 2011; Zhao, 2012).

Career readiness reports (Casner-Lotto & Barrington, 2006) similarly outlined the top five skills most desired by employers as: critical thinking, oral and written communication, collaboration, and professionalism. The Partnership for 21st Century Skills (2011), a national cooperative of business leaders and state department supervisors, published a similar list, dubbing them as

DOI: 10.4324/9781003236696-10

"21st-century skills." In addition, higher education has taken note and integrated these skills into postsecondary curriculum in many states. For example, The Texas Higher Education Coordinating Board (n.d.) recently approved six core curriculum objectives: critical thinking skills, communication skills, empirical and quantitative skills, teamwork, social responsibility, and personal responsibility.

These emphases on thinking, creating, and problem solving provide direction for educators who desire to prepare gifted students to lead a rapidly changing world. The skills learners need today go beyond the standard curriculum; their future and the well-being of our society depend on educational practices that foster these skills and abilities. Inquiry learning, including project- and problem-based learning, is a method for all students to acquire these outcomes; however, it is particularly well-suited to gifted students' inquiry-oriented learning style (Gallagher, 2009; Gallagher & Gallagher, 2013; Sak, 2004; Stepien & Gallagher, 1993). Inquiry learning provides the opportunity for true differentiation for exceptional learners (Swicord, n.d.b) and holds the promise of uncovering latent giftedness through developing intellectual character (Henderson, 2004; Ritchhart, 2001; VanTassel-Baska, 1995). For the purposes of this text, I will focus on inquiry learning as an effective strategy for optimizing and developing higher order thinking skills in gifted learners, differentiating curriculum in the inclusive classroom (with obvious parallel implications for the benefit of inquiry-based curriculum in cluster and exclusively gifted classroom environments), and the opportunity to reveal giftedness in unidentified learners. In a time of innovation, global connectedness, and technological possibility, educators have the opportunity to provide curriculum that fosters these skills and abilities for today's learners and nurtures the leaders of tomorrow.

Understanding Inquiry Learning

Inquiry learning is a theory grounded in Dewey's (1910) philosophy about experiential learning—people learn as a result of doing. Inquiry-based learning theory assumes that learners come with context and experiences that shape the processing and assimilation of information so that interactive dialogue, research, and problem solving are all optimized. Inquiry learning can be characterized by learning that is focused on active investigations and application of knowledge aligned to student interests while using fluid protocols (e.g., scientific method) and multiple resources to learn (Saunders-Stewart, Gyles, & Shore, 2012; Vygotsky, 1978).

Inquiry-based approaches in learning design have been recommended by national organizations (e.g., International Baccalaureate Organization, International Reading Association, National Council for the Social Studies, National Council of Teachers of Mathematics, and National Research Council; Barell, 2003; Saunders-Stewart et al., 2012; Zemelman, Daniels, & Hyde, 2005). Some studies have found that many teachers subscribe to a philosophy of learning that is "student-centered, experiential, expressive, reflective, authentic, holistic, social, collaborative, democratic, cognitive, developmental, constructivist, and challenging" (Zemelman et al., p. 227). Current research characterizes inquiry learning as a value-added learning design—at least as effective as traditional methods of acquiring knowledge and skills with the added benefit of being more effective than traditional methods for students to develop the critical thinking, analysis, synthesis, and problem-solving skills for this century of conceptual thinking and just-in-time information processing (Barron & Darling-Hammond, 2008; Saunders-Stewart et al., 2012; Zemelman et al., 2005). Although no one would deny the value of acquiring knowledge and skills, fostering inquiry and critical thinking are among the most important learning goals of our time (Barell, 2003).

What Is Project-Based Learning?

Dewey (1910) proposed a type of inquiry called project-based inquiry that specifies that a product will demonstrate results of an inquiry learning experience. Project-based learning (PBL) is focused, experiential learning organized around the investigation, explanation, and resolution of meaningful problems (Barrows, 1999; Torp & Sage, 2002). Problem-based and project-based learning were first used in medical school and architectural training respectively, and have been used increasingly in K–12 education as a curriculum model since the early 1980s (Thomas, 2000). Much has been written about the difference between problem-based and project-based learning, but for the purposes of this text, I will use a combined approach defined with common characteristics of both types and commonly found in current practice, denoted PBL. Therefore, PBL curriculum is characterized by a standards-aligned driving question or challenge delivered by an authentic audience. The challenge prompts students to plan collaboratively and conduct research to learn knowledge and skills. Ultimately, they apply the acquired knowledge and/or skills to meet the challenge, create a product, or solve the problem, which they share back with the authentic audience.

Research on the effectiveness of PBL is exacerbated by the myriad of approaches to implementation. However, in several summaries, reviews, and meta-analyses, PBL is deemed at least as effective as traditional approaches for short-term knowledge acquisition and more effective for long-term knowledge retention, application of knowledge, career readiness, and development of higher order thinking skills (Thomas, 2000; Strobel & van Barneveld, 2009; Swicord, n.d.b).

Higher Order Thinking Skills

When VanTassel-Baska and Brown (2007) conducted a study of curricular models in gifted education, they found six models that were effective with gifted learners that could be described as inquiry-based learning models. The research on inquiry-based learning and PBL supports the effectiveness of this type of curriculum and learning environment for enhancing the higher order thinking skills or 21st-century skills of all learners (Karnes & Bean, 2010; Sak, 2004). Specifically for gifted learners, this type of environment fosters development of the talents often cited as needs and/or abilities of exceptional learners (Bennett, 2014; Gallagher, 2009; Gallagher & Gallagher, 2013). The exhaustive list of identified outcomes for PBL in the literature includes the following (many of which were reported to have increased benefits for high-ability students):

- » increasing autonomy and choice (Bennett, 2014; Saunders-Stewart et al., 2012);
- » enhancing problem finding (Feldhusen & Kennedy, 1988; Hmelo-Silver, 2004; Jollands, Jolly, & Molyneaux, 2012);
- » application of knowledge (Aulls & Shore, 2008; Dochy, Segers, Van den Bossche, & Gijbels, 2003; Saunders-Stewart et al., 2012; Strobel & van Barneveld, 2009);
- » argumentation and understanding multiple perspectives (Barron & Darling-Hammond, 2008; Thomas, 2000);

» creativity and problem solving (Gallagher & Gallagher, 2013; Henderson, 2004; Saunders-Stewart et al., 2012; Thomas, 2000);
» critical thinking (Gallagher & Gallagher, 2013; Kettler, 2014; Mergendoller, Maxwell, & Bellisimo, 2006; Saunders-Stewart et al., 2012; Shepherd, 1988; Thomas, 2000; Tretten & Zachariou, 1995); and
» oral and written communication skills, research skills, advanced career goals, career readiness, and intrinsic motivation (Barron & Darling-Hammond, 2008; Bennett, 2014; Jollands et al., 2012; Sisk, 2009; Strobel & van Barneveld, 2009; Thomas, 2000).

Differentiated Curriculum

Arguably, one of the primary challenges in gifted education centers around truly differentiating curriculum for advanced learners in the mainstream classroom. Conklin and Frei (2007) outlined eight strategies based on Kaplan's depth and complexity model that may assist classroom teachers in differentiating. Most schools purport that differentiating in the heterogeneous classroom is the way they are serving gifted students; it is well-documented, unfortunately, that although the intention to differentiate is communicated often, the practice is rare, and the barriers to successfully differentiating are many (Bennett, 2014; Borland, 2003; Henderson, 2004; Sisk, 2009; VanTassel-Baska, Johnson, Hughes, & Boyce, 1996; VanTassel-Baska & Stambaugh, 2005; VanTassel-Baska, Zuo, Avery, & Little, 2002). The foremost barrier is that a teacher-directed classroom with whole-group instruction as the mode of operandi poses an impossibility; one person must direct the whole class while also meeting the individual needs of 25 or more students. As Sisk (2009) noted, in the context of accountability and standardization, the needs of the gifted are even more likely to be a low priority. In fact, several studies have shown that many learners identified as gifted early in their school career no longer exhibit those characteristics later in school (Gallagher & Gallagher, 2013; Robinson, 2011). For true differentiation, the one-size-fits-all teaching platform must become a more autonomous and self-directed learning environment that allows the teacher to assess and address varying needs and abilities, and frees individual learners to progress at a pace and depth of learning that is appropriately challenging.

Inquiry-based learning, specifically PBL, provides a naturally differentiated curriculum within the classroom because it is learner-centered and the structures, once learned, create autonomous learning opportunities. Individualized pacing, depth, complexity, roles, and responsibilities are hallmarks of a PBL classroom when the curriculum and instructional model are implemented with fidelity (Barron & Darling-Hammond, 2008; Borland, 2003; Sisk, 2009; Swicord, n.d.a). This personalized learning environment facilitates appropriate assessment, intervention, and enrichment during the course of a unit. Henderson (2004) reviewed VanTassel-Baska's Integrated Curriculum Model and identified common features that are shared by inquiry learning, including higher order thinking and processing skills, building learning experiences around major issues and themes, and real-world contexts combined with theoretical modeling. These common elements of learning design respond to needs of gifted learners as well as many of the needs of a spectrum of diverse learners. Finally, because inquiry and PBL are typically collaborative experiences, seamless peer ability-grouping can be intentional to address gifted learners' need for work with like-ability peers in an otherwise heterogeneous setting. Inquiry learning is an effective solution for truly differentiating for gifted learners, and it is incumbent upon educators to create the curriculum and learning environment with a balance of structure and choice to realize those benefits.

When used as the regular classroom instructional model, inquiry learning models also have the potential to reveal latent giftedness as teachers and learners are freed from one-size-fits-all pacing and assignments. In *Smart Schools: Better Thinking and Learning for Every Child*, Perkins (1992) outlined several ways that teachers can increase the inquiry quotient in classrooms. Teachers as facilitators interact with students more closely and are better able to assess and differentiate for individual needs; therefore, teachers in these environments are able to see more academic potential in students because they can observe how students process and interact with information (Gallagher & Gallagher, 2013). Students become engaged in learning, one of the undisputed outcomes of PBL, and underachieving or unidentified gifted learners who have been previously demotivated by an overly simplistic, fact-oriented classroom become intrigued and tuned in to the new opportunities to use their gifts in this environment (Gallagher & Gallagher, 2013; Schmidt, Rotgans, & Yew, 2011). Learners discover and have the opportunity to bring forward talents and cognitive abilities that have been stifled by only one way of thinking or demonstrating achievement. As some studies support, curriculum and learning environments for all students that promote analytical, creative, and experiential thinking provide opportunities to develop intellectual character and dispositions that may be latent due to lack of stimulating circumstances (Henderson, 2004; Ritchhart, 2001; Sternberg, 1996). In fact, the autonomy necessitated by PBL will foster behaviors that may even help close gender-based performance gaps in high-level mathematics problem solving (Gallagher, 1996).

Constraints Associated With Inquiry Learning

If the research is so compelling for implementing inquiry-based learning, why is it not the standard fare in every school? The literature also shows that making the shift from teaching platform to a learning model requires significant changes in systems as well. In fact, there are constraints to implementation that cause flat results, an implementation dip, or even lack of sustainability when left unaddressed (Hanney & Savin-Baden, 2013; Hmelo-Silver, 2004; Thomas, 2000).

In inquiry models, the primary change is an expansion and diversity of the roles of teacher and student and a blurring of those boundaries over time. Teachers become designers of experiential learning experiences and authentic assessments, which requires significant time in the beginning and in-depth knowledge of the standards and their relevance, as well as understanding of and access to differentiated learning and assessment resources. Time to design quality units, lack of a succinct process for design, and limited understanding of the depth and complexity of standards have all been cited as barriers to developing quality curriculum for inquiry and project-based learning as teachers transition to designers (Saunders-Stewart et al., 2008).

Once curriculum is designed and implemented, teachers must fill the role of facilitator or leader of the learning experiences, which requires yet another set of complex skills that research shows many teachers do not have the opportunity to gain from preservice training or in-service training (Barron & Darling-Hammond, 2008; Thomas, 2000). Implementation research indicates that teachers may struggle with a number of skills, especially in the beginning of implementation, including the following: (a) understanding of diverse needs of learners and methods for differentiating, (b) questioning at different levels of thinking to assess and prompt deeper investigations, (c) accessing information in just-in-time situations, (d) utilizing technology tools, (e) formatively assessing content and higher order thinking skills using varied methods, (f) providing feedback and guidance to students to adjust their learning and progress toward mastery and beyond, and (g) effectively monitoring and facilitating collaborative learning processes and conflict resolution (Aulls & Shore, 2008; Barron & Darling-Hammond, 2008; Hmelo-Silver, 2004; Strobel & van Barneveld, 2009; Swicord, n.d.b; Thomas, 2000). Studies have also indicated that if teachers are entrenched in current practice, they may have difficulty transitioning to the new model in spite of appropriate support and the proven promise of better results for students (Hattie, 2009; Ladewski, Krajcik, & Harvey, 1994). Additionally, they may struggle with balancing how much to direct students and control the information flow with giving students the opportunity to explore and problem solve on their own (Thomas, 2000).

Students do not automatically come to inquiry-based and collaborative PBL environments with the required skills to learn effectively either. Autonomous learning behaviors, critical thinking skills, collaboration skills, ability to apply knowledge, creative problem solving, ability to use technology productively, and metacognition skills are all necessary for successful learning in the self-directed inquiry environment and are learned behaviors that most students do not possess or have lost the ability to tap into as they have become accustomed to a teacher-directed educational experience (Hmelo-Silver, 2014; Saunders-Stewart et al., 2012; Strobel & van Barneveld, 2009; Thomas, 2000; Weng-yi Cheng, Lam, & Chan, 2008). In addition, teachers may think of PBL or inquiry learning as unstructured and fail to provide needed scaffolding and structures to students who are new to the model (Barron & Darling-Hammond, 2008; Hattie, 2009). This point deserves special attention because, as Hattie (2009) argued, if the conception of the teacher as a facilitator translates to leaving students to learn only on their own or from their peers, this faulty notion negatively impacts student achievement.

The traditional school systems that are in place can be barriers to effective implementation as well. Standardized time blocks and Carnegie unit scheduling, grading systems based on averages rather than growth, rigid facility structures, lesson planning requirements, lack of technology tools or infrastructure, district common assessments, and accountability pressures constrain teachers and students when it comes to inquiry learning (Barron & Darling-Hammond, 2008; Hanney & Savin-Baden, 2012; Sisk, 2009; Thomas, 2000).

Recommendations for Inquiry-Based Learning Design

In order to overcome the constraints outlined and to realize the benefits of inquiry and PBL curriculum and instruction for gifted learners in a standards-based system, I recommend the following: (1) redesign the curriculum development process to provide a framework for teachers to become effective designers; (2) immerse teachers and instructional support persons in adequate training *and* job-embedded coaching to assume the diversified roles of designers, facilitators, and leaders/systems thinkers; and (3) develop systems to support inquiry learning and strategically abandon those that inhibit the learning model.

Curriculum Design

Summer curriculum writing with a representative group of teachers creating lessons for themselves and their peers must be replaced by all teachers designing units that are relevant to the time, context, and their students within a conceptual, standards-based framework. The time to design PBL units is greatly diminished when teachers start from a concept-based cluster of standards that have been vertically and horizontally aligned and sequenced (see Appendices A–D for this chapter). The standards can be grouped based on priority for mastery and a conceptual lens that will readily translate to a relevant challenge or problem for students. Erickson's *Concept-Based Curriculum and Instruction for the Thinking Classroom* (2007) provided a helpful list of possible concepts to use when grouping standards by concept.

The steps recommended by Engage Learning, Inc. (2013) to create this concept-based curriculum framework are as follows:

1. Review all standards for a grade level/course across the disciplines for depth, complexity and conceptual connection.
2. Group standards by concept across disciplines, repeating standards in more than one grouping if appropriate.
3. Order "chunks" of standards in a sequence that is necessary for mastery.

Then, teachers need collaborative design time to create challenges and assessment tools that align to those "chunks" of standards for mastery. Thought partners collaborating on design spur creative ideas that build and integrate into engaging challenges for students (Johnson, 2010). Professionals from the local community, campus administrators, parents, and even students' ideas become catalysts for driving questions. Involving gifted learners in the design process of unpacking the standards to discover the relevance and application that will lead to engagement and mastery is one way to differentiate and stimulate their critical thinking.

Using a succinct design process that is aligned to standards, intentional about differentiation, and grounded in a culture of critique will both expedite the process and ensure higher quality iterations for learning units. One example of a structured process is detailed below (see Figure 8.1):

1. Analyze the standards identified for mastery to determine depth and complexity.
2. Brainstorm relevance of the standards to a real-in-time problem or issue and design a challenge brief for students containing a driving question, authentic audience, and project requirements.
3. Create a standards-aligned rubric and accompanying assessment tools (preassessment, formative assessments, summative assessment) that provide benchmarks for students. Ensure that assessment tools and rubrics for both content and discrete skills are scaffolded and that levels above "meeting expectations" are well-developed for challenging advanced learners.
4. With these pieces in place, allow an opportunity for critique and feedback from peers and a design coach.
5. Following iterations from critique, design differentiated learner tools aligned to each level of the rubric including research resources, do-it-yourself practice activities, small-group direct instruction workshops, and a calendar of protocols and progress checks for learners to use.

To support the design process, it is helpful if teachers have a bank of standards-aligned assessment tools including performance tasks and formative assessment options, access to a variety of research resources that are appropriately challenging, and a database of local volunteers who are willing to provide an authentic audience for student products and solutions. In most cases, teachers need professional development opportunities and coaching to design successfully.

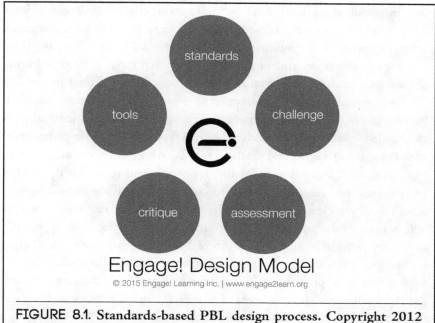

FIGURE 8.1. Standards-based PBL design process. Copyright 2012 Engage Learning. Reprinted with permission.

Professional Development and Coaching

Besides an intentional and supported design process, teachers and instructional support staff need training on making the transition to designers and facilitators or leaders of student-centered, personalized learning. The professional learning ought to mirror the inquiry-based classroom so teachers are immersed in experiences students will have, so they enhance their 21st-century skills during content acquisition, and so they are exposed to effective models of facilitation. Professional development that impacts student achievement has some distinct characteristics: (a) theory, underlying research base, or rationale; (b) demonstration or modeling; (c) practice and feedback during the workshop setting; and (d) coaching and follow-up during implementation that ensures the teacher is likely to make the strategy, skill, or concept part of his or her classroom practice (Cooper, 2014; Yoon, Duncan, Lee, Scarloss, & Shapley, 2007). Of all of these research-based components, Joyce and Showers (2002) identified coaching as the most critical to effective implementation, with 95% transfer attributed to coaching versus 0% transfer resulting from theory or demonstration alone. Interesting that research on effective professional learning parallels the research on inquiry and experiential learning for students in terms of transfer and application of knowledge. As Hattie (2009) suggested, "the biggest effects on student learning occur when teachers become learners of their own teaching, and when students become their own teachers" (p. 22).

Therefore, the professional learning plan for this implementation should be based on these research-based practices. Training before implementation needs to be collaborative and facilitated in the same type of learning environment and with the same protocols that teachers will use with students in an inquiry or PBL classroom. The classroom setting for training mirrors what the teachers will need to create curriculum that is conducive to an autonomous, learner-centered model with the accompanying hands-on, differentiated resources, technology tools, and visuals. Trainers need to model facilitation skills appropriate to inquiry including using clear protocols, project management, small-group instruction, assessment tools, ongoing corrective feedback, and effective questioning that foster problem analysis, autonomy, and informed choices for learning. Again, in considering this type of learning model, it is important to clarify the teacher role and demonstrate all of the skills necessary for moving from the narrow role of providing information to a more complex role of leading the learning. Teachers need to have opportunities during training to practice these skills of facilitation and receive feedback from each other and the trainer/coach.

Finally, job-embedded training during implementation and ongoing coaching are keys to successful implementation and sustainability (Joyce & Showers, 2002). Following implementation, teachers will have new needs and context for professional learning. Training scheduled to meet those needs in a just-in-time manner ensures that teachers are able and willing to persist beyond the rockiness of initial implementation (Landsberg, 2009; Whitmore, 2002). Coaching needs to be structured with individualized goals for growth, shared assessment of current effectiveness in relation to those goals, technical assistance for making progress toward those goals, agreed upon actions for making progress in between coaching sessions, and assessment of evidence to determine growth and next steps (Fine & Merrill, 2010; Renshaw & Alexander, 2005).

Systems Supporting Inquiry Learning

Lastly, as with any change in education, educators need to think about and support the change from a systemic viewpoint. As Senge and Suzuki (1994) wrote in *The Fifth Discipline: The Art and Practice of the Learning Organization*, "Business and human endeavors are systems . . . we tend to focus on snapshots of isolated parts of the system, and then wonder why our deepest problems never get solved" (p. 51). Purpose, process, product, place, and partnerships categorize the systems to transform for a foundation of sustainability for PBL and inquiry-based learning.

Purpose

In implementing a new curriculum, engage stakeholders in creating a shared purpose and measurable outcomes for the change. Once determined, communicate the shared purpose (why), measurable outcomes (what), and steps for implementation (how) to all stakeholders. Establish baseline and benchmark measurements for the desired outcomes as part of a strategic implementation plan. Provide the research base to stakeholders in accessible ways and be proactive and transparent. Saunders-Stewart and colleagues (2012) have compiled an inventory of 23 outcomes from inquiry derived from theoretical and empirical research that could be used as a starting point for identifying and even measuring outcomes.

Be strategic in terms of a responsible rollout plan if the curriculum change is going to be more than a classroom-by-classroom change. If the model will be scaled, develop a long-term plan that addresses who will be implementing it and how those educators will be supported with training, coaching, and design time. Include intentional preparation and readiness for teachers who will be implementing it in subsequent years of the rollout plan.

Process

For those classrooms in implementation, one of the most critical process support systems is project management. As mentioned earlier, students need scaffolding and support to manage a project successfully when it is not teacher-directed, and they need constant corrective feedback during the process (Hattie, 2009; Thomas, 2000). Online support systems for collaborative

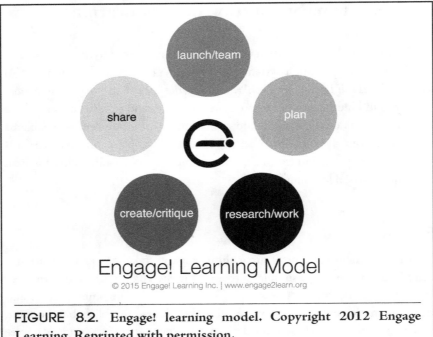

Engage! Learning Model

© 2015 Engage! Learning Inc. | www.engage2learn.org

FIGURE 8.2. Engage! learning model. Copyright 2012 Engage Learning. Reprinted with permission.

teamwork and/or organizing materials and documents in hard copy format can provide a guide for teams and individual students as they become more autonomous. The proliferation of handheld devices offers the opportunity for students to collaborate and access diverse resources seamlessly, as well as provides options for teachers to efficiently assess student work, thinking, and reflection and provide feedback systemically. In addition, following a structure and protocols for inquiry learning assists teachers and students, especially in the beginning. One five-step model used at Engage Learning, Inc. (2013) includes: (1) launch/team, (2) plan, (3) research/work, (4) create/critique, and (5) share. Each step follows a protocol that a teacher leads and then gradually releases until the students have developed the metacognitive and collaboration skills to autonomously go through the steps (see Figure 8.2).

For a curriculum product to be viable, it must be aligned vertically and horizontally, as well as aligned to required standards for mastery (Marzano, Waters, & McNulty, 2005). The standards for mastery include the state and/or federal standards and any local standards that have been established as outcomes. The two ways an inquiry-based curriculum can be aligned is through the conceptual framework of standards discussed above that guides unit design and through standards-aligned rubrics for each unit. The conceptual framework of standards, like a scope and sequence of chunks of standards, provides the basis for design of units. Developing vertically and horizontally aligned rubrics for assessment completes the curriculum-instruction-assessment alignment loop. If higher order thinking skills have been identified as learner outcomes for inclusion in the curriculum, rubrics need to be developed for these skills as well as content rubrics. Figure 8.3 is an example of an aligned rubric for collaboration. For example, if communication, collaboration, critical thinking, creativity, and professional ethics have been determined as measurable outcomes, vertically aligned rubrics for assessing these skills facilitate teachers in providing feedback to students over time as they become more sophisticated in their application of these skills and lay a foundation for monitoring the implementation as well.

Place

The setting or place in which learning happens can either facilitate collaboration, autonomy, and inquiry or inhibit these behaviors. Much has been written about the 21st-century classroom and campus learning environment and how the design of facilities, the integration of technology, and the structures of time must become more flexible and agile (e.g., Kelley, McCain, & Jukes, 2009; Pearlman, 2010). Creating spaces for collaboration, providing writable surfaces for displaying learning/thinking, repurposing corridor space, outdoor spaces, or spaces left by locker removal for teams or individuals to work, utilizing portable furniture and technology devices, and finding shared classroom spaces for combining groups of students are recommendations for redesigning learning environments conducive to collaborative inquiry and PBL. As a starting point, the classroom needs: (a) furniture to accommodate teams of three, (b) a station for students to access hands-on resources, (c) technology devices at a 1:3 ratio, and (d) a workshop space for the teacher to meet with a small group.

Partnerships

Lastly, inquiry learning and particularly PBL thrive with community partnerships for designing relevant challenges, accessing expert resources, sharing with authentic audiences, and collaborating on a vision for learning. Because inquiry-based learning is nontraditional and learner-centered, it is imperative to provide ongoing communication to parents and other stakeholders about the model and the results. Invite parents, community partners, and business leaders to be involved formally through an advisory board or informally through open house events, demonstration days, and parent nights. One of the most important things that educators can do to make the right decisions today about learning is to talk to the consumers: students, parents, and business leaders. A student advisory board that meets quarterly with the superintendent will ensure relevance and vitality in a district. A parent advisory committee will provide the opportunity for true partnership. A business advisory group that meets regularly with district leadership will ensure intentionality. Business leaders can articulate outcomes to prioritize in school that will ensure curriculum goals are aligned with skills valued for leadership in the current context.

Conclusion and Implications for Research

Advanced learners thrive in learning environments that stimulate critical thinking, creativity, problem solving, and inquiry. Unfortunately, they spend most of their time in teacher-directed classrooms where they are practicing skills concepts that they have already mastered. In an increasingly conceptual, global, and technologically advanced world, higher order thinking skills have become highly prized. Inquiry and project-based learning can be a truly differentiated solution for meeting the needs of exceptional learners and can be an exciting alternative to better meet the demands of life in the 21st century. Utilizing the available technology to create opportunities for innovative inquiry in the classroom can be an answer to challenging gifted learners to use their unique abilities in ways that positively impact the world and to develop those abilities to their fullest potential. The research on inquiry and project-based learning in meeting the needs of gifted learners is favorable, yet not expansive. One clear gap in the literature is focused assessment that could provide indicators of growth in the skills acquired through experiences in inquiry and project-based learning classrooms. Utilizing the literature-derived inventory of student outcomes from inquiry instruction by Saunders-Stewart et al., (2012), assessments and performance indicators could be designed that would measure growth of learners over time as it relates to each of these outcomes. With these assessment results, educators would have additional information beyond standardized test results to make more appropriate decisions about curriculum and pedagogy that would truly meet the needs of all learners.

Collaboration	1 Initiating Progress	2 Approaching Expectations	3 Meeting Expectations	4 Exceeding Expectations
Grades K–2	Works with diverse teams with guidance Practices compromising to accomplish a common goal with guidance Works as an individual even when part of a group	Demonstrates a willingness to work effectively and respectfully with diverse teams Exercises compromising to accomplish a common goal with encouragement Practices shared responsibility for collaborative work with consistent guidance	Demonstrates ability to work effectively and respectfully with diverse teams with guidance Exercises flexibility and willingness to be helpful in making necessary compromises to accomplish a common goal with some assistance Assumes shared responsibility for collaborative work with guidance, and values the individual contributions made by each team member	Demonstrates ability to work effectively and respectfully with diverse teams Exercises flexibility and willingness to be helpful in making necessary compromises to accomplish a common goal Assumes shared responsibility for collaborative work, and values the individual contributions made by each team member

FIGURE 8.3. Sample rubric for collaboration. Note. Copyright 2015 Engage Learning Inc. Reprinted with permission.

Collaboration	1 Initiating Progress	2 Approaching Expectations	3 Meeting Expectations	4 Exceeding Expectations
Grades 3–5	Works with diverse teams with guidance	Demonstrates a willingness to work effectively and respectfully with diverse teams	Demonstrates ability to work effectively and respectfully with diverse teams with guidance	Demonstrates ability to work effectively and respectfully with diverse teams
	Practices compromising to accomplish a common goal with guidance	Exercises compromising to accomplish a common goal with encouragement	Exercises flexibility and willingness to be helpful in making necessary compromises to accomplish a common goal with some assistance	Exercises flexibility and willingness to be helpful in making necessary compromises to accomplish a common goal
	Works as an individual even when part of a group	Practices shared responsibility for collaborative work with consistent guidance	Assumes shared responsibility for collaborative work with guidance, and values the individual contributions made by each team member	Assumes shared responsibility for collaborative work, and values the individual contributions made by each team member

FIGURE 8.3. Continued.

Collaboration	1 Initiating Progress	2 Approaching Expectations	3 Meeting Expectations	4 Exceeding Expectations
Middle School	Works with diverse teams with guidance	Demonstrates a willingness to work effectively and respectfully with diverse teams	Demonstrates ability to work effectively and respectfully with diverse teams	Improves a team's ability to work effectively and respectfully
	Practices compromising to accomplish a common goal with guidance	Exercises compromising to accomplish a common goal with encouragement	Exercises flexibility and willingness to be helpful in making necessary compromises to accomplish a common goal	Facilitates conflict resolution when necessary to accomplish a common goal
	Works as an individual even when part of a group	Practices shared responsibility for collaborative work with consistent guidance	Assumes shared responsibility for collaborative work, and values the individual contributions made by each team member	Leads team in sharing the collaborative work and support and encourages the individual contributions made by each team member

FIGURE 8.3. Continued.

Collaboration	1 Initiating Progress	2 Approaching Expectations	3 Meeting Expectations	4 Exceeding Expectations
High School	Works with diverse teams with guidance Practices compromising to accomplish a common goal with guidance Works as an individual even when part of a group	Demonstrates a willingness to work effectively and respectfully with diverse teams Exercises compromising to accomplish a common goal with encouragement Practices shared responsibility for collaborative work with consistent guidance	Demonstrates ability to work effectively and respectfully with diverse teams Exercises flexibility and willingness to be helpful in making necessary compromises to accomplish a common goal Assumes shared responsibility for collaborative work, and values the individual contributions made by each team member collaboratively while using teaming protocol with facilitation; writes and agrees to norms; uses the "Team Conflict Resolution" process to share responsibility	Demonstrates ability to work effectively and respectfully with diverse teams Exercises flexibility and willingness to be helpful in making necessary compromises to accomplish a common goal Assumes shared responsibility for collaborative work, and values the individual contributions made by each team member

FIGURE 8.3. Continued.

Discussion Questions

1. Inquiry models such as PBL claim to develop creative and critical thinking. What specific learning design elements need to be included within the PBL curriculum to ensure these thinking skills are developed?
2. Do some disciplines lend themselves more to PBL design than others? If so, how might curriculum designers think differently to support inquiry learning even in the disciplines that do not appear to be an easy fit?
3. What might be fears associated with implementing PBL learning design in gifted and advanced academics, and how might they be addressed?
4. This chapter devotes significant time to appropriate preparation and implementation. How might curriculum design for gifted and advanced students benefit from a focus on these elements?
5. Some critics of PBL might argue that content is sacrificed for process. How might you make arguments on both sides of this issue in ways to help educators understand how to implement PBL successfully?

References

Aulls, M. W., & Shore, B. M. (2008). *Inquiry in education, Volume I: The conceptual foundations for research as a curricular imperative.* New York, NY: Lawrence Erlbaum.

Barell, J. (2003). *Developing more curious minds.* Alexandria, VA: Association of Supervision and Curriculum Development.

Barron, B., & Darling-Hammond, L. (2008). *Powerful learning: Studies show deep understanding derives from collaborative methods.* Retrieved from http://www.edutopia.org/inquiry-project-learning-research

Barrows, H. S. (1999). *Problem-based learning applied to medical education.* Springfield: Southern Illinois University School of Medicine.

Bennett, V. (2014). Engaging and challenging gifted and talented students. *Teaching Geography, 39,* 30–31.

Borland, J. H. (2003). The death of giftedness: Gifted education without gifted children. In J. H. Borland (Ed.), *Rethinking gifted education* (pp. 105–126). New York, NY: Teachers College Press.

Casner-Lotto, J., & Barrington, L. (2006). *Are they really ready to work? Employers' perspectives on the basic knowledge and applied skills of new*

entrants to the 21st century U.S. workforce. Retrieved from http://www.
p21.org/storage/documents/FINAL_REPORT_PDF09-29-06.pdf

Conklin, W., & Frei, S. (2007). *Differentiating the curriculum for gifted learners.*
Huntington Beach, CA: Shell Education.

Cooper, J. D. (2014). Professional development: An effective research-based
model. *Current Research.* Retrieved from http://www.washingtonstem.
org/STEM/media/Media/Resources/Professional-DeveloPment-An-
Effective-Research-Based-Model-COOPER.pdf

Dewey, J. (1910). *How we think.* Lexington, MA: D. C. Heath.

Dochy, F., Segers, M., Van den Bossche, P., & Gijbels, D. (2003). Effects of
problem-based learning: A meta-analysis. *Learning and Instruction, 13,*
533–568.

Engage Learning. (2013). *Engage2learn.* Retrieved from http://engage2learn.
org/estudio/

Erickson, H. L. (2007). *Concept-based curriculum and instruction for the thinking
classroom.* Thousand Oaks, CA: Corwin Press.

Feldhusen, J. F., & Kennedy, D. M. (1988). Preparing gifted youth for leadership roles in a rapidly changing society. *Roeper Review, 10,* 226–230.

Fine, A., & Merrill, R. (2010). *You already know how to be great: A simple way
to remove interference and unlock your greatest potential.* New York, NY:
Penguin.

Gallagher, S. A. (1996). A new look (again) at gifted girls and mathematics
achievement. *Journal of Secondary Gifted Education, 7,* 459–475.

Gallagher, S. A. (2009). Problem-based learning. In J. S. Renzulli, E. J. Gubbins,
K. S. McMillen, R. D. Eckert, & C. A. Little (Eds.). *Systems and models
for developing programs for the gifted and talented* (2nd ed., pp. 193–210).
Waco, TX: Prufrock Press.

Gallagher, S. A., & Gallagher, J. (2013). Using problem-based learning to
explore unseen academic potential. *Interdisciplinary Journal of Problem-
Based Learning, 7*(1), 9.

Gardner, H. (2009). *Five minds for the future.* Boston, MA: Harvard Business
Review Press.

Hanney, R., & Savin-Baden, M. (2013). The problem of projects:
Understanding the theoretical underpinnings of project-led PBL. *London
Review of Education, 11*(1), 7–19.

Hattie, J. (2009). *Visible learning: A synthesis of over 800 meta-analyses relating
to achievement.* New York, NY: Routledge.

Henderson, L. (2004). Unleashing talent: An examination of VanTassel-
Baska's integrated curriculum model. *Post-Script, 5*(1), 54–73.

Hmelo-Silver, C. E. (2004). Problem-based learning: What and how do students learn? *Educational Psychology Review, 16*, 235–266.

Johnson, S. (2010). *Where good ideas come from: The natural history of innovation.* New York, NY: Riverhead Books.

Jollands, M., Jolly, L., & Molyneaux, T. (2012). Project-based learning as a contributing factor to graduates' work readiness. *European Journal of Engineering Education, 37*, 143–154.

Joyce, B. R., & Showers, B. (2002). *Student achievement through staff development.* Alexandria, VA: Association for Supervision and Curriculum Development.

Karnes, F. A., & Bean, S. M. (2010). *Developing leadership potential in gifted students.* Waco, TX: Prufrock Press.

Kelley, F. S., McCain, T., & Jukes, I. (2009). *Teaching the digital generation: No more cookie cutter high schools.* Thousand Oaks, CA: Corwin Press.

Kettler, T. (2014). Critical thinking skills among elementary gifted students: Comparing identified gifted and general education student performance. *Gifted Child Quarterly, 58*, 127–136.

Ladewski, B., Krajcik, J., & Harvey, C. (1994). A middle grade science teacher's emerging understanding of project-based instruction. *The Elementary School Journal, 94*, 498–515.

Landsberg, M. (2009). *The tao of coaching: Boost your effectiveness at work by inspiring and developing those around you.* London, England: Profile Books.

Marzano, R. J., Waters, T., & McNulty, B. A. (2005). *School leadership that works: From research to results.* Alexandria, VA: Association for Supervision and Curriculum Development.

Mergendoller, J. R., Maxwell, N. L., & Bellisimo, Y. (2006). The effectiveness of problem-based instruction: A comparative study of instructional methods and student characteristics. *The Interdisciplinary Journal of Problem-based Learning, 1*(2), 49–69.

Partnership for 21st Century Skills. (2011). *Framework for 21st century learning.* Retrieved from http://www.p21.org/storage/documents/1.__p21_framework_2-pager.pdf

Pearlman, B. (2010). Designing new learning environments to support 21st century skills. In J. Bellanca & R. Brandt (Eds.), *21st century skills: Rethinking how students learn* (pp. 117–147). Bloomington, IN: Solution Tree Press.

Perkins, D. (1992). *Smart schools: Better thinking and learning for every child.* New York, NY: The Free Press.

Pink, D. H. (2006). *A whole new mind: Why right-brainers will rule the future.* New York, NY: Penguin.

Renshaw, B., & Alexander, G. (2005). *Super coaching*. London, England: Random House.

Ritchhart, R. (2001). From IQ to IC: A dispositional view of intelligence. *Roeper Review, 23*, 143–150.

Robinson, K. (2011). *Out of our minds: Learning to be creative*. Chichester, West Sussex, England: Capstone.

Sak, U. (2004). A synthesis of research on psychological types of gifted adolescents. *Journal of Secondary Gifted Education, 15*(2), 70–79.

Saunders-Stewart, K. S., Gyles, P. D. T., & Shore, B. M. (2012). Student outcomes in inquiry instruction: A literature-derived inventory. *Journal of Advanced Academics, 23*, 5–31.

Schmidt, H. G., Rotgans, J. I., & Yew, E. H. J. (2011). The process of problem-based learning: what works and why. *Medical education, 45*, 792–806.

Senge, P. M., & Suzuki, J. (1994). *The fifth discipline: The art and practice of the learning organization*. New York, NY: Currency Doubleday.

Shepherd, H. G. (1988). The probe method: A problem-based learning model's effect on critical thinking skills of fourth- and fifth-grade social studies students. *Dissertation Abstracts International: Section A. Humanities and Social Sciences, 59*(3-A), 779.

Sisk, D. (2009). *Making great kids greater: Easing the burden being gifted*. Thousand Oaks, CA: Corwin Press.

Stepien, W., & Gallagher, S. (1993). Problem-based learning: As authentic as it gets. *Educational Leadership, 50*(7), 25–28.

Sternberg, R. J. (1996). *Successful intelligence: How practical and creative intelligence determine success in life*. New York, NY: Simon & Schuster.

Strobel, J., & van Barneveld, A. (2009). When is PBL more effective? A meta-synthesis of meta-analyses comparing PBL to conventional classrooms. *Interdisciplinary Journal of Problem-based Learning, 3*(1), 4.

Swicord, B. (n.d.a). *Problem-based learning: A promising strategy for gifted students*. Retrieved from http://www.nsgt.org/problem-based-learning/

Swicord, B. (n.d.b). *The puzzle of differentiating learning for gifted students*. Retrieved from http://www.nsgt.org/differentiating-learning-for-gifted-students/

Texas Higher Education Coordinating Board. (n.d.). *Elements of the Texas core curriculum*. Retrieved from http://www.thecb.state.tx.us/index.cfm?objectid=427FDE26-AF5D-F1A1-E6FDB62091E2A507

Thomas, J. W. (2000). *A review of research on project-based learning*. Retrieved from http://www.newtechnetwork.org.590elmp01.blackmesh.com/sites/default/files/dr/pblresearch2.pdf

Torp, L., & Sage, S. (2002). *Problems as possibilities: Problem-based learning for K–16 education* (2nd ed.). Alexandria, VA: Association for Supervision and Curriculum Development.

Tretten, R., & Zachariou, P. (1995). *Learning about project-based learning: Assessment of project-based learning in Tinkertech schools*. San Rafael, CA: The Autodesk Foundation.

VanTassel-Baska, J. (1995). The development of talent through curriculum. *Roeper Review, 18,* 98–102.

VanTassel-Baska, J., & Brown, E. F. (2007). Toward best practice: An analysis of the efficacy of curriculum models in gifted education. *Gifted Child Quarterly, 51,* 342–358.

VanTassel-Baska, J., Johnson, D. T., Hughes, C. E., & Boyce, L. N. (1996). A study of language arts curriculum effectiveness with gifted learners. *Journal for the Education of the Gifted, 19,* 461–480.

VanTassel-Baska, J., & Stambaugh, T. (2005). Challenges and possibilities for serving gifted learners in the regular classroom. *Theory Into Practice, 44,* 211–217.

VanTassel-Baska, J., Zuo, L., Avery, L. D., & Little, C. A. (2002). A curriculum study of gifted-student learning in the language arts. *Gifted Child Quarterly, 46,* 30–43.

Vygotsky, L. S. (1978). *Mind in society: The development of higher psychological processes.* Cambridge, MA: Harvard University Press.

Wagner, T. (2010). *The global achievement gap: Why even our best schools don't teach the new survival skills our children need—And what we can do about it.* New York, NY: Basic Books.

Weng-yi Cheng, R., Lam, S., & Chan, J. C. (2008). When high achievers and low achievers work in the same group: The roles of group heterogeneity and processes in project-based learning. *British Journal of Educational Psychology, 78,* 205–221.

Whitmore, S. J. (2002). *Coaching for performance: Growing people performance and purpose* (3rd ed.). London, England: Nicholas Brealey.

Yoon, K. S., Duncan, T., Lee, S. W.-Y., Scarloss, B., & Shapley, K. L. (2007). *Reviewing the evidence on how professional development affects student achievement* (Issues & Answers Report, REL 2007-No. 033). Washington, DC: U.S. Department of Education, Institute of Educational Sciences, National Center for Education Evaluation and Regional Assistance, Regional Educational Laboratory Southwest. Retrieved from http://ies.ed.gov/ncee/edlabs/regions/southwest/pdf/rel_2007033.pdf

Zemelman, S., Daniels, H., & Hyde, A. (2005). *Best practice: Today's standards for teaching and learning in America's schools* (3rd ed.). Portsmouth, NH: Heinemann.

Zhao, Y. (2012). *World class learners: Educating creative and entrepreneurial students.* Thousand Oaks, CA: Corwin.

Appendix A

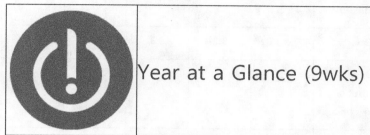

Year at a Glance (9wks)

Once you have grouped TEKS across disciplines according to concept, you can divide the "chunks" across the year and lay them out in a concept map. For each unit, you will list the driving question/real problem/concept idea, the approximate number of weeks you think this unit will take (2-4) and the standards that students will be expected to master in this unit. The concept map is a starting place to group and divide up units. The original map may have to be refined after writing PBL unit as standards shift during design work.

1st Quarter	1.1	1.2	1.3	1.4	1.5
Driving questions/ problem/concept					
Standards for mastery					
2nd Quarter	2.1	2.2	2.3	2.4	2.5
Driving questions/ problem/concept					

Standards for mastery					
3rd Quarter	3.1	3.2	3.3	3.4	3.5
Driving questions/ problem/concept					
Standards for mastery					
4th Quarter	4.1	4.2	4.3	4.4	4.5
Driving questions/ problem/concept					
Standards for mastery					

Appendix B

Reducing your Water Footprint

grade/course | 8/Archived Math K-12, Archived Math K-12, Archived Math K-12, Archived Math K-12

designer(s) | Lauren Hurt-Ashwin, Laura Dobbins, Shannon Buerk

✓ **design tasks:**
___ unit design complete
___ calendar created
___ rubric(s) complete
___ room/tech reserved
___ guest(s) contacted

---

project summary

Students will be researching how living things depend on and will compete for resource, including water, and how that connects to the global water crisis. They will determine their own water footprint and then research and work together to create a product that will help inform and persuade a local business of choice to create a water strategy plan to monitor, measure, manage, and reduce their water footprint.

---

pre-assessment

Your pre-assessment should focus on the readiness standards for mastery and contain questions at the rigor level of columns 1, 2, and 3 on the rubric to help you identify, not only what students know, but where their knowledge is in terms of working towards mastery.

You could also encourage students to leave answers blank on the pre-assessment, if they are unsure. This will help you gather data that best represents understanding and is not scued by guessing.

The pre-assessment will help you to map out the project, including which DIY scaffolding activities and workshops you will need to have prepared for which students. This pre-assessment, along with formatively assessing throughout the project, will help you differentiate materials, resoures, and workshops.

---

project standards
Archived Math K-12
Readiness 8.05.A predict, find, and justify solutions to application problems using appropriate tables, graphs, and algebraic equations
Process 8.14.A Identify and apply mathematics to everyday experiences, to activities in and outside of school, with other disciplines, and with other mathematical topics.
ELA & Reading
Supporting 8.18.A establishes a clear thesis or position
Supporting 8.18.C includes evidence that is logically organized to support the author's viewpoint and that differentiates between fact and opinion
Science
Knowledge/Skill Statement 8.11. Organisms and environments. The student knows that interdependence occurs among living systems and the environment and that human activities can affect these systems.
Readiness 8.11.B Investigate how organisms and populations in an ecosystem depend on and may compete for biotic and abiotic factors such as quantity of light, water, range of temperatures, or soil composition.

unit design template
Engage Learning Inc. © 2013

engage!
www.engage2learn.org

Supporting 8.11.D Recognize human dependence on ocean systems and explain how human activities such as runoff, artificial reefs, or use of resources have modified these systems.
Technology
Knowledge/Skill Statement 8.03 Research and information fluency. The student acquires, analyzes, and manages content from digital resources. (2012-13)
Standards 8.03.A Create a research plan to guide inquiry. (2012-13)
Standards 8.03.B Plan, use, and evaluate various search strategies, including keyword(s) and Boolean operators. (2012-13)
Standards 8.03.C Select and evaluate various types of digital resources for accuracy and validity. (2012-13)
Standards 8.03.D Process data and communicate results. (2012-13)
Standards 8.05.B Practice and explain ethical acquisition of information and standard methods for citing sources. (2012-13)

project requirements	driving question/challenge
To determine the ultimate importance of resources, use technology to create a research plan and investigate how organisms, including humans, and populations in an ecosystem depend on and may compete for biotic and abiotic factors such as: • quantity of light • water • range of temperatures • soil composition Use an appropriate algebraic equation, table, or graph that will allow you to find your average daily water usage, and predict the change in your average daily water usage to justify the implementation of a sustainable practice of choice. Write a multi-paragraph essay that recognizes human dependence and impact on water systems, and informs and persuades a local business of choice to reduce their water footprint, by supporting your essay with facts from different sources.	How can we create a product that will help inform and persuade a local business to reduce their water footprint?
hook 1. http://vimeo.com/64060204	**audience** Local business of choice

unit design template
Engage Learning Inc. © 2013

engage!
www.engage2learn.org

158

Reducing your Water Footprint | Challenge Brief

Engage! Learning | Learner Resources

Water is a resource that all living things need to survive, and living things will compete for their resources.

Freshwater is a scarce resource; its annual availability is limited and demand is growing. The water footprint of humanity has exceeded sustainable levels at several places and is unequally distributed among people. There are many spots in the world where serious water depletion or pollution takes place: rivers running dry, dropping lake and groundwater levels and endangering species because of contaminated water.

People use lots of water for drinking, cooking and washing, but even more for producing things such as food, paper, cotton clothes, etc. The water footprint is an indicator of water use that looks at both direct and indirect water use of a consumer or producer. The water footprint of an individual, community or business is defined as the total volume of freshwater that is used to produce the goods and services consumed by the individual or community or produced by the business.

As a consumer, you can reduce your direct and indirect water footprint by understanding first, all the different ways we use water. Then, by creating a customized plan and committing to reducing your personal usage. This is a great start, but the largest water footprints are coming from the businesses, not the consumer.

How can we create a product that will help inform and persuade a local business to reduce their water footprint?

Project Requirements:

1. To determine the ultimate importance of resources, use technology to create a research plan and investigate how organisms, including humans, and populations in an ecosystem depend on and may compete for biotic and abiotic factors such as:

- quantity of light
- water
- range of temperatures
- soil composition

2. Use an appropriate algebraic equation, table, or graph that will allow you to find your average daily water usage, and predict the change in your average daily water usage to justify the implementation of a sustainable practice of choice.

3. Write a multi-paragraph essay that recognizes human dependence and impact on water systems, and informs and persuades a local business of choice to reduce their water footprint, by supporting your essay with facts from different sources.

Considerations:

-Many variables go into calculating a true water footprint, so you might consider focusing on the more common wasteful water habits when completing the second project requirement.

-When sending your essay in the mail, you might want to include contact information, so the business owner could get back in touch with you for advice on their water strategy.

learner packet | secondary template
Engage Learning Inc. © 2012

1

engage!
www.engage2learn.org

Reducing your Water Footprint | Project Rubric

Engage! Learning | Learner Resources

	1 initiating progress	**2** approaching expectations	**3** meeting expectations	**4** exceeding expectations
Science 8.11B investigate how organisms and populations in an ecosystem depend on and may compete for	Identify how organisms, including humans, and populations in an ecosystem depend on and may compete for biotic and abiotic factors such as: • quantity of light • water • range of temperatures • soil composition	Research how organisms, including humans, and populations in an ecosystem depend on and may compete for biotic and abiotic factors such as: • quantity of light • water • range of temperatures • soil composition	Investigate how organisms, including humans, and populations in an ecosystem depend on and may compete for biotic and abiotic factors such as: • quantity of light • water • range of temperatures • soil composition	Compare and contrast how organisms, including humans, and populations in an ecosystem depend on and may compete for biotic and abiotic factors such as: • quantity of light • water • range of temperatures • soil composition
Writing 8.17A write a multi-paragraph essay to convey information about a topic that:	Brainstorm a multi-paragraph essay that lists human dependence and impact on water systems and informs and persuades a local business of choice to reduce their water footprint by supporting your	Draft and organize a multi-paragraph essay that outlines human dependence and impact on water systems and informs and persuades a local business of choice to reduce their water footprint by supporting your	Write a multi-paragraph essay that recognizes human dependence and impact on water systems and informs and persuades a local business of choice to reduce their water footprint by supporting your	Write and share a multi-paragraph essay that recognizes human dependence and impact on water systems and informs and persuades a local business of choice to reduce their water footprint by supporting your

project rubric template

Engage! Learning Inc. © 2013

1

	essay with facts from different sources.	essay with facts from different sources.	essay with facts from different sources.	essay with facts from different sources.
Math 8.05.A predict, find, and justify solutions to application problems using appropriate tables, g	Research an algebraic equation, table, or graph that shows users their average daily water usage, and predicts the change in their average daily water usage to determine the implementation of a sustainable practice of choice.	Identify an algebraic equation, table, or graph that will allow users to identify their average daily water usage, and predict the change in their average daily water usage to support the implementation of a sustainable practice of choice.	Use an algebraic equation, table, or graph that will allow users to find their average daily water usage, and predict the change in their average daily water usage to justify the implementation of a sustainable practice of choice.	Create an algebraic equation, table, or graph that will allow users to calculate their average daily water usage, and predict the change in their average daily water usage to compare the implementation of a sustainable practices of choice.
Science 8.11. The student knows that interdependence occurs among living systems and the environment and that human activities can affect these systems.				

project rubric template
Engagel Learning Inc. © 2013

2

Appendix C

"It's Sow Easy!"

grade/course | Algebra I
designer(s) | Engage Admin

✓ **design tasks:**
___ unit design complete
___ calendar created
___ rubric(s) complete
___ room/tech reserved
___ guest(s) contacted

---

project summary

This project uses gardening as the context for changing slope and y-intercepts and calculating changes in represented graphs, table and algebraic equations. Systems of equations compares two situations.

---

project standards
Algebra I
Supporting A.1.B gather and record data and use data sets to determine functional relationships between quantities
Readiness A.1.D represent relationships among quantities using ..., tables, graphs, ..., verbal descriptions, equations,...
Readiness A.2.B identify mathematical domains and ranges and determine reasonable domain and range values for given situations, ...discrete
Supporting A.5.A determine whether or not given situations can be represented by linear functions
Readiness A.6.B interpret the meaning of slope and intercepts in situations using data, symbolic representations, or graphs
Readiness A.6.C investigate, describe, and predict the effects of changes in m and b on the graph of y = mx + b
Supporting A.6.D graph and write equations of lines given characteristics such as two points, a point and a slope, or a slope and y?intercept
Readiness A.6.F interpret and predict the effects of changing slope and y?intercept in applied situations
Supporting A.8.A analyze situations and formulate systems of linear equations in two unknowns to solve problems
Readiness A.8.B solve systems of linear equations using concrete models, graphs, tables, and algebraic methods
Supporting A.8.C interpret and determine the reasonableness of solutions to systems of linear equations

---

project requirements	driving question/challenge
In a short PowerPoint and supporting working papers: • With two selected produce items, use a table, graph, verbal description and equation to represent the cost of repeatedly purchasing	How can you compare the costs of home gardening to grocery store produce purchases in a system of equations to convince the Sustainable Food Center's participants that home gardening is financially beneficial?

unit design template
Engage Learning Inc. © 2013

engage l
www.engage2learn.org

these items at the grocery store over a period of time representing the season of the items
- With the same two selected items, use a table, the same graph as above, verbal description and equation to represent the cost of planting and growing the produce in your own home over the same period of time
- Using graphs, tables, and algebraic methods, solve the system of equations and interpret the solution
- For both situations, identify the domains and ranges of each situation and interpret the meanings of their slopes and y-intercepts
- Consider factors that can affect the slopes and y-intercepts of each situation and graph the new system on a new coordinate plane to describe and predict a new solution to the system
- Using algebraic methods, solve the new system of equations to justify the prediction

hook	**audience**
http://www.howcast.com/videos/176423-How-to-Grow-Your-Own-Pineapple-at-Home http://realmilwaukeenow.com/2012/08/13/cheap-thoughts-grow-your-own-garden/ Generate, with students, a list of vegetables common in local home gardens.	Sustainable Food Center Community Relations Director Sustainable Food Center Youth

anticipated research questions	**anticipated resources**
How do we solve equations with more than 2 vegetables? What if the price at the grocery store changes? Why do grocery store prices change?	http://www.sustainablefoodcenter.org/ textbook Khan Academy

unit design template
Engage Learning Inc. © 2013

engage!
www.engage2learn.org

"It's Sow Easy!" | Challenge Brief

Engage! Learning | Learner Resources

www.engage2learn.org

Susan Leibrock, Community Relations Director

Sustainable Food Center

[Date]

[Teacher's Name]'s Algebra I Students

[School Name]

Dear Algebra I Students:

From seed to table, the Sustainable Food Center creates opportunities for individuals to make healthy food choices and to participate in a vibrant local food system. Through organic food gardening, relationships with area farmers, interactive cooking classes and nutrition education, children and adults have increased access to locally grown food and are empowered to improve the long-term health of Central Texans and our environment.

One goal of our organization is to encourage young adults and children to learn about gardening to understand how it can benefit them as adults. Although we have a lot of young participants, we feel we're lacking some education to help them adopt this practice as a lifestyle. This is where you come in!

Who doesn't want to save money on something they *have* to buy to spend it on something else they *want* to buy? We need you to use home gardening to show our youth and young adult participants how they can save money!

Challenge:

How can you compare the costs of home gardening to grocery store produce purchases in a system of equations to convince the Sustainable Food Center's participants that home gardening is financially beneficial?

Project Requirements:

In a short PowerPoint and supporting working papers:

- With two selected produce items, use a table, graph, verbal description and equation to represent the cost of repeatedly purchasing these items at the grocery store over a period of time representing the season of the items
- With the same two selected items, use a table, the same graph as above, verbal description and equation to represent the cost of planting and growing the produce in your own home over the same period of time
- Using graphs, tables, and algebraic methods, solve the system of equations and interpret the solution
- For both situations, identify the domains and ranges of each situation and interpret the meanings of their slopes and y-intercepts

learner packet | secondary template

Engage Learning Inc. © 2012

1

- Consider factors that can affect the slopes and y-intercepts of each situation and graph the new system on a new coordinate plane to describe and predict a new solution to the system
- Using algebraic methods, solve the new system of equations to justify the prediction

Variables (options):

- Your presentations will be different since you will all have different garden plants
- Your gardening expenses will vary due to the initial cost for purchasing gardening items and recurring costs to keep the garden fertilized and watered
- Your costs may vary since you may consider using different stores to buy your produce
- Your costs may vary since some of you may elect to use cost-free fertilizing and watering methods

Constraints (limitations):

- The PowerPoint should contain animation that contributes not distracts from your message
- The PowerPoint presentation should be between 3 and 5 minutes when presented in person

Considerations (food for thought):

- You may consider inviting someone to follow your recommended gardening ideas
- Grow your own garden and capture it on video
- Demonstrate how your harvest can be used in different recipes
- You may consider including the cost benefit on health expenses by growing your own garden
- You may consider joining our program
- You may consider teaching youth in your district schools about gardening with footage from your own gardening experience.

Sincerely,

Susan Leibrock

Community Relations Director

engage!
www.engage2learn.org

"It's Sow Easy!" | Project Rubric

Engage! Learning | Learner Resources

	1 initiating progress	2 approaching expectations	3 meeting expectations	4 exceeding expectations
Multiple Representations	For both the grocery purchase and the gardening expenses: represent relationships among quantities using tables, graphs, verbal descriptions, or equations.	For both the grocery purchase and the gardening expenses: represent relationships among quantities using tables, graphs, verbal descriptions, and equations.	For both the grocery purchase and the gardening expenses: correctly represent relationships among quantities using tables, graphs, verbal descriptions, and equations.	For both the grocery purchase and the gardening expenses: correctly represent relationships among quantities using tables, graphs, verbal descriptions, and equations. Support the information with your own gardening experience.
Systems of Equations	Solve systems of linear equations using concrete models, graphs, tables, or algebraic methods.	Solve systems of linear equations using concrete models, graphs, tables, and algebraic methods.	Correctly solve systems of linear equations using concrete models, graphs, tables, and algebraic methods.	Correctly solve systems of linear equations using concrete models, graphs, tables, and algebraic methods. Include an explanation of each process.
Linear Characteristics	Identify mathematical domains, ranges, slopes and y-intercepts.	Identify mathematical domains and ranges and determine reasonable domain and range values for given situations. Interpret the meaning of slope and intercepts in situations.	Correctly identify mathematical domains and ranges and determine reasonable domain and range values for given situations. Correctly interpret the meaning of slope and intercepts in situations.	Correctly identify mathematical domains and ranges and determine reasonable domain and range values for given situations. Correctly interpret the meaning of slope and intercepts in situations. Explain the process for identifying and interpreting this information.
Linear Effects	Interpret, investigate, describe, and predict the graphical effects of changes in m and b of $y = mx + b$.	Interpret, investigate, describe, and predict the graphical and solution effects of changes in m and b of $y = mx + b$.	Correctly interpret, investigate, describe, and predict the graphical and solution effects of changes in m and b of $y = mx + b$.	Correctly interpret, investigate, describe, and predict the graphical and solution effects of changes in m and b of $y = mx + b$. Demonstrate this with technology.

project rubric template
Engage! Learning Inc. © 2013

1

Appendix D

Rock and Roll, Kindergarten-Style!

grade/course | K/Archived Math K-12, Archived Math K-12

designer(s) | Engage Admin

project summary

Kindergarten students learn about rocks and their attributes and convey their findings in a mobile rock museum to be shared with students at another school.

project standards
Archived Math K-12
Readiness K.10.A compare and order two or three concrete objects according to length (longer/shorter than, or the same)
Readiness K.8.B compare two objects based on their attributes
Science
Process K.2.Collect data and make observations using simple equipment such as hand lenses, primary balances, and non-standard measurement tools
Readiness K.7.A Observe, describe, compare, and sort rocks by size, shape, color, and texture.

project requirements	driving question/challenge
<ul><li>observations of rocks using pictures, numbers, and words</li><li>descriptions of rocks</li><li>comparisons of rocks based on their attributes</li><li>sorting of rocks by size, shape, color, and texture</li><li>examples of how rocks are useful</li><li>recording and organization of data</li></ul>	How can we create a rock museum that we can share with kindergarten students at a neighboring school?
hook	**audience**
Have the principal present to kindergarten students to introduce them to the project. As part of the presentation, have him/her show different rocks or a rock collection to peak their interest.	Kindergarten students and teachers from near-by schools

unit design template
Engage Learning Inc. © 2013

anticipated research questions	anticipated resources
<ul><li>What are attributes?</li><li>What might be attributes of rocks?</li><li>Why are rocks different?</li><li>Where can we find rocks?</li><li>What is a museum?</li><li>How can we create a rock museum?</li><li>What is a data?</li><li>What kind of data can we collect about rocks?</li><li>How can we record observations and data?</li></ul>	If You Find a Rock (read-aloud book) Let's Go Rock Collecting (read-aloud book) Rocks: Hard, Soft, Smooth, and Rough (Amazing Science) Brain Pop Jr.: Rocks and Minerals

diy scaffolding activities

- Sorting activity
- How to do research
- Recording and organizing data
- Comparing two objects
- Labeling museum artifacts

protocols

	days	hours
launch	1.00	0.00
plan	1.00	1.00
research crit	10.00	10.00
design desk crit	2.00	2.00
publish/share	1.00	1.00
total	15.00	14.00

unit design template
Engage Learning Inc. © 2013

engage!
www.engage2learn.org

168

Rock and Roll, Kindergarten-Style! | Challenge Brief

Engage! Learning | Learner Resources

Dear Kindergarten Students,

All kindergarten students in Texas learn about rocks and their attributes. You will be learning about rocks very soon. I am asking you to work on a project that will help you learn about rocks and help other kindergarten students learn about them, too!

Each of our kindergarten classes will create a mobile rock museum. You will have three weeks to learn about rocks and make things to go into the museum. When your work is complete, each of our classes will visit each of the other rock museums. Then we will deliver the museum to the schools close to us. Those teachers and students will use your museums to help them learn about rocks.

The rock museum must show what you have learned while you were creating it. You must include these things in your museum:

- observations of rocks using pictures, numbers, and words
- descriptions of rocks
- comparisons of rocks based on their attributes
- sorting of rocks by size, shape, color, and texture, using hand lens and balances
- examples of rocks are useful
- recording and organization of data

I am excited about what you will learn about rocks, and how you will be able to help other students learn about them, too.

Thank you,

Your Principal

Rock and Roll, Kindergarten-Style! | Project Rubric

Engage! Learning | Learner Resources

www.engage2learn.org

	1 initiating progress	2 approaching expectations	3 meeting expectations	4 exceeding expectations
observe rocks using pictures, numbers, and words	museum creation recording of observations of rocks is limited, vague and/or unorganized	museum creation includes recording of observations of rocks using pictures, numbers, or words	museum creation includes recording of observations of rocks using pictures, numbers, and words	museum creation includes explanation of how observations were conducted and findings/conclusions
describe rocks	museum creation does not convey students ability to describe attributes of rocks	museum creation includes partial, inaccurate or vague description of rocks	museum creation includes description of rocks	museum creation includes multi-word descriptions of the attributes of rocks
organized comparison of attributes of two rocks	organization of the museum creation is not logical and does not convey understanding of "comparison" and "attributes"	museum creation is disorganized and/or shows little understanding of "comparison" and "attributes"	museum creation shows organization and comparison of artifacts, based on attributes	organization of the museum creation shows evidence of deep understanding of "comparison" and "attributes"
how rocks are useful	museum creation shows little or no evidence of understanding how rocks are useful	museum creation identifies a way that rocks are useful	museum creation includes an explanation of how rocks are useful	museum creation includes examples or explanations of how rocks are useful
recording and organization of data	museum creation does not include data	museum creation lacks organization of data	museum creation shows evidence of organizing and recording data	museum creation contains an original process to record and organize data logically

project rubric template
Engage! Learning Inc. © 2013

1

CHAPTER 9

INDEPENDENT RESEARCH, CREATIVE PRODUCTIVITY, AND PERSONALIZATION OF LEARNING

A STUDENT-CENTERED PEDAGOGY OF GIFTED EDUCATION

TAMARA FISHER

Independent study and independent learning projects are frequently among the suggested methods by which schools and teachers can accommodate their gifted and advanced students (Johnsen & Goree, 2015; National Association for Gifted Children [NAGC], 2010). The independent learning project is the featured culmination in three foundational models in the field of gifted education. In Renzulli's Enrichment Triad Model (1977), the independent research experiences are called Type III enrichment (with Type I being introductory experiences exposing students to new content and Type II being the how-to lessons that teach the skills of that profession). In Type III experiences, students self-select real-world problems to study or solve, and through a creative productive process, they formulate a product for an authentic audience. In Betts' Autonomous Learner Model (1985), in-depth study of a topic of personal interest to the student is the goal aimed for by the other features of the model (orientation, individual development, enrichment, and seminars). According to Betts, it is through this process, culminating in the in-depth study,

DOI: 10.4324/9781003236696-11

that students become life-long autonomous learners. In Feldhusen's Purdue Three-Stage Model (Feldhusen & Kolloff, 1986), the third stage centers on independent learning abilities developed through the student's involvement in a research project based on the student's own interests, culminating in communication to an authentic audience. Additionally, independent learning projects have been studied and touted by differentiation advocates including Tomlinson (1993), Delcourt (1993), Westberg (1995), and Fisher (2012; 2013a; 2013b) among others.

Independent Learning in 21st-Century Learning Design

In the technologically driven, knowledge-based economies of information, the ability to develop a deep level of expertise, create new ideas, and produce useful products and solutions is paramount. Modern curriculum for gifted and advanced learners includes a student-centered pedagogy of investigating and creating in areas of personal interest. Independent research and investigations are not new strategies in our field, but in an educational climate of narrow specializations and discrete skill development, they may be more important than ever in advanced learning design. Independent learning includes a collection of strategies where students are participants in selecting topics for investigation, designing plans and steps for procedures and products, establishing appropriate criteria for evaluation, engaging in the investigation, and ultimately sharing findings with interested audiences (Tomlinson, 1993). Independent learning culminates in creativity and problem solving. Renzulli (1984) described creative productivity as the process and outcome of independent learning in the Type III phase of the enrichment triad. Creative productivity includes participation and work focused on the development of original ideas, solutions to problems, and products purposefully designed to impact on one or more target audiences.

Independent learning when done appropriately is challenging and engaging to students. Some students may even clarify their interests and careers paths as a result of their projects (see Table 9.1). In the Autonomous Learner Model, the in-depth study dimension is an empowering process, where students pursue domains and topics of interest either individually or in small groups (Betts, 2004; Betts & Kercher, 1999). Johnsen and Goree (2015) also emphasized

172

TABLE 9.1

Student Evaluations of Independent Research

My least favorite part of this class was having to solve problems that in a normal classroom setting the teacher would solve for you. But I guess that was kinda the point. (11th grader)
I didn't really learn anything "the hard way" this time . . . However, that's only because I learned from the mistakes I made during last year's project! (8th grader)
I believe I have a little more respect for large projects and the time necessary to do them. I was humbled by this project! (7th grader)
The most important thing I learned was how to learn and have fun. This is important because if you don't enjoy something, then you won't want to continue to do it. (10th grader)
I have discovered patience buried in a place I hadn't thought to explore. (7th grader)
This class is thought-provoking, personalized, encourages creative thought, and encourages learning from mistakes. (9th grader who wrote and self-published a 188-page novel)
I had my project at the back of my mind constantly this year, always thinking of ways to overcome obstacles. (11th grader)
More than anything, my projects have allowed me to explore interests of mine and their real-world applications. (10th grader)

engaging students in topics of interest, and their model included the following specific steps: (a) introducing the independent study, (b) selecting a topic, (c) organizing the study, (d) asking questions, (e) choosing a study method, (f) gathering information, (g) developing a product, (h) sharing information, and (i) evaluating the study. In all descriptions, independent learning involves student-selected topics of personal interest, student-created plans of action for pursuing that topic, student choice in the final product, and student-led initiative in putting the product forth to an authentic audience. The key ingredient in all of this is the student, and independent learning projects are the most student-centered option available to teachers.

Essential Elements of Independent Learning Projects

There are a number of models available for implementing an independent learning project. As described above, some of these models have been widely utilized as part of a larger model of curriculum and instruction (e.g.,

Enrichment Triad and Autonomous Learner) and others have been developed as stand-alone learning design options to engage advanced learners (e.g., Johnsen & Goree, 2015). Some may prefer a tighter structure, but I prefer a relatively open-ended approach (Fisher, 2013a) including the following essential elements of design:

» *A blank slate of opportunity*: Truly independent student learning projects means there is little direction from the teacher about what *has* to be done and how it *should* be done. The student should be the one determining a topic, a direction, a goal, and how to overcome the obstacles along the way. It is the student who needs to gain those skills.

» *Student freedom to choose*: This does not mean the students are choosing from a few teacher-preselected or teacher-predesigned projects. It means the students are choosing essentially from scratch what to do, why to do it, how to do it, how to present it, and who the audience will be. Personalized learning projects do not include the teacher telling the students for instance, "Choose from one of these five mathematicians and write a report on that person." Personalized learning projects are personal by definition. The teacher encourages students to select a topic of interest on which they take advantage of an opportunity to focus on their interests and their pathways to expertise.

» *Flexibly structured support from the teacher*: This means giving guidance and backing off, then giving guidance and backing off. Opening this opportunity for students means the teacher has to let go of her need for complete control. The best way for students to learn how to be independent, to learn how to make decisions for themselves, to learn how to be self-reliant, to learn how to dream big and pursue it—*is to let them*. A K–12 classroom can and should be a safe and nurturing place in which to do just that.

» *Time, space, and resources*: Students seem to have dwindling free time. Their schedules are packed full with AP classes, Boy/Girl Scouts, leadership positions in clubs, sports, volunteering, chores, and family time. A student may want to learn deeply about the science of snowflakes or the physics of baseball, but simply just not have the time. In spite of increasing requirements regarding what teachers have to teach and how they have to teach it, the classroom remains many students' last best hope for finding their next direction in life. Carving time out for students to pursue personalized independent projects is not just essential in ways the core curriculum is, independent projects may actually be *more essential to each individual student on a very personal level.* Even if the only time for this option is the extra time a student has when finishing other work early, it can prove far more life-altering than *just* reading a book every day for days and years on end during that extra time (e.g., anchor projects).

The idea of cutting students loose to do and study whatever their hearts desire may strike fear in some teachers. Visions of mass chaos erupting bring on anxiety, fear, and trepidation. What about the standards? What about the curriculum? What about control of the classroom? How will I know what, if anything, students are really learning? These are normal and legitimate concerns, but they are not reasons to eliminate independent research from the learning design.

The prospect of a personalized, self-directed, self-selected, independent research or project opportunity is precisely the freedom of choice for which many gifted learners yearn. Even our most talented students may be capable of much more than we know. We don't know—we truly don't know—just how capable they are until and unless we cut them loose and let them show us how far they can go. As one of my seventh-grade students recently commented, "I learned that I was underestimating myself. When I discovered the things I was capable of, I was so surprised! That inspired me to do more, which I am grateful for."

Independent Learning Projects in the Classroom

Student-selected in-depth studies can be implemented in numerous ways in the classroom. For example, following the lead of Google's 20% Time, some classrooms have implemented Genius Hour (Kesler, 2013), a designated hour of the week (or day or month) when students can pursue their own self-selected topics and studies. In instances like this, typically all of the students in the class are involved. How in-depth the studies and projects go depends in part on how much class time is made available (and/or how much out-of-class time the student is able to access). Another option utilizes the strategy of curriculum compacting (Reis, Burns, & Renzulli, 1992; Reis & Renzulli, 2005) to condense the amount of time students have to be involved in the regular lessons when they can prove they already have mastery of some or all of the content. Through compacting, the students essentially *buy* time in the class-

175

room when they can then pursue their independent learning projects. A third option includes the creation of a separate class (such as an elective) focused solely on students' independent learning projects. This could be done as an independent study option for all students or as a time and place when gifted learners can come together to pursue their interests among other like minds (Fisher, 2013a). Finally, independent learning projects can be incorporated into the classroom learning design of the core content areas by connecting student projects (whether loosely or more directly) to the course's content (Johnsen & Goree, 2015). Designing independent learning into the core curriculum communicates that learning is not just remembering facts and details of the ideas and accomplishments of others; it is joining the conversation as one who is developing expertise in that domain.

The Value of Process

Although the final product is important, one goal for students engaged in independent learning is to help them understand the importance of process, especially a long-term process. Too often, gifted and advanced students can effortlessly complete homework the night before it is due and still earn a good grade. They (mistakenly) learn that serious effort isn't necessary for academic success, combined with the resulting belief that they will always be able to toss something into place at the last minute and still get a high grade. Sadly, life doesn't work that way. The long-term hard work and grueling trial and error that are necessary for creative innovations and masterpieces is rarely seen and even unknown. Students in our modern fast-food, immediate gratification society need to begin to develop an understanding of just what it takes—what it takes of the person—to produce those ideas and products. The independent project opportunity is a chance to play around with their own grand ideas and to see something big through to fruition. Even with this explained to them at the beginning of the project, they may not truly believe and understand it until they've actually been through the beginning-to-end process, including all of the ups and downs, of their project. However, they do come to understand it, and they are so much more independent, self-reliant, responsible, hard-working, and innovative as a result. Their big dreams that were once some-day aspirations become real, tangible, and within reach because they have a better idea of just what is and will be necessary to accomplish them.

Progressive independence is an amazing process to observe in students, in part because it requires them to make decisions they have not had to make before (because the teacher has typically been making those decisions). This decision-making aspect is important, as some students have come to rely on the teachers making so many of those decisions, even little ones like whether their poster should be oriented vertically or horizontally. The independent learning process they undergo encourages, nurtures, and even forces them to shoulder much more of the responsibility for their learning and final products. Additionally, they have to figure out how to organize their ideas, theories, problem-solving strategies, materials, schedule, and troubleshooting. They begin with a blank slate and a goal. Yes, the teacher is around for guidance and assistance. Yes, whatever students choose to do does have to be legal, appropriate to school, and have academic value, but essentially it is a blank slate. For gifted learners who may have unusual interests, talents, and ambitions (learning Latin, studying coccidiosis, trying to determine a formula for time travel, starting a web design business at age 16, taking college courses at age 15 in an effort to earn an early high school diploma and an associate's degree both within the same 3-year window, etc.), an independent learning project gives them the opportunity to fulfill those aspirations within school.

Why Independent Learning Projects for Gifted Learners?

All kids can benefit from this open-ended type of opportunity, so what makes independent learning distinctively important for the gifted and advanced learner? First, gifted youth often have unique and early interests that do not fit into normal curricula, interests they have a strong desire to pursue, but may need some freedom and flexible guidance to do so. Katie, for example, grew up on a ranch in Montana and by age 4 had developed a laser-sharp memory about the medical history of each cow and calf on the ranch—a memory that her father found himself relying on. By middle school, working on the family ranch, she had learned a little about coccidiosis, a parasitic disease of the intestinal tract of animals caused by coccidian protozoa. She wanted to know more to perhaps help other ranchers know how to prevent or treat these potential maladies in their calves. Through a personalized independent learning opportunity, Katie researched the topic; wrote a small booklet with information, photographs, and prevention and treatment options; and had a cattle specialist at Montana State University (MSU) review it for accuracy. She then obtained permission to distribute it to ranchers throughout Montana via the Extension Service, a project sponsored by MSU to disseminate research-based information to strengthen the social, economic, and environmental well-being of individuals, families, and communities in the state. Today, Katie is a recent graduate of the nation's top veterinary school and is splitting her time working as a veterinarian in a western state and serving as a mission/relief veterinarian in Rwanda (Fisher, 2014).

Another student, Clint, became interested in computer science at an early age when he became fascinated with the computer at his daycare. "I wanted to know how it worked and why," he said. "Shortly after, I realized that I wanted to help people and use computers as my medium." He took advantage of self-directed, personalized, independent learning project opportunities throughout his K–12 years to learn almost a dozen programming languages, to design and build his own operating system using a Linux kernel, to learn how to make iPhone apps, and to assist others in furthering their tech skills. Today, he is studying computer science on a full scholarship, with the aspiration of working for the FBI doing white hat cyber security. As one student who used his independent learning opportunity to work toward his private pilot's license has said, "I am getting closer to my dream by doing a project about it. Once you start getting closer to your career, you feel more accomplished" (Fisher, 2014).

Second, personalized independent learning projects help to build life skills—important life skills that gifted learners may not have acquired because their high ability has insulated them from needing the skills. For example, gifted students who have been through the process report they have learned organizational skills, patience, creative processes, time management skills, and confidence. Others students have reported that they learned a better work ethic, how to avoid procrastination, and independence.

One of my former students who currently is a medical school student and a soccer coach stated,

> Advanced Studies [the independent project class] helped to prepare us for college in ways that other classes couldn't. The structure of the class enabled us to pick a topic we were passionate about, find a way to expand our knowledge on it, and pursue it. It required us to have the self-motivation to push ourselves since our projects were often individual efforts, where we strived to answer questions and solve problems for ourselves. In college, students receive an education and

knowledge base proportional to the effort they put in during those years. Students who are self-motivated are able to push themselves and accomplish, or even exceed, the goals they set in life. Advanced Studies helped me to develop this self-motivation and prepared me for a successful career in my undergraduate years, and now medical school education. (Fisher, 2014)

Personalized independent learning projects stretch gifted learners in ways no other school experience can. Placing the responsibility for the project on the *students'* shoulders radically alters their investment in the process. Opening for them the door to freedom—freedom to learn what they want—inspires them to go further and reignites their motivation and love of learning, lending to how far they will stretch themselves. Gifted learners naturally dream big—it is human nature, and they have exceptional talent and ideas to bring to the table. However, much of the gifted learner's experience in school reinforces the notion that he or she is able to get by with mediocre effort and production. A self-selected, self-directed independent project is a different story, though, because the student is more *personally* invested. As one student said,

> I learned that I don't have to give up if I run into a major problem. I just need to come up with a solution even if it takes a while. Now, since doing my project, I try to go big in everything I do and I don't really need a boost to do it anymore. Plus, I'm more confident in my abilities to deal with problems in school and in life now. (Fisher, 2014).

The inherent lesson of dreaming big hits home when they are young and follows them into adulthood:

> The chance to do my own personalized independent projects in middle school was my safe haven. Middle school can be a scary, nasty place for a lot of girls, and with lots of drama, my parents going through a divorce, and constant bullying, my only happy place was in that one classroom, the classroom where I believed anything was possible. I felt free to be myself and dream as big as I wanted without the fear of anyone criticizing me for doing so. (Fisher, 2014)

Another reason to utilize independent learning projects with gifted students is because they have been shown to reverse underachievement in this population. The student with so much potential who does not achieve to his or her abilities often baffles parents and teachers. Baum, Renzulli, and Hébert (1995) found that underachieving gifted students who became involved in an independent learning project (Type III) were more likely than not to reverse their underachievement. Gifted students tend to learn faster, seek out-of-the-box topics, and soldier through the doldrums of too-slow classes. Learning designs that include opportunities for independent research gives them sustenance and breathes life back into their desire to learn with passion. One of the 11th-grade female students reported,

> It's the one place that approves of my embracing of myself and my talents and interests, something that isn't approved of in other places. This opportunity means that I am in a safe haven where I don't have to listen to laughs of disapproval and rejection. (Fisher, 2014)

Similarly, a ninth-grade student commented on the chance to do her personal project,

> [It] makes school bearable as without it I think the routine and 'you do this' attitude would make school stale and dull. This class gives me so much more. I can have an intelligent conversation with someone almost every day, and people understand issues and can help me with them much more often, which really helps my well-being, I think. (Fisher, 2014)

Another former student who currently is a West Point cadet suggested the simple learning pleasure found in the independent research program may have saved him from dropping out.

> I undoubtedly would have dropped out of public school if not for the chance to do independent projects through the gifted program at my high school. If it weren't for all I gained through my projects, I also highly doubt I would have had the courage to take the positive risk of applying to West Point Military Academy. (Fisher, 2014)

Finally, independent learning projects provide gifted students a direct and early link into their possible career trajectory. As Taylor (1995) found, students who had participated in creative productivity had significantly heightened career aspirations. In my own work with gifted students doing independent learning projects, I've found that about two-thirds of them end up in a college major and/or career that is somehow connected to at least one of their independent projects (Fisher, 2014). Despite assumptions that gifted learners will have obvious and easy decisions about which career to pursue, the reality is that they more typically struggle with the career planning process (Kerr, 1990), in part due to their multipotentiality. Independent learning projects provide an opportunity whereby these advanced students with multipotentiality can begin the career exploration process earlier and more deeply, which in turn allows them to get a boost into a career or to cross a few options off their list before it starts costing mom and dad thousands of dollars a semester. A student who participated in the independent research program and now works as a graphic designer commented,

> I was in the Advanced Studies program for 5 years and they were the most beneficial years of my public education. Through those years, I studied miniature modeling, mycology, music, and fine art. The opportunity enables students to explore their own academic interests. As a result, I was more creatively mature going into design school. (Fisher, 2014)

Independent Learning in a Standards-Driven Climate

It is not only possible, but relatively simple for student-selected independent learning projects and the step-by-step structure of standards to intersect and coordinate. Several of the processes students undergo while pursuing an independent learning project are specifically called for in the Common Core State Standards and Next Generation Science Standards (National Governors Association Center for Best Practices & Council of Chief State School Officers, 2010a, 2010b; NGSS Lead States, 2013). For example, ELA Writing Anchor Standard 7 asks for students to *conduct short as well as more sustained research projects based on focused questions, demonstrating understanding of the subject under investigation* (CCSS.ELA-Literacy.CCRA.W.7). This is accompanied by ELA Writing Anchor Standard 8, which calls upon students to *gather relevant information from multiple print and digital sources, assess the credibility and accuracy of each source, and integrate the information while avoiding plagiarism* (CCSS.ELA-Literacy.CCRA.W.8). Reading Informational Text Anchor

Standard 1 will often be met by students doing independent learning projects as they *read closely to determine what the text says explicitly and to make logical inferences from it,* and then *cite specific textual evidence when writing or speaking to support conclusions drawn from the text* (CCSS.ELA-Literacy.CCRA.R.1).

More broadly, specific projects will allow students to demonstrate mastery of specific standards. For example, a student who is researching and writing a brochure about coccidiosis and distributing it to ranchers across the state would demonstrate how to *integrate and evaluate content presented in diverse media and formats, including visually and quantitatively, as well as in words* (CCSS.ELA-Literacy.CCRA.R.7), in addition to learning how to *write informative/ explanatory texts to examine and convey complex ideas and information clearly and accurately through the effective selection, organization, and analysis of content* (CCSS.ELA-Literacy.CCRA.W.2). A student building a scale model would be learning to *represent proportional relationships by equations* (CCSS.Math. Content.7.RP.A.2.c), as well as learning to *apply geometric methods to solve design problems* (CCSS.Math.Content.HSG.MG.A.3). A student comparing the hatching outcomes of hen versus incubator would inevitably be meeting the Next Generation Science Standard of learning to *construct a scientific explanation based on evidence for how environmental and genetic factors influence the growth of organisms* (NGSS MS-LS1-5).

It is certainly reasonable for students (particularly middle and high school students) pursuing independent learning projects to find and make note of the specific standards they expect to meet (or have met) by doing their projects. This not only gives them a deeper understanding of the academic basis of their independent pursuits, but it also provides an opportunity for them to demonstrate to parents and administrators that their projects have value beyond personal interest. For more than a decade now, I have been asking my independent project students to note for me which standards they are meeting through their projects, and while at first the task can seem daunting for them, they actually find the search to be interesting. For example, they find themselves developing an understanding of why they are learning what they're learning in some of their other classes. The process of noting standards met through their projects also gives the students a foundation for understanding the academic and content connections between pretty much anything they may ever want to pursue. Essentially, by way of coming to know the standards a little bit, they are coming to see the big picture of knowledge and how it all fits together.

Implications for Research

For an area that is so widely suggested and recognized as important for gifted and advanced learners, research on gifted students and independent learning projects is slim, getting old, and/or short-term focused. We need longitudinal (multiyear) studies following students who have done such projects. Although more research could certainly be done on the short-term impacts on students (e.g., self-efficacy, motivation, engagement with school, etc.), any long-term (i.e., following them into college and career) research would be beneficial to empirically anchor the practice. Based on my own classroom research (Fisher, 2014), I know that many of my students who have completed an independent learning project have gone on to pursue a college major and/or career that is somehow related to at least one of the independent projects they did as a K–12 student. I have also repeatedly witnessed the growth in self-reliance and independence that results for them throughout the independent learning. However, few if any studies have examined changes in these affective/psychosocial characteristics over time. We also need long-term studies of the impact of independent learning projects on identity formation or development, college/career decisions, drop-out rates, family dynamics, entrepreneurial motivations, and changes in the scope of students' aspirations (and pursuit of those aspirations). Additional longitudinal studies may examine broader societal impacts (economic growth, patent applications, political activism, business development, and innovations) of the career pathways of students who began their interests and talent development with an independent learning project.

Another related research need is case study examination to document the different ways independent learning projects are implemented in various school settings. Some teachers structure the process (and even the topics and other requirements) more significantly for their students, while other teachers essentially provide an open-ended structure and give students a blank slate with minimal guidance and requirements. It would be quite interesting to study how these different styles affect the students and/or the outcome of the projects. Similarly, it would be helpful to examine factors that influence which style a teacher employs in implementing independent learning projects. For instance, do teachers in different disciplines vary in the amount of structure they provide? What types of training are beneficial and related to the implementation of independent learning projects?

Additionally, I think it would be fascinating to look into how students discover their passion for learning in a domain of practice (Coleman & Guo,

2013). How early in life do students identify their passion area, and how sustaining it is throughout their lives? There are several areas of needed research regarding effective implementation. For instance, what school-level factors support and/or hinder implementation of independent learning projects? What support systems, technologies, and policies need to be in place for effective implementation? What concerns/fears inhibit teachers' willingness to adopt the student-centered approach to independent learning? What concerns/fears are associated with students' willingness to take on the challenge of long-term, independent projects? Which skills and habits of mind in both the student and teacher best support effective implementation of independent learning projects? What training, materials, and support mechanisms need to be developed to help teachers adopt practices of independent learning?

It is somewhat surprising that student-centered, independent learning has been advocated in gifted education learning design for decades; yet as a field, we have very little empirical evidence associated with this practice. Anecdotal evidence and teacher stories have sustained the practice over time. Perhaps the nature of independent learning prevents it from large sample, quantitative study, and qualitative or case study approaches are needed. Given systematic inquiry and gradual improvements to practice, student-centered, independent learning projects may prove to be one of our most powerful teaching and learning tools for advanced and gifted learners.

Discussion Questions

1. What obstacles do teachers, schools, and gifted programs face in their efforts to offer or implement independent learning projects for gifted and advanced learners? What strategies can be employed to overcome these obstacles?

2. What characteristics and supports are necessary for the teacher/school/program to have in order for students to more successfully take on the challenge of pursuing an independent learning project? How can these characteristics and supports be developed and nurtured?

3. What prior preparations and/or habits of mind do you think students might need as they embark on an independent learning project?

4. In what ways might personalized independent learning projects look different for younger students compared to older students? Or, would it really

need to be different? What are the essential elements that would/should be the same?

5. What implications does a personalized independent project have for a student's (a) college prospects and readiness, (b) career prospects and readiness, (c) personal development, and (d) social and emotional needs?

References

Baum, S. M., Renzulli, J. S., & Hébert, T. P. (1995). *The prism metaphor: A new paradigm for reversing underachievement* (CRS 95310). Storrs: University of Connecticut, The National Research Center on the Gifted and Talented.

Betts, G. T. (1985). *The autonomous learner model.* Greeley, CO: Autonomous Learning Publications Specialists.

Betts, G. T. (2004). Fostering autonomous learners through levels of differentiation. *Roeper Review, 26,* 190–191.

Betts, G. T., & Kercher J. J. (1999). *The autonomous learner model: Optimizing ability.* Greeley, CO: ALPS Publications.

Coleman, L. J., & Guo, A. (2013). Exploring children's passion for learning in six domains. *Journal for the Education of the Gifted, 36,* 155–175. doi:10.1177/0162353213480432

Delcourt, M. A. B. (1993). *Creative productivity among secondary school students: Combining energy, interest, and imagination. Gifted Child Quarterly,* 37, 23–31.

Feldhusen, J. F., & Kolloff, M. B. (1986). The Purdue three stage model. In J. S. Renzulli (Ed.), *Systems and models for developing programs for the gifted and talented* (pp. 126–152). Mansfield Center, CT: Creative Learning Press.

Fisher, T. J. (2012, July 12). *Unwrapping the gifted: Advice from kids for kids* [Web log post]. Retrieved from http://blogs.edweek.org/teachers/unwrapping_the_gifted/2012/07/advice_from_kids_for_kids.html

Fisher, T. J. (2013a, June 18). *Unwrapping the gifted: The gift of independent learning projects* [Web log post]. Retrieved from http://blogs.edweek.org/teachers/unwrapping_the_gifted/2013/06/reciprocating_saw.html

Fisher, T. J. (2013b, July 3). *Unwrapping the gifted: Student feedback regarding independent learning projects* [Web log post]. Retrieved from http://blogs.edweek.org/teachers/unwrapping_the_gifted/2013/07/student_feedback_regarding_ind.html

Fisher, T. J. (2014). [Independent learning in advanced studies]. Unpublished raw data.

Johnsen, S. K., & Goree, K. K. (2015). Teaching gifted students through independent study. In F. A. Karnes & S. M. Bean (Eds.), *Methods and materials for teaching the gifted* (4th ed., pp. 445–478). Waco, TX: Prufrock Press.

Kerr, B. (1990). *Career planning for gifted and talented youth.* Retrieved from ERIC Database. ED321497

Kesler, C. (2013, March 31) *Genius hour ideas* [Web log post]. Retrieved from http://www.geniushour.com/2013/03/31/genius-hour-ideas/

National Association for Gifted Children. (2010). *Pre-K–grade 12 gifted education programming standards.* Retrieved from http://www.nagc.org/sites/default/files/standards/K-12%20programming%20standards.pdf

National Governors Association Center for Best Practices, & Council of Chief State School Officers. (2010a). *Common Core State Standards for English language arts.* Washington, DC: Authors. Retrieved from http://www.corestandards.org/ELA-Literacy

National Governors Association Center for Best Practices, & Council of Chief State School Officers. (2010b). *Common Core State Standards for mathematics.* Washington, DC: Authors. Retrieved from http://www.corestandards.org/Math

Next Generation Science Standards Lead States. (2013). *Next generation science standards: For states, by states.* Washington, DC: The National Academies Press.

Reis, S. M., Burns, D. E., & Renzulli, J. S. (1992). *Curriculum compacting: The complete guide to modifying the regular curriculum for high ability students.* Waco, TX: Prufrock Press.

Reis, S. M., & Renzulli, J. S. (2005). *Curriculum compacting: An easy start to differentiating for high potential students.* Waco, TX: Prufrock Press.

Renzulli, J. S. (1977). *The enrichment triad model: A guide for developing defensible programs for the gifted and talented.* Mansfield Center, CT: Creative Learning Press.

Renzulli, J. S. (1984). *The three-ring conception of giftedness: A developmental model for promoting creative productivity* (ERIC Document Reproduction Service ED249728). Retrieved from ERIC database.

Taylor, L. A. (1995). *Undiscovered Edisons: Fostering talents of vocational-technical students* (RM95214). Storrs: University of Connecticut, The National Research Center on the Gifted and Talented.

Tomlinson, C. A. (1993). Independent study: A flexible tool for encouraging academic and personal growth. *Middle School Journal, 25*(1), 55–59.

Westberg, K. L. (1995). Meeting the needs of the gifted in the regular classroom: The practices of exemplary teachers and schools. *Gifted Child Today, 18*(1) 27–29, 41.

CHAPTER 10

RESEARCH EXPERIENCES FOR HIGH SCHOOL STUDENTS

A CURRICULUM FOR EXPERTISE AND AUTHENTIC PRACTICE

TODD KETTLER AND JEB S. PURYEAR

In the knowledge economy of the 21st century, creating knowledge is a valued skill across virtually all disciplines. With information widely and freely available, the expert is not necessarily the one with the information. Experts are the ones who use the information and research skills to generate new knowledge to solve problems, offer new perspectives, and design innovative products and performances. Gifted and advanced students attending special high schools like the Texas Academy of Mathematics and Science systematically engage in research with faculty members. Research experiences have helped those students win awards, publish papers, and gain entry into subsequent prestigious learning opportunities (Kettler, Sayler, & Stukel, 2014). Modern curriculum innovation for gifted and advanced high school students ought to include authentic research practices across the core curriculum areas regardless of whether students attend specialized schools or comprehensive high schools with gifted education services.

DOI: 10.4324/9781003236696-12

Research Experiences in Advanced Curriculum

Student Engagement in Research

Undergraduate student research is an emergent practice across all levels of postsecondary education, including community colleges and large research universities. Kuh (2008) found that students rated student-faculty collaborative research at the highest level of academic challenge in a cluster of the most effective educational practices. Kuh also found that college seniors reported their undergraduate research experiences as the most engaging component of their learning experiences. The goal of undergraduate student research is to involve students in authentic work on "actively contested questions, empirical observations, cutting-edge technologies, and the sense of excitement that comes from working to answer important questions" (Phelps & Prevost, 2012, p. 102).

Hu, Kuh, and Gayles (2007) found evidence of undergraduate research across several types of postsecondary institutions, including liberal arts colleges, comprehensive universities, and Tier I research universities. According to their data, students were just as involved at smaller liberal arts colleges as they were at larger research universities. A number of universities address engagement of students in research as part of their undergraduate mission (Gonzalez, 2001; Pascarella & Terenzini, 2005), but not all undergraduates participate in authentic research with faculty. Merkel (2003) found that top students are the most likely to be engaged in research projects.

Engagement in authentic research also impacts the practices of high school teachers. Columbia University partnered with New York City Public Schools, allowing science teachers to apply for a summer program at which they worked directly with Columbia scientists on research projects. The teachers were assigned to research projects in their areas of interest and specialty and participated in the research over multiple summers. The goal of the project was to involve high school teachers in authentic research and encourage them to take those ideas and practices back to their classrooms. Teachers in the program increased hands-on science activities in class, introduced new laboratory experiences and new technologies in their classes, and increased requirements for students to write formal science reports and deliver oral reports of their research. Additionally, these teachers increased the amount of time they read scientific journals and spent more time discussing science careers with their students. Perhaps most significantly, the students of the teachers who participated in the program passed the New York State Regents science exams at a rate that was 10% higher ($p = 0.049$) than the comparison group with nonparticipating teachers (Silverstein, Dubner, Miller, Glied, & Loike, 2009).

Standards Supporting Student Research

Developing and implementing authentic research experiences with gifted and advanced high school students aligns with national gifted education standards. The third standard in the National Association for Gifted Children's (NAGC; 2010) Pre-K–Grade 12 Gifted Education Programming Standards recommends educators create curriculum applying an array of evidence-based instructional strategies to both develop students' talents and help them become independent learners. The NAGC curriculum and instruction student outcomes recommend that students become independent investigators employing creative thinking, critical thinking, problem-solving models, and inquiry models.

Student research is also an explicit standard in the Common Core State Standards for Language Arts (National Governors Association Center for Best Practices [NGA] & Council of State School Officers [CCSSO], 2010a). Students are expected to conduct short, as well as more sustained, research projects based on focused questions, demonstrating understanding of the subject under investigation (Writing Anchor Standard 7). The Common Core State Standards for Mathematics (NGA & CCSSO, 2010b) encourage high school student engagement in authentic research, particularly in the modeling standards and the statistics and probability standards where students are expected to apply quantitative reasoning to investigate specific questions and solve complex problems. The Next Generation Science Standards (NGSS; NGSS Lead States, 2013) articulated eight practices for science and engineering. These practices represent the intersection of knowledge and skill in science disciplines and require students to (1) ask questions and define problems, (2) develop and use models, (3) plan and carry out investigations, (4) analyze and interpret data, (5) use mathematics and computational thinking, (6) construct explanations and design solutions, (7) engage in argument from evidence, and (8) obtain, evaluate, and communicate information. Lastly, the National Council for the Social Studies (NCSS; 2008) published curriculum guidelines for social studies teaching and learning. Those guidelines call for social studies curriculum to be (1) meaningful, (2) integrated, (3) value-based, (4) challenging, and (5) active. Clarifying *active* as a curriculum standard for social studies, the curriculum guidelines state that students should have opportunities to formulate hypotheses and test them by gathering and analyzing data (5.2). Additionally, the program should stimulate students to investigate and respond to the human condition in the contemporary world (5.7).

Standards and curriculum guidelines in all four core content disciplines articulate expectations that students should be actively involved in some type of discipline-specific, authentic research practices. A modern curriculum design for gifted and advanced students emphasizes the importance of building expertise in knowledge creation through authentic research. Although standards call for all students to engage in discipline specific research practices, a differentiated curriculum approach for gifted and advanced students involves more complex and sophisticated skills and research protocols leading to elite levels of products and performances.

Types of Research

Research is systematic inquiry to collect and analyze data in order to investigate hypotheses, offer new interpretations, and suggest solutions to complex problems. Research may be thought of as creative work that seeks greater knowledge and understanding of a phenomenon. Researchers in all disciplines systematically analyze and interpret data to provide insights into the nature of humanity, culture, and society, and the development of new products and applications to solve problems or enhance experiences (National Science Foundation, n.d.).

Although all disciplines share a common concept of research as systematic inquiry, each discipline has a history of established research traditions and methodologies (see Table 10.1). Arts disciplines conduct research differently than science disciplines. Although history and the humanities have much in common, they each have some discipline-specific methodologies. Mathematics research may be the most unique of the core curriculum, focusing on developing proofs and models. The practical application of these discipline-specific research traditions is that each curriculum area will approach teaching authentic research slightly differently. Thus, an advanced curriculum design includes teaching the structures of a discipline, including its methodologies for conducting research and generating new knowledge. In this way, authentic research becomes a type of creative productivity in a field of study.

We have created a hierarchy of research to characterize a progression from the most simple to the more complex types of inquiries. Table 10.2 displays the distinctions from summary reports to professional-level original research.

TABLE 10.1

Authentic Research Traditions

The Art Disciplines	These disciplines consist of different fields of fine arts and liberal arts including painting, music, film, literature, and music. The researcher may use empirical approaches to conduct surveys of public opinions, tastes, or habits. Additionally, researchers can use theoretical approaches to perform analysis or application of theory to works of art, literature, music, film, etc.
The Science Disciplines	The scientific disciplines of medicine, engineering, physics, biology, and chemistry are just a few sciences on which researchers use empirical inquiry to conduct research. Scientific research may involve experimental or quasi-experimental studies in laboratory or field settings. Students need to understand research design, measurement theory, and analytic techniques to conduct scientific research.
The Discipline of History	Historical research may involve analysis of existing data or generation of new data (e.g., oral history projects). Historical research includes questions of how a phenomenon has changed over time, how time has led to a new interpretation of an event or phenomenon, or how patterns can be illuminated to better understand our past and present. A student can conduct local history research or study archival records housed in physical or digital formats. Almost everything has a history, so students may study the history of phenomena of interests (e.g., baseball, ballet, dress making, or video games).
The Disciplines of Humanities and Philosophy	Research in humanities and philosophy is generally based on analytical thinking, interpretation, or applications of theories and ideas. Students may conduct analyses of religious beliefs, ethical theories, political philosophies, or aesthetics. Research of this type includes proposing new interpretations or connections that may not previously have been considered. It may also include analysis of ideas and behaviors against standards of logic and reason. Classical philosophical analyses may include the fundamental meanings of everyday phenomena we take for granted, such as love, friendship, duty, and honor.
The Discipline of Mathematics	Mathematics research involves developing proofs or models or the application of mathematics to solve practical problems. For instance, beginning mathematical research might require a student to prove that a statement is true or to give an example of a phenomenon. Similarly, students might conduct research to answer, "Under what conditions is X true?" Other mathematical research may involve the creation of models. Mathematical models are a way to describe the behavior of a system. Thus, given a complex system of behaviors, students may be charged with developing a mathematical model to accurately represent the behaviors in mathematical language and functions.

TABLE 10.2

Hierarchy of Research

Type of Research	General Description
Summary Report	» Students search the Internet or other sources to write a summary report about a topic. » No systematic methodology is employed for gathering or analyzing data. » Generally considered the lowest level of research activity. » Mostly recreational value, but not exactly academic. » May employ skills of data collection, source validation, and summarization.
Systematic Review	» Differs from summary report in the use of a systematic methodology for gathering and analyzing data. » Analyzing secondary data that already exists in order to make a type of meta-analysis of the information. » Systematic methodology is determined in advance and guides the researcher throughout the process. » Systematic methodology adds validity to the findings and value to the final product.
Original Research: Novice	» Original research involves a theoretical, descriptive, experimental, or quasi-experimental design. » It can be quantitative, qualitative, or mixed methods. » Each discipline has traditions of research that guide authentic practice in those fields. » At the novice level, the research questions and analyses are less complex, and the new information generated typically has little or no value in the field.
Original Research: Expert	» Differs from the novice level of original research in that the research questions are grounded in previous research in a way that the product may add a new layer of understanding. » It can be theoretical, quantitative, qualitative, or mixed methods. » Involves some type of review of previous research to validate the importance of the research question(s). » Research questions and analyses are generally more complex and authentic than research at the novice level.
Original Research: Professional	» Professional-level original research includes domain specific methodologies that are utilized with rigor and precision. » This level of research builds on previous research and adds new knowledge to the discipline-specific knowledge base on the topic studied. » Generally, professional-level research is publishable and valued in the specific field of study in which it was conducted. » Novice and developing researchers often develop expert and professional levels of expertise by working with professional-level mentors to guide and teach research techniques for data collection and analyses.

Too often, research experiences for students are limited to summary reports. Summary reports are the lowest level of research in a discipline primarily because there is little use of systematic data collection and analysis. Students may Google search a topic and obtain more than 100,000 results from which they somewhat randomly select two or three to count as their sources. From these sources, the students' analyses are generally limited to making summary statements with no technique for resolving or even recognizing conflicting data or ideas in the sources. Further, due to the lack of systematic retrieval and analysis of data, summary reports have a very low capacity for replication, a hallmark of quality research in any discipline.

Beyond the summary report is the systematic review. The distinguishing quality of a systematic review is the methodological attempt to include all relevant literature or sources of information and conduct a technically unbiased review of the data to generate answers to a specific research question. In a systematic review, students begin with a clear research question and clearly defined boundaries within which they will seek data for the analysis. By clearly defining these boundaries and methods of data collection and analysis, the systematic review has a high degree of replicability; thus, the conclusions derived or the knowledge created in a systematic review has more validity and less bias than information generated in a summary report. Summary reports have little variability across disciplines because they have no distinct methodology. There may be some slight variations in data sources and analyses across disciplines in systematic reviews, but most importantly, teaching students to conduct systematic reviews as part of the curriculum places value on methodology, analysis, and the creation of valid conclusions.

The highest level of the research hierarchy is original research, and we have established three increasingly complex levels of original research: novice, expert, and professional. At the original research stage of the hierarchy, discipline-specific methodologies emerge. Original research could be theoretical, such as studies in literature and philosophy. It could be qualitative in fields such as history or education. Scientific research is generally experimental or quasi-experimental. The critical defining feature of original research is the dedicated use of discipline-specific methodologies for data collection and analysis. When making original research a component of an advanced curriculum, teachers will need to teach research traditions and theories. Science students should acquire skills in areas of experimental design, measurement theory, and statistical analysis. In other disciplines, students may learn skills of interviewing, document analysis, and interpretation. Although some of these topics may be new for teachers and students alike, technology has made learning and applying these techniques accessible in ways that simply were not possible a decade ago. For instance, a Google search for "ethnographic research techniques" yields approximately 800,000 results including papers, books, videos, and step-by-step guides.

Table 10.3 provides a few examples of what each of the levels of research might look like in the core curriculum disciplines. Ultimately, we advocate a pedagogy of gifted or advanced learning that involves building capacity as a creative producer in one or more fields of inquiry. Learning to conduct research is one way to practice creative productivity; furthermore, learning the methodologies of knowledge creation and participating in those traditions moves students along discipline-specific continuums from novice toward expert.

Examples of Elite-Level Student Research

The annual Intel Science and Engineering Fair is widely considered the biggest stage for high school student research in science and engineering disciplines. Students from around the world compete for the top prize, which includes $75,000 in scholarship funds. In 2014, a 15-year-old high school student from Boston, MA, took the top prize for his research and development of a machine-learning software tool to study mutations of a gene linked to breast and ovarian cancer. His project included applications for the fields of genomics, bioinformatics, and big data analysis. In 2014, there were two runner-up prizes in the Intel competition ($50,000 scholarships for each). The first runner-up prize was awarded to a high school student in Germany who developed a new mathematical tool for smartphones and tablets. The tool allowed handheld devices to perform mathematical processes previously only performed on more sophisticated and expensive computers. The second runner-up prize went to a student in Singapore who developed a new electrocatalyst capable of improving batteries of the future through the use of zinc-air technologies that are lighter and safer and include more storage capacity than lithium ion batteries. Her research has tremendous potential to improve the energy performance of hybrid vehicles.

These examples are the work of high school students—high school students who challenge our imagination of what constitutes a gifted and talented high school science program. Intel Science and Engineering Fair projects include finalists who developed an experimental vaccine for colon cancer, a student who combined mechanical and electrical engineering to create a finger-

TABLE 10.3

Examples of Different Types of Research in the Core Curriculum

	Type of Research	Example
Language Arts	Summary Report	Students do research and write an essay/report about the historical time period in which F. Scott Fitzgerald's *The Great Gatsby* was set.
	Systematic Review	Students survey the top 10 literature study guides (e.g., SparkNotes) and identify similarities and differences in their explanations of theme in *The Great Gatsby*.
	Original Research	Students study the classical Greek literary structure of tragedy and compose a theoretical literary analysis to argue that *The Great Gatsby* does or does not resemble the tragic narrative structure.
Social Studies	Summary Report	Students do research and write an essay/report on the significance of the Vietnam War.
	Systematic Review	Students identify songs written about the Vietnam War between 1970 and 1975 and conduct a textual analysis of the lyrics to identify pop culture opinions of the war.
	Original Research	Students identify 10 veterans of the Vietnam War and interview them using a phenomenological research approach and a structured interview protocol to complete a historical research paper on postwar experiences of Vietnam War veterans.
Science	Summary Report	Students do research and write a position paper on stem cell research.
	Systematic Review	Using the National Institute of Health (NIH) website, students locate and summarize the five most common themes in stem cell research in the years 2011–2014.
	Original Research	Student studies mutations of a gene linked to breast and ovarian cancer and develops software to differentiate between mutations that cause disease and those that do not.

TABLE 10.3

Continued

	Type of Research	Example
Mathematics	Summary Report	Students do research and write a summary report of the differences between observations, conjectures, and theorems.
	Systematic Review	Utilizing online math resources, students generate as many conjectures as possible about convex polygons.
	Original Research	Using Hilgemeier's Likeness Sequence students will generate a conjecture and attempt to prove it so that it becomes a theorem.

print lock for firearms, and multiple projects on Earth-friendly biofuels that use algae but no chemicals or processing.

The Concord Review publishes the most outstanding examples of social studies research conducted by high school students. The best of the best compete for the Emerson Prize. The work of these students represents the use of authentic methods of historical research and professional writing. Emerson Prize essays include an essay from a high school student in New Jersey who studied the English monarch during the English Reformation, resulting in a paper titled, "The Paradox of Power: An Analysis of the Rise of Parliamentary Power With the Consolidation of the Monarch in the English Reformation." Another student from Tennessee conducted historical research on Apartheid in South Africa resulting in a prize-winning essay titled, "The Nazi Influence in the Formation of Apartheid in South Africa." The work of these gifted social studies students paints a compelling picture of the outcomes of authentic research in history or political science.

Some of the most talented mathematics students participate in the PRIMES program sponsored by the Massachusetts Institute of Technology (MIT). Through the program, high school students interact with other gifted/advanced mathematics students and engage in mathematics research. They learn how to use computers to conduct pure and applied mathematics research, learn how to write mathematics research papers, give oral presentations of their mathematics research, and learn how to format and submit their work for potential publication in mathematics journals. Through the PRIMES program, students have conducted research and written papers on cylindric young tableaux (combinatorial objects), linear homogeneous equations, the Sierpinski triangle, the Ulam-Warburton automata, and Nim fractals. The work of these high school mathematics students engaged in mathematics research presents a contrasting image to gifted mathematics culminating in Advanced Placement calculus classes.

We share these examples of the highest levels of student research to raise the ceiling on our collective vision of what gifted and advanced students are capable of when they are afforded opportunities. Certainly not all students are going to achieve at this level, but some are capable and willing. Authentic research at these levels is not common practice and is rarely systematically implemented in most high school gifted education programs. However, our conception of innovation and excellence in gifted high school education makes this type of advanced research central to the talent development process.

Fostering a Curriculum Embedded With Authentic Research

Educators are likely to respond to our suggestions with a range of sentiments from a jubilant, arms-wide *let's get started* to arms-folded harrumph and chorus of *how are we supposed to do that?* Clearly, we share the sense of excitement of the former, but the caution offered by the latter deserves our dedicated attention as well. Indeed, even the willing idealists should be careful that a rush to get such a program of authentic research off the ground will require deliberate efforts and planning in order to avoid pitfalls and outcomes below expectations. The curriculum advocated here is not something to be implemented overnight—although the philosophy would likely emerge much faster with proper staff training. It is a learning design that thrives on vertical integration of curriculum across all grade levels and attention to potential interdisciplinary opportunities. Perhaps most importantly, it is a curriculum element that we argue could succeed with or without other curriculum changes such as reworked course offerings or pathways. This may make it appealing to advocates and practitioners seeking systems of talent development with minimal levels of disruption.

Foundational faculty training would be needed to implement an effective scheme of authentic research in a school or school district. Traditional schooling has proceeded for a long time with students completing "research projects" that largely resemble what we call summary reports. Even in advanced academic settings, the change and specificity in nomenclature alone could be a hurdle. We would suggest a core group of teachers or courses be included in initial discussions of an authentic research program. These faculty should come from across the four main content areas. Also, if a high school plans to implement such a scheme, teachers across all grade levels should be included. This will lay the groundwork for later K–12 vertical planning and alignment. Diversity with respect to teacher age/experience and time in the school or district might also contribute to generating an eclectic mix of teachers and courses. We believe this would best allow for those teachers, in turn, to train other teachers how to implement authentic research in their classrooms. Although it might be the case that those students in gifted or advanced academics classrooms would see the greatest successes in authentic research outcomes, those designing such schemes should apply the term *gifted* liberally to broaden the scope of opportunities for students and the pool of faculty talent on which to draw.

In our estimation, a program of authentic research would generate initial gains in academic outcomes based on the differences in expectations for generativity and depth of study. However, once established, the gains in the richness of experiences would be dependent on continued staff training and a coherent vision of an authentic program of research across subject domains and grade levels. This sort of interdisciplinary and vertical alignment creates an environment for quality gifted education. The interdisciplinary opportunities could take a number of forms. Beginning a program of authentic research in a comprehensive high school could foster traditional connections across subjects such as mathematics and science or English and social studies. Additionally, multiple sciences could work together, and different fields in social studies (e.g., history and economics) might also find common ground for research options. More rich experiences might arise from developing new courses dedicated to skills in research. These could be taught collaboratively by faculty from several disciplines and be structured around thematic skills common across types of inquiry. Students could study different ontologies, epistemologies, and viewpoints in metaphysics (e.g., positivism, postpositivism, interpretive hermeneutics) to become complex thinkers who engage in authentic research as an outgrowth of this intellectualism.

If you view these core thinking skills and this philosophical awareness as central to the rationale for a program of authentic research, then it follows that you would want to develop them early and reinforce them often. With the desired outcomes of developing students into researchers, the school or district should work backward from that point, deciding what expectations are appropriate for each level. In this way, the focus remains on doing the research itself.

We believe this captures much of the benefit from other schemes of research focused on the completion of independent study as a means to support the needs of gifted students. However, because the authentic research process itself can be seen as an outcome of a developed, vertically aligned program, the system we suggest also engenders cognitive skills that serve learners in multiple levels of study.

Lastly, as we envision a system of authentic research, we should be mindful of the other curricular structures, both macro and micro, that influence the education of students in advanced academic programs. Creating a system of authentic research *can* be viewed as a process to take on in the context of current schools, although the ideas are a bit beyond the status quo. One could generate experiences in the context of current course offerings. These would most likely end up taking the form of subject collaborations and interdisciplinary approaches. A further step would be creating local electives based on research skills. We believe the outcomes of the authentic research program are in line with ambitious goals of talent development. Teaching students the skills of research is one thing. Generating time in their school schedule to implement these research skills is another. We suggest developing alternate course pathways allowing students to concentrate on research in their primary interest area. Through aggressive curriculum compacting and acceleration, students can meet state graduation requirements and create time in their schedules to pursue their passion in a subject and to deepen that interest. Our view on a program of authentic research aims to nourish budding scholars in the skills of their chosen discipline—a time-honored goal in gifted education.

Implications for Research

Areas of study related to authentic research include the following: talent development models in school settings, cognitive skills, and student belief systems regarding approaches to learning. Research on models of talent development often focuses on finding specific characteristics of programs that lead to short-term and long-term academic and personal outcomes. We need field-based research to validate how an authentic research program contributes to the talent development process. Although there are some studies on this topic for undergraduate research, we found no empirical studies involving high school students.

Development of authentic research programs in middle school and high school could be investigated quantitatively by defining and measuring desired academic outcomes. It may also be studied qualitatively by describing and interpreting the experiences of students in authentic research programs. For instance, developing cognitive skills and conceptual understandings of content domains could be an outcome for quantitative research. We may also investigate which curriculum interventions change the trajectories of talent development in students who participate in authentic research. Ultimately, we view the authentic research program as a means of fostering more complex epistemologies in students. We want students to view a creative-productive research process as an outlet for deeper thinking and understanding that spills over into other endeavors. In what ways might we compare students engaged in authentic research with similar students who study advanced content in the same discipline, but do not engage in research?

Discussion Questions

1. What are some systemic barriers that would make it difficult to develop and implement a program of authentic student research in school settings?
2. Most teachers are not actively engaged in research in their disciplines. What types of training and institutional support would be necessary to prepare faculty to mentor students in authentic research activities?
3. What student outcomes would align with a dedicated program of authentic research for gifted and advanced students?
4. How might you make the argument that a program of authentic research is well-aligned with information/technology initiatives (e.g., 21st-century skills)?

References

Gonzalez, C. (2001). Undergraduate research, graduate mentoring, and the university's mission. *Science, 293,* 1624–1626.

Hu, S., Kuh, G. D., & Gayles, J. G. (2007). Engaging undergraduate students in research activities: Are research universities doing a better job? *Innovative Higher Education, 32,* 167–177. doi:10:1007/s10755-007-9043-y

Kettler, T., Sayler, M., & Stukel, R. (2014). Gifted education at the Texas Academy of Mathematics and Science: A model for STEM talenst development. *Tempo, 35*(1), 8–16.

Kuh, G. D. (2008). *High-impact educational practices: What they are, who has access to them, and why they matter.* Washington, DC: Association of American Colleges and Universities.

Merkel, C. A. (2003). Undergraduate research at the research universities. In J. Kinkead (Ed.), *Valuing and supporting undergraduate research* (pp. 39–53). San Francisco, CA: Jossey-Bass.

National Association for Gifted Children. (2010). *NAGC pre-K–grade 12 gifted education programming standards: A blueprint for quality gifted education programs.* Retrieved from http://www.nagc.org/sites/default/files/standards/K-12%20standards%20booklet.pdf

National Council for the Social Studies. (2008). NCSS position statement: Curriculum guidelines for social studies teaching and learning. *Social Education, 72,* 211–212.

National Governors Association Center for Best Practices, & Council of Chief State School Officers. (2010a). *Common Core State Standards for English language arts.* Washington, DC: Authors.

National Governors Association Center for Best Practices, & Council of Chief State School Officers. (2010b). *Common Core State Standards for mathematics.* Washington, DC: Authors.

National Science Foundation. (n.d.). *Definitions of research and development: An annotated compilation of official sources.* Retrieved from http://www.nsf.gov/statistics/randdef/fedgov.cfm

Next Generation Science Standards Lead States. (2013). *The next generation science standards: For states, by states.* Washington, DC: The National Academies Press.

Pascarella, E. T., & Terenzini, P. T. (2005). *How college affects students: A third decade of research.* San Francisco, CA: Jossey-Bass.

Phelps, L. A., & Prevost, A. (2012). Community college—research university collaboration: Emerging student research and transfer partnerships. *New Directions for Community Colleges, 157,* 97–110. doi:10.1002/cc

Silverstein, S. C., Dubner, J. Miller, J., Glied, S., & Loike, J. D. (2009). Teachers' participation in research programs improves their students' achievement in science. *Science, 326*(5951), 440–442. doi:10.1126/science.1177344

CHAPTER 11

AUTHENTIC, FORMATIVE, AND INFORMATIVE

ASSESSMENT OF ADVANCED LEARNING

TRACY F. INMAN AND JULIA L. ROBERTS

Each chapter so far has addressed one fundamental question: How should we design learning experiences for our most advanced academic students in the foundational curriculum areas? Assessment, this chapter's topic, plays an integral role in all aspects of the learning experience. Once planning has occurred, assessment begins with a preassessment to determine what the individual student already knows, understands, and is able to do so that the learning experience is designed for the learner to make continuous progress. Students cannot learn what they already know. Then formative assessments take place throughout the lesson; these growth checks critically determine what learning occurs and the next appropriate steps. Formative assessment results dictate daily alterations of the learning experiences to ensure continuous progress. Finally, differentiated summative assessments determine what has been learned at the culmination of the learning experience; ideally these are product-based or performance-based in nature. They are the requisite grades in the grade book. Without informative, intentional, authentic, and appropriate assessment, learning experiences may be designed, implemented, and evaluated without our advanced academic students learning much at all.

When the National Association for Gifted Children (NAGC; 2010) developed the Pre-K–Grade 12 Gifted Education Programming Standards in

DOI: 10.4324/9781003236696-13

programming, services, and teacher preparation, the organization fully realized how foundational assessment is to learning, listing it as one of six standards. Emphasizing identification, learning progress and outcomes, and evaluation of programming, the standard stresses that "knowledge about all forms of assessment is essential for educators of students with gifts and talents" (NAGC, 2010, p. 2). Because the focus of this chapter is neither identification nor program evaluation, the most important piece of this standard addresses learning: "Students with gifts and talents demonstrate advanced and complex learning as a result of using multiple, appropriate, and ongoing assessments" (p. 2). Five evidence-based practices complete this standard: (a) using pre- and post-performance-based assessments to measure progress, (b) using differentiated product-based assessments to measure progress, (c) using off-level standardized assessments to measure progress, (d) using and interpreting qualitative and quantitative assessment information to develop a profile of the strengths and weaknesses of each student to plan appropriate intervention, and (e) communicating and interpreting assessment information to students and their parents/guardians.

Assessment of Learning, Assessment for Learning, and Assessment as Learning

Perhaps one of the most important concepts to understand from the start is the critical difference among assessment *for* learning, assessment *of* learning, and assessment *as* learning. Too often when educators, students, and parents think of assessment, they think only of grades that go in the gradebook or on the report card. This certainly qualifies as assessment, in particular, assessment *of* learning, according to Chappius, Stiggins, Arter, and Chappius (2005). Assessment of learning equates with summative assessment, an important component to be sure, but not necessarily the most important. Chappius and his colleagues emphasized the difference between this type of assessment and assessment *for* learning—that ongoing piece key to continuous progress. Assessment for learning occurs when "teachers use the classroom assessment process and the continuous flow of information about student achievement that it provides in order to advance, not merely check on, student learning" (Stiggins, 2002, p. 5). Assessment *as* learning means that "assessment becomes a key part of teaching and learning" (Tomlinson & Moon, 2013, p. 21); students examine their growth via feedback to set new learning goals and develop new skills. Assessment *as* and *for* learning, then, are formative assessments, "assessment carried out during the instructional process for the purpose of improving teaching or learning" (Shepard et al., 2005, p. 275). Assessment *of* learning certainly has a place in the educational process, but assessment *for* and *as* learning guides the actual learning and encourages continuous progress.

Formative Assessment

While preassessment diagnoses what students know, understand, and/or are able to do in relation to the learning outcomes, formative assessment allows the teacher to monitor progress students make in reaching those outcomes. Formative assessment informs instruction for all students, as no students should have learning goals they can readily achieve without any academic stretch or challenge.

Popham (2008) offered a definition of formative assessment: "Formative assessment is a process used by teachers and students during instruction that provides feedback to adjust ongoing teaching and learning to improve students' achievement of intended instructional outcomes" (p. 5).

Popham (2008) described four levels of formative assessment by functions that differ:

>   Level 1 calls for teachers to use formative assessment to collect evidence by which they can adjust their current and future instructional activities.

>   Level 2 deals with students' use of formative assessment evidence to adjust their own learning tactics.

>   Level 3 represents a complete change in the culture of a classroom, shifting the overriding role of classroom assessment from the means to compare students with one another for grade assignments to the means to generate evidence from which teachers and students can, if warranted, adjust what they're doing.

>   Level 4 consists of schoolwide adoption of one or more levels of formative assessment, chiefly through the use of professional development and teacher learning communities.

>   The classroom teacher controls Levels 1–3.

Formative assessment strategies are many (Dodge, 2009): learning logs, exit slips, entrance slips, homework, etc. (See Appendix A of this chapter for more examples). The key is for the educator to assess multiple times throughout the learning experience in order to modify teaching so that continuous progress occurs. Studies have indicated clear gains in student achievement when formative assessment is utilized effectively (Black & Wiliam, 1998).

Preassessment

An essential component of formative assessment, preassessment (or diagnostic assessment) serves as the linchpin to defensible differentiation. How can an educator possibly match learning experiences to students' levels of readiness, strengths, or interests if those levels of readiness, strengths, or interests are not determined? Once the educator knows who already knows, understands, and/or can use the content or demonstrate the skills and who needs additional support, modifications can be made. McTighe and O'Connor (2005) presented a medical analogy to stress the importance of preassessment: "Diagnostic assessment is as important to teaching as a physical exam is to prescribing an appropriate medical regiment" (p. 14). None of us would (or should) trust a physician who makes blind diagnoses, perhaps relying on typical ailments or issues for people our age. Nor should students trust educators who blindly create learning experiences, perhaps relying on standards designed for typical readiness for students of a certain age or grade.

Educators can preassess a multitude of areas, ideally focusing on that aspect they plan to differentiate. For example, if the match will be the complexity of manipulating fractions, then a level of readiness preassessment would help facilitate that match. If students will have appropriate choices of product to demonstrate their understanding of the unit, then a learning profile preassessment is in order.

One of the most critical areas to preassess for continuous progress is levels of readiness for learning a particular concept or standard. For example, some students come to the classroom having already mastered the concept. In fact, a curriculum compacting study (Reis et al., 1993) found gifted students knew as much as 50% of the curriculum before school started; when that content was omitted, these students scored just as well as control students on achievement tests. Because students cannot learn what they already know, when educators preassess the levels of readiness and modify instruction to address only those areas not known, continuous progress occurs. Skills, concepts, and content knowledge fall into this area.

Educators should also preassess learning profiles. According to Tomlinson and Imbeau (2010), the learning profile comprises four areas of influence on how students approach learning: gender, culture, intelligence preferences, and learning style (pp. 17–18). Learning styles can readily be matched to differentiation of process (how a student cognitively processes what he is learning) and differentiation of product (how a student demonstrates what he has learned). Although research does not necessarily link learning style to achievement, it has shown that providing multiple avenues to access content improves learning (Hattie, 2014). Work preference can also be preassessed and differentiated: Does the student prefer working alone, in pairs, or in small groups? The educator cannot always accommodate this preference, but oftentimes the work configuration does not matter. Likewise, educators can preassess the product preferences a student has in order to offer appropriate choices.

A third area for preassessment is interests. At the beginning of the year, an interest inventory can facilitate a teacher getting to know her students as they describe such things as what they do after school, their favorite books, or the ability to access the Internet from home. Ideally, though, educators will also preassess a learner's interest in the learning experience. What previous experience does the student have with the content to be studied, the learning process, or the product? Is the student interested in learning about the content? Interest preassessment, then, is twofold: overall interests and particular interests in a certain learning experience or area of content.

In order to match learning with individual students, preassessment strategies must be written and individual. From end-of-unit assessments to Five Hardest Questions (Winebrenner, 1992), a multitude of strategies work in a variety of content areas and across grades. See Appendix B of this chapter for preassessments including templates and student samples.

Oftentimes a little preteaching can jog students' memories, so their preassessments are more accurate. The learner may not remember if the content was studied a year ago. With a 5-minute refresher, however, information comes flooding back. How often have readers picked up a book, scanned the cover, then reached the second or third chapter before remembering that they already read the book a few years ago? The same is true for students; preteaching helps them make connections to previous learning.

In addition to preteaching, students should understand that they are not expected to know all of the information or all of the answers on this diagnostic tool. The preassessment gives them the opportunity to show what they know as well as what their interests are in the topic and their preferred ways of learning. They should also understand that this is formative; a grade will not be given.

Summative Assessment

While formative assessment is assessment *for* learning, summative assessment is assessment *of* learning. These measures transfer to grade books and ultimately report cards, indicating mastery level of content studied. Therefore, each summative assessment should accurately reflect the learning objectives. Wiggins and McTighe (2005) suggested a backward design model wherein the assessments are created before the learning experiences. Those assessments parallel the learning objectives and direct the teacher to plan all learning experiences to facilitate students demonstrating the learning outcomes at high levels. And, just as learning objectives have been differentiated for students, assessments should be as well. The words *multiple* and *appropriate* embedded in the Gifted Education Programming Standards (NAGC, 2010) certainly come into play. Appropriate means that the measurement matches the content and learning objectives, and, where possible, brings into play the student's strengths, learning profile, and/or interests. When multiple differentiated assessments are offered, students can demonstrate mastery in myriad ways such as performance-based or product-based (Tomlinson & Imbeau, 2010).

Most educators feel comfortable with traditional pencil and paper measures, typically composed of multiple choice and short answers. Well-designed assessments such as these are certainly valid, but they may be limiting to some students. Consider the student with test anxiety or students who overanalyze, for example. Think of the student who fought with his parents that morning or is sick. This "snapshot in time" (Dueck, 2014) may not truly indicate a learner's level of mastery or his complexity of thinking about the concept.

Ideally, educators utilize a variety of summative assessments without relying solely on the pencil/paper type. Performance-based (Stanley, 2014) and product-based (Roberts & Inman, 2015) assessments provide strong avenues for students to demonstrate mastery of learning. Choice in how they demonstrate that learning empowers the student: "There is no question of academic integrity. The goal would be to demonstrate that they could learn a particular concept. How they demonstrated this would be their decision. Kids fly on their strengths" (Fay & Funk, 1995, p. 211).

Rubrics or grading criteria must be distributed at the time of the assignment so that students fully understand the expectations of the performance or product from the beginning. A learner cannot create an exemplary collage unless he knows what one looks like. Moreover, the rubrics should be product focused (with the content language general) so that the educator can use them across content and grade levels. Educators must be wary of the beautifully crafted Prezi hiding incorrect content; advanced students can typically whip out a summative assessment without much time or effort that far exceeds the product another student creates. All students must be held to appropriately high expectations, not the same expectations.

Retesting. Dueck's *Grading Smarter, Not Harder* (2014) argued the pros of allowing students the option of retesting in order to demonstrate mastery or the learning of objectives. Students focus only on those sections that proved problematic, taking another version of that section of the test at a mutually agreed upon time. Dueck claimed that retesting has many benefits including student ownership of learning, less cheating, tangible results, and fewer grading conflicts. If the goal of learning is mastering skills and content, then "new evidence of achievement should replace old evidence. Classroom assessments and grading should focus on *how well*—not on *when*—the student mastered the designated knowledge and skill" (McTighe & O'Connor, 2005, p. 17). Consider the newly licensed driver. Nowhere on the license does it indicate whether the person passed the first or third time or if the two scores were averaged; the license simply indicates the driver can demonstrate all necessary skills and understanding to drive safely (McTighe & O'Connor, 2005).

Authentic Assessment

Authentic assessment, so important that it is in the title of this chapter, has been interpreted in multiple ways. Frey, Schmitt, and Allen (2012) examined more than 100 articles that included definitions of the term with specific characteristics of what made the assessment authentic; their intent was to explore what experts and researchers agreed upon and to provide a more unified definition and understanding. Frey and colleagues found "the context of assessment" (p. 5) to be a broad category in the meta-analysis (i.e., the assessment should be a realistic activity, performance-based, and "cognitively complex" [p. 5]). The student's role in authentic assessment, the second category, is a collaborative one between students and teacher, wherein they can defend their product or their responses on the assessment. Students also understand that assessment is formative. The last category, scoring, included the idea that students know the scoring criteria before the assessment or they play a role in the development of the criteria. With the "performance expectation (being) mastery" (Frey et al., 2012, p. 5), scoring should comprise multiple indicators or portfolios.

McTighe and O'Connor (2005) explained the importance of authentic assessment providing evidence of learning:

When we call for authentic application, we do not mean recall of basic facts or mechanical plug-ins of a memorized formula. Rather, we want students to transfer knowledge—to use what they know in a new situation. Teachers should set up realistic, authentic contexts for assessment that enable students to apply their learning thoughtfully and flexibly, thereby demonstrating their understanding of the content standards. (p. 12)

In short, then, authentic assessment, ideally performance-based or product-based (because very few careers utilize multiple-choice or true-false format), provides learners with an important, valid way of demonstrating their understanding. The link to learning and the real world is evident.

Growth Assessment: Remove the Learning Ceiling

Assessing growth is essential for all students, and, in order to assess growth, there must be room in the assignments or learning experiences for students to make growth in achievement. It is as wrong to assume that all students with gifts and talents will have exceeded grade-level expectations as it is to assume that grade-level learning is the perfect match for all students. Advanced learners often encounter barriers to their academic growth in classrooms and schools in which educators have formally or informally established proficiency as their goal. If assessing growth is the goal, teachers must consider various ways to ensure that students have room in the assessment to demonstrate growth in learning. Otherwise, advanced students spend time in classrooms running in place rather than advancing.

Off-level testing is one way to provide opportunities for students to demonstrate what they know and are able to do without being limited by a learning ceiling. Off-level assessments are designed for an older population but are administered to a younger group, thus, lifting the learning ceiling. In spite of its importance in measuring growth among advanced learners, Olszewski-Kubilius and Kulieke (2008) stated, "Off-level testing as an assessment practice within gifted education is not widely used by educators, particularly to analyze a student's knowledge before instruction or to evaluate growth as a result of a program or intervention" (p. 90). The measurement of growth becomes so important when explaining student progress or the lack of progress to parents or to inform decision makers as to the impact of the instructional programming.

Performance assessment is another way to remove the learning ceiling, yet all performance assessment will not allow for continuous progress. It is essential that the tasks be constructed to allow for the highest level of performance, and that the rubrics provide the opportunity for all learners, including the most advanced, to work hard to reach the learning goal. VanTassel-Baska (2008) stated, "The incorporation of performance-based assessment in core content areas would appear a necessary part of designing effective programs for gifted learners" (p. 285).

Product assessment also provides an avenue for measuring growth. Renzulli and Callahan (2008) described product assessment as most frequently being thought of as summative assessment but stated:

> product assessment also can inform the next instructional steps. . . . The planning process should incorporate tasks that are just beyond the point where the student can do the task without any assistance and should incorporate activities that should require some guidance by an adult or peer in execution so that some new learning will occur. (p. 261)

The assignment should not be to complete another product at the same level, but rather to stretch the student to enhance knowledge, understanding, and skills.

Creating a rubric for professionals yet using it with students also raises the possibilities of performing at exceptional levels. The Developing and Assessing Product (DAP) Tool (Roberts & Inman, 2015) has seven levels of performance with the highest being that of a professional. Although no students are expected to have products matching the level of professionals who use that product in their careers, this level allows all students, no matter how advanced, to continue striving to meet higher standards.

Feedback

Feedback, in both formative and summative assessment, is important for teachers to master in order to guide students in their learning. The purposes of instructional feedback are to enhance understanding and improve performance. "Feedback says to the student, 'Somebody cared enough about my work to read it and think about it!' Most teachers want to be that 'somebody.' Feedback matches specific descriptions and suggestions with a particular student's work"

(Brookhart, 2008, p. 1). Wiggins (2012) stated "feedback is information about how we are doing in our efforts to reach a goal" (p. 10). Hattie and Timperley (2007) argued that feedback is a very key influence on achievement.

Characteristics of effective feedback. For feedback to have the greatest impact on learning, several things must occur:

1. Feedback must be specific to the learners. It may be directed to the individual, a cluster of learners, or the class; however, feedback will only be effective if it matches the student's or students' performance.
2. Feedback should occur soon after the performance. Of course, it would not be possible to always provide a class of students with individual feedback immediately, but it is best to offer feedback as soon as possible.
3. Feedback must focus on what is most important. Too much feedback at one time may result in overwhelming students, and the result may be that they pay attention to none of it.
4. Feedback must be ongoing to be most effective. Students should expect feedback, considering it part of learning. It should not come only at the conclusion of a unit of study, typically when the end-of-the-unit test is the only assessment.

Types of feedback. Much feedback will occur in conversations with students, and some feedback will be written on their work. It is the mix of feedback, the tone in the presentation of it, and the focus on learning that will make the huge difference in student learning. So one way to look at types of feedback would be to look at the giver of the feedback—teacher, peer, self, or other.

Another way to examine feedback would relate to whether it is individual or group. Providing feedback to a class or group is appropriate only when the message matches what all individuals in the class or group need to hear. Individual feedback is generally more effective as it relates to a specific student's work.

Hattie and Timperley (2007) described a four-tiered model of feedback: feedback about the task, the processing of the task, self-regulation (i.e., self-evaluation or self-confidence), and the student as a person. These are different in their focus and in their effectiveness in supporting continuous progress and improving performance. For example, feedback such as "good job" does not direct the student to anything specific that would facilitate doing a better job the next time. Grades are not feedback, as they do not suggest ways in which the student will enhance learning. Evaluative comments are not feedback either.

Not all feedback will come from teachers. Self-reflection will lead students to determine their own progress toward learning targets. Peers may also provide feedback; however, they must be prepared to offer effective feedback. Dueck (2014) suggested that providing opportunities to assess work is helpful before giving feedback to others or perhaps to self-assess or reflect:

> Students will best process the criteria that they themselves need to meet if they are first asked to assess someone else's work. One very effective technique is to display an example of a completed project and challenge students to reverse-engineer it. (p. 83)

Feedback includes self-reflection, a process that is useful for enhancing learning and improving performance over a lifetime. McTighe and O'Connor (2005) suggested the following way to encourage self-reflection:

> Initially, the teacher models how to self-assess, set goals, and plan improvements by asking such prompting questions as,
> - What aspect of your work was most effective?
> - What aspect of your work was least effective?
> - What specific action or actions will improve your performance?
> - What will you do differently next time? (pp. 16–17)

See Appendix C of this chapter for the reflection section of the DAP Tool. Over time, it is hoped that the individual will internalize those questions and use them to improve. For most people, learning to reflect will become a habit only if it is modeled and encouraged as can be done through class projects and performances within the school and beyond in sports, music, or other endeavors.

Developing and Assessing (DAP) Tool

Products provide an opportunity for students to engage in high-level learning that is engaging and that can result in the opportunity to showcase strengths and interests. The DAP Tool (Roberts & Inman, 2015) is a protocol to use with product assessment. The D stands for developing as the student uses the DAP Tool to guide the development of the product, and the A denotes the assessing role as teachers use the DAP Tool to assess products (P is for product). It is designed to use at all grade levels and in all content areas, so it is a protocol that takes away the need to create rubrics for various assignments.

There are three innovations that the DAP Tool offers. First is the consistency of the components—content, presentation (i.e., specific criteria of the product), creativity, and reflection. All DAP Tools focus on these four components with content always the first consideration, as content is the key reason for assigning products to be developed. Second, each DAP Tool has three tiers, making varying levels readily available for teachers to differentiate the rubrics for students with varying levels of experience and expertise with the content and product. Third, the performance scale includes two levels above proficiency or meeting the grade-level standard—advanced and professional. Although students are not expected to perform at the level of professionals, highlighting that professionals use products sets students' sights higher than grade-level expectations. See Appendix D of this chapter for sample DAP Tools.

Grading

Not synonymous terms, grading and assessment differ greatly, with grading being "one moment in a long progression of assessment decisions" (Tomlinson & Imbeau, 2010, p. 145). Although preassessments and formative assessments are recorded, they do not factor into the grade. A grade should reflect the learning achievement—period. It should not reflect points lost to late work or no name on the homework, nor should it be inflated with extra credit or points for effort. Problems with grading arise when best practices and principles are ignored. Tomlinson and Imbeau (2010) outlined these based on experts in the field:

>> The nature of a teacher's decisions about assessment will affect grading.
>> Instruction should be differentiated.
>> Assessments should be differentiated.
>> Grading should stem from, not dictate, effective assessment practices.
>> Grades should be based on clear and specific learning goals.
>> Evidence that contributes to grading should be valid.
>> Students should be graded on clear criteria, not norms.
>> Grade later in a cycle rather than earlier.
>> Report key elements of learner development, but report them separately. (pp. 145–147)

Couple these concepts with common sense, and grading should naturally mirror the learning that has occurred.

Implications for Research

Research possibilities in assessment of learning are many. Studies focusing on assessment could be replicated using advanced learners as the population. Product-based assessment is an open arena with little research completed, especially with advanced learners. Moreover, research studies designed to implement best practices with preassessment and formative assessment could be conducted with advanced learners.

Discussion Questions

1. "As we look to our future, if we wish to create a different reality and tap the full potential of assessment as our ally in improving student learning, we must refocus our efforts around a new overarching assessment belief: we must strike a balance between standardized tests *of* learning and classroom assessment *for* learning" (Stiggins, 2004, p. 26). Describe what might be the appropriate balance.
2. Why is preassessment considered the cornerstone of defensible differentiation?
3. In what ways can educators ensure that summative assessments are authentic reflections of student learning?
4. What must be in place for assessment to facilitate removing the learning ceiling?
5. After examining the DAP Tool in Appendix D, describe features that could be implemented to enhance learning for all students, including those who are advanced.
6. What aspects of providing feedback are the most effective for enhancing learning?
7. Justify this statement: Grading and assessment are not synonymous.

References

Black, P., & Wiliam, D. (1998). Inside the black box: Raising standards through classroom assessment. *Phi Delta Kappan, 80*, 130–148.

Brookhart, S. (2008). *How to give effective feedback to your students.* Alexandra, VA: Association for Supervision and Curriculum Development.

Chappius, S., Stiggins, R. J., Arter, J., & Chappius, J. (2005). *Assessment for learning: An action guide for school leaders.* Portland, OR: Educational Testing Service.

Dodge, J. (2009). *25 quick formative assessments for a differentiated classroom.* New York, NY: Scholastic.

Dueck, M. (2014). *Grading smarter, not harder.* Alexandria, VA: Association for Supervision and Curriculum Development.

Fay, J., & Funk, D. (1995). *Teaching with love and logic: Taking control of the classroom.* Golden, CO: Love and Logic Press.

Frey, B. B., Schmitt, V. L., & Allen, J. P. (2012). Defining authentic classroom assessment. *Practical Assessment, Research, & Evaluation, 17*(2), 1–18. Retrieved from http://pareonline.net/getvn.asp?v=17&n=2

Hattie, J. (2014). *Visible learning: A synthesis of over 800 meta-analysis relating to achievement.* Thousand Oaks, CA: Corwin.

Hattie, J., & Timperley, H. (2007). The power of feedback. *Review of Educational Research, 77,* 81–112.

McTighe, J., & O'Connor, K. (2005). Seven practices for effective learning. *Educational Leadership, 63*(3), 10–17.

National Association for Gifted Children. (2010). *Pre-K–grade 12 gifted education programming standards.* Retrieved from http://www.nagc.org/sites/default/files/standards/K-12%20programming%20standards.pdf

National Governors Association Center for Best Practices, & Council of Chief State School Officers. (2010). *Common Core State Standards for English language arts.* Washington, DC: Author. Retrieved from http://www.corestandards.org/ELA-Literacy

Olszewski-Kubilius, P., & Kulieke, M. J. (2008). Using off-level testing and assessment for gifted and talented students. In J. VanTassel-Baska (Ed.), *Alternative assessments with gifted and talented students* (pp. 89–106). Waco, TX: Prufrock Press.

Popham, W. J. (2008). *Transformative assessment.* Alexandria, VA: Association for Supervision and Curriculum Development.

Reis, S. M., Westberg, K. L., Kulikowich, J., Caillard, F., Hébert, T., Plucker, J., . . . Smist, J. M. (1993). *Why not let high ability students start school in January? The curriculum compacting study* (RM93106). Storrs: University of Connecticut, The National Research Center on the Gifted and Talented.

Renzulli, J. S., & Callahan, C. (2008). Product assessment. In J. VanTassel-Baska (Ed.), *Alternative assessments with gifted and talented students* (pp. 259–283). Waco, TX: Prufrock Press.

Roberts, J. L., & Boggess, J. R. (2011). *Teacher's survival guide: Gifted education.* Waco, TX: Prufrock Press.

Roberts, J. L., & Boggess, J. R. (2012). *Differentiating instruction with centers in the gifted classroom.* Waco, TX: Prufrock Press.

Roberts, J. L., & Inman, T. F. (2009). *Strategies for differentiating instruction: Best practices for the classroom* (2nd ed.). Waco, TX: Prufrock Press.

Roberts,, J. L., & Inman, T. F. (2015). *Assessing differentiated student products: A protocol for development and evaluation* (2nd ed.). Waco, TX: Prufrock Press.

Shepard, L., Hammerness, K., Darling-Hammond, L., Rust, F., Snowden, J. B., Gordon, E., . . . Pacheco, A. (2005). Assessment. In L. Darling-Hammond & J. Bransford (Eds.), *Preparing teachers for a changing world: What teachers should learn and be able to do* (pp. 275–326). San Francisco, CA: Jossey-Bass.

Stanley, T. (2014). *Performance-based assessment for 21st-century skills.* Waco, TX: Prufrock Press.

Stiggins, R. J. (2002, June 6). Assessment crisis: The absence of assessment for learning. *Phi Delta Kappan.* Retrieved from http://electronicportfolios. org/afl/Stiggins-AssessmentCrisis.pdf

Stiggins, R. (2004, September). New assessment beliefs for a new school mission. *Phi Delta Kappan.* Retrieved from http://www.sd5.k12.mt.us/ cms/lib3/MT01001507/Centricity/Domain/8/Grading%20Practices/ gpg5%205.pdf

Tomlinson, C. A., & Imbeau, M. (2010). *Leading and managing a differentiated classroom.* Alexandria, VA: Association for Supervision and Curriculum Development.

Tomlinson, C. A., & Moon, T. R. (2013). *Assessment and student success in a differentiated classroom.* Alexandria, VA: Association for Supervision and Curriculum Development.

VanTassel-Baska, J. (2008). Using performance-based assessment to document authentic learning. In J. VanTassel-Baska (Ed.), *Alternative assessments with gifted and talented students* (pp. 285–305). Waco, TX: Prufrock Press.

Wiggins, G. (2012). Seven keys to effective feedback. *Educational Leadership, 70*(1), 10–16.

Wiggins, G., & McTighe, J. (2005). *Understanding by design* (2nd ed.). Alexandria, VA: Association for Supervision and Curriculum Development.

Winebrenner, S. (1992). *Teaching gifted kids in the regular classroom.* Minneapolis, MN: Free Spirit.

Appendix A

Formative Assessment Examples

- » **3-2-1 summary:** Students write down three concepts or ideas, two examples or uses, and one question.
- » **Conference:** Teachers meet with students individually or in small groups to assess understanding.
- » **Discussion:** Students participate in an open discussion regarding concepts, ideas, or content.
- » **Exit slip:** Students must turn in the slip before leaving class; the slip contains specific questions related to the learning objectives.
- » **Graphic organizer:** Students visually represent their understanding of the learning objectives.
- » **Learning log:** Students answer specific prompts concerning learning objectives or summarize thoughts and voice concerns.
- » **Observation:** Teachers observe student progress by making notations.
- » **Think-Pair-Share:** Students consider the question or topic presented, pair with another to discuss, then openly share with class.
- » **Think-Write-Pair-Share:** Students consider the question or topic presented, write down those thoughts, pair with another to discuss, then openly share with class.
- » **Top 10 list:** Students jot down the top 10 ideas or concepts they've learned or jot down questions they have.
- » **Ungraded quiz:** Students answer questions with pen-and-paper quiz.
- » **Venn diagram:** Students compare and contrast main concepts or ideas using one to four ovals in the diagram.

Online Resources for More Ideas

- » http://wvde.state.wv.us/teach21/ExamplesofFormativeAssessment.html
- » http://www.levy.k12.fl.us/instruction/Instructional_Tools/60FormativeAssessment.pdf
- » http://www.edutopia.org/groups/assessment/250941
- » http://www.nwea.org/blog/2013/22-easy-formative-assessment-techniques-for-measuring-student-learning/

Appendix B
Preassessment Examples

End-of-the-unit assessment

If a student shows mastery of learning objectives prior to instruction, he does not need to participate in the unit the way it is planned. When the end-of-unit exam is directly linked to the learning objectives, it serves as an effective preassessment strategy. As a rule of thumb, if a student scores 80% or better, then accommodations must be made.

Open-ended questions

A simple strategy, the open-ended question, may be posed days prior to the unit. Students simply write what they know about the states of matter, determining an author's style, imperialism in Africa—whatever the topic may be. The educator can quickly skim the papers, determining who is ready to learn what in the unit.

K-W-L and T-W-H charts

Many educators are familiar with the traditional K-W-L chart wherein students list what they know about the concept or content (the K), what they want to know (the W), and then, after the learning experience, what they learned (L). The L, as it is used here, is more summative in nature than formative; in a preassessment, it proves more diagnostic to use the L differently. Figure 11.1 shows a revamped K-W-L chart where the L stands for how you want to learn in lieu of what did you learn. This gleans information about whether the student wants to work alone or in groups, do research via the Internet or through books, or create a written piece or a Prezi to demonstrate learning. Another variation, the T-W-H chart (see Figure 11.2), changes "know" to "think" so that students can jot down ideas they believe may go with that concept even if they are not certain. They can also include their personal beliefs about the concept. Figure 11.3 shows a completed T-W-H chart on world religions.

K - W - L CHART

Topic/Unit_____   Name_____

What do you **K**now about this topic?	What do you **W**ant to learn about this topic?	How do you want to **L**earn about this topic?

FIGURE 11.1. K-W-L chart. From *Strategies for Differentiating Instruction: Best Practices for the Classroom* (2nd ed., p. 50), by J. L. Roberts and T. F. Inman, 2009, New York, NY: Taylor & Francis. Copyright 2009 by Taylor & Francis. Reprinted with permission.

T - W - H CHART

Topic/Unit _____

Name _____

What do you **T**hink about this topic?	What do you **W**ant to learn about this topic?	**H**ow do you want to learn about this topic?

FIGURE 11.2. T-W-H chart. From *Teacher's Survival Guide: Gifted Education* (p. 91), by J. L. Roberts and J. R. Boggess, 2011, New York, NY: Taylor & Francis. Copyright 2011 by Taylor & Francis. Reprinted with permission.

T - W - H CHART

Topic/Unit __World Religions__   Name __Maddie__

What do you **Think** about this topic?	What do you **Want** to learn about this topic?	**How** do you want to learn about this topic?
Christianity – intense Bibe study – 10 commandments – Story of Paul – Jesus crucified – Jesus is Gods son – single God	– about Purgatory (in depth) – sin in eyes of God	– readings – discussion
Islam – Muhammad was prophet – 6 prayers a day facing a holy way	– how they worship – how they live life	– videos – visit worship places – discussion
Hinduism – multiple Gods (?) – Quran	– more about religion in general	– readings – visit worship places – discussion

FIGURE 11.3. T-W-H chart: World religions.

Interest and experience inventory

An interest inventory can be as simple as having language arts students analyze short stories and rank order their preference of topic: characterization, theme, style, plot, and setting. The educator would organize the groups according to individual preference, so each group analyzes the short story but focuses on a specific aspect. Groups share at the end of the activity so that all gain understanding.

Inventories, when used prior to the learning experience, can also provide a plethora of information: interests, experiences with the topic or product, or preference for a final product. Figure 11.4 shows an example of such an inventory for a fifth-grade language arts classroom addressing Reading Literature Standard 5.2: *Determine a theme of a story, drama, or poem from details in the text, including how characters in a story or drama respond to challenges or how the speaker in a poem reflects upon a topic; summarize the text* (National Governors Association & Council of Chief State School Officers, 2010).

Five hardest questions

Designed by Winebrenner (1992), this strategy encourages the educator to create the five most difficult questions about the unit. This could be five challenging math applications of the Pythagorean Theorem or five short answer questions probing the causes of the French Revolution. If students can accurately answer four of the five, they need to have different assignments that extend or enrich their learning about the concept. This is the only preassessment strategy discussed here that should not be used with the entire class. Educators should invite those interested to take the preassessment in order to open up alternative assignments about the topic; it may be overwhelming to some students.

Exploration of Theme Preassessment

Content:
1. What kind of literature do you enjoy reading? (This could be genre, subject matter, or author.)
2. Do you prefer to read stories or plays?

Process:
1. On the back of the paper, define theme. Then, explain a theme in one of the works you've read in the past year. Be sure to give examples from the work to support the theme.
2. On the back of the paper, summarize a fairy tale of your choice.

Product:
1. Circle those products that you have created before.
2. Put a star beside those products that interest you that you have not created before.

Diorama	Mask	Model	Sculpture
Debate	Interview	Monologue	Oral Presentation
Computer Graphic	Movie	Podcast	PowerPoint
Cartoon	Collage	Pamphlet	Poster
Diary	Essay	Letter	Written Interview

FIGURE 11.4. Exploration of theme preassessment. From "Language Arts: Differentiation Through Centers and Agendas" by T. F. Inman (p. 44), in *Differentiating Instruction With Centers in the Gifted Classroom* by J. L. Roberts & J. R. Boggess (Eds.), 2012, New York, NY: Taylor & Francis. Copyright 2012. Reprinted with permission.

Appendix C
Student Reflection Sheets

Student Reflection: Tier 1

Please answer the following questions fully.

Content: **What connections can you make between what you have learned by completing this project and previous learning?**

_____

_____

_____

_____

_____

_____

_____

_____

_____

_____

_____

_____

_____

_____

Product: In what ways could you improve your product when completing this product with a different assignment?

_____

_____

_____

_____

_____

_____

_____

_____

_____

Learning: How did the amount of effort affect your learning about the content and creating the product?

_____

_____

_____

_____

_____

_____

_____

_____

_____

Student Reflection: Tier 2

Please reflect on the content, the product itself, and yourself as a learner.

Content: Reflections include connections to previous learning and questions raised for future learning.

How do the concepts and content relate to previous things you have studied? What connections can you make to other content areas or issues in the real world? What questions has this content raised for you? What aspect of the content do you want to learn more about?

_____

_____

_____

_____

_____

_____

_____

_____

Product: Reflections include improvements made over other times the product was created as well as suggestions for improvements when creating the same product in a future learning experience.

If you have ever created this product before, how does this one compare? How is it better? How is it worse? What improvements could you make next time to have an even better product? Why is that important?

_____

_____

Learning: **Reflection includes analysis of self as a learner, including effort, work habits, and thought processes.**

What have you realized about yourself as a learner? How much effort did you put into learning the content and developing the product? How could that be improved? Describe your work habits that were successful and those that were not. Describe your thought processes as you learned the content and created the product.

Student Reflection: Tier 3

Please reflect on the content, the product itself, and yourself as a learner.

***Content:* Reflections analyze and evaluate connections to previous learning and project insightful future connections.**

How do the concepts and content relate to previous things you have studied? What connections can you make to other content areas or issues in the real world? What questions has this content raised for you? Is there some aspect of the content you want to learn more about?

_____

_____

_____

_____

_____

_____

_____

_____

***Product:* Reflections analyze and evaluate the product components in light of past and future creations of the same product.**

If you have ever created this product before, how does this one compare? How is it better? How is it worse? What improvements could you make next time to have an even better product? Why is that important?

_____

_____

_____

_____

_____

_____

_____

_____

_____

_____

Learning: **Reflections include analysis of self as a learner and project how changes to the process would increase capacity as a learner.**

What have you realized about yourself as a learner? How much effort did you put into learning the content and developing the product? How could that be improved? Describe your work habits that were successful and those that were not. Describe your thought processes as you learned the content and created the product.

_____

_____

_____

_____

_____

_____

_____

_____

_____

From *Assessing Differentiated Student Products: A Protocol for Development and Evaluation* (2nd ed., pp. 235–240), by J. L. Roberts and T. F. Inman, 2015, New York, NY: Taylor & Francis. Copyright 2015 Taylor & Francis. Reprinted with permission.

Appendix D
Poster DAP Tools (Tiers 1–3)

POSTER TIER 1—DAP TOOL

CONTENT									
	◆ Is the content correct?	0	1	2	3	4	5	6
	◆ Has the content been thought about in a way that goes beyond a surface understanding?	0	1	2	3	4	5	6
	◆ Is the content put together in such a way that people understand it?	0	1	2	3	4	5	6
PRESENTATION									
TEXT	◆ Is the title easy to see, clear, and well placed? Do labels clearly explain the graphics?	0	1	2	3	4	5	6
GRAPHICS	◆ Are the graphics (e.g., illustrations, photos) important and appropriate to the topic?	0	1	2	3	4	5	6
LAYOUT	◆ Are the images carefully selected and emphasized? Is the labeling linked to the graphic? Is it pleasing to the eye? Is the spacing deliberate to draw attention to main parts of the poster?	0	1	2	3	4	5	6
CORRECTNESS	◆ Is the poster mostly free from usage, punctuation, capitalization, and spelling errors? If sources are used, are they cited correctly?	0	1	2	3	4	5	6
CREATIVITY									
	◆ Is the content seen in a new way?	0	1	2	3	4	5	6
	◆ Is the presentation done in a new way?	0	1	2	3	4	5	6
REFLECTION									
CONTENT	◆ What connections can you make between what you have learned by completing this project and previous learning?	0	1	2	3	4	5	6
PRODUCT	◆ In what ways could you improve your product when completing this product with a different assignment?	0	1	2	3	4	5	6
LEARNING	◆ How did the amount of effort affect your learning about the content and creating the product?	0	1	2	3	4	5	6

Comments:

_____

_____

Meaning of Performance Scale:
6—**PROFESSIONAL LEVEL:** level expected from a professional in the content area
5—**ADVANCED LEVEL:** level exceeds expectations of the standard
4—**PROFICIENT LEVEL:** level expected for meeting the standard
3—**PROGRESSING LEVEL:** level demonstrates movement toward the standard
2—**NOVICE LEVEL:** level demonstrates initial awareness and knowledge of standard
1—**NONPERFORMING LEVEL:** level indicates no effort made to meet standard
0—**NONPARTICIPATING LEVEL:** level indicates nothing turned in

POSTER TIER 2—DAP TOOL

CONTENT									
	◆ Content is accurate and complete.	0	1	2	3	4	5	6
	◆ Content has depth and complexity of thought.	0	1	2	3	4	5	6
	◆ Content is organized.	0	1	2	3	4	5	6
PRESENTATION									
TEXT	◆ Title enhances the poster's purpose and is well placed. Text highlights most important concepts.	0	1	2	3	4	5	6
GRAPHICS	◆ Graphics (e.g., illustrations, photos) add information and are relevant to the topic.	0	1	2	3	4	5	6
LAYOUT	◆ Layout design clearly emphasizes graphics in an organized and attractive manner. Text is placed to clearly describe/explain all graphic images. Spacing is carefully planned with consideration of space not used.	0	1	2	3	4	5	6
CORRECTNESS	◆ The poster is free from usage, punctuation, capitalization, and spelling errors. Sources, when used, are thoroughly cited.	0	1	2	3	4	5	6
CREATIVITY									
	◆ Originality is expressed in relation to the content.	0	1	2	3	4	5	6
	◆ Originality is expressed in relation to the presentation.	0	1	2	3	4	5	6
REFLECTION									
CONTENT	◆ Reflections include connections to previous learning and questions raised for future learning.	0	1	2	3	4	5	6
PRODUCT	◆ Reflections include improvements made over other times the product was created as well as suggestions for improvements when creating the same product in a future learning experience.	0	1	2	3	4	5	6
LEARNING	◆ Reflections include analysis of learning, including effort, work habits, and thought processes.	0	1	2	3	4	5	6

Comments:

_____

_____

_____

Meaning of Performance Scale:

6—PROFESSIONAL LEVEL: level expected from a professional in the content area

5—ADVANCED LEVEL: level exceeds expectations of the standard

4—PROFICIENT LEVEL: level expected for meeting the standard

3—PROGRESSING LEVEL: level demonstrates movement toward the standard

2—NOVICE LEVEL: level demonstrates initial awareness and knowledge of standard

1—NONPERFORMING LEVEL: level indicates no effort made to meet standard

0—NONPARTICIPATING LEVEL: level indicates nothing turned in

POSTER TIER 3—DAP TOOL

CONTENT									
	◆ Content is accurate and thorough in detail.	0	1	2	3	4	5	6
	◆ Product shows complex understanding and manipulation of content.	0	1	2	3	4	5	6
	◆ Product shows deep probing of content.	0	1	2	3	4	5	6
	◆ Organization is best suited to the product.	0	1	2	3	4	5	6
PRESENTATION									
TEXT	◆ Title, clearly reflecting purpose, is strategically placed. Text highlights most important concepts in clear, concise manner.	0	1	2	3	4	5	6
GRAPHICS	◆ Graphics (e.g., illustrations, photos) enhance meaning and are best suited for the purpose.	0	1	2	3	4	5	6
LAYOUT	◆ Successful composition of graphic images and design concepts communicates the purpose. Text is strategically placed to enhance the message of the poster. Negative space is used to highlight key points.	0	1	2	3	4	5	6
CORRECTNESS	◆ The poster is error free, with correct usage, punctuation, capitalization, and spelling used. All sources are cited correctly with the citation placed appropriately.	0	1	2	3	4	5	6
CREATIVITY									
	◆ Innovation is evident in relation to the content.	0	1	2	3	4	5	6
	◆ Innovation is evident in relation to the presentation.	0	1	2	3	4	5	6
REFLECTION									
CONTENT	◆ Reflections analyze and evaluate connections to previous learning and project insightful future connections.	0	1	2	3	4	5	6
PRODUCT	◆ Reflections analyze and evaluate the product components in light of past and future creations of the same product.	0	1	2	3	4	5	6
LEARNING	◆ Reflections include analysis of self as a learner and project how changes to the process would increase capacity as a learner.	0	1	2	3	4	5	6

Comments:

_____

_____

_____

Meaning of Performance Scale:
6—PROFESSIONAL LEVEL: level expected from a professional in the content area
5—ADVANCED LEVEL: level exceeds expectations of the standard
4—PROFICIENT LEVEL: level expected for meeting the standard
3—PROGRESSING LEVEL: level demonstrates movement toward the standard
2—NOVICE LEVEL: level demonstrates initial awareness and knowledge of standard
1—NONPERFORMING LEVEL: level indicates no effort made to meet standard
0—NONPARTICIPATING LEVEL: level indicates nothing turned in

From *Assessing Differentiated Student Products: A Protocol for Development and Evaluation* (2nd ed., pp. 48–50), by J. L. Roberts and T. F. Inman, 2015, New York, NY: Taylor & Francis. Copyright 2015 Taylor & Francis. Reprinted with permission.

CHAPTER 12

BLENDED LEARNING
A NEW FRONTIER OF
DIFFERENTIATED CURRICULUM

LAILA Y. SANGURAS

In 2008, Christiansen, Horn, and Johnson summoned educational leaders to the table of innovation in their provocative book, *Disrupting Class*. In it, the authors explained the difference between sustaining innovation, a modern adaptation of an existing product (i.e., rechargeable batteries), and disruptive innovation, a life-changing revolution (i.e., smartphones). They also challenged readers to consider the American educational system, highlighting the chasm between the desire to be globally competitive and the painstakingly slow pace at which the educational system evolves. Imagine the classrooms of your youth; physically, they are not too different from the classrooms of today, or even from the one-room schoolhouses in the early part of the 20th century.

This gradual progression of the current educational system extends to how schools respond to special populations, particularly gifted students. Since the 1980s, differentiation for gifted learners has largely been the recommendation of how to meet the needs of varying abilities within a traditional classroom (Jacobs & Borland, 1986; Maker, 1982; Passow, 1982; VanTassel-Baska, 1989; VanTassel-Baska et al., 1988). Whether through curriculum compacting, acceleration, independent study, or varying levels of depth and complexity, despite teachers' commitment to excellence and dedication to their students, differen-

DOI: 10.4324/9781003236696-14

tiation within traditional models of instruction have been largely unsuccessful in meeting the needs of gifted learners (Westberg, Archambault, Dobyns, & Salvin, 1993). However, by leveraging technology in order to develop the talents of the gifted, perhaps the current system can be comfortably disrupted enough to narrow the chasm and compete in global markets.

In its most basic definition, blended learning is a model of instruction that combines face-to-face with online learning environments. Also called hybrid learning, blended learning is the umbrella over several models in K–12 education: rotation, flex, self-blend, and enriched virtual. These models run the continuum of disruption to the current system. The rotation model refers to station and lab rotations in addition to the flipped classroom model and is the least disruptive to the current system. The flex model relies on individualized face-to-face instruction when needed by the student. The self-blend model is one that allows students to attend traditional classes while also taking a course online. The enriched virtual model, the most disruptive within K–12 education, provides on-site enrichment opportunities to extend students' online learning (Staker & Horn, 2012).

Despite a general understanding of these models, blended learning is still a rarely used method of instruction at the K–12 level, perhaps because of issues related to the definition of the term. It is still unclear what exactly is being blended, what constitutes a blended learning experience versus an online activity, and what is the purpose of blended learning. In fact, the term by itself suggests an emphasis on the learner, when definitions and recommendations for blended learning typically focus on the instructor (Oliver & Trigwell, 2005). Perhaps a more accurate term would be blended instructional design.

Effective educators within the blended model are those with a strong pedagogical base and an intense desire to personalize the educational experiences of all learners. In a time when understanding what it means to learn and when the rate of information available to the public are at their highest, this is when educators need to view themselves as facilitators and designers of instruction. With a priority on designing blended learning experiences that are "cognitively complex" (Kirkley & Kirkley, 2004, p. 42), lessons should be rooted in social and individual constructivism. At its core, the constructivist framework capitalizes on the interaction between the student and the environment (Savery & Duffy, 1995); by altering the environment based on student need, instructors are able to maximize student learning, removing the ceiling that leads to exceptionality and, eventually, eminence.

As is the case with most instructional models, blended learning design requires intentional planning of both online and face-to-face components

(Picciano, 2011). The term *blended* is more than creative semantics; instructors who effectively blend their instruction find ways to connect online learning to face-to-face content and vice versa. Voegele (2014) reported that students felt their learning experiences were most positive when there were strong curricular connections between both formats. For example, in an environmental science class, the instructor may have students conduct online research on the effects of oil spills on the environment and oceanic life as well as the financial incentives behind drilling for oil. In pairs, the students may explore the causes and effects of the Exxon Valdez oil spill and then analyze the Dawn Saves Wildlife commercial campaign for propaganda techniques. After the preliminary research is completed, students can conduct an experiment in class, analyzing the effects of vegetable oil and water on feathers. The teacher can then ask students to debate one another from the perspectives of environmentalists and representatives of the oil industry, using information gained from their research and propaganda techniques. In this example, both online and face-to-face learning experiences build upon one another rather than existing in isolation, creating a sense of community within the class.

Identifying student need can be difficult, especially within a traditional classroom. Consider Shulman's (2002) Table of Learning, a taxonomy that considers both cognitive and affective interactions with content. The elements of this table include engagement and motivation, knowledge and understanding, performance and action, reflection and critique, judgment and design, and commitment and identity. Shulman clarified that, although the table is presented in a certain order, actual learning does not always happen the same way. Perhaps it is most effective to think of Shulman's taxonomy as a nexus; it is the responsibility of the educator to determine the starting point of each learner and then extend learning from there.

However, even when gifted learners are clustered together, there is natural variance of ability and interest among them. Suppose that a classroom educator successfully identified the nexus for each child in the room. In a traditional classroom model where the teacher directs lessons and maintains control over pacing and complexity, it is very difficult to authentically differentiate at the individual level. In a more progressive model that provides students with opportunities to construct meaning, the teacher becomes more of a facilitator, but there are still limits to the authenticity and variety of differentiation. However, the power of a blended instructional design becomes apparent when technology is leveraged in order to provide personalized experiences based on each student's nexus of learning.

In addition to recognizing student need, this model of instruction requires an understanding of task commitment, a facet of giftedness first introduced by Renzulli in 1978. Although successful blended instructional design relies on individualization of learning experiences, it can be difficult for an educator to prioritize each student's needs and strengths. Asking each gifted student to complete a Gifted Learner Profile (see Figure 12.1) can be a way to identify and create an individualized plan of instruction.

Blended Instructional Design as a Continuum of Services for Gifted Learners

In its most basic form, a blended instructional design allows for differentiation of content. Because most of the content is housed online in a learning management system, students are often unaware of what the others in the class are studying. For example, a language arts teacher could give all students a grade-level pretest on vocabulary. Based on their results, each student can complete individualized activities and tests. In this example, the teacher creates a template for all students to complete; they list their words for the week, definitions, and an extension (i.e., a visual representation or an example of the word in context). The students then create their own vocabulary tests, listing the words for the week, and turn these in to the teacher. This list acts as a contract, or a commitment to study these words. At the end of the week, the teacher passes back the learner created tests, asks the students to write the definitions of the words, and then provides an open-ended writing prompt for students to respond to, using a certain number of words. Students who are gifted or advanced in language arts will likely be studying a more advanced set of words and will also be required to use more of their words in their written responses.

With the breadth of information available online, an instructor teaching within the blended model must rethink assessments. A test that requires memorization of facts is antiquated, both in the teacher's assumption that students cannot search quickly for the answers and in the belief that memorization is the goal. The blended instructional model is most successful when the teacher leverages technology in order to further students' thinking. For example, in a history class, the students may be required to know the causes and effects of the American Revolution. Because a quick search online can provide a fairly comprehensive list, the teacher should create leveled assessments for her students

Gifted Learner Profile

Please answer the following questions so that we can understand you as a gifted learner.

How long have you been in the gifted and talented program?

_____

_____

What gifted courses have you taken?

_____

_____

Evaluation of Data
What does the data (i.e. state assessments, benchmarks, etc.) say about you?

_____

_____

Manifestation of Giftedness
In what way(s) are you gifted and/or talented (i.e. math, science, language arts, social studies, fine arts, leadership, etc.)?

_____

_____

What are your strengths?

_____

_____

What are your weaknesses?

_____

_____

Classroom Implications
In what way(s) would you like to be challenged in the classroom? Please check all that apply.

❑   I want to move through the curriculum at a faster pace, even if that means I have to work alone.

FIGURE 12.1. Gifted learner profile.

Classroom Implications, continued

❏ I want to be required to show deeper understanding of the content than what is asked of everyone else.

❏ I want choice in whether I attempt a more difficult assignment.

❏ I want my teachers to hold me accountable and require that I complete the more difficult assignments.

❏ I want to work ahead on my assignments so that I can focus on an independent study project.

❏ I want creative options to demonstrate my learning.

❏ I do not want any specialized services at this time. I prefer to complete the same assignments as my peers.

What are some of your short-term academic goals (i.e., can be attained this year)?

_____

_____

What is a long-term goal that you have for yourself?

_____

_____

Is there anything else that we should know?

_____

_____

_____

FIGURE 12.1. Continued.

that require extensions of the essential information. The most basic assessment could be a ranking of the causes and effects with brief explanations of the order. The average history student could extend his understanding of the causes of the war by creating a survival guide for the American soldiers during the war. The gifted history student could compose a brief, cautioning the United States Department of Defense on the ways the events of the American Revolution can be seen in current events throughout the nation. In this example, the educator recognizes and uses the power of technology to further challenge her students while also differentiating based on ability.

An important component of the blended framework is student control (Smith & Suzuki, 2014; Staker & Horn, 2012). This control can take many forms, depending on the instructional need of the student and the design of the course. Students may have control over the pacing and order of the content. This may mean that a teacher provides a module for a developmentally appropriate length of time; a module in an elementary class may last a few days, whereas a module in a high school course may last a month. The student can then work through the material at a comfortable pace, revisiting content as needed and moving quickly through it as appropriate. It is important to recognize that, while some control is given to the student, the teacher-as-facilitator remains an essential element in the learning process (Dzubian, Hartman, & Mahaffy, 2014).

Another piece of a blended instructional design is flexibility in the time spent online and the time spent face-to-face. In a college course, students attend classes on campus while also completing work online off campus. Because this is not feasible in the K–12 setting, it is important to create a learning space outside of the classroom, but within the school, where students can complete work online. Typically, schools designate a blended learning lab that is a supervised independent learning space away from the primary instructor. Although students often describe control over pacing and order as a benefit to a blended course, they also explain that this freedom requires a level of responsibility they may not have (Lewis, Whiteside, & Dikkers, 2014). Creating a workspace such as a blended learning lab facilitates autonomy and independence for all levels of learners. An additional benefit of this supervised learning space is that the educator can organize workshops for small groups of students. The purposes of these workshops should vary based on need: enriching, scaffolding, reteaching, and extending learning. For gifted learners in a math class, these workshops can create small learning communities within the regular classroom focused on fueling passion for mathematics in a challenging and rewarding environment. Even if these workshops only happen several times a month, the educator is using the blended instructional design to allow for talent development within these gifted learners.

In its most radical form, a blended instructional model allows for an environment that is fully individualized with the intent of enhancing the talents of gifted learners within the classroom. The educator can customize the experiences of the learner with the goal of focusing the learning on the required standards so that the student can sufficiently demonstrate mastery and then concentrate on developing talent and pursuing passion. Although the process sounds daunting, the framework of the blended instructional model allows the teacher to leverage technology in order to curate these learning experiences. For example, an English teacher could organize her learning standards into modules that require a gifted student to analyze texts and write in a variety of genres. This student, whose talents and interests lie outside of language arts, could connect to others who are wrestling with these same texts via social media, conference with the teacher about questions, and reflect on new learning throughout the process. He could meet the speaking standards by presenting his learning to the class or perhaps to a more authentic audience. His teacher then requires assessments that allow him to demonstrate mastery of all mandated standards. In this scenario, the teacher takes on the role of an instructional coach, creating experiences designed to maximize individualization in order to minimize the time spent on English—ultimately creating time for the student to dedicate to his true passion. And all of this could take a fraction of the time it would take to learn these same standards in a traditional classroom, while still maintaining a level of interest for the gifted learner.

Implications for Research

Existing research has generally indicated that although differentiation of curriculum and instruction in mixed-ability classrooms is a common service model for gifted education, teachers most often implement the same curriculum for all students (Westberg et al., 1993). Additional research is needed to investigate under what conditions curriculum and instruction are most likely to be modified for gifted learners. Blended learning models of instruction are one of the conditions that should be investigated as a robust learning design for implementing differentiated curricula. At this time, anecdotal evidence and action research projects suggest that blended learning models provide teachers flexible arrangements to group and regroup and modify or personalize learning experiences. These are not necessarily research agendas embraced in the field of educational technology, but these agendas should be developed and systematically studied by those interested in teaching gifted and advanced students and developing advanced levels of talent.

Research designs with gifted education teachers need to explore under what conditions teachers are more or less likely to modify curriculum. In what ways might flexible time and space captured through the use of technology enhance teachers' capacity for curriculum modification? In what ways can blended learning models allow curriculum designers to create opportunities for independent investigations, personalization of learning outcomes, and customized learning experiences based on core mastery complemented with optional pathways of specialization? Typically, teachers understand curriculum as a relative static sequence of learning events. However, the customization made possible through blended learning models propagates a more fluid understanding of curriculum. Have teachers been adequately prepared to think differently, less linearly about curriculum? How might a hierarchical understanding of curriculum with a labyrinth of customized pathways require different pedagogy skills than those associated with linear curriculum?

Studies of talent development and proposed models of talent development in gifted education have often relied upon out-of-school training and experiences to push performance to elite levels. Blended instructional models and their capacity for customized learning design have the potential to facilitate development of advanced, even elite, talent in school settings. How might research designs explore the capacity for customized advanced learning to develop domain-specific talents? Can a verbally gifted student with a compelling motivation to become a writer accelerate rapidly through the basic curriculum standards of an English course and then devote the recaptured time to developing her talents as a fiction writer within the structures of a blended learning classroom? Could a talented science student with a motivation to compete in prestigious science competitions use blended learning to customize a pathway to master the essential core of his biology class, then devote the recaptured time and flexible space to conducting experiments for a device capable of early detection of Alzheimer's disease?

These are the bold potentials of blending instructional designs and talent development. It is a great time to think differently about curriculum, talent development, and the power of technology. We need innovative approaches to learning to remove the ceilings that have been levied by static time and space, and we need systematic investigation to document our trials and successes at customized talent development in school settings.

Discussion Questions

1. How do traditional learning environments differ from blended learning environments in ways that influence the implementation of differentiated curriculum?

2. How might blended instructional designs push educators to think differently, less linearly, about curriculum?

3. Are there some disciplines or domains of student personalities that seem better suited to the flexibility of blended instruction design?

4. What are the implications for professional development and teacher training in order to prepare teachers to leverage technology to increase customization and differentiation?

References

Christensen, C. M., Horn, M. B., & Johnson, C. W. (2008). *Disrupting class: How disruptive innovation will change the way the world learns.* New York, NY: McGraw-Hill.

Dzubian, C. D., Hartman, J. L., & Mahaffy, G. L. (2014). Blending it all together. In A. G. Picciano, C. D. Dzubian, & C. R. Graham (Eds.), *Blended learning research perspectives* (Vol. 2, pp. 93–103). New York, NY: Routledge.

Jacobs, H., & Borland, J. (1986). The interdisciplinary concept model: Theory and practice. *Gifted Child Quarterly, 30,* 159–163.

Kirkley, S. E., & Kirkley, J. R. (2004). Creating next generation blended learning environments using mixed reality, video games and simulations. *TechTrends, 49*(3), 42–53.

Lewis, S., Whiteside, A. L., & Dikkers, A. G. (2014). Autonomy and responsibility: Online learning as a solution for at-risk high school students. *International Journal of E-Learning & Distance Education, 29*(2).

Maker, C. J. (1982). *Curriculum development for the gifted.* Rockville, MD: Aspen.

Oliver, M., & Trigwell, K. (2005). Can 'blended learning' be redeemed. *E-learning, 2*(1), 17–26.

Passow, A. H. (1982). Differentiated curricula for the gifted/talented. In *Curricula for the gifted: Selected proceedings for the First National Conference on Curricula for the Gifted/Talented* (pp. 4–20). Ventura, CA: National/State Leadership Training Institute on the Gifted and Talented.

Picciano, A. G. (2011). Introduction to the special issue on transitioning to blended learning. *Journal of Asynchronous Learning Networks, 13*(1), 7–18.

Renzulli, J. S. (1978). What makes giftedness? Reexamining a definition. *Phi Delta Kappan, 60,* 180.

Savery, J. R., & Duffy, T. M. (1995). Problem based learning: An instructional model and its constructivist framework. *Educational Technology, 35*(5), 31–38.

Shulman, L. S. (2002). Making differences: A table of learning. *Change: The Magazine of Higher Learning, 34*(6), 36–44. doi:10.1080/000913802096 05567

Smith, J. G., & Suzuki, S. (2014). Embedded blended learning within an Algebra classroom: A multimedia capture experiment. *Journal of Computer Assisted Learning.* doi:10.1111/jcal.12083

Staker, H., & Horn, M. B. (2012). *Classifying K–12 blended learning.* Retrieved from http://www.innosightinstitute.org/innosight/wp-con tent/uploads/2012/05/Classifying-K-12-blended-learning2.pdf

VanTassel-Baska, J. (1989). Appropriate curriculum for the gifted. In J. Feldhusen, J. VanTassel-Baska, & K. Seeley (Eds.), *Excellence in educating the gifted* (pp. 175–191). Denver, CO: Love.

VanTassel-Baska, J., Feldhusen, J., Seeley, K., Wheatley, G., Silverman, L., & Foster, W. (1988). *Comprehensive curriculum for gifted learners.* Needham Heights, MA: Allyn & Bacon.

Voegele, J. D. (2014). Student perspectives on blended learning through the lens of social, teaching, and cognitive presence. In A. G. Picciano, C. D. Dziuban, & C. R. Graham (Eds.), *Blended learning research perspectives* (Vol. 2, pp. 93–103). New York, NY: Routledge.

Westberg, K. L., Archambault, F. X., Dobyns, S. M., & Salvin, T. J. (1993). The classroom practices observation study. *Journal for the Education of the Gifted, 16,* 120–146.

SECTION 3

DEVELOPING DOMAIN EXPERTISE THROUGH RIGOROUS CURRICULUM DESIGN

CHAPTER 13

DIFFERENTIATING ENGLISH LANGUAGE ARTS STANDARDS FOR GIFTED AND ADVANCED STUDENTS

ELIZABETH SHAUNESSY-DEDRICK
AND CLAIRE E. HUGHES

Conceptualizing Differentiation

Broadly speaking, in a differentiated classroom, the teacher plans and carries out varied approaches to content, process, and product in anticipation of, and in response to, student differences in readiness, interest, and learning need (Tomlinson, 1999). This philosophy, which appeals to educators working with students in general, special, and gifted education, reflects earlier work by Maker and Nielson (1996), which organized curriculum differentiation into four clusters—content, process, product, and learning environments. VanTassel-Baska (2003) later articulated essential elements of curriculum differentiation: acceleration (i.e., pace, depth), complexity, depth, challenge, creativity, and abstractness. In contrast, Kaplan's (2009) vision of differentiation is more malleable, as she suggested that teachers maintain a core curriculum for all learners, but differentiate learning for students with advanced learning needs by enhancing depth, content, or complexity based on learners' needs. In this chapter, we provide a systematic approach to planning curriculum and instruction of gifted and advanced learners that honors each student's learning needs and maxi-

 DOI: 10.4324/9781003236696-16

mizes each student's learning capacity based on the key features evident in the above models.

Within the field of ELA, there are also specific learning goals to guide differentiation efforts, including domain expertise, complex thinking, advanced product and performance development, and cultivating intellect (VanTassel-Baska, Hughes, Kettler, & Shaunessy-Dedrick, 2013). Domain expertise in ELA is related to a variety of language tasks for advanced students, such as avid reading, proficient communication, and discourse that reflects critical consideration of culture. Individuals who engage in complex thinking are able to examine multiple perspectives and can articulate logical, rational arguments. Through ELA, teachers of gifted/advanced learners seek to cultivate skills in writing and publishing in for a variety of audiences and genres and can express insightful, complex understandings of literature.

In this chapter, we apply these theories and practices to the Common Core State Standards in English Language Arts (CCSS-ELA; National Governor's Association Center for Best Practices [NGA] & Council of Chief State School Officers [CCSSO], 2010). Although the CCSS-ELA have been deemed more challenging and rigorous for most students than previous state standards (Porter, McMaken, Hwang, & Yang, 2011), we take the stance that they are necessary, but not sufficient, for learners who are advanced/gifted. The CCSS-ELA is not a curriculum, but merely a set of guiding content standards for lessons and experiences that are to be adapted for individual contexts.

In this chapter, we offer strategies for differentiating the ELA Common Core through defensible differentiation efforts—or those based on theoretical and empirical evidence for teaching students who are advanced/gifted. Examples of lessons are provided as applied demonstrations of strategy-driven instruction that is designed to challenge, advance, and enrich the educational experiences of students who are advanced/gifted. Although these lesson concepts offer initial ideas to guide teachers' differentiation efforts, they are not designed to be replicated in total, but to serve as resources for teachers and researchers to craft specific learning experiences based on the context of the child, the teacher, and the school.

Grouping

There are many perspectives about the optimal instructional environments often framed around issues of grouping, inclusion, and justice. In this chapter, we do not advocate for a particular grouping arrangement, but provide examples of appropriate learning experiences to be implemented once a child is placed in a setting for his or her cognitive and affective needs as an advanced/gifted learner. Thus, our emphasis is not *where*, but *how* a teacher engages a learner who is advanced/gifted in ELA in a manner that is appropriate for that student's level of learning. Although we include grouping decisions in the learning experiences, these are not intended to be prescriptive, but rather as a frame that educators may further contextualize.

Defensible Differentiation

Differentiation does not occur by happenstance; it is a deliberate act teachers consider not only in response to serendipitous opportunities that emerge with students, but primarily a purposeful pre-planning of instruction that addresses the varying needs of students—including levels of advanced student learning. This chapter provides a model of differentiation in the language arts that is rooted in elements from gifted education, but also includes general curriculum and assessment principles. In a course developed by one of the authors, teacher candidates are to prepare, for each lesson plan, the appropriate version of the following sentence:

> Because (<u>relevant preassessment data</u>), I differentiated the following lesson by adapting the (<u>elements of instruction</u>) by (<u>tools</u>) and providing (<u>management plan</u>), and determined its effectiveness by (<u>assessment plan</u>).

Each of the above five elements represents an instructional decision made by a teacher while adapting curriculum for advanced/gifted learners. This chapter will focus primarily on the elements of readiness determined by preassessment and the inclusion of advanced concepts and specific thinking skills, such as creativity, critical thinking skills, and choice. Implications for assessment and grouping will be determined relevant to the individual lessons, but it is understood that such efforts are highly context-dependent. We include with the examples below specific differentiation statements modeled after the generic italicized statement above to show how a teacher may differentiate.

Developing Differentiated Curriculum in Reading Foundational Skills

Grade 1 Unit Example Framework

The teacher should identify the required objective for core curriculum. For example, learners may be asked to focus on phonics and word recognition in a text. From the foundational standard, teachers should then determine the appropriate progression of skills (see Table 13.1), or complementary skills.

TABLE 13.1.

Sequence of CCSS Literacy Standards From Grades 1–2: Phonics and Word Recognition

CCSS.ELA-Literacy. RF1.2A	Distinguish long from short vowel sounds in spoken single-syllable words.
CCSS.ELA-Literacy. RF2.3A	Distinguish long and short vowels when reading regularly spelled one-syllable words.

Instructional Overview

Teachers may require all students to read the same story of *Green Eggs and Ham* (Seuss, 1960), although the process and activities will be differentiated according to those who are gifted or advanced in demonstrating mastery of the grade-level standard. Teachers should preassess students on the grade-level skill of RF1.2A above. Based on student performance data specific to this skill, teachers can then determine each student's mastery of these standards and begin to differentiate learning experiences using the appropriate standard of RF2.3A. The teacher may adjust the lesson according to specific thinking skills and opportunities for advanced reading material as illustrated in Table 13.2. Note that learning experiences for students who are on grade level in ELA development (hereafter described as "typical") are indicated on the left, while learning experiences for advanced ELA students are provided on the right. We recommend that teachers identify students with advanced ELA skills—as opposed to those with advanced skills in other areas—as those needing appropriately challenging learning experiences based on their abilities in reading, writing, speaking/listening, and/or language. Some advanced learners

TABLE 13.2

Differentiated Learning Experiences for Grade 1 Students on Distinguishing Long and Short Vowels

Typical Learner	Advanced ELA Learner
Introduction Read *Green Eggs and Ham* (Seuss, 1960) aloud, with great flair and drama. **Direct Instruction** Provide students with two different popsicle sticks, one with a "long" label that is written horizontally and one with a "short" label that is written vertically. Use a green marker for the long label and a red marker for the short label. Give direct instruction that a "long" popsicle stick is raised when you hear the vowel say its name and your mouth moves, as in "goat," and the short one is raised when you hear it make another sound when your mouth is just opened, such as "Sam" and "box." **Practice—Guided and Independent** Reread the story, stopping at significant vocabulary words, such as "ham," "boat," "fox," "chair," etc. Ask students to raise their popsicle stick that states whether it's a long vowel or a short vowel. Keep track of individual student responses to determine who is struggling. In small groups, give each student a different page from the story. Have them read the story aloud to their group, and lead the long and short discussions. Each student will take a turn reading and directing the raising of the popsicle sticks. **Assess** On a checklist, monitor which child masters the long vowels and which child masters the short vowels.	**Introduction** Read *Green Eggs and Ham* (Seuss, 1960) aloud, with great flair and drama. Pause every now and then to encourage advanced students to fill in the rhyme. "I will not eat them in a _____" **Direct Instruction** Provide students with a green marker for long vowel sounds and a red marker for short vowel sounds. Ask them if they notice anything about the words that are long. If they do not notice, highlight the use of the second vowel—either the silent "e" or the paired vowel that makes the vowel long. Ask them why they think that a green marker would signify the long vowel sound and a red marker might signify the short vowel sound. **Practice—Guided and Independent** Give the advanced students a copy of *Green Eggs and Ham* (Seuss, 1960) and have advanced students highlight each of the words in the text with either a green marker or a red marker. Model the first page for them. Ask students to create two more pages for the book, one that uses short vowel sounds, such as "fox/box" and one that uses long vowel sounds, such as "goat/boat." **Assess** The colored copy of the book will act as an assessment to determine mastery of the advanced standard. In addition, the "new" pages will provide evidence of creativity.

may develop more rapidly in one or more of these ELA dimensions, but not necessarily all areas.

Differentiation statement. Because of pretest data that demonstrated which students had mastered the concept of *short and long vowel sounds in read-aloud stories* and because of the interest advanced students have in *creating rhymes* (preassessment), I differentiated the following lesson by *creating more advanced content* (<u>elements of instruction</u>) by using *advanced standard RF2.3A* and an *opportunity for creative output* (<u>tools</u>) and using a *small group to provide instruction* (<u>management plan</u>), and determined its effectiveness by collecting *the created pages* (<u>assessment plan</u>).

Developing Differentiated Curriculum in Literature

Grade 2 Unit Example Framework

The teacher should identify the required objective for core curriculum. For example, learners may be asked to describe character responses. From the foundational standard, teachers should then determine the appropriate progression of skills (see Table 13.3), or complementary skills.

TABLE 13.3

Sequence of CCSS Literacy Standards From Grades 2–3: Character Responses

CCSS.ELA-Literacy. RL2.3	Describe how characters in a story respond to major events and challenges.
CCSS.ELA-Literacy. RL3.3	Describe characters in a story (e.g., their traits, motivations, or feelings) and explain how their actions contribute to the sequence of events.

Instructional Overview

Teachers should preassess students on the grade-level skill of RL2.3. Based on student performance data specific to this skill, teachers can then determine each student's mastery of these standards and begin to differentiate learning experiences accordingly. Teachers may then require all students to read *Sarah,*

Plain and Tall (MacLachlan, 1985), although the process and activities will be differentiated according to those who have demonstrated mastery of the grade-level standard. To adjust the lesson, teachers should consider how to challenge students who are advanced in ELA. The teacher may adjust the lesson according to specific thinking skills as illustrated below.

Differentiation statement. Because of preassessment data based on students' reading comprehension skills in *identifying key ideas and details* (relevant preassessment data), I differentiated the following lesson in Table 13.4 by *adapting the level of abstraction, depth of textual analysis, and depth of writing development* (elements of instruction) by *creative production* (tools) and *providing for grouping based on mastery of the standard* (management plan). I determined the lesson's effectiveness by evaluating the degree that students were able to *develop original descriptive details* about characters in their writing, reading, and discussion and the degree to which they are able to discuss this aspect of their work in a reflection (assessment plan).

TABLE 13.4

Differentiated Learning Experiences for Grade 2 Students on Character Responses

Typical Learner	Advanced ELA Learner
Introduce Visualization Introduce the concept of visualizing—or imagining pictures in our minds of the stories that we read. Explain to students the rationale for visualizing in relationship to developing comprehension, particularly in stories that are written without pictures.	**Introduce Character** Tell students: Sometimes we experience moments of great happiness or excitement, while other times we experience disappointment, regret, or even loss. These ups and downs are part of life, but how we react to these events reflects our character.
Model Model how to visualize by reading an excerpt from *Sarah, Plain and Tall* (MacLachlan, 1985), and illustrating the picture in your mind after you read the selection aloud.	The teacher should share a description of a major event from his or her life, how he or she felt during the event, and what he or she believes this reaction conveys about his or her character.
Practice Read another excerpt, but this time ask students to imagine pictures for the story in their minds as you read, and then to pick one after you've finished reading to	**Prewriting** Tell students: Our lives are defined by critical moments and our reactions to these moments. It is through these events we learn about ourselves and others come to know who we are. What are some major

TABLE 13.4

Continued

Typical Learner	Advanced ELA Learner
draw. Ask students to explain their illustrations to shoulder partners. Circulate as students talk and identify potential examples of students who understand the concept. Ask 2–3 students who you deem comprehended the visualizing (without providing this assessment aloud to others) and ask them to share their illustrations and explanations for what part of the excerpt they envisioned in their illustration.	events that you've experienced during the last year? How did you react to these?
	Independent Reading
	Tell students: For two of the main characters in the text, *Sarah, Plan and Tall* (MacLachlan, 1985), identify the most critical events that they experience and their reaction to these events. As you read each chapter, note these critical events and how each character reacts. Note specific words and phrases the author uses to convey both the event and the author's reaction to the event.
Independent Reading and Visualizing	
Assign Chapter 1 of *Sarah, Plain and Tall* (MacLachlan, 1985) and encourage students to imagine the story in their mind as they read. When they finish reading, they are to select one of the mental images generated during Chapter 1 to illustrate and provide a caption to describe the image.	**Group Discussion**
	At various junctures as students progress through the text, they will convene in small groups to consider the running character notes and compare with those selected by classmates. During these group meetings, students should identify what personality traits the selected character seems to have and use words and phrases from the text to support these conclusions.
Assess	
As students work, assess whether they could draw an illustration representative of a scene in Chapter 1, add a sentence to the illustration, and explain the illustration and sentence aloud. Check for comprehension following the illustration experience by asking students to identify the characters, major events, and challenges each character encounters/confronts.	**Individual Writing**
	Students will revisit their initial prewriting assignment and identify how their work reflects character description. Students will continue to refine writing to show the ability to create characters through specific words and phrases embedded within the text.
	Assess
	In addition to listening to small-group discussions of character analysis from the text, the teacher will also analyze the degree to which the student is able to develop character in writing. The student will indicate in a separate reflection how

TABLE 13.4
Continued

Typical Learner	Advanced ELA Learner
	his or her understanding and development of character evolved from the prewriting to the current form and where additional development could occur in the original piece.

Developing Differentiated Curriculum in Reading for Information

Grade 5 Unit Example Framework

The teacher should identify the required objective for core curriculum. For example, learners may be asked to describe point of view and argument evidence. From the foundational standard, teachers should then determine the appropriate progression of skills (see Table 13.5), or complementary skills.

TABLE 13.5.

Sequence of CCSS Literacy Reading for Information Standards From Grades 5: Point of View and Supporting Details

CCSS.ELA-Literacy. RI5.6	Analyze multiple accounts of the same event or topic, noting important similarities and differences in the point of view they represent.
CCSS.ELA-Literacy. RI5.8	Explain how an author uses reasons and evidence to support particular points in a text, identifying which reasons and evidence support which point(s).
CCSS.ELA-Literacy. RI6.6	Determine an author's point of view or purpose in a text and explain how it is conveyed in the text.
CCSS.ELA-Literacy. RI6.8	Trace and evaluate the argument and specific claims in a text, distinguishing claims that are supported by reasons and evidence from claims that are not.

Instructional Overview

Teachers should preassess students on the skills above. Based on student performance data specific to this skill, teachers can then determine each student's mastery of these standards and begin to differentiate learning experiences accordingly as the sample below is described.

Teachers may require all students to read an article about food waste, although the process and activities will be differentiated according to those who are gifted or advanced in demonstrating mastery of the grade-level standard. To adjust the lesson, teachers should consider how to challenge students who are advanced in ELA. The teacher may adjust the lesson according to specific thinking skills and opportunities for advanced reading material as illustrated in Table 13.6 below. Note that learning experiences for students who are on grade level in ELA development (hereafter described as "typical") are indicated on the left, while learning experiences for advanced ELA students are provided on the right. Thinking skill adaptations are bolded following the differentiated experience.

Differentiation statement. Because of pretest data that demonstrated which students had mastered the *concept of stating opinions and student interest in school food* (preassessment), I differentiated the following lesson by *creating a debate* (<u>elements of instruction</u>) by *using advanced levels of Bloom's of evaluation* and *higher reading level content* (<u>tools</u>) and using a *small group to provide instruction* (<u>management plan</u>), and determined its effectiveness by *collecting the debate format* (<u>assessment plan</u>).

TABLE 13.6.

Differentiated Learning Experiences for Grade 5 Students on Points of View and Supporting Details

Typical Learner	Advanced ELA Learner
Introduction Have students discuss how much food they eat and how much they throw away at lunch. Have them read the article: "Solutions Sought to Reduce Food Waste at Schools" (Watanabe, 2014) and "Letters: Why is so much food wasted at LAUSD?" (*Los Angeles Times*, April 6, 2014).	

TABLE 13.6
Continued

Summarize, Compare and Contrast	Points of View and Original Sources
1. Ask students to summarize the main arguments and evidence used in the article, using a graphic organizer that has the central idea in the center and supporting details coming from the central idea.	1. Ask them to identify two different points of view, or "sides," in this argument presented in the Letters to the Editor using details from the article and the letters.
2. Ask them to identify two different points of view, or "sides," in this argument presented in the Letter to the Editors.	2. Ask students to review the standards required of healthy school lunches in the law itself (U.S. Department of Agriculture, 2012).
3. Using the same graphic organizer, have students respond to the main point of two of the arguments and add supporting details.	3. Students will use the main idea graphic organizer to determine key points within the law.
Assess	**Assess**
Ask students to compare and contrast the differing viewpoints through a written paper or a graphic organizer.	Students will outline a debate with major pros and cons and rebuttal arguments clarified, using a written format. They will take a stand at the conclusion of the article, basing their opinion on what they perceive to be the stronger argument.

Developing Differentiated Curriculum in Listening and Speaking

Grade 7 Unit Example Framework

The teacher should identify the required purpose for core curriculum. For example, learners may be asked to describe main ideas and details. From the foundational standard, teachers should then determine the appropriate progression of skills (see Table 13.7), or complementary skills.

Teachers should preassess students on the grade-level skills above. Based on student performance data specific to this skill, teachers can then determine each student's mastery of these standards and begin to differentiate learning experiences accordingly as described below.

TABLE 13.7

Sequence of CCSS Literacy Standards From Grades 7 to 8: Main Idea and Purpose

CCSS.ELA-Literacy. SL.7.2	Analyze the main ideas and supporting details presented in diverse media and formats (e.g., visually, quantitatively, orally) and explain how the ideas clarify a topic, text, or issue under study.
CCSS.ELA-Literacy. SL.8.2	Analyze the purpose of information presented in diverse media and formats (e.g., visually, quantitatively, orally) and evaluate the motives (e.g., social, commercial, political) behind its presentation.

Instructional Overview

As seen in Table 13.8, teachers may require all students to find an infographic (see Daily Infographic's website, http://dailyinfographic.com for the two used in the lesson), although the process and activities will be differentiated according to those who are gifted or advanced in demonstrating mastery of the grade-level standard. To adjust the lesson, teachers should consider how to challenge students who are advanced in ELA. The teacher may adjust the lesson according to specific thinking skills as illustrated in Table 13.8 below.

Differentiation statement. Because of *data that demonstrated that certain students had already mastered SL7.2* and *student interest in graphics* (<u>relevant preassessment data</u>), I differentiated the following lesson by *adapting the higher standard of SL 8.2* (<u>elements of instruction</u>) by using a *higher level of Bloom's taxonomy of analysis, comparison and contrast, and creativity* (<u>tools</u>) and providing *choice and small-group instruction* (<u>management plan</u>), and determined its effectiveness by having student *submit to a real world audience* (<u>assessment plan</u>).

TABLE 13.8

Differentiated Learning Experiences for Grade 7 Students on Key Ideas and Details/Purposes

Typical Learner	Advanced ELA Learner
Introduce Infographics Main Idea	**Introduce Infographic Purpose**
Introduce the concept of infographics— visually representing relationships or infor-	Infographics create discussion and share information, often for a particular purpose

TABLE 13.8

Continued

Typical Learner	Advanced ELA Learner
mation, using bright colors and elements of "flow." Several examples from Daily Infographic (http://dailyinfographic.com; check for appropriate content) could be placed on student desks to stimulate conversation.	through visual representation. Several examples from Daily Infographic (http://dailyinfographic.com; check for appropriate content) could be placed on student desks to stimulate conversation.

Typical Learner

Model

Present the infographic "How to Teach English" (or a similar one of the teacher's choosing from the Daily Infographic site). Present the concept of "main idea" and ask students how they know what the main ideas of the infographic are. How are they demonstrated? How are details presented? What roles do the pictures and the colors play?

Practice

In small groups of 3–4, provide students with another infographic. Each group should have a different infographic. Ask students to explain the main idea and supporting details to group partners. Circulate as students talk and identify potential examples of students who understand the concept. Ask those 2–3 students who you deem comprehended the main idea and how supporting details are presented.

Independent Activity/Extension

For extra credit, ask students to take something with steps or information and create an infographic. Students could use the infographic maker at http://piktochart.com. Be sure to discuss how to demonstrate main idea and supporting details. If their infographic is particularly good, they can submit it to the Daily Infographic website for consideration.

Advanced ELA Learner

Model

Present the infographic "How to Teach English" (or a similar one of the teacher's choosing from the Daily Infographic site). Present the concept of "purpose and motive" and ask students how they know what the purposes of the infographic are. What elements are used to clarify this purpose? Are there other points of view that might not be presented?

Practice

In small groups of 3–4, provide students with another infographic that has a very specific "message" or purpose, such as "An Average Day in the Life of Nursing" (found on the Daily Infographic site). Each group should have a different infographic. Ask students to explain the purpose, motive, and any other possible points of view that might not be included. Circulate as students talk and identify potential examples of students who understand the concept. Ask those 2–3 students who you deem comprehended the concept of purpose and motive and how supporting details are presented.

Independent Activity/Extension

Ask students to pick a headline of the day—political, social, etc.—and create an infographic that has a specified purpose—communicate, influence, etc. Students could use the infographic maker at http://piktochart.com. If their infographic is

TABLE 13.8

Continued

Typical Learner	Advanced ELA Learner
Assess As students work, assess whether they are determining the main ideas and not just reading the infographic word-by-word, or headline-by-headline. Check for comprehension following the illustration experience by asking students to identify how the pictures and elements contribute to main idea.	particularly good, they can submit it to the Daily Infographic website for consideration. **Assess** As students work, assess whether they are determining the purposes and motivations of the various infographic by examining the authors of the infographics. Check for analysis by asking students to identify how the pictures and elements might be different if the infographic was for another purpose.

Developing Differentiated Curriculum in Writing

Grade 9 Unit Example Framework

The power of the personal narrative has spanned centuries, whether spoken or written. The power of an individual's experience will be explored through considering examples and writing personal narratives, consistent with CCSS writing standards noted in Table 13.9. Differentiated learning is addressed through text complexity and students' previously documented writing ability.

TABLE 13.9.

Sequence of CCSS Literacy Writing Standards From Grades 9–10

CCSS.ELA-Literacy. W9-10.3	Write narratives to develop real or imagined experiences or events using effective technique, well-chosen details, and well-structured event sequences.
CCSS.ELA-Literacy. W11-12.3	Write narratives to develop real or imagined experiences or events using effective technique, well-chosen details, and well-structured event sequences.

Instructional Overview

Throughout the learning experience detailed in 13.10, teachers should use evidence from previous reading comprehension assessments to guide selection of texts and also allow for multiple levels of advanced writing groups based on students' prior writing to guide group placement. If writing response groups are already a central consideration in the classroom, then this type of arrangement would lend itself well to the pre-established format. Alternately, reading groups may differ from writing groups; advanced readers and advanced writers are not a mutually exclusive group, so levels of advanced groupings should be a consideration based on the scope and sequence of skills on this standard at this grade level and beyond.

Differentiation Statement. Based upon *students' reading comprehension and history of writing* (relevant preassessment data), I differentiated the following lesson by *adapting the level of reading selections, depth of concept exploration, and written production* (elements of instruction) by *creative production* (tools) and providing for *grouping based on mastery of the writing standard* (management plan). I determined the lesson's effectiveness by evaluating the degree that students were able to develop original narratives and related visual or textual extensions.

TABLE 13.10

Differentiated Learning Experiences for Grade 9 Students on Writing Narratives

Typical Learners	Advanced Learners
Teacher will read aloud an excerpt from *I am Malala: The Girl Who Stood Up for Education and Was Shot by the Taliban* (Yousafzai & Lamb, 2013).	Teacher will read aloud an excerpt from *I am Malala: The Girl Who Stood Up for Education and Was Shot by the Taliban* (Yousafzai & Lamb, 2013).
Reading: Students will select two published personal narratives based on topical lists provided by the teacher. *Concept options:* Teachers, Encouragement, Loyalty *Resources:* StoryCorps (NPR; http://www.storycorps.org) • "A Homeless Teen Finds Solace in a Teacher and a Recording" (NPR, 2014)	*Reading:* Students will select two published personal narratives based on topical lists provided by the teacher. *Concept options:* Loss, family *Above-level reading options:* • Excerpt of *I Will Plant You a Lilac Tree: A Memoir of a Schindler's List Survivor* (Hillman, 2008) • Excerpt of *Learning Joy From Dogs Without Collars: A Memoir* (Summer,

TABLE 13.10

Continued

Typical Learners	Advanced Learners
• "Remembering When a Teacher had His Back" (NPR, 2013) *On-grade-level reading options:* • "Bully thwarted by suburban district 129 employee" (Cohen, 2012) • "Dear Jillian: Letter to a Young Bully" (Parra, 2011)	2004) • Excerpt of *The Boy Who Invented Skiing: A Memoir* (Wolfe, 2006)

Small-Group Discussions

From the selection provided, identify the subject or situation that is the central focus, narrator's role in the narrative, characters, use of dialogue, and transitions. Then identify how the author developed the plot through beginning, middle, and end. Groups will reflect shared reading interests. Each group will provide an overview to the class of the text selected and detail (briefly) how these elements were established by the authors.

Individual Brainstorming

To begin the writing process, the teacher will post options for writing based on the following prompts; students will select one prompt to brainstorm.

A. Jot down the most pivotal events in your life; beside each, bullet why these events were critical to you and some of the memories you have of the event.

B. Courage can be a profound subject for personal narratives—as both courage shown and courage unexplored can remain in our memories for many years. Identify examples

Individual Brainstorming, continued

of times when you've been courageous and times you lacked courage. Beside each, note specific recollections of the event, people involved, and the nature of your response. What do you recall as memorable about it?

C. Encountering certain people in our lives—even if briefly—can be memorable, particularly if a specific interaction with them comes to mind. Recall times when you encountered someone, whether a positive, negative, or otherwise memorable experience occurred. Describe the encounters, the circumstances that brought you together, and how you interacted with this person—possibly via dialogue.

D. Conflicts are sometimes troublesome and make a powerful impact on our lives, even if briefly. List conflicts you've had with others, the nature of the conflict, and how your conflict unfolded and ended.

Writing Groups

Organize students according to writing ability (not reading, speaking, listening, or other ability), preferably with 3–4 people per group.

Mini-Lessons

To address the standard and sub-skills noted in W7.3A-E or E9-10.3A-E, the teacher may offer writing workshops to develop specific skills based on student need and skill.

TABLE 13.10

Continued

Typical Learners	Advanced Learners
Publication Students will have the option of sharing their narrative with a selected audience: the teacher, teacher and writing response group, teacher and whole class, or teacher and other audience as appropriate to the content (guided by teacher).	**Publication** Students will have the option of sharing their narrative with a selected audience: the teacher, teacher and writing response group, teacher and whole class, or teacher and other audience as appropriate to the content (guided by teacher).
Extension Students may opt to locate a photograph, illustrate a picture, or create a piece of artwork that represents a concept explored in the narrative.	**Extension** Personal narratives may serve as the basis for other writing efforts, including drama (such as one-act play, reader's theatre), screenplay, historical nonfiction, or a short story. Students will adapt the narrative in an alternate format.

Developing Differentiated Curriculum in Language

Grade 11 Unit Example Framework

To support students' continued use of language conventions included in Table 13.11, the learning experiences provided in Table 13.12 are shaped around a common topic: technological innovation. As there are no above-level standards to guide teachers whose students in grades 11 and 12 have achieved the on-level skills, the learning experience is differentiated according to levels of concept abstraction, reading selections, and writing products. The central strategies addressed relate to the literacy skill of persuasion.

TABLE 13.11

Sequence of CCSS Literacy Standards From Grades 11–12

CCSS.ELA-Literacy. L11-12.6	Acquire and use accurately general academic and domain-specific words and phrases, sufficient for reading, writing, speaking, and listening at the college and career readiness level; demonstrate independence in gathering vocabulary knowledge when considering a word or phrase important to comprehension or expression.

Instructional Overview

To begin the learning experience, teachers should use evidence from previous reading comprehension assessments to guide selection of texts, and should also allow for multiple levels of advanced writing groups based on students' prior writing to guide group placement. If writing response groups are already a central consideration in the classroom, then this type of arrangement would lend itself well to the pre-established format. Alternately, reading groups may differ from writing groups; advanced readers and advanced writers are not a mutually exclusive group, so levels of advanced groupings should be a consideration based on the scope and sequence of skills on this standard at this grade level and beyond. See Table 13.12 for an example.

Differentiation statement. Because of *previous writing* (relevant pre-assessment data), I differentiated the following lesson by *adapting the level of reading selections, level of abstraction, depth of concept exploration, analysis of text and theme, and written production* (elements of instruction) by *critical analysis and generation of a persuasive argument* (tools) and providing for *grouping based on mastery of persuasive writing* (management plan). I determined the lesson's effectiveness by evaluating the degree that students were able to develop persuasive arguments that include domain-specific words, adhere to the conventions of language in writing, and through different purposes of writing (essay, Op-Ed, response to Op-Ed).

TABLE 13.12.

Differentiated Learning Experiences for Grade 11 Students on Using Persuasive Words and Phrases

Typical Learners	Advanced Learners
Overview/Introduction	**Overview/Introduction**
The Internet has revolutionized society as we know it, including the educational landscape. In this learning experience, students will identify recent technological innovations and argue for or against the addition of this innovation in their school.	The Internet has revolutionized society as we know it, including the educational landscape. In the Romantic period, novelists cautioned the rapid acquisition of new technologies, as reflected in Shelley's (2008) *Frankenstein, or the Modern Prometheus.* The American vision of progress, however, suggests that economy in thinking and action and scientific discovery is desirable, as described in *The Autobiography of Ben Franklin* (Franklin, 1916).
Reading	
Review recent technological innovations as reported in local, national, or international newspapers or magazines. Check technology sections of publications to locate descriptions of developments.	

TABLE 13.12

Continued

Typical Learners	Advanced Learners
Craft a Persuasive Argument Consider the potential benefits for students and acknowledge the arguments against the use of this innovation in schools. Identify a recent development, such as MOOCs, and develop a letter to a newspaper of a school, school district, university, or local community, and present a persuasive argument in the form of an Op-Ed piece that advocates for or against the implementation of MOOCs. **Draft, Review, Publish** Using conventions of persuasive arguments and English language, students will draft their Op-Ed piece, work with student writing-response groups to refine it, and ultimately publish through an outlet of their choice or disseminate to the entire class. **Responses** Classmates will select an Op-Ed selection written by a classmate and develop a letter to the editor that provides a response to the initial submission, either supporting, challenging, or further illuminating the idea(s) advanced in the initial article.	**Reading** Review recent sociological analyses of the effect of technological innovations on society or segments of society. Check technology sections of publications to locate descriptions of developments. **Craft a Persuasive Argument** In view of the rapid pace and adoption of recent technological innovations, consider the historical views of progress and innovation and the implications for society, business, education, or the country's aspirations to remain an economic superpower. Connect the works above or more contemporary texts with your argument about the role of technology in a persuasive essay. **Draft, Review, Publish** Using conventions of persuasive arguments, effective communication, and rhetorical skills, students will draft their essays and develop iteratively within student writing-response groups. Students will then present their arguments in an Op-Ed to the class and respond to the Op-Eds of classmates.

Implications for Future Research: Differentiating English Language Arts for Advanced Learners

As schools continue to group students of all abilities in homogenous classrooms—perhaps even more so with the reduction of funding for specialized programs for students who are gifted, the need for learning opportunities that address the needs of a wide range of student abilities in ELA remains and may even be more needed now than in prior years. Recent research has shown that classrooms may have learners who have different, often varying abilities. For example, in a study of more than 1,100 elementary students in grades 3 through 5, Firmender, Reis, and Sweeney (2013) found a wide range of reading levels—from nine to 11 different levels of readers—within a single classroom. Several researchers have advanced theoretical positions about differentiation as a practice in education, including researchers in the field of gifted education (Tomlinson, 1999). Beyond these positions, models of differentiation have also been advanced (Kaplan, 2009; Maker & Schiever, 2010; VanTassel-Baska, 2003), and evidence supporting differentiated reading as a purposeful approach has also been published (Reis & Boeve, 2009; Reis, Eckert, McCoach, Jacobs, & Coyne, 2008; Reis et al. 2007; Reis, McCoach, Little, Muller, & Kaniskan, 2011). Despite this history of strong theoretical and empirical support for differentiation, there is limited evidence that differentiated ELA instruction is a widely adopted practice. Although individuals with knowledge of statewide practices in gifted education have participated in surveys about the most-often utilized models for services, there is no evidence specific to the field of ELA for gifted students regarding the extent to which teachers differentiate instruction in various strands (i.e., reading, writing, speaking/listening, or language development). More research is also needed to illustrate the efficacy of differentiation as an effective instructional approach, the frequency that teachers adopt these strategies, and the effect of these modifications within various ELA strands. As there is an absence of research about why teachers may or may not differentiate, this remains a potential area of research that may guide subsequent efforts to implement professional development and other teacher-education opportunities.

Although the acquisition of ELA skills rarely includes a dimension of one skill (i.e., reading, writing, speaking and listening, or language), research on reading comprehension has been the focus of the majority of publications to date (see Reis et al., 2011). Given the central foundational role of reading comprehension and fluency in the development of literacy, as well as the emphasis on this skill in achievement tests, the rationale for the initial focus on reading among advanced learners is a logical point of origin for the field of gifted education and beyond. To broaden and deepen understanding about the theories and practices in writing, speaking and listening, and language, additional research in differentiation instruction in these areas is needed.

Conclusion

As reflected in the description of differentiation provided above and the subsequent examples of learning experience examples for each ELA strand, teachers can address the CCSS for all learners with modifications to instruction for typical and advanced learners. As our examples show, modifications may include above-grade-level text selections, incorporation of advanced standards based on the scope and sequence of learning, integration of critical and creative thinking opportunities, research, and the infusion of related CCSS in ELA (reading literature, reading for information, writing, speaking/listening, and language). Teachers should consider the individual student's readiness level and interests in differentiating learning.

Discussion Questions

1. How is differentiation in language arts similar to, and different from, differentiation in other content areas?
2. Do the Common Core State Standards for English language arts need differentiating when they are already rigorous and challenging? Why or why not?
3. How can a teacher describe the differentiation process?
4. What might differentiation in language arts look like at the different grade levels? Or in the different strands?

References

Cohen, J. C. (2012). *Bully thwarted by suburban district 129 employee*. Retrieved from https://dearbully.wordpress.com/2012/01/18/new-story-bully-thwarted-by-suburban-district-129-employee/

Firmender, J. M., Reis, S. M., & Sweeney, J. M. (2013). Reading comprehension and fluency levels across diverse classrooms: The need for differentiated instruction and content. *Gifted Child Quarterly, 57*, 3–14. doi:10.1177/0016986212460084

Franklin, B. (1916). *The autobiography of Ben Franklin*. New York, NY: Henry Holt and Company. Retrieved from http://www.gutenberg.org/files/20203/20203-h/20203-h.htm

Hillman, L. (2008). *I will plant you a lilac tree: A memoir of a Schindler's list survivor*. New York, NY: Simon Pulse. Retrieved from http://www.barnesandnoble.com/w/i-will-plant-you-a-lilac-tree-laura-hillman/1102343711?ean=9781416953661

Kaplan, S. (2009). Layering differentiated curricula. In F. A. Karnes & S. M. Bean (Eds.). *Methods and materials for teaching the gifted* (3rd ed., pp. 107–135). Waco, TX: Prufrock Press.

Letters: Why is so much food wasted at LAUSD? (2014, April 6). *Los Angeles Times*. Retrieved from http://articles.latimes.com/2014/apr/06/opinion/la-le-0406-sunday-lausd-food-20140406

MacLachlan, P. (1985). *Sarah, Plain and Tall*. New York, NY: HarperCollins.

Maker, C. J., & Nielson, A. (1996). *Curriculum development and teaching strategies for the gifted* (2nd ed.). Austin, TX: Pro-Ed.

Maker, C. J., & Schiever, S. W. (2010). *Curriculum development and teaching strategies for gifted learners* (2nd ed.). Austin, TX: Pro-Ed.

National Governors Association Center for Best Practices, & Council of Chief State School Officers. (2010). *Common Core State Standards for English language arts*. Washington, DC: Author. Retrieved from http://www.corestandards.org/the-standards

National Public Radio. (2013). *Remembering when a teacher had his back*. Retrieved from http://www.npr.org/2013/11/24/246984890/remembering-when-a-teacher-had-his-back

National Public Radio. (2014). *A homeless teen finds solace in a teacher and a recording*. Retrieved from http://www.npr.org/2014/03/07/286921391/a-homeless-teen-finds-solace-in-a-teacher-and-a-recording

Parra, K. (2011). *Dear Jillian: Letter to a young bully*. Retrieved from http://www.dearbully.wordpress.com/2011/12/13/448

Porter, A., McMaken, J., Hwang, J., & Yang, R. (2011). Common core standards: The new U.S. intended curriculum. *Educational Researcher, 40*, 103–116. doi:10.3102/0013189X11405038

Reis, S. M., & Boeve, H. (2009). How academically gifted elementary urban students respond to challenge in an enriched, differentiated reading program. *Journal for the Education of the Gifted, 33*, 203–240.

Reis, S. M., Eckert, R. D., McCoach, D. B., Jacobs, J. J., & Coyne, M. (2008). Using enrichment reading practices to increase reading fluency, comprehension, and attitudes. *The Journal of Educational Research, 101*, 299–314. doi.org/10.3200/JOER.101.5.299-315

Reis, S. M., McCoach, D. B., Coyne, M., Schreiber, F. J., Eckert, R. D., & Gubbins, E. J. (2007). Using planned enrichment strategies with direct instruction to improve reading fluency, comprehension, and attitude toward reading: An evidence based study. *The Elementary School Journal, 108,* 3–24. doi:10.1086/522383

Reis, S. M., McCoach, B. D., Little, C. A., Muller, L. M., & Kaniskan, R. B. (2011). The effects of differentiated instruction and enrichment pedagogy on reading achievement in five elementary schools. *American Educational Research Journal, 48,* 462–501. doi:10.3102/0002831210382891

Shelley, M. W. (2008). *Frankenstein, or the modern Prometheus.* Project Gutenberg. Retrieved from http://www.gutenberg.org/files/84/84-h/84-h.htm

Seuss, D. (1960). *Green eggs and ham.* New York, NY: Random.

Summer, L. (2004). *Learning joy from dogs without collars: A memoir.* New York, NY: Simon & Schuster. Retrieved from http://www.barnesandnoble.com/w/learning-joy-from-dogs-without-collars-lauralee-summer/11032 76271?ean=9780743257923

Tomlinson, C. A. (1999). *The differentiated classroom.* Alexandria, VA: Association for Supervision and Curriculum Development.

U.S. Department of Agriculture. (2012). Nutrition standards in the national school lunch school breakfast programs (7 CFR Parts 210 and 220). *Federal Register, 77*(17), 4088. Retrieved from http://www.gpo.gov/fdsys/pkg/FR-2012-01-26/pdf/2012-1010.pdf

VanTassel-Baska, J. (2003). *Curriculum planning and instructional design for gifted learners.* Denver, CO: Love.

VanTassel-Baska, J., Hughes, C., Kettler, T., & Shaunessy-Dedrick, E. (2013, November). *Modifying the national standards for high-ability learners: Examples and strategies for K–12 educators.* Session presented at preconference workshop of the National Association for Gifted Children annual conference, Indianapolis, IN.

Watanabe, T. (2014, April 1). Solutions sought to reduce food waste at schools. *Los Angeles Times* [Electronic version]. Retrieved from http://www.latimes.com/local/la-me-lausd-waste-20140402-story.html#page=1

Wolfe, S. (2006). *The boy who invented skiing: A memoir.* New York, NY: St. Martin's Press.

Yousafzai, M., & Lamb, C. (2013). *I am Malala: The girl who stood up for education and was shot by the Taliban.* London, England: Little, Brown and Company.

CHAPTER 14

ROMANCE, PRECISION, AND INTEGRATION
DEVELOPING TALENT AND EXPERTISE IN WRITING

TODD KETTLER

Margaret Atwood chose to be a writer walking home from school one day. She said it was sudden, not contemplated as one would choose to be a lawyer or a dentist. "I wrote a poem in my head and then I wrote it down, and after that, writing was the only thing I wanted to do" (Atwood, 2003, p. 9). She said the poem was not any good, but that didn't matter, it was the experience that hooked her: "it was electric" (Atwood, 2003, p. 9). She announced her career transition to writer the next day with a group of girls in the high school cafeteria. James Tate became a writer in his dorm room during his freshmen year in college. "The thing that was magic about it was that once you put down one word, you could cross it out" (Simic, 2006, p. 55). He described his initial draw to writing as a desire to create another world. A month later, Tate was sitting alone in a bar when some guys approached him and asked, "What do you do?" Tate answered, "I looked up at them and I said, I'm a poet. That was it. My identity was already formed" (Simic, 2006, p. 56).

Recognizing and embracing identity as a writer seems to be an important moment in the journey to developing writing talent. The proclamation both internal and external that "writing is what I do" confirms commitment and intent; it's the illumination of a budding romance to seek expertise, per-

DOI: 10.4324/9781003236696-17

haps eminence, perhaps self-satisfaction. In our traditions of gifted education, there appears to be an unquestioning constancy to ask how the gifted students should be identified. In a talent development approach, developing the talent takes primacy over identification of the gifted. When seeking to develop talented writers, we begin by seeking those who identify themselves as writers. Furthermore, we create environments that invite potential writers to come to the table and toy with the electricity of creating new worlds.

Benjamin Bloom (1985a) wrote what is arguably the most seminal work on talent development after conducting intensive case studies with 120 eminently talented individuals across multiple domains of performance. In an interview conducted shortly after the publication of *Developing Talent in Young People*, Bloom said, "In most schools, we ignore what Whitehead was trying to tell us. We begin almost all instruction with precision and accuracy when we should begin with something more exciting, romantic, and playful" (Brandt, 1985, p. 35).

Bloom was influenced by the Whitehead (1929) model of talent development in which Whitehead described three distinct phases of the process: romance, precision, and integration. Bloom (1985b) similarly found three general qualities that seemed to appear in the development of advanced or elite talent regardless of the domain. First, individuals who develop elite levels of talent display a strong interest and commitment to the particular domain of talent. Second, individuals who develop elite levels of talent express a desire to reach a high level of attainment in the domain of talent. Third, individuals who develop elite levels of talent are willing to commit great amounts of time and effort needed to reach the highest levels of achievement in the domain of talent. When Bloom stated that schools ignore what Whitehead was telling us by beginning with precision and accuracy, he meant that little or no attention was devoted to the romance phase of the process. By evidence and inference, we know that without the passion (Coleman & Guo, 2013) and desire for a talent domain that is the result of the romance phase, individuals are not likely to commit great amounts of time and effort to attain elite levels of performance.

More recently, Subotnik, Olszewski-Kubilius, and Worrell (2011) have also proposed a three-stage model for developing elite or eminent levels of talent: (a) developing an interest and love for the subject, (b) honing skills and techniques, and (c) mentoring for personalized niche in the final stage. This model clearly bears the lineage of Whitehead and Bloom. To this point, much of the research on how to apply this three-phase model of talent development has examined the process largely in out-of-school settings. One of the challenges facing the talent development approach to gifted education is to articulate how we might apply what we know about developing advanced or elite levels of talent to the structures of school settings and the implementation of curriculum (Dai & Chen, 2014).

In this chapter, I offer an approach to developing learning experiences for gifted and advanced learners in English language arts that is theoretically grounded in the talent development model (Bloom, 1985a; Subotnik et al., 2011; Whitehead, 1929). The approach takes seriously the comment from Bloom, that schools and curriculum too often ignore Whitehead and attempt to develop advanced talent while neglecting to build a love for the discipline. Furthermore, it might be argued that honing skills and techniques and the final phase of mentoring for a personalized niche are largely conducted after students have completed the K– 12 curriculum. Thus, we might project that the greatest task of a curriculum for advanced talent development in the language arts domain in elementary and secondary education is to cultivate the interest and love for work in communicating, critiquing, and creating artifacts of intellect and culture.

Talent Development and Giftedness

The field of gifted education suffers no shortage of conceptions of giftedness. Dai and Chen (2014) characterized three competing paradigms of gifted education, each of which may define giftedness differently. Competing conceptions of giftedness vary in several ways, but one important facet of divergence is whether giftedness is constitutional or dynamic. In the constitutional view, giftedness is innate and rather permanent. In the dynamic view, giftedness is changing, evolving, and subject to influences both personal and environmental. Dai and Chen (2014) characterized the constitutional view of giftedness as the predominant view throughout most of the 20th century. However, the dynamic view began with studies of talent development and talent development conceptions of giftedness in the 1980s (Dai & Renzulli, 2008; Renzulli, 1978; Subotnik et al., 2011) and has gained significant momentum for designing gifted education practices in the 21st century.

This emergent view of giftedness in the talent development paradigm is developmental and requires performance or production recognized as outstanding or elite relative to a particular domain of practice (Subotnik et al., 2011). A child's potential matters in early stages, but eventually potential must be developed to result in achievement to validate giftedness (Coleman & Cross, 2005). Subotnik et al. (2011) made the following points regarding this dynamic, developmental view of giftedness and talent development:

» Ability is necessary for giftedness but not sufficient for the development of special talent.

» Interest in and commitment to a domain are essential to becoming a gifted achiever.

» Gifted levels of achievement depend on appropriate teaching and coaching of psychosocial skills including persistence and exertion of effort.

» The development of advanced talent requires substantial time and commitment. (p. 7–8)

Thus, the practical question becomes how to develop systematic learning experiences that support the development of specialized talent in the language arts domain. Even more specifically, how might we develop interest, passion, and drive to achieve in the language arts domain? What types of educational experiences nurture passion for learning and producing in the language arts domain while at the same type fostering development of required psychosocial skills?

Domain of Language Arts Talent

It is generally agreed that talent development is domain specific (Dai & Chen, 2014; Subotnik et al., 2011). Thus, we must understand and define the boundaries of the talent domain associated with language arts curriculum. Domains may be viewed as general categories of thinking and processing, but they may also be viewed as specific areas of work and production, such as professions and narrow specialties within those professions. General categories may derive from those areas of giftedness offered in the Marland (1972) definition: general intellectual ability, specific academic aptitude, creative or productive thinking, leadership ability, visual and performing arts aptitude, and psychomotor ability. Gagné (2003) also suggested four broad categories or domains of ability: intellectual, creative, socioaffective, and sensorimotor. Dai and Renzulli (2008) argued that we may lose appreciation for the complexity of talent development by seeking a unitary ability as the foundation for domain specific talent. It seems most reasonable that the domain of language arts includes some general intellectual ability, particularly verbal ability, as well as some creative/productive thinking. Moreover, when we think of the skills of the talented writer, surely Gagné's (2003) socioaffective ability, which includes perceptiveness, is critical to understanding character, emotion, and the dramatic rendering of human complexity.

From those conceptions of domain as general abilities, we further consider language art talent through the lens of professional specificity. When we develop talent in language arts, we are developing young people capable of being outstanding professionals in fields that require communication through writing. These fields may be as obvious as literary writers, historical-political writers, and journalists. The fields associated with language arts talent development also include screenwriters, travel writers, essayists, bloggers, critics, researchers, humorists, cartoonists, and even translators. Although the development of talent for work in these professions and fields of practice will include specific training and practice beyond the realm of the K–12 curriculum, the curricular experiences in school ought to develop the foundational talents in writing, thinking, and creating.

How Does Writing Talent Develop?

Analyses of talent development suggest three phases of the process (see Table 14.1). Although there are some differences in each of these three models (Bloom, 1985b; Subotnik et al., 2011; Whitehead, 1929), generalizations may be inferred through their commonalities. In all three models, the first phase is to develop a strong interest in the domain or a love for the domain. This interest or love for the domain is the foundation on which serious commitment will be built. In the second phase, the person learns precision and technique. This is characterized by the honing of skills, building a deep understanding of the concepts, knowledge, methods, and structures of the domain. Bloom (1985b) characterized this phase uniquely as a desire for high levels of attainment. In the third phase, the person takes an already advanced level of talent and works toward elite or eminent levels of accomplishment in the domain. As Whitehead (1929) said, the person integrates herself into the role of recognized expert, and Bloom clarified that such expertise is found through great amounts of work and commitment.

TABLE 14.1

Phases of Talent Development

Model	Phase 1	Phase 2	Phase 3
Whitehead (1929)	Romance	Precision	Integration
Bloom (1985b)	Strong interest and commitment to the domain of talent	Express a desire to reach a high level of attainment in the domain of talent	Willing to commit great amounts of time and effort as needed to develop the talent
Subotnik et al. (2011)	Develop an interest and love for the subject	Honing skills and techniques	Mentoring for personalized niche

These phases of talent development have been consistently recognized across domains, and studies of talented writers offer evidence to support the validity of these pathways (Kaufman, & Kaufman, 2009; Piirto, 1998, 2002). A recent study of adolescent creative writers (Garrett & Moltzen, 2011) found high levels of intrinsic motivation. The participants expressed a love for the acts of writing, thinking, and creating. Edmonds and Noel (2003) similarly found an intense love for writing in their case study of a child writer prodigy. Where does this romance with the discipline arise? In her biographical analysis of eminent U.S. writers, Piirto (1999) found a consistent positive impact of teachers who nurture writing talents. Similarly, Csikszentmihalyi (1990) suggested that teachers who support writing talent development know how to create conditions that foster and sustain motivation to write. Potter, McCormick, and Busching (2001) found that adolescent writers are motivated to write in ways that make sense of their own experiences. In other situations, students built a love for "real writing" as opposed to "school writing," suggesting that authentic tasks with student choices and format flexibility contributed to developing motivation and commitment (Garrett & Moltzen, 2011). Perhaps the most interesting description of the romance or love for writing comes from Olthouse (2013). In her qualitative study of adult writers in a Master's of Fine Arts (MFA) program, Olthouse asked the subjects to describe their relationship with writing using a metaphor. Responses included, "a spouse, a strange but innocuous stalker, the seductive call of ocean, a prey that must be circled carefully" (p. 271).

Olthouse (2014) studied the development of writing talent in children. She found that children (grades 3 through 6) who were engaged in writing talent development were influenced by teachers who made writing fun and engaging, parents who supported and encouraged story writing outside of school, and attendance at enrichment programs for creative writing. Additionally, the child writers were avid readers. The children Olthouse (2014) studied expressed intrinsic motivation and personal goals for improving their own writing. They also valued the idea of creativity as a trait or skill worth cultivating for their writing development.

Olthouse (2012) also studied talented high school writers. The high school writers in her study were also avid readers who described modeling their own writing after the writing of their favorite authors. The high school students in her study described influential teachers who supported creative responses and provided structured practice and serious critiques of student writing. The high school writers in Olthouse's study participated in writing competitions and in writing enrichment programs. These students shared a value of openness that helped them to be open to criticism of their work and to creating stories about characters with diverse perspectives. Olthouse found the high school writers had personal goals to express emotions, develop writing talent, mediate emotions, and have fun with writing. By high school, these students had built an identity as a writer, and they saw writing as prominent in their future. Olthouse characterized their relationship with writing as personal, positive, and context dependent. One student described the relationship as a love affair and another described it as a best friend.

Gifted writers not only display attraction and commitment to the domain of writing, but they have also developed technical proficiencies advanced for their age. Piirto (1989, 1992) found evidence that the writing of young writers included advanced qualities, such as the following: (a) use of paradox, (b) use of parallel structure, (c) use of rhythm, (d) use of visual imagery, (e) melodic combinations, (f) unusual use of figures of speech such as alliterations and personification, (g) confidence with reverse structure, (h) unusual adjectives and adverbs, (i) feeling of movement, (j) evidence of insight or wisdom, (k) sophisticated syntax and advanced use of punctuation, (l) prose lyricism, (m) a natural ear for language, (n) sense of humor, (o) a philosophical or moral bent, and (p) a tendency to play with words and language.

The existing research on developing talent in writing seems to support the three phase models of talent development (see Table 14.1). From elementary school to MFA writing programs, developing writers talk about their love for the practice of writing. They commit significant time to writing and build identities as writers. The romance with the domain appears to be a significant foundation on which they establish goals for writing, create consistent routines for writing, attend enrichment programs in writing, and submit their writing to competitions. Intrinsic motivation flows from this love of writing and sustains them through the cruelties of rejection. Their influences include supportive parents and teachers who not only encourage writing, but also find ways to make it a fun and worthwhile endeavor. These writers have deep and significant relationships with writing and may have a tendency to approach reading not only as a reader, but also as a writer reading to study the craft and thinking of other writers.

Narratives of Developing Writing Talent

To further understand the development of writing talent in school, we turn briefly to insightful narratives. Narrative inquiry connects theory to practice through embedded and contextual understandings of a phenomenon (Clandinin & Connelly, 2000). I share the following stories I have collected to describe young people developing their advanced writing talents and to provide a heuristic for understanding the process (Czarniawska, 1997).

Tommy

Tommy traversed elementary school with little special attention from his teachers. His grades were good, not exceptional. His demeanor was pleasant, humble, and unassuming. He was almost always chosen in the middle of the pack during daily kickball matches in fifth grade. Tommy liked to read, and *The Boxcar Children* books were his favorite. Tommy remembers his parents reading all of the time during his childhood. He said he started writing because he wanted to create something that his parents would love, and they clearly loved books. The house was full of books. His first book was a dual biography of the two best kickball players in his fifth-grade class. He read a book from the school library titled, *The Homerun Kings* about Babe Ruth and Hank Aaron, and thought, "I can totally do that." A week later he used the stapler on his teacher's desk to secure the binding on *The Kickball Kings*. In middle school, he discovered Stephen King, despite his disapproving mother, who thought King too crude for his middle school mind, but Tommy said the hint of rebellion pushed him to read King even more. In addition to reading King, Tommy began writing tales of horror, mimicking King's style. Tommy's middle school hosted a talent show each fall, and after 2 years of mimicking Stephen King stories in his private notebook, Tommy signed up to read what he considered his best short story, "Don't Trust a Clown at Halloween." In describing his influence for the story, he said he had read two of Stephen King's short story collections, *Night Shift* and *Everything's Eventual*. He once went through roughly 25 King short stories writing down the first sentence because he wanted to learn how King tried to capture the reader's attention right out of the shoot. He tried to imitate how King used common settings to perpetuate the fear of monsters and horror in our everyday surroundings. "Don't Trust a Clown" was a big hit, and from that day on, everybody knew Tommy was a writer. Tommy continued writing tales involving high school characters, many based on his friends. He entered a regional writing competition in both his freshman and sophomore years in high school and received honorable mention for his short stories. He described his English teachers as supportive but uninspiring for the most part. His tenth-grade teacher encouraged him to write and share more stories, but Tommy described narrative writing as a low priority compared to the emphasis on expository and persuasive writing. During his final year of high school, Tommy won first place in the regional writing competition. When asked how he improved from his honorable mention stories, he said he read a wider variety of short stories online, including those in literary publications such as *The New Yorker*, *A Public Space*, and the online literary journal, *Narrative*. He commented that while Stephen King set the table, the literary journals polished the silver.

Kathryn

Kathryn knew she wanted to be a writer in middle school, where she participated in the school's gifted education program. In her gifted language arts classes, she was fortunate to have teachers who lauded and supported her interest in writing. Her eighth-grade English teacher asked her to share her writing ideas in class and suggested she enter a local writing competition for middle school and high school students. Kathryn was excited by the encouragement and submitted an entry in the short story category. Kathryn won first place in the middle school short story competition, and said at that moment, she knew she was a writer.

In high school, she chose journalism as her freshman year elective and practiced writing narratives in a new way, experimenting with creative nonfiction. Spring of freshman year, she entered the same local writing competition and won first place again in the high school short story category. During her sophomore year, she continued in the journalism program at her school, and she applied and was accepted to a program for student editorial writers for the city's major newspaper. Over the course of the year, she had four editorials published. Still working on her fiction writing, she submitted a short story for her high school's literary magazine, and it was accepted and published.

In her junior year, she took creative writing and began working on the staff of the high school literary magazine. She published a short story in the magazine again as a junior and also entered the same writing competition. She did not win, but received honorable mention from the judges in the high school short story category. During her senior year, she became the assistant editor of the high school literary magazine and won the local short story competition for a third time in 5 years. When describing her success in writing as a high school student, Kathryn said she wrote lots of stories. Some she said were worth revising over and over and others are in a drawer at home dying a slow death. She said that over time, she learned from practice and extensive reading how to discern which ones to edit and submit and which ones to put aside.

Kathryn had opportunities through her school to develop writing talent. She described the journalism program as one of the best in the state, regularly having students write for the city newspaper and go on to study at prestigious journalism programs in college. She also had the chance to take 2 years of creative writing and work on the editorial staff of a high school literary magazine. She described her creative writing teacher as the most influential teacher in her life so far. The creative writing competition also presented an outlet for Kathryn to share her work and build her identity as a writer. The creators of the competition said that prior to Kathryn, no one else had won three times in the same category. They jokingly added that many students were happy to see her graduate.

Alexa and Alex

The Blue Pencil is an online literary magazine for high school writers. The publication is supported by the Walnut Hill School for the Arts, but contributing authors come from high schools across the United States as well as abroad. *The Blue Pencil* is a good example of what elite levels of writing talent might look like in high school as well as a cast of those we might consider gifted writers in the adolescent years. Take, for example, Alexa, a 2014 graduate of Westfield High School in Westfield, NJ. Alexa published an innovative short story titled, "Sixteen Ways of Looking for Sarah" in the Spring 2014 issue of *The Blue Pencil*. Alexa has also had her work published in *Word Riot*, *Hanging Loose*, *The Apprentice Writer*, *Polyphony HS*, *The Postscript Journal*, *Winter Tangerine Review*, and *The Adroit Journal*, where she recently was named as the managing editor. Although *The Blue Pencil* and *Polyphony HS* are literary publications for high school writers, Alexa's other publication outlets are all adult literary journals. Additionally in *The Blue Pencil*, we find Alex, poet and high school student at Ethical Culture Fieldston School in New York City. Alex has been twice the runner-up in the Cape Farewell Poetry Competitions and has been recognized by the Young Poets Society, Scholastic Arts and Writing Awards, and the Foyle Young Poets of the Year Award. In addition to the poem "Visiting Hour" published in *The Blue Pencil*, Alex has had poems published in *Able Muse*, *Spinning Jenny*, *Spittoon*, and *The Boiler*.

Tommy, Kathryn, Alexa, and Alex are examples of gifted writers. They earn this designation by their production and performance at elite levels compared to their typical high school peers. Highlighting them in these narratives paints a picture of what gifted levels of performance might entail in the writing domain. Giftedness as a high school writer is not determined by an intelligence test, an achievement test, or even a teacher checklist. Rather, these students developed as gifted writers because of a love for writing, commitment, practice, and opportunities to participate in the arena where writing performances are on display and validated for excellence. The qualifying criteria are their activities as writers and the advanced quality of their products and performances.

Developing Writing Talent in School

How can we apply understanding of the three phases of talent development and design learning experiences to foster the development of gifted writers? Developing writing talent in school is not a clearly articulated formula or step-by-step mechanistic process. Attempts to make it such are misguided; rather, developing gifted writers is a complex process involving commitments by the students and dedicated instruction and mentorship by teachers. The following principles are guidelines characteristic of the process. These principles may take on slightly different appearances in each school, but their application to the learning design process is fundamental to developing giftedness in language arts.

Focus on Motivation

In order to develop writing talent, we need to design learning experiences that build and sustain motivation to engage as writers. Boscolo and Gelati (2007) argued that motivation to write is an attitude or view toward writing based on beliefs the students develop through their writing experiences. Students generally come to view writing as either engaging or repetitive and boring and more or less important for their future (Bruning & Horn, 2000). In other words, attitudes and motivations to engage or avoid writing are formed largely based on experiences at school. Furthermore, students' attitudes toward writing influence the way they engage and commit to writing tasks.

When designing learning experiences to foster motivation to write, focus on tasks that are authentic and interesting. Writing tasks that are authentic consists of three critical features. First, authentic writing tasks allow and encourage students to express personal points of view and feelings. These tasks give voice to the student writer. Students are asked to not just complete assignments, but to say something meaningful, reflective of their personal analysis and commitments. Second, authentic writing tasks engage students in the immediate uses of writing for enjoyment and communication. For example, students may write to the school board to communicate how they are using technology in the classroom as a result of a new laptop or tablet initiative. Students who participate in youth sports may write sports articles for the classroom in which they analyze their games from the previous weekend. Third, authentic writing tasks are those that address a real problem that can be solved using writing. Perhaps the students want to petition the city council for improved bike trails in the local park or innovative youth activities such as disc golf or beach volleyball tournaments to encourage active youth lifestyles.

In addition to those that are authentic, writing learning experiences that are interesting build and sustain motivation attitudes. There is a difference between asking students to write about interesting topics and actually making writing interesting. We generally find that just because students are interested in a topic, we cannot assume they are also interested in writing about it. Interesting topics are a good starting point, but curriculum design needs to also address ways to make writing on the interesting topic worthwhile and useful (Boscolo & Gelati, 2007). We can also make writing interesting through thought-provoking ideas and collaboration systems where students work together to produce innovative written products and performances. For instance, the English department at a middle school might start an annual Halloween tradition of literacies of the macabre. Students would work in groups to produce innovative and thought-provoking multimedia productions of poems, flash fiction, and movies exploring what makes us afraid, and the school community of teachers, students, and parents come to the literacy fair where students display and perform their works and interpretations of fear itself.

The curriculum goal to emphasize motivation to write seeks to help students build positive beliefs about writing. Sometimes, these activities are needed to start replacing negative beliefs that have already formed. Designing writing curriculum that is authentic and interesting builds a foundation on which students can build a romance with the discipline and begin the journey of developing talent capable of advanced or elite performance.

Teach and Model Advanced Writing Habits

Developing gifted levels of talent in any domain is founded on discipline, commitment, and practice. Thus, a simple principle applies when developing writing talent. Teach students to have writing discipline. Most adult writers commit to writing every day and do not consider their work done until they reach their daily word count expectation or time expectation. The discipline and commitment to establish and follow through on a consistent writing routine is a foundational skill for becoming a talented writer. In order to develop advanced or elite writing skills, students must practice regularly with focus and discipline. When creating curriculum for gifted writing programs, include expectations for establishing the daily routines, habits, and commitments of a writer (Silva, 2007).

Most writers are avid readers, but they do not just read for comprehension and literary critique. Writers learn to read like writers (Bunn, 2011); therefore, students wanting to be writers need to be taught how to read like a writer. This includes analyzing and mimicking writing styles. Although mimicking may not sound exciting or especially creative, many or even most established and successful writers have talked about mimicking their favorite writers in the early days while searching for their own voice and style. When creating curriculum for gifted writing programs, include "reading like a writer" learning experiences. Ask students to look at how to write a beginning, how to write dialogue, and how to infer character traits from events and dialogue. Have students describe authors' styles and voices using text examples to verify their analyses. Ultimately, reading like a writer must lead to writing practice that applies what was learned in the reading.

In addition to teaching advanced writing habits, teachers need to model writing habits. Teachers themselves need to establish and talk about their own writing practices. For instance, talk about how and when you write best. Is it morning or evening? When you write, do you have a particular desk, or do you like writing in the backyard, in a coffee shop, or in public spaces where you observe people and overhear dialogue and conversation? Show students how to read like a writer. Bring in poems, short stories, or books that you have been reading and model how you think like a writer while reading those texts. Share your own writing as part of the writing workshop in your classroom. If you teach young students, write books and stories for your class. If you work with older students, share your triumphs and struggles as a writer. Show students how you personally are creating texts. Model revising and editing through think aloud exercises with your class. Become one of the peer editors in the writing workshop and model for students how to provide valuable comments and criticisms to writers in the group. Teachers can inspire students to follow their lead and adopt positive attitudes toward writing when teachers are open and honest about their lives as writers (Allison, 2009; Bandura, 1986).

Advanced writing habits can be taught by studying writers and their thought processes as writers. Build the study of writers and the writing process into the curriculum. A great tool for understanding writing and identity as a writer is to read interviews with writers. *The Paris Review* is famous for interesting and thought provoking interviews with writers, and many of those interviews are available online. National Public Radio (NPR) has collected interviews with some of the world's best writers. Simple online searches can lead teachers and students to publically available interviews with the likes of Stephen King, J. K. Rowling, Dan Brown, and John Grisham. Reading and discussing interviews helps students not only understand the process of writing, but also to imagine their own identity as a writer. In addition to studying writers, students learn about the practice and identity as a writer through peripheral participation in the writing community. Organizations like Poets & Writers (http://www.pw.org) and The Write Life (http://www.thewritelife.com) offer tools for writers, writing prompts for fiction and creative nonfiction, lists of contests, places to submit work, and ways to connect with other writers.

To develop advanced writing talent, learning experiences should introduce writing habits and connect students to a community of writers within and beyond the school. Students interested and committed to developing writing talent need opportunities to learn not only about writing, but the profession of writing. What types of work do writers do? How do writers connect with each other? These experiences and connections are facets of writing talent development, and school programs dedicated to developing gifted writers can build these components into the curriculum of learning experiences.

Create a School Culture of Advanced Writing Achievement

Writing development is fueled through social and cultural interaction (Graham, MacArthur, & Fitzgerald, 2007). Writers write for audiences and long for readers. Writers want to influence and affect others; they want to entertain, enlighten, even shock and surprise. How do we create school and classroom cultures to support development of advanced writing talent?

Educational research (e.g., Graham & Perin, 2007) has documented effective instructional strategies to improve writing skills. Although much of the research on these strategies has involved developing writing competency, these approaches can also inform how we develop beyond competency and support elite levels of achievement. In addition to the curriculum experiences to support writing competency, schools can also create a culture of advanced writing achievement though the consistent implementation of several elements in the learning experiences of writing students (see Table 14.2). It is unlikely and perhaps accidental that students should develop advanced or elite writing talent in a curriculum designed to only develop writing competency. The Common Core State Standards for English Language Arts are well-aligned and perhaps more advanced than previous iterations of writing standards. However, they should be considered the foundation upon which advanced training in writing talent should be built.

Gifted programs for the development of advanced writing talent should train teachers to provide advanced writing instruction across multiple genres and provide targeted feedback to support the skill development of young writers. In addition to advanced instruction in writing, teachers should make writing workshops a regular feature of the writing curriculum. In the writing workshop, students of similar ability would be grouped together to share their work and provide specific feedback on what works and what could be improved. Students build a schedule that designates when each person is to submit work to the rest of the group. The submission of work is in advance of the date at which the group meets to discuss the text and provide feedback so that each participant has time to read and generate comments. Writing workshop is the most common pedagogy of advanced writing programs in colleges and universities.

TABLE 14.2

Elements of a Gifted Writing Program

Program Component	Description
Advanced writing instruction	» Teach students to plan, revise, and edit across multiple genres as well as innovative techniques to blend genres. » Teach students advanced techniques of composition. » Provide targeted feedback on specific elements of writing.
Writing workshop approach	» Students write and share their work with a group of writing peers on a regular basis. » Students learn to be effective critics and supporters. » Students learn to meet writing deadlines according to schedule.
Publication opportunities	» In elementary years, teachers publish handmade books, classroom collections, and digital collections of student work. » Middle school and high school years should include a school literary journal to annually publish work of talented writers at the school. » By middle school and high school, teachers help students find journals that publish student work. » Schools may create partnerships with local newspapers to regularly publish high-quality student work. » Students may establish blogs and writer websites to showcase their portfolio of work. » Some elite-level writers will begin to publish in adult literary publications by the end of high school.
Writing competitions	» Schools and teachers make lists of all age appropriate contests with deadlines and guidelines. » Use competition deadlines to influence curriculum calendar so that students learn and prepare for contests and competitions.
Collaboration and community	» Collaborative writing activities with similar ability peers can be both engaging and instructive. » Student collaborative projects may include: novels, screenplays, multimedia story presentations, edited collections of student work, and blogs or other online writing outlets. » Students are encouraged and taught to connect with other writers both within and beyond the school.

TABLE 14.2

Continued

Program Component	Description
Advanced writing coursework	» Gifted high school writing programs may include advanced journalism courses, creative writing courses, and independent study/mentorship opportunities to work on advanced writing projects. » Program options should also include concurrent enrollment with colleges for writing classes. » Schools may have extracurricular writing programs that meet beyond the traditional school hours or calendar.

In addition to advanced instruction and writing workshops, students should be educated in the practical activities of developing writing talent. Specifically, they need to understand the publication process: preparing work for submission, finding publication outlets appropriate for their work, and dealing with rejection. Most writers admit that the adrenaline is in publication, and progressive acts of publishing can begin a romance with the discipline at a young age. Elementary writing programs should include individual and group publications beginning with simple stories and picture books leading to more sophisticated literary and nonfiction publications in upper elementary grades. Gifted writing programs may take on a more formalized look in middle school with school-sponsored literary publications, readings, and talented premieres. The goal is to provide more advanced instruction while building a community of writers who find writing and publishing an exciting adventure in creation, critique, and collaboration. These writing experiences continue into high school where students submit and publish in school-sponsored journals. Additionally, many talented high school students will begin to submit to regional and national publications for high school students. Ideally, gifted students have opportunities to work with writing teachers who are also engaged in the creation and publication of their own.

Writing competitions are a great way for young writers to practice their skills and build a reputation for quality work. Although there are national and international competitions available, one way a gifted program can nurture writing talents is to sponsor campus or district-level competitions. These local competitions can include divisions for elementary students all the way through high school students. I worked with a school district that partnered with a local organization that provided financial support to publish the work of the winners in each category and at each grade level. Another district I worked with had a corporate sponsor who gave prize money to the winners of the annual fiction and poetry contests. Ideally, teachers in the gifted program can organize a listing of the competitions by submission deadline and include guidelines for submission and participation.

Collaborative writing projects have been found to improve student skills (Graham & Perin, 2007), and collaborative projects are also engaging and interesting for students to build positive attitudes about writing. Professional models of collaborative writing work are most prominent in the television and film industry; however, student writers can collaborate on fiction, poetry, and creative nonfiction work as well. Collaborative writing projects should include students of similar abilities who push each other for mutual benefit throughout the process. Students can collaboratively write screenplays, documentaries, and collections of essays on topics. I have seen students collaborate to create wiki sites on topics and blogs where each student is assigned to post on a regular schedule on a range of topics. Collaborative writing should encompass high interest with the intent of both skill development and deepening the love of writing.

Lastly, high school gifted programs for language arts talent development should include courses of advanced study. Advanced courses may include Advanced Placement courses in English Language and English Literature as well as specialized courses in creative writing. Advanced courses in journalism and film may also allow students opportunities to develop diverse writing talents. Concurrent enrollment occurs when high school students are concurrently enrolled in college courses; thus, college courses in writing or creative writing are ways to supplement the standard high school curriculum. Online courses in creative writing are widely available and may vary in quality and intensity, and these can be excellent opportunities for gifted students to further develop their writing talents. A well-designed high school program for gifted writers will include multiple options of advanced study in writing. In many ways, the role of the school is not to provide each opportunity, but to facilitate and support the connection between the student and the opportunity.

Conclusion and Implications for Research

Gifted education services in language arts should develop advanced skills in literacy. A talent development approach to curriculum and instruction in language arts seeks to identify capable students wanting to move through the phases of development toward advanced or elite levels of performance as a writer. Talent development as a writer requires discipline, commitment, and practice. Furthermore, talent development as a writer requires ongoing work with teachers and mentors capable of both instructing and instilling attitudes of excitement and engagement in writing. Writing curriculum should be engaging, interesting, and challenging. Experiences in the writing curriculum should provide students with opportunities to build an identity as a writer with the appropriate habits and attitudes associated with an interest and love for work in communicating, critiquing, and creating artifacts of intellect and culture.

Research on developing writing competency is more advanced than research on developing advanced writing talent. Research is needed on all aspects of writing talent development, including how students develop identities as writers and how authentic tasks foster advanced development. What skills are required for faculty members working in the gifted writing program? What curriculum resources are available to support advanced writing tasks? What is the impact of specific facets of instruction such as vocabulary development and the use of rubrics for self-assessment and peer feedback? We need case studies of talented young writers to understand the complexity of the journey toward success as a writer. We need intervention designs to measure the efficacy of online writing programs that are becoming more and more prominent as tools to developing talent. We need programmatic research to identify barriers and benefactors to establishing and developing gifted writing programs within diverse public school settings.

Developing writing talent may concurrently appear simple, with three clear and distinct phases, and vastly complex, with hours and years of practice writing and revising with capable mentors. Gifted programs play the role of talent development funnel. Throughout the process, we attract numerous students to the electricity of creating new worlds, but for every hundred students we attract to the process, perhaps only a few will move on to elite levels of achievement. That is in no way a weakness; it is simply the nature of the process of developing giftedness. Trying to determine in advance who those few will be seems both unfair and a poor use of educational resources.

Discussion Questions

1. In what ways does the development of writing talent seem to follow the three-stage model, and in what ways does it seem to deviate from the three-stage model?
2. How might school or class groupings and arrangements support the implementation of the talent development approach to developing gifted writers?
3. In what ways might differentiated instruction play a role in the day-to-day implementation of the talent development approach to language arts gifted education?
4. How might we clarify or operationalize the descriptors of engaging, interesting, and challenging as important characteristics of writing tasks in the curriculum?

References

Allison, P. (2009). Be a blogger: Social networking in the classroom. In A. Herrington, K. Hodgson, & C. Moran (Eds.), *Teaching the new writing: Technology, change, and assessment in the 21st-century classroom* (pp. 75–91). New York, NY: Teachers College Press.

Atwood, M. (2003). A path taken, with all the great certainty of youth. In J. Smiley, *Writers on writing* (Vol. II, pp. 9–12). New York, NY: Times Books.

Bandura, A. (1986). *Social foundations of thought and action: A social cognitive theory.* Englewood Cliffs, NJ: Prentice Hall.

Bloom, B. S. (Ed.). (1985a). *Developing talent in young people.* New York, NY: Ballantine Books.

Bloom, B. S. (1985b). Generalizations about talent development. In B. S. Bloom (Ed.), *Developing talent in young people* (pp. 507–549). New York, NY: Ballantine Books.

Boscolo, P., & Gelati, C. (2007). Best practices in promoting motivation to write. In S. Graham, C. A. MacArthur, & J. Fitzgerald (Eds.), *Best practices in writing instruction* (pp. 202–221). New York, NY: Guilford Press.

Brandt, R. J. (1985). On talent development: A conversation with Benjamin Bloom. *Educational Leadership, 43*(1), 33–35.

Bruning, R., & Horn, C. (2000). Developing motivation to write. *Educational Psychologist, 34,* 75–85.

Bunn, M. (2011). How to read like a writer. In C. Lowe & P. Zemliansky (Eds.), *Writing spaces: Readings on writing* (Vol. 2, pp. 71–86). Anderson, NC: Parlor Press.

Clandinin, D. J., & Connelly, E. M. (2000). *Narrative inquiry: Experience in story and qualitative research.* San Francisco, CA: Jossey-Bass.

Coleman, L. J., & Cross, T. L. (2005). *Being gifted in school: An introduction to development, guidance, and teaching* (2nd ed.). Waco, TX: Prufrock Press.

Coleman, L. J., & Guo, A. (2013). Exploring children's passion for learning in six domains. *Journal for the Education of the Gifted, 36,* 155–175. doi:10.1177/0162353213480432

Csikszentmihalyi, M. (1990). Literacy and intrinsic motivation. *Daedalus, 119,* 115–140.

Czarniawska, B. (1997). *Narrating the organization: Dramas of institutional identity.* Chicago, IL: University of Chicago Press.

Dai, D. Y., & Chen F. (2014). *Paradigms of gifted education: A guide to theory-based, practice-focused research.* Waco, TX: Prufrock Press.

Dai, D. Y., & Renzulli, J. S. (2008). Snowflakes, living systems, and the mystery of giftedness. *Gifted Child Quarterly, 52,* 114–130.

Edmonds, A. L., & Noel, K. (2003). The child writer prodigy: An exceptional case among exceptional cases. *Roeper Review, 25,* 185–194.

Gagné, F. (2003). Transforming gifts into talents: The DMGT as a developmental theory. In N. Colangelo & G. A. Davis (Eds.), *Handbook of gifted education* (3rd ed., pp. 60–74). Boston, MA: Allyn & Bacon.

Garrett, L., & Moltzen, R. (2011). Writing because I want to, not because I have to: Young gifted writers' perspectives on the factors that matter in developing expertise. *English Teaching: Practice and Critique, 10*(1), 165–180.

Graham, S., MacArthur, C. A., & Fitzgerald, J. (2007). Introduction: Best practices in writing instruction now. In S. Graham, C. A. MacArthur, & J. Fitzgerald (Eds.), *Best practices in writing instruction* (pp. 1–9). New York, NY: Guilford Press.

Graham, S., & Perin, D. (2007). *Writing next: Effective strategies to improve writing of adolescents in middle and high school.* A report to Carnegie Corporation of New York. Washington, DC: Alliance for Excellent Education.

Kaufman, S. B., & Kaufman, J. C. (Eds.). (2009). *The psychology of creative writing.* New York, NY: Cambridge University Press.

Marland, S. P., Jr. (1972). *Education of the gifted and talented: Report to the Congress of the United States by the U.S. Commissioner of Education and back-*

ground papers submitted to the U.S. Office of Education, 2 vols. Washington, DC: U.S. Government Printing Office. (Government Documents, Y4.L 11/2: G36)

Olthouse, J. M. (2012). Talented young writers' relationships with writing. *Journal for the Education of the Gifted, 35,* 66–80. doi:10.1177/01623532 11432039

Olthouse, J. M. (2013). MFA writer's relationships with writing. *Journal of Advanced Academics, 24,* 259–274.

Olthouse, J. M. (2014). Gifted children's relationships with writing. *Journal for the Education of the Gifted, 37,* 171–188.

Piirto, J. (1989). Does writing prodigy exist? *Creativity Research Journal, 2,* 134–135.

Piirto, J. (1992). Does writing prodigy exist? How to identify and nurture children with extraordinary writing talent. In J. Piirto (Ed.), *Talent development proceedings from the 1991 Henry B. and Jocelyn Wallace national research symposium on talent development* (pp. 387–388). San Francisco, CA: Trillium Press.

Piirto, J. (1998). Themes in the lives of successful contemporary U.S. women creative writers. *Roeper Review, 21*(1), 60–70.

Piirto, J. (1999). *Talented children and adults: Their development and education* (2nd ed.). Upper Saddle River, NJ: Merrill.

Piirto, J. (2002). *My teeming brain: Understanding creative writers.* Cresskill, NJ: Hampton Press.

Potter, E. F., McCormick, C. B., & Busching, B. A. (2001). Academic and life goals: Insights from adolescent writers. *High School Journal, 85,* 45–56.

Renzulli, J. S. (1978). What makes giftedness? Re-examining a definition. *Phi Delta Kappan, 60,* 180–184, 261.

Silva, P. J. (2007). *How to write a lot: A practical guide to productive academic writing.* Washington, DC: American Psychological Association.

Simic, C. (2006). The art of poetry no. 92: Interview with James Tate. *The Paris Review, 177,* 43–76.

Subotnik, R. F., Olszewski-Kubilius, P., & Worrell, F. C. (2011). Rethinking giftedness and gifted education: A proposed direction forward based on psychological science. *Psychological Science in the Public Interest, 12,* 3–54. doi:10.1177/1529100611418056

Whitehead, A. N. (1929). *The aims of education.* New York, NY: The Free Press.

CHAPTER 15

DIFFERENTIATING MATHEMATICS STANDARDS FOR GIFTED STUDENTS

SUSAN K. JOHNSEN AND GAIL R. RYSER

In 2010, the National Governors Association (NGA) and the Council of Chief State School Officers (CCSSO) released the Common Core State Standards in Mathematics (CCSSM; NGA & CCSSO, 2010a, 2010b). Designed by teachers, administrators, and content experts, the CCSSM are intended to incorporate knowledge and skills required for the 21st century and prepare K–12 students for college and the workplace.

Standards development at the national level was stimulated by the inconsistencies across state standards and the United States' poor performance on international assessments such as the Program for International Student Assessment (PISA). In fact, in PISA's (2014) most recent report, only 9% of 15-year-old students in the United States scored at proficiency, which was lower than the average for all countries. For these reasons, the new standards stress rigor, depth, clarity, and coherence and draw from national and international studies. To date, 43 states, the District of Columbia, four territories, and the Department of Defense Education Activity have adopted the CCSSM (Common Core State Standards Initiative [CCSSI], n.d.b).

Some educators would suggest that these standards are already at such a high level that they do not need to be differentiated for most learners who are

DOI: 10.4324/9781003236696-18

advanced or gifted in mathematics. Although the standards are strong, math educators stress that modifications are necessary for students who might accelerate through the standards before the end of high school (NGA & CCSSO, 2010b), as well as students who may need more enrichment and open-ended opportunities (Johnsen & Sheffield, 2013). The major purpose of this chapter is to describe how the CCSSM might be differentiated for students who are gifted and advanced in mathematics.

The CCSM Standards

According to the Common Core State Standards Initiative (n.d.a), the CCSSM differ from previous standards in three key ways: focus, coherence, and rigor. Teachers are asked to *focus* on fewer topics so that students deepen their knowledge and gain a strong foundation. The standards are also organized into *coherent* progressions from grade to grade and across topics. The third key word—*rigor*—does not refer to "making math harder" but to fostering students' acquisition of a solid understanding of concepts, a high degree of procedural skill and fluency, and important problem-solving skills that can be applied inside and outside the classroom. To address these key shifts in mathematics education, two sets of standards have been developed: Standards for Mathematical Content (CCSSM-C) and Standards for Mathematical Practice (CCSSM-P).

Standards for Mathematical Content

The CCSSM-C are organized by grade and secondary levels, standards, clusters, and domains (NGA & CCSSO, 2010a). Standards define what students should understand and be able to do at specific levels, clusters summarize groups of related standards, and domains are larger groups of related standards. For example, at the fourth-grade level, within the *domain* of Number and Operations—Fractions (4.NF), the student is expected to "Extend understanding of fraction equivalence and ordering" (*cluster heading*) by "explaining why a fraction a/b is equivalent to a fraction $(n \times a)/(n \times b)$ by using visual fraction models" and by "comparing two fractions with different numerators and different denominators" (*standards*; NGA & CCSSO, 2010a, p. 30).

The standards, clusters, and domains are related to one another at different grade levels and at the same grade level, forming learning progressions and interconnections across concepts (Johnsen, Ryser, & Assouline, 2014). For example, with fractions, students develop an "understanding of fraction equivalence, addition and subtraction of fractions with like denominators, and multiplication of fractions by whole numbers" (NGA & CCSSO, 2010a, p. 27) at the elementary level; "divide fractions by fractions" (p. 41), "use negative fractions to form rational numbers" (p. 58), and then "augment rational numbers with irrational numbers to form real numbers" (p. 58) at the middle school level; and then "augment real numbers by imaginary numbers to form complex numbers" at the high school level (p. 58). Similarly, at the fourth-grade level, fractions are not only within the domain of Number and Operations—Fractions ("extend understanding of fraction equivalence and ordering," "build fractions from unit fractions," and "understand decimal notation for fractions"; NGA & CCSSO, 2010a, pp. 30–31) but also within the domain of Measurement and Data ("Use the four operations to solve word problems involving distances, intervals of time, liquid volumes, masses of objects, and money, including problems involving simple fractions or decimals . . ."; NGA & CCSSO, 2010a, p. 31). Educators need to be aware of these vertical and lateral alignments when teaching the CCSSM-C. The vertical alignments are presented in Table 15.1.

Standards for Mathematical Practice

The Standards for Mathematical Practice define the thinking skills that educators need to develop in their students (NGA & CCSSO, 2010a). These eight practice standards are for all students in kindergarten through high school:

1. Make sense of problems and persevere in solving them.
2. Reason abstractly and quantitatively.
3. Construct viable arguments and critique the reasoning of others.
4. Model with mathematics.
5. Use appropriate tools strategically.
6. Attend to precision.
7. Look for and make use of structure.
8. Look for and express regularity in repeated reasoning.

A ninth standard was proposed by Sheffield (2006) to develop more innovative and creative mathematicians: *Solve problems in novel ways and pose new*

TABLE 15.1

Vertical Alignment of Mathematical Domains

K	1	2	3	4	5	6	7	8	High School
Counting and Cardinality									
	Number and Operations in Base Ten					Ratios and Proportional Relationships			Number and Quantity
			Number and Quantity			The Number System			
Operations and Algebraic Thinking						Expressions and Equations			Algebra
								Functions	
Geometry									
Measurement and Data						Statistics and Probability			

mathematical questions of interest to investigate. Students need to build on a deep understanding of mathematics in posing new mathematical questions, adding new ideas for solving problems, and creating innovative solutions (Johnsen & Sheffield, 2013). To encourage this type of creative thinking, teachers need to encourage and support risk taking, ask open-ended questions that are of interest to investigate, and focus on fluency, flexibility, originality, elaboration or elegance, generalizations, and extensions (Chapin, O'Connor, & Anderson, 2009; Sheffield, 2000). Moreover, they need to develop students' enjoyment, interest, and passion by engaging them in math circles, clubs, competitions, online games and activities, challenging puzzles and problems, research opportunities, mentors, and afterschool math programs where they interact with mathematicians and others with similar interests and abilities. In this way, positive attitudes toward mathematics develop along with mathematical abilities (Gavin & Sheffield, 2010).

The Standards of Mathematical Practice might be developed in gifted and advanced students through the problem-solving process described below (Johnsen & Sheffield, 2013). First, pose questions that can be answered with data. Then, have the students design and use a research plan to collect relevant data. Following the collection of data, ask the students to analyze the data using methods that relate to the questions. Finally, have them interpret the results, summarize conclusions, and pose future questions for further research.

All of these practices have longstanding importance in mathematics education. The National Council of Teachers of Mathematics included the following process standards in their principles and standards for school mathematics: problem solving, reasoning and proof, communication, connections, and representation (NCTM, n.d.a). Moreover, the National Research Council (2001) recommended the following strands of mathematical proficiency: adaptive reasoning, strategic competence, conceptual understanding, procedural fluency, and productive disposition. They are important to mathematical educators who will not only want to develop these proficiencies in their students, but also model them.

Differentiating the CCSSM Standards

Although gifted educators will use the CCSM and other core curriculum that is aligned with local, state, and national standards, they will still need to differentiate for gifted and advanced students because of individual variations in experiences, abilities, and responsiveness to learning activities. No single scope and sequence or learning progression is appropriate for every student. Therefore, they will need to adapt and modify curriculum structures (i.e., goals, outcomes, and activities) to address each student's characteristics for optimal learning (Johnsen et al., 2014). A variety of ways have been described to differentiate the CCSSM standards for students who are gifted and advanced in mathematics (Johnsen, 2013; Johnsen et al., 2014; Johnsen & Sheffield, 2013). Some of these strategies include:

1. *Accelerating standards and clusters of standards across grade levels and across courses* (Colangelo, Assouline, & Gross, 2004). By studying the vertical alignment of clusters and individual standards, teachers can identify concepts that are above level. They can include these above-level concepts on pre- and ongoing assessments to raise the ceiling, which allows them to determine which students are ready for more advanced work (Assouline & Lupkowski-Shoplik, 2011). Teachers can then integrate these more advanced concepts into math problems or allow students to do alternative problems using compacting or other strategies. For example, a third-grade student who understands fractions as numbers (3.NF) might be solving problems using fractions with different denominators and numerators (grade 4 standard). In some cases where the students may be learning concepts that are two or more grade levels beyond the typical learner, decision makers may want to consider other acceleration options such as single subject, grade skipping, or early entrance into secondary or higher education courses. At the high school level, four pathways are described in CCSSM Appendix A (NGA & CCSSO, 2010b). The compacted version of the more traditional pathway allows students to complete the content of the seventh- and eighth-grade course in the seventh grade and the high school algebra course (Algebra I) in the eighth grade so that they can reach calculus or other college-level courses by their junior or senior year. Similarly, the compacted integrated pathway combines the seventh- and eighth-grade math courses into a single compacted course in the seventh grade so that students are able to take Mathematics I at the eighth-grade level (see Appendix A of the CCSSM for an overview of each pathway and other acceleration options at the secondary level). It should be noted that students who take advanced courses in high school, such as precalculus and calculus, tend to do better in the STEM fields in college than those who do not (Colangelo et al., 2004).

2. *Varying the pace within learning activities* (Johnsen, 2015). In addition to acceleration, the teacher needs to attend to the rate at which material is taught to gifted and advanced learners. Because they are often capable of reaching mastery more quickly than typical learners, ongoing assessment needs to be used to determine (a) the number of examples used for a particular concept, (b) the depth and complexity of the concepts, (c) the number of concepts presented in a single lesson, and (d) areas of interest for investigations. Students with similar rates of learning might also be grouped homogeneously with instruction matched to their abilities. Full-time ability grouping produces substantial academic gains for gifted students and encourages critical thinking and creativity (Kulik, 2004; Rogers, 2007). Students need to advance at an appropriate pace so that they are challenged and not bored with the material.

3. *Building complex problems* (Saul, Assouline, & Sheffield, 2010). Teachers can develop more complex problems by including abstract concepts, more than one operation, more variables to study, more higher order skills, multiple resources, irrelevant information, and novel situations (Chamberlin, 2010). With ambiguous, multifaceted problems, students are able to think more deeply about both the process and possible solutions and work on problems for longer periods of time. For example, advanced students may be presented with a problem such as building an aquarium within budget constraints. By including more variables (variety of equipment, variety of fish, and different size tanks), students are given the opportunity to think critically while developing creative solutions (e.g., NCTM, n.d.c).

4. *Encouraging creativity by developing open-ended problems* (Sheffield, 2006). To enhance creativity, the teacher might want to develop open-ended problems that mirror real-world professional work and offer opportunities for students to pose their own questions and find new problems. Students might use multiple ways of solving problems, representing their data, and creating their own questions. Advanced learners need to become proficient in the skills of becoming a creator or innovator. Sheffield (2000) identified some of these skills as fluency, flexibility, originality, elaboration or elegance, generalizing, and extending. Grade-level ceilings should not be imposed during the creative process. Rather, the teacher should consider the student's atypical development and include more advanced curriculum.

5. *Adding depth* (Kaplan, 2009). In adding depth, the teacher might use specialized mathematical vocabulary, ask students to find more details,

look for trends and patterns across problems, or identify a new mathematical rule. For example, students might develop a rule that explains how a pattern grows (e.g., bowling pin patterns, T patterns, Pascal's triangle) or collect data about population demographics such as age, socioeconomic status, and ethnicity to predict future trends.

6. *Making connections and integrating math across domains* (Kaplan, 2009; VanTassel-Baska, 2004). Because mathematics is a tool subject, it can be naturally integrated into other domains. For example, students can summarize survey results about favorite authors' plots (math and language arts); use descriptive statistics in describing the number of calories consumed during lunch and examine their relationship to weight gain (math and health); and identify the economic effects from global warming when action or no action is taken (math, science, economics).

7. *Identifying themes or concepts within and across domains* (VanTassel-Baska, 2004). Teachers might develop learning activities and units of study around broader mathematical concepts or themes within and across domains. The concepts of "patterns" and "structures" can develop understanding across standards and clusters of standards within the CCSM and also connect to other core disciplines. For example, in the third grade, students are asked to look for "patterns in arithmetic" (NGA & CCSSO, 2010a, p. 22), "generate and analyze patterns" at the fourth-grade level (NGA & CCSSO, 2010a, p. 28), and "investigate patterns of association in bivariate data" at the eighth-grade level (NGA & CCSSO, 2010a, p. 53). "Patterns" can then be connected to science (e.g., patterns in tidal waves), to English (patterns when writing stories), to the arts (patterns when composing music), to social studies (patterns in population growth), and so on.

8. *Using questioning to encourage higher level thinking and mathematical processes* (Johnsen & Sheffield, 2013; Sheffield, 2003). Teachers need to use deliberate questioning techniques to elevate thinking. Sheffield (2003; Johnsen & Sheffield, 2013) has provided a heuristic for innovative and creative mathematicians that might be used for asking questions related to problem solving:

» Relate: How is this problem similar to other problems you have seen? How is it different?

» Investigate: What questions might you ask about this problem?

» Evaluate: Does the answer relate to the question? Does it make sense?

>> Communicate: How might you let others know about your solution?

>> Create: What other questions do you have about the problem?

By asking questions, the teacher can guide students through solving problems by using the same processes mathematicians might use.

9. *Solving problems that relate to global issues* (Partnership for 21st Century Skills, n.d.). Many problems that relate to global issues have quantitative aspects (e.g., endangered species, climate change, population growth, military spending). Students can conduct interdisciplinary investigations and share their results with audiences within or outside their community.

10. *Engaging students in problems of interest to them* (Gavin, Casa, Adelson, Carroll, & Sheffield, 2009). Solving interesting problems encourages students' enjoyment and interest in mathematics and often leads to higher achievement gains (Gavin et al., 2009). Interest can be incorporated into learning activities by allowing students to choose their own research projects, decide on the ways they might solve problems, and/ or decide on the products or performances that represent their data.

11. *Involving students in extracurricular activities* (Barbeau & Taylor, 2009). Extracurricular activities often develop passion as well as the expertise and creativity of students who are gifted and advanced in math. Extracurricular activities might include mathematical clubs and circles, mentorships and apprenticeships, scientific research, online games and courses, Saturday and summer programs, and competitions such as the American Mathematics Competitions, International Mathematical Olympiad, or Mathcounts®. These activities provide students with opportunities to interact with other students who have talents in mathematics and other STEM fields in a stimulating environment. Mentors can stimulate students' interests and involve them deeply in the methods of the discipline.

Process and Examples for Differentiation

The following two examples are provided to show how a teacher might differentiate a learning activity for typical and advanced students in math. The fourth-grade example focuses on the domain of Number and Operations-Fractions. Although both groups receive the same initial problem, the teacher differentiates the lesson by having the advanced students use skills from the fifth-grade level (*acceleration*), consider more variables in the problem such as calories and sugar (*complexity*), examine consumption of beverages over a longer period of time (*depth*), solve problems related to the issue of obesity, and create their own table or graph. This problem also connects the domain of Number and Operations to the domain of Measurement and Data by requiring students to solve problems involving measurement (see 4.MD).

The eighth-grade example focuses on the domain of Expressions and Equations. As in the fourth-grade example, both groups receive the same initial problem. The teacher differentiates the lesson for the advanced students by including skills from Algebra (see A-CED.2; *acceleration*), adding additional variables to the initial problem (*complexity*), asking students to solve the problem in multiple ways (*creativity*), and asking higher level thinking questions (*questioning*). Suggestions for both examples are also made for possible preassessments and ongoing assessment so that each learning activity is matched to the needs of the students.

In designing these learning experiences, it's important to find a problem that is interesting to the students and is open-ended so that a variety of smaller problems might be identified and multiple solutions are possible. Some good sources for problems are the National Council for Teachers of Mathematics' "Illuminations" newsletter (see http://illuminations.nctm.org), and the Noyce Foundation's "Inside Mathematics" (see http://www.insidemathematics.org).

Subject: Math Learning Progression
Domain: Number and Operations–Fractions (Grades 3–5)

Grade 4 Problem	Both typical and advanced students collect data and compare the costs of beverages from fast-food restaurants. The typical students will share their conclusions using visual fraction models.	
Extend understanding of fraction equivalence and ordering Standard 4. NF.2.	*Advanced students also compare the calories and sugar for each of the beverages and calculate the number consumed each day for a week. They create their own table to share the results.*	
Compare two fractions with different numerators and different denominators.	**Typical Learner**	**Advanced Learner**
	Students are going to make comparisons to decide which fast-food restaurants offer the best value for beverages. Select one beverage cup from at least five fast-food restaurants and show the students how to record each cup's size and price. Next, fill one of the beverage cups with water and transfer the water to a large measuring cup. Show the students how to record the amount of water to the nearest ounce (capacity), how to calculate the price per ounce (unit price), and then have them set up a fraction illustrating the total number of ounces to the total price and a second fraction illustrating the unit price. Finally, show them how to return the water in the measuring cup back to the water pitcher for the next measurement. *continued*	Students are going to make comparisons to decide which fast-food restaurants offer the best value for beverages. Select one beverage cup from at least five fast-food restaurants and show the students how to record each cup's size and price. Next, fill one of the beverage cups with water and transfer the water to a large measuring cup. Show the students how to record the amount of water to the nearest ounce (capacity), how to calculate the price per ounce (unit price), and then have them set up a fraction illustrating the total number of ounces to the total price and a second fraction illustrating the unit price. Finally, show them how to return the water in the measuring cup back to the water pitcher for the next measurement. *continued*

Typical Learner	Advanced Learner
Give each team or pair of students a recording sheet and five cups from different fast-food restaurants. Have them record their observations. Have each team create visual fraction models to share their conclusions.	Give each team or pair of students a recording sheet and five cups from different fast-food restaurants. Have them record their observations. *When they complete their observations, give each team a list of the number of calories and sugar for each of the beverages. Have them calculate the calories and sugar for each of the beverages if two beverages were consumed each day for a week. Have them create a table to visually display their data. Have them predict what might happen if two beverages were consumed each day for a month, a year, etc.? If time permits, they might pursue further questions or pose their own questions for research (see enrichment activities below).* Have each team create visual fraction models to share their conclusions about the cost comparisons and a table to share their results about the calories and sugar consumed.

Further enrichment: Have students develop a survey for the students in the class, asking them about how many beverages they consume in a day, a week, and a month? Have them calculate the number of beverages, the total amount of liquid, calories, and sugar for the class and develop a graph to share their results.

Have students research how the sizes of fountain drinks have changed over time and graph their results; or how sugary drinks can make you fat and graph their results; or how the mayor of New York City banned oversize sodas and share the results in a class debate. |

	Typical Learners	Advanced Learners
Formative Assessment	**Preassessment:** Prior to the lesson, give a preassessment to determine students' knowledge and skills with fractions (include problems with like and unlike denominators that require students to make comparisons using >, =, and <). **Ongoing assessment:** Were the students able to measure accurately? Did they complete the record form with the correct information? Were they able to make conclusions that related to the data? Were they able to organize their information using visual fraction models?	**Preassessment:** Prior to the lesson, give a preassessment to determine students' knowledge and skills with fractions (include problems with like and unlike denominators that require students to make comparisons using >, =, and <). **Ongoing assessment:** In addition to the ongoing questions for the typical student, were the students able to create a table that included calories and sugar? Did the table display their data accurately? Did they pose additional questions for research? Were the questions at a higher level of thinking and related to the problem?
Implementation Materials needed: 1. Drinking cups from fast-food restaurants with the price of the drink marked on the outside of the cup 2. Measuring cups (quart size) 3. Water pitcher (quart size) 4. Recording sheets 5. Menus from fast-food restaurants	Based on your preassessment, put the students into homogeneous groups or in pairs. Those who already have an understanding of comparing fractions with unlike denominators and numerators would be in the advanced group. Those who do not understand how to compare fractions would be in the typical group. Tell the entire class that they will be making comparisons about fast-food beverages. Model how to record data on the chart, then have the students work independently. As the advanced students complete their data chart, provide them with the information regarding the calories and sugar for each beverage. While the advanced learners continue their work, bring the typical learners together to share their results orally. Have them work together in planning their visual fraction models. When all are finished, have the students share their results and conclusions.	

Subject: Math Learning Progression
Domain: Expressions and Equations (Grades 6–8)

Grade 8 Problem	Both typical and advanced students set up a table illustrating a proportional relationship, graph the relationship in one quadrant, write an equation of the relationship, and share the results in a poster.
Understand the connections between proportional relationships, lines, and linear equations. **Standard 8EE.5.** Graph proportional relationships, interpreting the unit rate as the slope of the graph. Compare two different proportional relationships represented in different ways.	*Advanced students also graph and write the equation of a second relationship. They next solve an advanced problem using both the graphical representation and the two equations and share the results in a poster.*

	Typical Learner	Advanced Learner
	Students are going to solve a problem involving a person who walks at a steady rate. Tell the students that the average grade 8 student can walk 90 feet in 30 seconds. Show them how to set up a table with x = time in seconds and y = distance in feet. As a group, fill in 30 under the x variable and 90 under the y variable. Now have the teams complete four additional ordered pairs on their own. When finished, show students how to graph *continued*	Students are going to solve a problem involving a person who walks at a steady rate. Tell the students that the average grade 8 student can walk 90 feet in 30 seconds. Show them how to set up a table with x = time in seconds and y = distance in feet. As a group, fill in 30 under the x variable and 90 under the y variable. Now have the teams complete four additional ordered pairs on their own. When finished, ask students to graph the *continued*

Typical Learner	Advanced Learner
the results and then have them write the equation of the relationship on their own. Students will create a poster of their results. When they have completed their posters review them with the students by asking the following questions: Did you include any negatives? Why or why not? If the student could walk faster or slower how would the graph change? What is the slope of the line? How would you use the graph to find the distance a student could walk in a given amount of time? How would you use the equation to find the distance a student could walk in a given amount of time?	results and then have them write the equation of the relationship. *Students in the advanced group will solve the following additional problem: Jared and Alisha are in classrooms on opposite ends of the school hallway. The classrooms are 60 feet apart. Jared walks 90 feet in 30 seconds while Alisha walks at a rate of 2 feet per second. If the students walk toward each other at a constant rate, how far from Jared's classroom will they be when they meet? Write the equation for Alisha (Hint: We are calculating the distance from Jared's classroom so Alisha's distance will decrease as time passes and the slope will be negative. The equation is $y=60-2x$). Graph Alisha's relationship on the same graph as for Jared. Use the graph and the equation to figure out the solution to the problem.* Students will create a poster of their results. When they have completed their posters review them with the students by asking the following questions: *Why was the slope for Alisha negative? If Jared and Alisha were traveling at the same rate, how would the slopes of their lines compare? Why did Alisha's graph and equation have the y-intercept of (0, 60)? Was it easier to figure out the answer to this problem from the graphs or the equations?*

	Typical Learner	Advanced Learner
Formative Assessment	**Preassessment:** Prior to the lesson, give a preassessment to determine students' knowledge and skills with proportions and graphing linear or proportional relationships. Include questions about the slope. **Ongoing assessment:** Were the students able to find ordered pairs that made sense? Did they complete the table with the correct information? Were they able to make the connection that the slope was the unit rate of speed? Were they able to write an equation for the relationship? Were they able to organize their information using a poster?	**Preassessment:** Prior to the lesson, give a preassessment to determine students' knowledge and skills with proportions and graphing linear or proportional relationships. Include questions about the slope. **Ongoing assessment:** In addition to the ongoing questions for the typical student, were the students able to create the graph for Alisha? Were the students able to answer the problem using both the graphical representation and the equations?
Implementation Materials needed: 1. Graph paper 2. Colored pencils 3. Posters 4. Recording sheets	Based on your preassessment, put the students into homogeneous groups or in pairs. Those who already have an understanding of how to graph a linear or proportional relationship and how to find the slope of the line would be in the advanced group. Those who do not understand how to graph a linear or proportional relationship and/or how to find the slope of the line would be in the typical group. Tell the entire class that they will be graphing proportional relationships. Model how to begin a table with ordered pairs, then have the students work independently to complete the table. Model how to graph the proportional relationship for the typical learners by plotting two of the ordered pairs, then have the students work independently to complete the graph. As the advanced students complete their first graph and equation, provide them with the problem. While the advanced learners continue their work, bring the typical learners together to share their results orally. Have them work together in planning their posters. When all are finished, have the students share their results and conclusions.	

Implications for Research

Areas for future research have been suggested by mathematics educators, professional associations, and professionals in the field of gifted education (Johnsen & Sheffield, 2013; NCTM, n.d.b; NGA & CCSSO, 2010a). The suggestions relate to the content of the standards and their sequence, curriculum, assessments, acceleration, and the school culture.

Sequence of standards. More research is needed about the grade placement of standards and *specific learning progressions* (NCTM, n.d.b). The NGA and CCSSO (2010a) report that the learning progressions in the CCSSM are based on state and international comparisons, but not necessarily on research.

Interventions and curricular effects. Research is needed not only to identify important sequences of knowledge and skills, but also learning trajectories—how does each student's progression change in response to interventions? What *interventions* are key in changing and accelerating the learning trajectories of gifted and advanced students? Are they similar to typically developing students? In addition, what curriculum seems to be effective with gifted and advanced students that might influence their trajectories in mathematics? How does the integration of mathematics in other domains affect students' achievement in math? Some curriculum programs have yielded promising results. For example, Project M^3: Mentoring Mathematical Minds, which incorporates acceleration and the mathematical practice standards, has shown significant increases in mathematical concept acquisition at the elementary level (Gavin et al., 2009; Gavin et al., 2007). What has happened to these students as they have progressed through secondary school? What curricula and interventions are most effective with secondary students?

Assessments. Another area for future research is how *assessments* influence responses to the standards, which include the state, the school district, and individual teachers (Johnsen & Sheffield, 2013). Because educators are more likely to teach content related to state and national tests, how might these assessments be designed to focus on higher level thinking skills? How might nontraditional forms of assessments such as performance and product assessments, which tend to measure more complex problem solving, be designed so they meet psychometrically sound criteria? Moreover, what types of informal, ongoing assessments yield results that are useful in designing and implementing learning activities that meet each student's strengths and weaknesses?

Acceleration. Many research-based articles have shown the benefits of *acceleration* both academically and affectively (Colangelo et al., 2004; Lee,

Olszewski-Kubilius, & Peternel, 2010; Neihart, 2007; Steenbergen-Hu & Moon, 2010). More students are taking advanced classes in middle and high school. Although the number of students who are successfully passing Advanced Placement exams in calculus has increased, those who take the second or third course in calculus has declined (Bressoud, 2009). What are the factors that contribute to this decline in course taking? Researchers suggest that when students with potential in mathematics participate in accelerated classes that are taught by experienced teachers who are aware of their needs, they are more likely to take rigorous college courses, complete advanced degrees, and feel academically challenged and socially accepted (Colangelo et al., 2004; Gross, 2006; Kolitch & Brody, 1992; Swiatek, 1993). Therefore, what are the characteristics of teachers who develop this interest and passion for mathematics? How might we recruit these teachers so that they encourage students to continue in advanced math courses and enter the STEM fields in college?

School culture. In spite of this rich research evidence, schools, parents, and teachers have not accepted the idea of acceleration. What are the factors that tend to contribute to this rejection of research-based practices in schools? What system practices encourage and support the development of math talent? What are the most effective classroom practices that support acceleration? How might a teacher manage multiple strategies in meeting the diverse needs of students in the classroom?

Conclusion

The new CCSSM hold great promise for providing services to gifted and advanced students in mathematics. They provide guidance for educators in organizing the major concepts and skills within and across grade levels and in defining the thinking skills that need to be developed in students. However, they still need to be differentiated for most learners who are advanced or gifted in mathematics.

This chapter provided specific examples and a variety of ways that the standards might be differentiated through acceleration, pacing, depth, complexity, creativity, interdisciplinary connections, major concepts and themes, higher level questioning, interest, and extracurricular activities. Although all of these strategies are recommended in the literature, more research is needed to determine which strategies are most effective in developing the next generation of STEM professionals.

Discussion Questions

1. When a school tightly aligns its curriculum to the school year—pacing topics week by week, how might a teacher differentiate for gifted and advanced students?
2. In what ways might assessments be harmful and helpful in designing differentiated math lessons for gifted and advanced students? Consider pre-assessments, ongoing or interim assessments, school-district benchmark assessments, and state-required tests.
3. If you only had one day of professional learning to develop teachers' abilities to differentiate in mathematics, what topics would you include?
4. Some math educators believe that acceleration should be used sparingly, if at all. What are your thoughts about acceleration and enrichment? What do you support and why?
5. If you were planning the ideal program for gifted and advanced learners in mathematics, what components should be included and why?

References

Assouline, S. G., & Lupkowski-Shoplik, A. E. (2011). *Developing math talent: A comprehensive guide to math education for gifted students in elementary and middle school* (2nd ed.). Waco, TX: Prufrock Press.

Barbeau, E., & Taylor, P. J. (Eds.). (2009). *Challenging mathematics in and beyond the classroom: The 16th ICMI study*. New York, NY: Springer.

Bressoud, D. M. (2009). Is the sky still falling? *Notices of the AMS, 56*, 20–25.

Chamberlin, S. (2010). Mathematical problems that optimize learning for academically advanced students in grades K–6. *Journal for Advanced Academics, 2*, 52–76.

Chapin, S. H., O'Connor, C., & Anderson, N. C. (2009). *Classroom discussions: Using math talk to help students learn*. Sausalito, CA: Math Solutions.

Colangelo, N., Assouline, S. G., & Gross, M. U. M. (Eds.). (2004). *A nation deceived: How schools hold back America's brightest students* (Vol. 2). Iowa City: University of Iowa, The Connie Belin and Jacqueline N. Blank International Center for Gifted Education and Talent Development.

Common Core State Standards Initiative. (n.d.a.). *Key shifts in mathematics.* Retrieved from http://www.corestandards.org/other-resources/key-shifts-in-mathematics

Common Core State Standards Initiative. (n.d.b.). *Standards in your state.* Retrieved from http://www.corestandards.org/standards-in-your-state

Gavin, M. K., Casa, T. M., Adelson, J. L., Carroll, S. R., & Sheffield, L. J. (2009). The impact of advanced curriculum on the achievement of mathematically promising elementary students. *Gifted Child Quarterly, 53*, 188–202.

Gavin, M. K., Casa, T. M., Adelson, J. L., Carroll, S. R., Sheffield, L. J., & Spinelli, A. M. (2007). Project M^3: Mentoring Mathematical Minds—A research-based curriculum for talented elementary students. *Journal of Advanced Academics, 18*, 566–585.

Gavin, M. K., & Sheffield, L. J. (2010). Using curriculum to develop mathematical promise in the middle grades. In M. Saul, S. Assouline, & L. J. Sheffield (Eds.), *The peak in the middle: Developing mathematically gifted students in the middle grades* (pp. 51–76). Reston, VA: National Council of Teachers of Mathematics.

Gross, M. U. M. (2006). Exceptionally gifted children: Long-term outcomes of academic acceleration and nonacceleration. *Journal for the Education of the Gifted, 29*, 404–429.

Johnsen, S. K. (2013). The Common Core State Standards: Where do gifted and advanced learners fit? *Parenting for High Potential, 3*(1), 4–7.

Johnsen, S. K. (2015). Gifted education and programming standards. In F. A. Karnes & S. M. Bean (Eds.), *Methods and materials for teaching the gifted* (4th ed., pp. 3–41). Waco, TX: Prufrock Press.

Johnsen, S. K., Ryser, G. R., Assouline, S. (2014). *A teacher's guide to using the Common Core State Standards with mathematically gifted and advanced learners.* Waco, TX: Prufrock Press.

Johnsen, S. K., & Sheffield, L. J. (Eds.). (2013). *Using the Common Core State Standards for mathematics with gifted and advanced learners.* Waco, TX: Prufrock Press.

Kaplan, S. N. (2009). Layering differentiated curricula for the gifted and talented. In F. A. Karnes & S. M. Bean (Eds.), *Methods and materials for teaching the gifted* (3rd ed., pp. 107–135). Waco, TX: Prufrock Press.

Kolitch, E. R., & Brody, L. E. (1992). Mathematics acceleration of highly talented students: An evaluation. *Gifted Child Quarterly, 36*, 78–86.

Kulik, J. A. (2004). Meta-analysis studies of acceleration. In N. Colangelo, S. G. Assouline, M. U. M. Gross (Eds.), *A nation deceived: How schools hold back America's brightest students* (Vol. II, pp. 13–22). Iowa City: University of Iowa, The Connie Belin and Jacqueline N. Blank International Center for Gifted Education and Talent Development.

Lee, S. Y., Olszewski-Kubilius, P., & Peternel, G. (2010). The efficacy of academic acceleration for gifted minority students. *Gifted Child Quarterly, 54*, 189–208. doi:10.1177/0016986210369256

National Council of Teachers of Mathematics. (n.d.a). *Process standards*. Retrieved from http://www.org/standards/content.aspx?id=322

National Council of Teachers of Mathematics. (n.d.b). *Research clips and briefs*. Retrieved from http://www.nctm.org/clipsandbriefs.aspx

National Council of Teachers of Mathematics. (n.d.c). *Welcome to the aquarium: Planning a classroom aquarium to practice decimal operations*. Retrieved from http://illuminations.nctm.org/Lesson.aspx?id=3649

National Governors Association Center for Best Practices, & Council of Chief State School Officers. (2010a). *Common Core State Standards for mathematics*. Washington, DC: Authors. Retrieved from http://www. corestandards.org/the-standards.

National Governors Association Center for Best Practices, & Council of Chief State School Officers. (2010b). *Appendix A. Common Core State Standards for mathematics*. Washington DC: Authors. Retrieved from http://www. corestandards.org/the-standards

National Research Council. (2001). *Adding + it up: Helping children learn mathematics*. Washington, DC: National Academy Press.

Neihart, M. (2007). The socioaffective impact of acceleration and ability grouping: Recommendations for best practice. *Gifted Child Quarterly, 51*, 330–341. doi:10.1177/0016986207306319

Partnership for 21st Century Skills. (n.d.). *Framework for 21st century learning*. Retrieved from http://www.p21.org/overview

Program for International Assessment. (2014). *Selected findings from PISA 2012*. Washington, DC: National Center for Education Statistics. Retrieved from http://nces.ed.gov/surveys/pisa/pisa2012/pisa2012highlights_1. asp

Rogers, K. B. (2007). Lessons learned about educating the gifted and talented: A synthesis of the research on educational practice. *Gifted Child Quarterly, 51*, 382–396.

Saul, M., Assouline, S. G., & Sheffield, L. J. (Eds.). (2010). *The peak in the middle: Developing mathematically gifted students in the middle grades.* Reston, VA: National Council of Teachers of Mathematics.

Sheffield, L. J. (2000). Creating and developing promising young mathematicians. *Teaching Children Mathematics, 6,* 416–419, 426.

Sheffield, L. J. (2003). *Extending the challenge in mathematics: Developing mathematical promise in K–8 students.* Thousand Oaks, CA: Corwin Press.

Sheffield, L. J. (2006). Developing mathematical promise and creativity. *Journal of the Korea Society of Mathematical Education Series D: Research in Mathematical Education, 10,* 1–11.

Steenbergen-Hu, S., & Moon, S. M. (2010). The effects of acceleration on high-ability learners: A meta-analysis. *Gifted Child Quarterly, 55,* 39–53. doi:10.1177/0016986210383155

Swiatek, M. A. (1993). A decade of longitudinal research on academic acceleration through the Study of Mathematically Precocious Youth. *Roeper Review, 15,* 120–123.

VanTassel-Baska, J. (Ed.). (2004). *Curriculum for gifted and talented students.* Thousand Oaks, CA: Corwin Press.

CHAPTER 16

DEVELOPING MATHEMATICAL TALENT
A PRACTICAL, RESEARCH-SUPPORTED APPROACH

KAREN E. RAMBO-HERNANDEZ

When I was a classroom teacher, I worked with students whom I affectionately termed the hyper-gifted. Travis and Jared were two of those students. Travis's small, sixth-grade frame entered my classroom with more energy than should ever be legally bottled into one body. Jared came in my classroom so quietly that he was barely noticeable, but his wit was sharper than my brand new No. 2 pencils. Both boys were already accelerated in mathematics by 2 and 3 years respectively. In so many ways, they both epitomized stereotypical awkward middle school boys on very different ends of the spectrum, but one thing separated them from most of their peers. They both possessed tremendous raw mathematical talent. During instruction, Travis rarely needed to take notes but would instead stand (or more frequently jump) at the back of my classroom while simultaneously responding to my questions and asking insightful ones of his own. Jared, on the other hand, was often deep in thought and would typically only ask questions one on one. Travis, Jared, and I shared a common love—mathematics—and we immediately bonded.

As we continued to work together along with several other students who also loved mathematics, I watched the love of mathematics strengthen. They were also part of a team of students that I coached for Mathcounts®. I worked

DOI: 10.4324/9781003236696-19

with these students every day during a shortened class period. We prepared for competitions and worked through numerous rich problems that required mathematics well beyond typical middle school curriculum (e.g., combinatorics, probability theory). This group began to be quite proud of their love and skill in mathematics and started calling each other "nerds" as a compliment. Jared was so proud of his new nerd status that he only wore mathematics competition shirts to school. Being a nerd in my classroom was respected and encouraged. This group of students consistently performed well in local and state Mathcounts® competitions. At least one student from this group was among the top 10 individuals in the state every year that we competed, and our team was also consistently among the top 10 teams in the state. They trained with the same rigor as any state-ranking athletic teams, so much so that they called themselves "mathletes." They organized out-of-school practice sessions and stayed late after school to practice with me. Travis's parents once told me that they had to check on him after he went to bed because he would frequently be working problems under his comforter by flashlight.

Travis and Jared have both gone on to success in mathematics, although their paths looked quite different. Travis took a more traditional route. He finished high school in his hometown, participated in engineering competitions (at one point he worked on a team of high school students to build an solar-powered car that could drive more than 1,000 miles without needing to be serviced), and eventually went to college to major in engineering on a partial scholarship that he earned while competing in Mathcounts® in middle school. Jared was further accelerated and completed his last 2 years of high school while concurrently completing his first 2 years of college. He went on to graduate college with a degree in mathematics. He chose to stay an extra year in his undergraduate program to earn a double major, and, ironically, so he could be at least one year older than the freshman undergraduate students whom he would teach while pursuing his Ph.D. in mathematics. Both young men love mathematics. Both young men are incredibly hard working and successful. And both of them point to their time in middle school as turning points in their respective journeys.

Even though I taught for several years before I met Travis and Jared, had more training than most in working with gifted students, and had the mathematical prowess to challenge them and their classmates, I did not know exactly what to do to develop this latent talent. Now I know much more about what the research says works and how theory suggests that practitioners encourage talent. In this chapter, I will combine what I have since gleaned from research and theory regarding how to develop mathematical talent and discuss how that aligns with my classroom teaching experience working with emerging mathematicians. It is my hope that this chapter is both practically and intellectually informative and motivating for those who wish to develop mathematical talent in students.

The Purpose

The purpose of this chapter is to present options to develop mathematical talent. As is constantly repeated in both research and media, more students need to pursue science, technology, engineering, and mathematics (STEM) fields to fill gaping holes in the workforce. A recent study found that while some of these STEM areas are seeing a slight uptick in the number of students pursuing degrees, the number of the most able students pursuing STEM undergraduate degrees has actually fallen (Lowell, Salzman, Bernstein, & Henderson, 2009). Talented mathematics students are failing to pursue STEM degrees at the rate necessary to keep up with the demand (Lowell et al., 2009). For this reason, those who work with talented students need to consider developing mathematical talent differently.

Recently, a refocusing of gifted education surfaced. Rather than expending energy on identifying those students who are gifted and creating services for those students, some leaders in gifted education have called for the complete removal of labeling students as gifted and simply working to meet the needs of diverse learners. Included in this group of diverse learners are those students for whom the standard curriculum is insufficient (Borland, 2005; Peters, Matthews, McBee, & McCoach, 2013). Gifted education would still exist for the purpose of making the curriculum more effective and fair for all students, but a label for students would cease to be necessary. From a practitioner's standpoint, I did not care how one of my students was identified for a program or even if they had ever been given the label. Like most teachers, I saw talent that needed developing. I can probably safely assume that if you are reading this chapter you have considered at least one student whom you know (or knew) who demonstrated some mathematical ability that could be developed, whether that student had been given a label or not.

It is in that spirit that this chapter is written. Rather than focusing on how to identify which students should be identified as having mathematical talent, this chapter focuses on which programs and structures should be in place to develop mathematical talent. Before I discuss some of the options for structures for developing mathematical talent, I want to make one assumption explicit. The primary basis for developing and offering programs to develop mathematical talent would be because the local education agency (LEA) values developing mathematical talent. This may seem obvious, but if the LEA does not value developing mathematical talent and does not plan to put a program or plan in place to do so, then there is no need to identify students who could benefit from such a program or plan. The goals of the program or plan also need to be created. For example, if an LEA decided to develop a system for allowing students to easily subject accelerate in mathematics, then the LEA needs to decide the desired goal of easy access to acceleration. Once the goals are identified, as early as possible, then the LEA can evaluate the success of the program. Finally, during this whole process, the LEA should keep in mind the particular characteristics of the population that they serve. For example, if the LEA is located near a large corporation like Exxon-Mobile or Intel, the LEA should consider those resources when creating effective programs. These three pieces should be in place (values, program, and goals) before identifying students who would benefit from the program (Peters et al., 2013).

Theoretical Framework

Building on the work of many others who sought to develop talent (Bloom, 1985b; Gagné, 2005; Tannenbaum, 1983), Subotnik, Olszewski-Kubilius, and Worrell (2011) developed a comprehensive mega model that integrates the most promising components of previous talent development models. In this talent development model, ability leads to competence, which leads to expertise, which eventually should lead to eminence. In addition to eminence being the ultimate outcome, some of the key elements of this model include the ideas that ability exists and can be developed, psychosocial issues matter (e.g., motivation is important), developmental trajectories differ by domain, and opportunities to develop talent are critical.

McBee, McCoach, Peters, and Matthews (2012) have suggested that this framework should be further specified. Giftedness would be better served by creating an "amicable schism in theory if not in organization" (p. 211) and recommend a distinction between high-ability psychology and advanced academics. The former research would center on the students with high ability, and the latter would center on those with unmet academic needs. My intent in this chapter is to explicitly focus on mathematical talent development; thus, I will focus on advanced academics and those students who have some latent talent, but not readily available or insufficient methods of developing it.

Two Levers for Developing Mathematical Talent

The two levers that will universally work to set students on a solid trajectory for developing their mathematical talent are taking advantage of opportunities and having a healthy motivation for learning (Subotnik et al., 2011). Before discussing some common opportunities that have been shown to be successful and healthy motivational dispositions that promote developing mathematical talent, it is important to understand the range of mathematical ability in the talent pool. For the sake of illustration, assume for a second that researchers and educators used an extremely exclusive (and archaic) definition of who qualifies as gifted in mathematics—only the top 1% of students on some nationally standardized assessment of IQ. In this top 1% lies one third of the range of mathematical ability (Lubinski & Benbow, 2006). On its face, this seems impossible. But the top 1% of an IQ test would have scores that could range from 135 to 200 (or higher depending on the ceiling of the assessment). For students that fall into this top 1%, static curriculum, singular approaches, and inflexible teaching will not meet the needs of these learners. These learners are much too diverse to benefit from a one-size-fits-all approach.

The Study of Mathematically Precocious Youth (SMPY; Lubinski & Benbow, 2006) is a 40-year longitudinal study of students identified as having exceptional mathematical talent at a young age (most students were identified in middle school). One finding in particular is worth noting relative to developing mathematical talent—ability matters. Students qualified by earning an SAT mathematics score in the top 1% and individual differences in the top 1% mattered. Those students who were in the top quartile of the top 1% earned more doctorates (and more doctorates in mathematics, science, engineering, and technology), more patents, more money, and secured tenure at top-tier universities at higher rates than those who were in the bottom quartile of the top 1% (Lubinski & Benbow, 2006). Again, a one-size-fits-all approach to developing talent is not going to meet the needs of even those in the top 1%.

Opportunity

Given the wide variety of talent at the very top of the talent distribution, the importance of taking advantage of opportunities to develop mathematical talent cannot be overstated. Researchers in gifted education point to a link between success and participating in opportunities when they present themselves (Lubinski & Benbow, 2006; Subotnik et al., 2011; Wai, Lubinski, Benbow, & Steiger, 2010). One longitudinal study found that for extremely high-ability students (0.5% or higher on the SAT mathematics at age 13) exposure to STEM experiences in high doses impacted the likelihood of an occupation, publication, Ph.D., and tenure in a STEM field. Dosage was defined by the number of STEM-related activities in high school (e.g., mathematics competition, participation in a STEM-related AP class, early enrollment in a college STEM course; Wai et al., 2010). Taking advantage of opportunities is important when developing mathematical talent. In this section, I provide nonexhaustive practical options for developing mathematical talent with hopes of exposing more curriculum designers to the opportunities that are available for developing mathematical talent. The most empirically supported and/or potentially transformative are highlighted. Assouline and Lupkowski-Shoplik (2010) also provided an excellent list of opportunities for mathematical talent development.

Acceleration. The method for developing mathematical talent that has the most research supporting its use is acceleration. Acceleration occurs when a student proceeds through curriculum at a faster pace or at a younger age than normally expected (Southern, Jones, & Stanley, 1993). More than 30 years ago, Stanley and Benbow (1982) made recommendations about how to educate mathematically precocious youth. Of the 12 recommendations, more than half involved either acceleration or early admission to programming (summer institutes or college). In fact, many of my mathletes like Travis and Jared were accelerated 2 or more years.

The vast amount of research supporting acceleration is impressive (Colangelo, Assouline, & Gross, 2004); however, acceleration is incredibly underused (Colangelo et al., 2004; Southern & Jones, 2004; Vialle, Ashton, Carlon, & Rankin, 2001). Instead, students are more likely to be given exposure to specific mathematical content based on their age rather than because of their academic need. One study found that teachers were much more likely to give importance to the potential negative consequences than to the positive ones when considering a student for acceleration—even though the teachers in the study generally believed that acceleration was good for students (Rambo

& McCoach, 2012). Thus, teachers were more inclined to keep the status quo than recommend acceleration. When considering acceleration options, parents and teachers should try to ensure that the teachers working with accelerated students are supportive of and have realistic expectations for the maturity level of the younger accelerated student (Brody, Muratori, & Stanley, 2004). Students should also be thoroughly assessed for readiness before acceleration (Brody et al., 2004). Despite the fact that many teachers are still resistant to using acceleration, it remains one of the best options for developing mathematical talent.

Acceleration should not be optional. Acceleration should be the expectation and the foundation for developing mathematical talent. There are many different types of acceleration ranging from early admission to kindergarten, to subject-specific acceleration, to whole-grade acceleration, to curriculum compacting, to early entrance to college (Southern & Jones, 2004). Early admission to college could take many forms, such as taking courses at the local community college or university, enrolling in online college courses, or attending a residential program for talented mathematics students. The first two are options that could be integrated into a current high school system. Although not discussed in detail here (as it is a more classroom-based intervention), grouping for tailored instruction also has a rich history of success with improving student performance, particularly with advanced students (Huang, 2009; Kulik & Kulik, 1992; Lou, Abrami, & Spence, 2000; Mulkey, Catsambis, Steelman, & Crain, 2005). Thus, if acceleration is used more systemically, another benefit is that students will gain academically from being grouped with like students for instruction.

Collaboration and competition. Two critical pieces in developing mathematical talent are engaging students in rich problems worth solving and engaging students in collaborative work (Bloom, 1985b). Working with other talented students can take on many forms—such as grouping for instruction, summer camps for students wanting to improve their mathematics skills, math circles, or mathematics competitions. Some summer camps are also a great way for students to be accelerated and to have curriculum compacting simultaneously. Math circles are a relatively new way to connect professional mathematicians with precollege students to solve nonformulaic problems.

One of best examples of a mathematics competition that encourages teamwork is Mathcounts®. This program was started because some engineers were dissatisfied with the quality of newly minted engineers. Rather than complain about it, they chose to do something. Designed to get middle school students interested in and deepen their understanding of mathematics, Mathcounts involves students as individuals and teams to solve problems competitively. The Mathcounts program began in 1980, and the first competition was held in 1982. Mathcounts has capitalized successfully on the need for rich problems, competition, and collaboration.

Other competitions are available for elementary, middle, and high school. Math Olympiad (http://www.moems.org) is also a strong program, and students in fourth through eighth grade are eligible to participate. The program is team-based, and competitions are held at the school five times a year. Thus, one of the potential advantages of this program over Mathcounts is that no travel is required. Math Olympiad fosters collaboration among students by requiring that students participate as a team rather than as individuals. American Mathematics Competitions (AMC) is available for students in sixth to 12th grade, although students as young as 8 years old have participated. These competitions are also held at the students' school, but unfortunately are not team based. Students who perform exceptionally well are eligible for more competitions including invitation-only summer programs from which an elite group of six students are selected for international competitions (Mathematical Association of America, n.d.).

Acceleration, collaboration, and team-based competition should all be components of an LEA's program for developing mathematical talent. The intensity and the specific flavor of these components will vary by LEA, but they each uniquely contribute to developing mathematical talent. The LEA needs to work creatively to ensure that the structures are in place both administratively and physically (e.g., coordinating bussing between schools) to support student acceleration. Further, the LEA needs to be prepared to financially support student collaboration and competition (e.g., sending students to competitions and dedicating teacher time).

Motivation

The second lever for developing mathematical talent is not related to mathematical content but to how students approach mathematics. Dweck (Grant & Dweck, 2003; Mueller & Dweck, 1998) has contributed substantially to the understanding of motivation in student academic development. Mindset is a framework (Dweck, 2006; Mueller & Dweck, 1998) that proposes that belief about ability influences motivation and ultimately achievement. Some people believe that intelligence is fixed, while others believe that intelligence can grow. Those with a fixed mindset believe that intelligence is largely fixed at birth and is a result of your genetic code. People who have fixed mindsets tend to see failure as a direct reflection on them and are more likely to quit or give up early on challenging tasks. People with a growth mindset tend to believe that their brain is like a muscle—that the more a person's brain is used, the more intelligent that person becomes. Thus, those with a growth mindset view failure as an opportunity to exercise this "muscle" and become smarter. Numerous interventions have shown that teaching students to have a growth view of intelligence has positive outcomes for students (e.g., Grant & Dweck, 2003; Mueller & Dweck, 1998; Yeager & Dweck, 2012). Students see problems as opportunities to learn, that effort is necessary, and are more willing to persist in difficult problems. Within the mindset framework, I want to highlight traits that are essential to helping students persist in mathematics. I conclude this section on motivation by describing the critical role that teachers, parents, and coaches play in motivating students.

Effort. First, students need to recognize that mathematics takes a lot of effort. In one groundbreaking study (Mueller & Dweck, 1998), praising students for effort instead of praising them for being smart resulted in greater persistence, less inclination to cheat, and increased willingness to engage with more difficult work. Educators of burgeoning mathematicians must be aware of the need to encourage effort. Praising intelligence is likely to be demotivating to students when tasks become difficult. To use a common analogy in gifted education, developing mathematical talent is much like developing athletic talent (Bloom, 1985a). Gifted athletes have a natural proclivity toward a particular skill but have dedicated a lot of time and effort to develop those talents. No one would rightly expect young athletes (who show promise) to maximize their talent without extensive practice. And those many, many hours of practice would need to be coached by an expert in the field and often alongside other promising athletes. However, some students in particular seem to think that promising mathematicians should be successful with little practice—that mathematics should come naturally and with little effort. There seems to be an exception made to the need for effort for promising mathematicians, but this should not be the case.

If students perceive mathematics as something that is only for the smart (a fixed mindset), then they are unlikely to be successful in mathematics. In a retrospective study of highly successful research mathematicians (Bloom, 1985b; Gustin, 1985), only a handful of the 20 study participants would have been considered child prodigies by parents, teachers, or experts in their eventual field, but all of the participants came to love the subject and spent enormous amounts of time devoted to learning and eventually creating mathematics. No matter how talented the student, there will come a point where that student can no longer be as successful without considerable practice. Like mastering a sport, a student must pour hours into mastering the skills and mental flexibility necessary for mathematics. Jared, one of the two talented students whom I discussed in the introduction, said that he used to think that being gifted in mathematics was about solving problems quickly, but he later realized that it is about solving problems that can take weeks, months, or even years. For mathematics students of all levels and abilities, effort should be the norm.

Mistakes. Secondly, students need to expect, be comfortable with, and learn from mistakes. Those working with talented mathematics students need to normalize failure. To be a successful mathematician, one has to be comfortable learning from failure. Rarely will the first approach to a problem be the best one (or even work). In classrooms, teachers must allow making mistakes to be a normal and acceptable part of the classroom culture. In fact, persistence is one of the characteristics that differentiates those who are most successful at developing their talent from those who do not (Calderon, Subotnik, Knotek, Rayhack, & Gorgia, 2007; Subotnik, Kassan, Summers, & Wasser, 1993). Parents and teachers who work with emerging mathematicians can help those students see that mistakes are not failures but opportunities to learn something new. Again borrowing an athletic term, parents and teachers need to develop a "coachability" sense in their students. Students need a safe place to make mistakes and have a coach who can come alongside them to provide help and encouragement. Like effort, normalizing failure is important regardless of the level of mathematical talent a student processes.

The role of adults. Those working with talented mathematics students, such as teachers and coaches, need to be intentional about normalizing the amount of effort needed to be exceptional in mathematics and the crucial role that mistakes play in a student's mathematical journey, but teachers need to do much more. Classroom teachers can deliberately structure their classrooms to encourage students to have an adaptive, healthy, and productive view of learning. Similar to the mindset framework, achievement goal orientation is a theoretical framework that helps to explain what motivates students (Kaplan & Maehr, 2007; Meece, Anderman, & Anderman, 2006; Pintrich, Marx, & Boyle, 1993), and students' motivation for learning is likely hinged in their belief about intelligence (Dweck, 1986). The essence of achievement goal theory is that students want to either display competence (performance orientation) or develop competence (mastery orientation). Simple tasks such as praising students for effort, being creative, and learning from their mistakes can help students adopt a healthy perspective on learning. See Kaplan and Maehr (2007) for more suggestions for how to encourage students to adopt mastery orientations toward learning.

In addition to classroom teachers structuring their classrooms for optimal motivation, the scholarly productivity/artistry model of talent development (Subotnik & Jarvin, 2005) highlights the critical role that parents, teachers, coaches, and mentors play in talent development. This model illustrates three stages through which talented students must progress to develop their talent. The three stages are transformation of abilities to competencies, competencies to expertise, and expertise to scholarly productivity and artistry (Calderon et al., 2007). In the first stage, parents, teachers, and coaches play the role of inspiring a love for the discipline. Most mathematics students in middle school and in high school are still in this first stage, and some students begin to progress to the second stage during high school (Gustin, 1985; Subotnik et al., 2011). Teachers should help students to see the beauty and creativity that is innate within mathematics, to appreciate the elegance of simple solutions, and enjoy the journey of discovering mathematics personally (Mann, 2006). Most of the top research mathematicians previously mentioned (Gustin, 1985) began their love of mathematics in middle school or high school. With few exceptions, the primary jobs of middle and high school teachers are to inspire students to love mathematics and prepare students to move from competencies to expertise.

Implications for Research

Many opportunities exist for those interested in doing research in developing mathematical talent. For example, despite the wealth of research on acceleration, many teachers are still reluctant to recommend that students be accelerated. New research could examine potential biases toward specific groups or other factors that might impact whether a student is recommended for acceleration. Also, as LEAs begin to develop plans and programs for developing mathematical talent, it would be beneficial to know how various barriers were overcome (e.g., resistance from stakeholders, transportation concerns related to acceleration, and access to college courses for rural communities). Knowing how these issues were overcome would help other LEAs expand their programming options for developing mathematical talent in their districts.

Finally, given the overwhelming positive results of acceleration and mindset interventions, a natural next step is to combine them. Here are some sample research questions that combine them: Are teachers with a growth mindset more likely to recommend students for acceleration than teachers with a fixed mindset? If accelerated students are taught to approach learning with a growth mindset, are these accelerated students more successful?

The Larger Impact

This chapter on developing mathematical talent serves as a complement to the previous chapter on differentiating mathematics standards. The previous chapter made recommendations for what teachers can do in their classrooms to better meet the needs of their talented mathematics students. This chapter examines what can be done from a more systemic perspective, such as building infrastructure to support acceleration.

The time for developing mathematical talent is now. One of the 16 university-based residential programs for advanced students in mathematics is the Texas Academy of Mathematics and Science (TAMS; Jones, 2011; Kettler, Sayler, & Stukel, 2014). In this program, students complete their last 2 years of high school while essentially completing their first 2 years of college. All coursework is at the university level. Students who have applied to TAMS have cited frustration with their current educational options, citing that high school is too simple and that the repetition is soul crushing. One particularly confident student stated, "I am going to find a cure for AIDS or cancer. Two more years in public school are millions of lives wasted" (Jones, 2011, p. 522). Although this may seem overly dramatic, the student is summarizing what acceleration advocates have stated for years. What talents are being held back, thwarted, or otherwise distinguished because students are inappropriately challenged? Many schools may measure their success in developing mathematical talent by the number of students taking calculus (and passing the Advanced Placement exam). Getting more students to take calculus in high school is a great goal, but this is short sighted. The larger goal is to develop mathematicians who solve real problems.

Discussion Questions

1. What can middle and high teachers do to become incubators of mathematical talent? What can administrators do to help schools become incubators of mathematical talent?
2. Who is responsible for determining the goals of developing mathematical talent? What are some possible goals of developing mathematical talent?
3. How can schools use technology to provide some of the opportunities mentioned in this chapter to capitalize on mathematical potential?
4. Should all promising mathematicians be provided unique opportunities to develop their talent by the local education agency? Why or why not?
5. What are the critical components that should be included in a local education agency's plan for developing mathematical talent?
6. What is the primary purpose of the classroom teacher in developing mathematical talent? Why?

References

Assouline, S., & Lupkowski-Shoplik, A. (2010). *Developing math talent: A comprehensive guide to math education for gifted students in elementary and middle school* (2nd ed.). Waco, TX: Prufrock Press.

Bloom, B. S. (Ed.). (1985a). *Developing talent in young people.* New York, NY: Ballantine.

Bloom, B. S. (1985b). Generalizations about talent in young people. In B. S. Bloom (Ed.), *Developing talent in young people* (pp. 507–549). New York, NY: Ballantine.

Borland, J. H. (2005). Gifted education without gifted children. In R. J. Sternberg & J. E. Davidson (Eds.), *Conceptions of giftedness* (pp. 1–19). New York, NY: Cambridge University Press.

Brody, L. E., Muratori, M. C., & Stanley, J. C. (2004). Early entrance to college: Academic, social, and emotional considerations. In N. Colangelo, S. Assouline, & M. U. M. Gross (Eds.), *A nation deceived: How schools hold back America's brightest students* (Vol. 2, 97–107). Iowa City: The University of Iowa, The Connie Belin and Jacqueline N. Blank International Center for Gifted Education and Talent Development.

Calderon, J., Subotnik, R. F., Knotek, S., Rayhack, K., & Gorgia, J. (2007). Focus on the psychosocial dimensions of talent development: An important potential role for consultee-centered consultants. *Journal of Educational and Psychological Consultation, 17*, 347–367.

Colangelo, N., Assouline, S., & Gross, M. U. M. (Eds.). (2004). *A nation deceived: How schools hold back America's students* (Vols. 1 and 2). Iowa City: The University of Iowa, The Connie Belin and Jacqueline N. Blank International Center for Gifted Education and Talent Development.

Dweck, C. (1986). Motivational processes affecting learning. *American Psychologist, 41*, 1040.

Dweck, C. (2006). *Mindset: The new psychology of success*. New York, NY: Random House.

Gagné, F. (2005). The DMGT as a developmental model. In R. J. Sternberg & J. E. Davidson (Eds.), *Conceptions of giftedness* (2nd ed., pp. 98–119). New York, NY: Cambridge University Press

Grant, H., & Dweck, C. S. (2003). Clarifying achievement goals and their impact. *Journal of Personality and Social Psychology, 85*, 541–553. doi:10.1037/0022-3514.85.3.541

Gustin, W. C. (1985). The development of exceptional research mathematicians. In B. S. Bloom (Ed.), *Developing talent in young people* (pp. 270–331). New York, NY: Ballantine.

Huang, M.-H. (2009). Classroom homogeneity and the distribution of student math performance: A country-level fixed-effects analysis. *Social Science Research, 38*, 781–791.

Jones, B. M. (2011). The Texas Academy of Mathematics and Science: A 20-year perspective. *Journal for the Education of the Gifted, 34*, 513–543.

Kaplan, A., & Maehr, M. L. (2007). The contributions and prospects of goal orientation theory. *Educational Psychology Review, 19*, 141–184. doi:10.1007/s10648-006-9012-5

Kettler, T., Sayler, M., & Stukel, R. (2014). Gifted education at the Texas Academy of Mathematics and Science: A model for STEM talent development. *Tempo, 35*, 9.

Kulik, J. A., & Kulik, C.-L. C. (1992). Meta-analytic findings on grouping programs. *Gifted Child Quarterly, 36*, 73–77. doi:10.1177/001698629203600204

Lou, Y., Abrami, P. C., & Spence, J. C. (2000). Effects of within-class grouping on student achievement: An exploratory model. *The Journal of Educational Research, 94*, 101–112.

Lowell, B. L., Salzman, H., Bernstein, H., & Henderson, E. (2009). *Steady as she goes? Three generations of students through the science and engineering pipeline.* Paper presented at the Annual Meetings of the Association for Public Policy Analysis and Management Washington, DC on November.

Lubinski, D., & Benbow, C. P. (2006). Study of mathematically precocious youth after 35 years: Uncovering antecedents for the development of math-science expertise. *Perspectives on Psychological Science, 1,* 316–345.

Mann, E. L. (2006). Creativity: The essence of mathematics. *Journal for the Education of the Gifted, 30,* 236–260.

Mathematical Association of America. (n.d.). *About AMC.* Retrieved from http://www.maa.org/math-competitions/about-amc

McBee, M. T., McCoach, D. B., Peters, S. J., & Matthews, M. S. (2012). The case for a schism: A commentary on Subotnik, Olszewski-Kubilius, and Worrell (2011). *Gifted Child Quarterly, 56,* 210–214.

Meece, J. L., Anderman, E. M., & Anderman, L. H. (2006). Classroom goal structure, student motivation, and academic achievement. *Annual Review of Psychology, 57,* 487–503. doi:10.1146/annurev.psych.56.091103.070258

Mueller, C. M., & Dweck, C. S. (1998). Praise for intelligence can undermine children's motivation and performance. *Journal of Personality and Social Psychology, 75,* 33.

Mulkey, L. M., Catsambis, S., Steelman, L. C., & Crain, R. L. (2005). The long-term effects of ability grouping in mathematics: A national investigation. *Social Psychology of Education, 8,* 137–177.

Peters, S., Matthews, M., McBee, M., & McCoach, D. B. (2013). *Beyond gifted education: Designing and implementing advanced academic programs.* Waco, TX: Prufrock Press.

Pintrich, P. R., Marx, R. W., & Boyle, R. A. (1993). Beyond cold conceptual change: The role of motivational beliefs and classroom contextual factors in the process of conceptual change. *Review of Educational Research, 63,* 167–199. doi:10.3102/00346543063002167

Rambo, K. E., & McCoach, D. B. (2012). Teacher attitudes toward subject-specific acceleration: instrument development and validation. *Journal for the Education of the Gifted, 35,* 129–152. doi:10.1177/0162353212440591

Southern, W., & Jones, E. (2004). Types of acceleration: Dimensions and issues. In N. Colangelo, S. Assouline, & M. U. M. Gross (Eds.), *A nation deceived: How schools hold back America's brightest students* (Vol. 2, 5–12). Iowa City: The University of Iowa, The Connie Belin and Jacqueline N. Blank International Center for Gifted Education and Talent Development.

Southern, W., Jones, E., & Stanley, J. (1993). Acceleration and enrichment: The context and development of program options. In K. A. Heller, F. J. Mönks, & A. H. Passow (Eds.), *International handbook of research and development of giftedness and talent* (pp. 387–409). Oxford, England: Pergamon Press.

Stanley, J. C., & Benbow, C. P. (1982). Educating mathematically precocious youths: Twelve policy recommendations. *Educational Researcher, 11*(5), 4–9.

Subotnik, R. F., & Jarvin, L. (2005). Beyond expertise. In R. J. Sternberg & J. E. Davidson (Eds.), *Conceptions of giftedness* (2nd ed., pp. 343–357). New York, NY: Cambridge University Press

Subotnik, R. F., Kassan, L. S., Summers, E., & Wasser, A. (1993). *Genius revisited: High IQ children grown up.* Norwood, NJ: Ablex.

Subotnik, R. F., Olszewski-Kubilius, P., & Worrell, F. C. (2011). Rethinking giftedness and gifted education: A proposed direction forward based on psychological science. *Psychological Science in the Public Interest, 12,* 3–54. doi:10.1177/1529100611418056

Tannenbaum, A. J. (1983). *Gifted children: Psychological and educational perspectives.* New York, NY: Macmillan.

Vialle, W., Ashton, T., Carlon, G., & Rankin, F. (2001). Acceleration: A coat of many colours. *Roeper Review, 24,* 14–19. doi:10.1080/02783190109554119

Wai, J., Lubinski, D., Benbow, C. P., & Steiger, J. H. (2010). Accomplishment in science, technology, engineering, and mathematics (STEM) and its relation to STEM educational dose: A 25-year longitudinal study. *Journal of Educational Psychology, 102,* 860.

Yeager, D. S., & Dweck, C. S. (2012). Mindsets that promote resilience: When students believe that personal characteristics can be developed. *Educational Psychologist, 47,* 302–314.

CHAPTER 17

DEVELOPING ADVANCED SCIENCE CURRICULUM FOR GIFTED STUDENTS

DEBBIE DAILEY AND ALICIA COTABISH

The need for improved science education is well documented. A recent report found that 20% of all U.S. jobs required a significant background in at least one of the STEM (science, technology, engineering, mathematics) disciplines (Rothwell, 2013). Unfortunately, our education system appears to be falling short when preparing students for science-related careers. Recently, Change the Equation (2014) reported that only 32% of fourth graders, 29% of eighth graders, and 20% of 12th graders were proficient in science, and only 30% of students in grade 12 who took the ACT were prepared for college-level science courses. In addressing gifted programs, Callahan, Moon, and Oh (2014) reported that out of 371 districts, the majority of elementary programs identified language arts as the most well-developed content area used in their program (47.2%), while a mere 10.5% of schools identified science and technology as the primary content area. Although we are beginning to show signs of improvement, we still lag behind other nations in the number and percentages of STEM graduates (National Science Board, 2014). Between the years 1997–2007, 15.6% of U.S. bachelor's degrees were awarded in science, technology, engineering, and mathematics (STEM); whereas China, South Korea, and Germany awarded 46.7%, 37.8%, and 28.1%, respectively

 DOI: 10.4324/9781003236696-20

(Business-Higher Education Forum [BHEF], 2010). Moreover, 61% of grade 12 students who demonstrated a proficiency or greater on the ACT indicated they were not interested in STEM (BHEF, 2010). With the number of STEM jobs expected to increase over the next 5 years by 17%, it is vital that we work to increase students' interest in STEM majors and careers (Feder, 2012).

To meet our nation's increasing demand for skilled STEM workers, our advanced learners, in particular, need opportunities to facilitate their interest and desire to learn science. Many times, science is not taught until the middle school grades and by then, many learners have lost their initial interest. The necessity of early science experiences is made poignantly clear in a recent study by Maltese and Tai (2010). In interviews with 85 scientists and science graduate students, the researchers found that 65% of those interviewed developed their interest in science before middle school. This is particularly disconcerting with the reduced amount of time elementary classrooms typically devote to science (Griffith & Scharmann, 2008). Additionally, these early science courses often do cursory science lessons that are focused on a superficial coverage of facts without time for students to explore the meaning behind the facts (Banilower, Smith, Pasley, & Weiss, 2006).

Science Curriculum for Gifted Learners

To increase the number of students interested in pursuing STEM as a career, gifted learners need more than a fact-based, didactic approach to learning science. With this in mind, researchers suggested that gifted learners have frequent opportunities with investigative science that includes in-depth studies of content; active learning with real-world, meaningful connections; and experiences with the practices of science (Robbins, 2011; Robinson, Shore, & Enerson, 2007; VanTassel-Baska, 1998). Consequently, a strong curriculum is paramount to providing quality instruction and increasing interest in science for gifted learners (Brandwein, 1995; Robinson et al., 2007; Subotnik, Olszewski-Kubilius, & Worrell, 2011; VanTassel-Baska, 1998).

Using the NGSS to Develop Curriculum for Advanced Learners

With the release of the Next Generation Science Standards (NGSS), strides are being made to improve science education and provide students early opportunities to engage in investigative, real-world experiences in science. To make learning meaningful and mimic the practices of real scientists, the NGSS encourages science learning across three dimensions: science and engineering practices, crosscutting concepts, and disciplinary core ideas. Incorporating three dimensions of science learning is not new to gifted educators. VanTassel-Baska (1992, 1998) suggested science curriculum focus on three dimensions (advanced content, process/product, and overarching concepts) in her Integrated Curriculum Model. Similar to the recommendations made in the NGSS, VanTassel-Baska suggested science curriculum for advanced learners focus on conceptual understanding. This is accomplished through deep exploration of content that is scaffolded and linked to previous and future content areas by overarching concepts. Additionally, content exploration is not learned in isolation but is supported with real-world investigations engaging students in the processes of science.

The NGSS can be used to guide the development of science curriculum, but it can be limiting to advanced learners. Throughout the performance expectations are assessment boundaries that suggest teachers and curriculum developers not extend the learning past the boundaries. Gifted educators, however, see this as a point of differentiation for advanced learners (Adams, Cotabish, & Dailey, 2015; Adams, Cotabish, & Ricci, 2014). Educators can use the assessment boundaries to extend learning for advanced learners. For example, in a grade 3 performance expectation (3-PS2-2: *Make observations and/or measurements of an object's motion to provide evidence that a pattern can be used to predict future motion*), the assessment boundary states that assessment does not include technical terms such as period or frequency. If students demonstrate their understanding of an object's motion, learning can be extended by using the appropriate technical terms and calculating their values.

Additionally, the disciplinary core ideas, practices, and crosscutting concepts are arranged by grade-band endpoints. These endpoints describe what students should know by the end of the grade-band. For example, in the physical science disciplinary core idea addressing chemical reactions (PS1.B), grades 3–5 students focus on the properties of the products of a chemical reaction, whereas grades 6–8 students focus on how the molecules are arranged in the products of the reaction (NGSS Lead States, 2013). Additionally, students in early grades may conduct simple investigations and ask questions about what would happen if a variable were changed, whereas students in upper grades generate questions from careful observations that can be empirically tested (NGSS Lead States, 2013). Overall, the learning progressions across the three dimensions take students from concrete phenomena that can be directly observed and investigated to more complex and abstract phenomena, such as subatomic particles (National Research Council, 2012). The arrangement of progressions lends itself well to advanced learners who are capable of more complex, abstract thinking, allowing them to accelerate to the next grade-band to challenge their learning as needed.

Engineering

An interesting addition to science instruction is the inclusion of engineering design practices. The NGSS placed engineering design on equal footing with physical science, life science, and Earth and space science. It is emphasized in the science and engineering practices as well as the disciplinary core ideas. The NGSS Lead States (2013) described how engineering design progresses across grade-band endpoints. In grades K–2, engineering is focused on solving simple problems, developing solutions, and evaluating the best solutions. In the study of motion, students could design a track to increase or decrease the speed of a toy car. For an additional challenge, students could explore the effects of friction using various materials added to the track or wheels of the toy car. In grades 3–5, engineering is focused on solving problems with specific criteria, researching and exploring multiple solutions, and improving solutions based on testing. In the study of energy, students could design sound insulators to reduce the amount of sound traveling out of a container. For added challenge, constraints could include materials, size of the container, and criteria for measuring the sound.

In grades 6–8, the problems involve more precise criteria and constraints for added challenge. For example, in the study of ecosystems, students could design a water filtration system. The constraints might include the materials used, the amount of purification (macro–micro), cost, and safety. Advanced learners could be challenged to use quantitative measures to determine the purity of the water, design a solar still to further purify water, and examine why water treatment facilities are sparse in third world countries. In grades 9–12, the problems are more complex and often involve issues of social and global significance. The testing involves quantitative methods of comparison, and the solutions must be weighed against societal and environmental impacts. In a study of thermodynamics, students could design a hand warmer. The constraints might include the type of products used—acknowledging both cost, safety, the degree of temperature increased, and the effects on the environment. To increase the societal affects, students could use a product such as this as a fundraiser for specific causes.

Overall, the inclusion of engineering practices in the science standards is beneficial to advanced learners. Engaging gifted learners in real-world problem solving, reflection and collaboration, and creative and critical thinking is complementary to their learning needs (Robbins, 2011; VanTassel-Baska, 1998). As demonstrated above, teachers could easily differentiate these types of learning experiences by adding complexity and constraints to the trajectory of the science and engineering design progressions.

21st-Century Skills

To prepare students to work in a STEM-related field, all challenging science instruction should be supported by the following 21st-century skills (Partnership for 21st Century Skills, 2009):

» *Collaboration*: Students are encouraged to work with partners and small groups to carry out tasks and projects, to pose and solve problems, and to plan presentations.

» *Communication*: Students are encouraged to develop communication skills in written, oral, visual, and technological modes in a balanced format within each unit of study.

» *Critical thinking*: Students are provided with models of critical thought that are incorporated into classroom instructional experiences, questions, and assignments.

» *Creative thinking*: Students are provided opportunities to think creatively so that they can develop skills that support original, innovative thinking, elaboration of ideas, flexibility of thought, and problem posing and solving.

» *Problem solving*: Students are engaged in real-world problem solving embedded in scientific processes in sample learning tasks.

> » *Technology literacy*: Students use technology in multiple forms and formats as a tool in solving problems and to create generative products.
> » *Information media literacy*: Students use multimedia to express ideas, research results, explore real-world problems, and evaluate information presented in media (graphs and diagrams) for scientific accuracy.
> » *Social skills*: Students work in small groups and develop the tools of collaboration, communication, and working effectively with others on a common set of tasks.

Through the science and engineering practices, the NGSS clearly emphasize creativity and innovation, critical thinking and problem solving, and communication and collaboration. These 21st-century skills are typical of scientists and engineers. Regrettably, many of these skills have been missing in science classrooms, where much emphasis has been on an accumulation of abundant knowledge with little depth and insight. Science curriculum for advanced learners should model the NGSS and encourage these skills to be practiced in all grade levels.

The inclusion of technology into the science curriculum should be seamless, especially when utilizing 21st-century skills such as inquiry-based learning, problem solving, and critical thinking (Periathiruvadi & Rinn, 2012). Commonly, technology can be used in the science classroom to: (a) conduct research, (b) collect and analyze data during investigations, (c) design models for explaining and solving problems, (d) make multimedia presentations, and (e) collaborate with others to solve problems. Furthermore, technology can provide teachers additional ways to differentiate instruction (Periathiruvadi & Rinn, 2012). Colombo and Colombo (2007) suggested teacher blogs could be used to extend instruction time, providing enrichment opportunities and accelerated learning. Moreover, the use of flipped classrooms can be an advantage for gifted learners. In a flipped classroom, students receive their instruction via audio or video blogs at home and do their assignments in class where they can receive help from the teacher. In a survey among teachers who utilized flipped classrooms, teachers indicated they had more time for authentic research activities and in-depth investigations (Herreid & Schiller, 2013).

Many web-based activities and online simulations can promote student understanding, interest, and engagement in science. Simulations allow students to manipulate variables, analyze data, and immediately see results. These are especially effective in schools where laboratory space and materials are in need. One such example is an Explore Learning product called Gizmos. Gizmos is a highly individualized experience that guides students through inquiry and exploration to understanding content and concepts (Explore Learning, n.d.). One such lesson allows students to recreate Galileo's famous experiment by dropping objects off the Tower of Pisa. Students can choose among a variety of objects to drop, such as golf balls, watermelons, and soccer balls. Through the exploration, students discover that objects in a vacuum fall at the same rate, objects accelerate as they fall, and they explore the effects of air resistance on each tested item. This lesson can be further extended for advanced learners by allowing them to calculate the terminal velocity of the items dropped.

Life and career skills should also be infused into the science curriculum for gifted students. This is especially important when meeting the needs of culturally diverse, scientifically advanced learners. Cultural, as well as intellectual, diversity can be embraced through collaborative opportunities—allowing students to practice the skills of flexibility and adaptability, productivity and accountability, leadership, and responsibility. In particular, students will need these skills when working with groups to design and evaluate the best solutions to presented problems.

Problem and Project-Based Learning Experiences for Advanced Science Learners

Two increasingly popular inquiry-based modes of instruction are problem-based and project-based learning. Both are viable options to employ with advanced learners in the science classroom. Finkle and Torp (1995) described problem-based learning as a "curriculum development and instructional system that simultaneously develops both problem solving strategies and disciplinary knowledge bases and skills by placing students in the active role of problem solvers confronted with ill-structured problems that mirror real-world problems" (p. 1).

A similar concept, project-based learning is an instructional strategy in which students work cooperatively over time to create a product, presentation, or performance. The fundamental difference between problem-based and project-based learning is in the application. Both provide opportunities for differentiation, are open-ended in nature, follow a list of steps, and utilize inquiry for the basis of student-centered instruction; however, there are some differences to note. Project-based learning is always grounded in an authentic real-world problem, whereas problem-based learning may use a fictitious scenario to present a problem. In addition, project-based learning experiences always culminate in the presentation of a product, whereas problem-based learning experiences may result in a solution rather than a product. In project-based learning, students may be involved in the development of rubrics, through which assessment of outcomes, including student self-assessment, may be conducted. Like problem-based learning, project-based learning is grounded in 21st-century skills, engages students in metacognitive thinking, and may likely improve scientific habits of mind and higher order thinking. Figure 17.1 presents the similarities and differences between the two inquiry methods or PBLs.

Both PBLs lend themselves to the sciences and the STEM disciplines with STEM content, science big ideas, engineering practices, and mathematical computations. The NGSS performance expectations can also be integrated seamlessly into a PBL experience. At the centerpiece of instruction, science comes to life through PBL frameworks (science content, science and engineering practices, and essential questions and understandings) while applying them to problems that will meaningfully engage students.

Problem-Based Learning

Problem-based learning has taken root in gifted education. VanTassel-Baska and Bass (1998) and VanTassel-Baska, Avery, Hughes, and Little (2000) both examined science units utilizing problem-based learning. Both studies documented significant gains in student learning, particularly in the implementation of scientific processes.

Typically in a group setting, students are presented real-world problems that may or may not be presented as a fictitious scenario. Many times, the problem may be tied to an authentic community-based issue, and when acted upon, can serve as a service-learning project. Working as a facilitator of learning, the teacher would guide the learning process and promote an environment of inquiry. An open-ended challenge would be presented with no specific "right" answer. As self-directed, active investigators, students identify a significant problem and work to derive a solution through a process of six steps (Finkle & Torp, 1995). Adams, Cotabish, and Dailey (2015) proposed a seventh (optional) step, resolution/action, because an additional step may be necessary to carry out the solution. The seven steps are:

1. Introduce an ill-structured problem.
2. Identify the three "What's," also known as "Need to Know." Students list what is known, what they need to know, and what they need to do.

Problem-Based Learning Versus Project-Based Learning	
Similarities	
Both:	
Provide opportunities for differentiation	
Are open-ended in nature	
Address 21st-century learning competencies	
Are task driven	
Employ entry events	
Are typically conducted in groups	
Are student-centered	
Are used as a formative assessment	
Include the three "What's" or "Need to Knows"	
Involve research of subject matter	
Spur in-depth inquiry	
Follow steps	
Prompt critical and creative thinking	
Differences	
Problem-Based Learning	**Project-Based Learning**
Typically shorter in duration	Often longer in duration
Choice is tied to possible solutions	Frequently employs student choice throughout
Often single subject	Often interdisciplinary/integrative
Products are often in the form of solutions	Emphasis on final product
Multiple paths for solving ill-structured problem	Centered around driving questions
Newfound information may redirect or pose additional questions	Final products are often presented to public audiences
Often uses case studies or fictitious scenarios to set up the problem	Typically involves real-world problem
May require an additional action step to carry out and resolve the issue(s)	Employs revision and reflection
May or may not utilize technology	Utilizes technology

FIGURE 17.1. Problem-based versus project-based learning. From *A Teacher's Guide to Using the Next Generation Science Standards with Gifted and Advanced Learners in Science,* by C. Adams, A. Cotabish, & D. Dailey, 2015. Waco, TX: Prufrock Press. Copyright 2015 by National Association for Gifted Children. Reprinted with permission.

3. Gather information.
4. Generate possible solutions.
5. Determine the best fit solution.
6. Present the solution.
7. Resolution/action (optional).

Steps 2–5 are not necessarily sequential and may be conducted simultaneously, as new information may redefine the original problem.

Project-Based Learning

Like problem-based learning, students engaging in a project-based learning environment respond to a complex question, problem, or challenge that is guided by a set of steps that direct teacher and student experiences. Once again, the teacher acts as facilitator, guiding students through the process. Furthermore, project-based learning experiences are framed around essential/driving questions. The teacher scaffolds the learning for students through labs, lectures, technology applications, and instructional activities. Students generate a list of "need to know" elements in order to proceed with the investigation. Through collaborative means, students engage in a process called "voice and choice," where they choose an artifact they want to produce utilizing technology, one of the noted defining differences between the two PBLs. Toward the end of the project-based learning experience, students engage in reflection and utilize feedback to inform their learning. Lastly, students present their work to an audience, often professionals in a related field of study. According to the Buck Institute for Education (n.d.), the essential elements of project-based learning include:

» *Significant content*: At its core, the project is focused on teaching students important knowledge and skills, derived from standards and key concepts at the heart of academic subjects.

» *21st-century competencies*: Students build competencies valuable for today's world, such as critical thinking/problem solving, collaboration, and communication, and creativity/innovation, which are taught and assessed.

» *In-depth inquiry*: Students are engaged in a rigorous, extended process of asking questions, using resources, and developing answers.

> » *Driving question*: Project work is focused by an open-ended question that students understand and find intriguing, which captures their task or frames their exploration.
> » *Need to knows*: Students see the need to gain knowledge, understand concepts, and apply skills in order to answer the driving question and create project products, beginning with an entry event that generates interest and curiosity.
> » *Voice and choice*: Students are allowed to make some choices about the products to be created, how they work, and how they use their time, guided by the teacher and depending on age level and project-based learning experience.
> » *Revision and reflection*: The project includes processes for students to use feedback to consider additions and changes that lead to high-quality products, and think about what and how they are learning.
> » *Public audience*: Students present their work to other people, beyond their classmates and teacher.

Differentiating the Two PBLs

With regard to advanced learners, student buy-in can be garnered by tapping students' personal interests, and there are many opportunities to provide appropriate levels of challenge. Both PBL experiences can be easily differentiated, offer opportunities for acceleration of content, and promote problem solving, collaboration, and critical thinking. Advanced learners are not limited by "ceilings," and the modes to conduct inquiry investigations are limitless.

In terms of problem-based learning, the experiences can be arranged in terms of readiness, interests, and learning profiles. Scaffolding opportunities exist to meet the individual needs of gifted learners, and there are multiple opportunities for teachers' to adapt science learning experiences according to students' learning styles.

With regard to project-based learning experiences, the use of technology applications provide opportunities for gifted students to excel without imposed limitations. Additionally, gifted students have a voice about their choices, and are often involved in the assessment process, creating their own rubrics and monitoring plans tied to individualized project goals.

In conclusion, problem-based and project-based learning experiences are both engaging and appropriate options for meeting the needs of scientifically advanced students. The practical application of content, engaging key elements, and authentic real-world experiences are excellent instructional avenues for addressing the NGSS and offer opportunities for students to acquire 21st-century skills. In an enriched inquiry-based science classroom, both experiences can augment science talent development, contribute to students' scientific literacy, reinforce scientific and mathematical practices, and provide gifted students an outlet for innovation and independent learning.

Conclusions

In summary, opportunities for integrating science content, the NGSS, and 21st-century skills into advanced curriculum is plentiful. Opportunities abound for creating avenues for gifted students to be enriched, accelerated, and challenged. However, the act of promoting science, particularly in the early grades, falls on the shoulders of classroom teachers and administrators alike. Creating an excitement and love for science is imperative as well as recognizing student talent in the science disciplines. Commercially available differentiated curriculum, such as the William & Mary problem-based learning units and Clarion units, USTARS science curriculum, and others, do exist in the field of gifted education and should be considered. Additionally, there are other popular and relevant science curricula that are commercially available, that when differentiated for advanced learners, can be beneficial in teaching science content, scientific literacy, and 21st-century skills. Regardless of the curricular materials or mode of delivery that is utilized, teachers of gifted learners are charged with delivering challenging instruction that develops and hones science talent. One aspect of fulfilling that purpose is to clarify, define, and deliver advanced opportunities for such learners as they progress from kindergarten through high school.

Implications for Research

Research opportunities in science education for advanced learners are plentiful. As states begin to implement the NGSS, research studies are needed to analyze their impact on science education and specifically, advanced learners. Will the implementation of the standards increase quality science experiences in general and gifted classrooms? Will these experiences increase student engagement and enthusiasm for science? How will these experiences translate into science achievement as measured by state-mandated science assessments and college entrance examinations? And finally, what impact will these experiences have on student interest in science as measured by the number of students seeking and receiving science degrees?

Discussion Questions

1. How can teachers of the gifted provide the level of rigor and relevance within the NGSS as they translate them into experiences for gifted learners?
2. How can teachers of the gifted provide creative and innovative opportunities that will nurture the thinking and problem solving of advanced learners?
3. Teachers of the gifted need to be sensitive to the ideas that science talent may not apply exclusively to identified gifted students. Many gifted children go unidentified, especially if they are culturally diverse and/or from low socioeconomic status groups. In what ways can the teacher of advanced learners develop and identify science talent?
4. In what ways can local educational reform (e.g., district policies and practices) in your district elevate learning in science to higher levels of passion, proficiency, and creativity for all learners?

References

Adams, A. Cotabish, A., & Dailey, D. (2015). *A teacher's guide to using the next generation science standards with gifted and advanced learners.* Waco, TX: Prufrock Press.

Adams. C., Cotabish, A., & Ricci, M. C. (2014). *Using the next generation science standards with advanced and gifted learners.* Waco, TX: Prufrock Press.

Banilower, E. R., Smith, P. S., Pasley, J. D., & Weiss, I. R. (2006). The status of K–12 science teaching in the United States: Results from a national observation survey. In D. Sunal & E. Wright (Eds.), *The impact of state and national standards on K–12 teaching* (pp. 83–122). Greenwich, CT: Information Age Publishing.

Business-Higher Education Forum. (2010). *Increasing the number of STEM graduates: Insights from the U.S. STEM education & modeling project.* Washington, DC: Author. Retrieved from http://www.ncci-cu.org/downloads/BHEF_STEM.pdf

Brandwein, P. F. (1995). *Science talent in the young expressed within ecologies of achievement* (RBDM9510). Storrs: University of Connecticut, The National Research Center on the Gifted and Talented.

Buck Institute for Education. (n.d.). *What is project-based learning (PBL)?* Retrieved from http://bie.org/about/what_pbl

Callahan, C., Moon, T., & Oh, S. (2014). *Status of elementary gifted programs.* Retrieved from http://www.nagc.org/sites/default/files/key%20reports/ELEM%20school%20GT%20Survey%20Report.pdf

Change the Equation. (2014). *STEMtistics–Science.* Retrieved from http://changetheequation.org/stemtistics/science

Colombo, M. W., & Colombo, P. D. (2007). Using blogs to improve differentiated instruction. *Phi Delta Kappan, 89,* 60–63.

Explore Learning. (n.d.). *Gizmos: Freefall tower.* Retrieved from http://www.explorelearning.com/index.cfm?method=cResource.dspDetail&ResourceID=650

Feder, M. (2012). *One decade, one million more STEM graduates.* Washington, DC: Office of Science and Technology Policy. Retrieved from http://www.whitehouse.gov/blog/2012/12/18/one-decade-one-million-more-stem-graduates

Finkle, S. L., & Torp, L. L. (1995). *Introductory documents.* Aurora, IL: Illinois Math and Science Academy.

Griffith, G., & Scharmann, L. (2008). Initial impacts of No Child Left Behind on elementary science education. *Journal of Elementary Science Education, 20*(3), 35–48.

Herreid, C. F., & Schiller, N. A. (2013). Case studies and the flipped classroom. *Journal of College Science Teaching, 42,* 62–66.

Maltese, A. V., & Tai, R. H. (2010). Eyeballs in the fridge: Sources of early interest in science. *International Journal of Science Education, 32,* 669–685. doi:10.1080/09500690902792385

National Research Council. (2012). *A framework for K–12 science education: Practices, crosscutting concepts, and core ideas.* Washington, DC: The National Academies Press.

National Science Board. (2014). *Science and engineering indicators 2014.* Arlington, VA: National Science Foundation.

Next Generation Science Standards Lead States. (2013). *Next generation science standards: For states, by states.* Washington, DC: The National Academies Press.

Partnership for 21st Century Skills. (2009). *P21 framework definitions.* Retrieved from http://www.p21.org/storage/documents/P21_Frame work_Definitions.pdf

Periathiruvadi, S., & Rinn, A. N. (2012). Technology in gifted education: A review of best practices and empirical research. *Journal of Research on Technology in Education, 45,* 153–169.

Robbins, J. I. (2011). Adapting science curricula for high-ability learners. In J. VanTassel-Baska & C. A. Little (Eds.), *Content-based curriculum for high-ability learners* (2nd ed., pp. 217–238). Waco, TX: Prufrock Press.

Robinson, A., Shore, B. M., & Enerson, D. L. (2007). *Best practices in gifted education.* Waco, TX: Prufrock Press.

Rothwell, J. (2013, June 10). *The hidden STEM economy.* Retrieved from http://www.brookings.edu/research/reports/2013/06/10-stem-economy-rothwell

Subotnik, R. F., Olszewski-Kubilius, P., & Worrell, F. C. (2011). Rethinking giftedness and gifted education: A proposed direction forward based on psychological science. *Psychological Science in the Public Interest, 12,* 3–54. doi:10.1177/1529100611418056

VanTassel-Baska, J. (1992). *Planning effective curriculum for gifted learners.* Denver, CO: Love Publishing.

VanTassel-Baska, J. (1998). *Planning science programs for high ability learners* (ED425567). Retrieved from http://www.ericdigests.org/1999-3/science.htm

VanTassel-Baska, J., Avery, L. D., Hughes, C. E., & Little, C. A. (2000). An evaluation of the implementation of curriculum innovation: The impact of William and Mary units on schools. *Journal for the Education of the Gifted, 23,* 244–272.

VanTassel-Baska, J., & Bass, G. (1998). A national study of science curriculum effectiveness with high ability learners. *Gifted Child Quarterly, 42,* 200–211.

CHAPTER 18

DEVELOPING SCIENCE TALENT

AN INNOVATIVE APPROACH TO LEARNING FOR EXPERTISE AND ELITE PERFORMANCE

JEB S. PURYEAR

Programs intended as long-term, self-sufficient models for meeting the needs of gifted and talented students, like other educational ventures, ought to be based on solid theoretical foundations and supported by empirical evidence. Perhaps ironically, pinning down these theoretical foundations and/or reaching consensus on belief systems in gifted education is often problematic. Additionally, to compound the challenge of solid empirical foundations, recent scholarship has highlighted the sparse efforts at replication research in the field of education in general, including gifted education (Makel & Plucker, 2014). Dai and Chen (2013) outlined the emergence of three broad distinguishable paradigms in the field of gifted education: the gifted child paradigm, the talent development paradigm, and the differentiation paradigm. Other works in this volume take varied views of gifted education and its application to curriculum practices. For example, the previous chapter by Dailey and Cotabish focused on curriculum differentiation as a means of meeting gifted student needs in science. Alternatively, in this chapter, I will focus on a talent development approach to science.

The relative merit of these paradigms of practice is certainly debatable, but the breakdown used by Dai and Chen (2014) in their attempts to bring

 DOI: 10.4324/9781003236696-21

clarity provides guidance that can be applied to issues across gifted education. The questions of why, who, what, and how raise issues of purpose, students to be included, tacit assumptions, and strategies, respectively. Differences in the treatment of these questions lead to altered advocacies. Paradigmatic differences can lead to dissimilar practices for developing science talent—if they formally exist at all. Even my own advocacy and presentation here, while steeped in the talent development tradition, may press even those typically in such a camp to consider new implications and applications of such a paradigm to the education of gifted students in science.

Operationalizing Talent Development in Science

Consider Ben. Compared to other students, he has shown less outward aptitude in science and school, but he scores above average across the board when it comes to academic screening assessments. He likes to tinker with electronics and is fascinated by science-related shows he consistently watches on television. He knows he wants to go to college, but is still mostly ambivalent toward any specific pathway or course of study. Beginning in late elementary through high school, Ben's school district offers enrichment courses on weekends and during the summer that focus on specific areas of interest. Attending these courses fostered the default bent toward science he has in his free time. Teachers in science (and other) courses are encouraged to employ problem- or project-based approaches to add context to the material when possible. The district makes specific efforts to encourage contributions and connections with community partners including two nearby universities. These efforts are on top of course sequences tailored toward specific interests—all of which are open enrollment. Counselors cast a wide net in suggesting upper level courses as an end goal. Ben is optimistic his educational needs both inside and outside of high school will be met by his district's programs.

When using a talent development approach, one goes beyond the traditional school experience as an endgame. That is not to say the schooling experience lacks importance, in fact Bloom (1985) suggested that talent emerges under the "tutelage and supervision of a remarkable series of teachers" (p. 543). It's been suggested, however, that we keep in mind what we mean when we define giftedness in the context of school. There may be important differences in such identification practices and the subsequent educational interventions when compared to those occurring out of a more practical, real-world approach (Renzulli, 1986, 1994). Ben doesn't meet traditional definitions of giftedness, nor does it seem that differentiation alone will meet his intellectual needs particularly when a lack of real-world applications will stifle his natural proclivity for science from being noticed. The talent development approach, by casting a wide net, focusing on higher long-term goals and contributions, and by forming and reinforcing connections between classroom learning experiences and the environment outside of school as much as possible, seems a good fit for Ben. But does it meet our goals? Does the narrative of Ben's experiences *really* paint a picture of someone building capacity in the skills of a discipline? Should that not be our goal in developing science talent (or any talent)? How do we know Ben and other students in the programs are reaching the goal of "doing science?" Or is this not *really* our goal? Or are we content with curriculum structures and options that tilt toward building science interest (as opposed to capacity) and rarely move further due to the comfortable, bells-and-whistles inertia the focus on affect provides?

Four Questions

The remainder of this chapter provides a specific advocacy for a robust talent development approach to learning design aimed at building *both* interest and capacity in the domain of science. Unique benefits of the approach are articulated, exemplar programs currently in use are described, and research in the field is described, whenever possible. By focusing on the questions of why, who, what, and how, I hope to make concrete connections to research and practice from what at first glance, or thought, may seem a nebulous approach.

The Why of Developing Science Talent

The National Academy of Sciences, together with other agencies, has reported problems in the system of science talent development in the United States (Committee on Prospering in the Global Economy of the 21st Century, 2007). Among the challenges are lagging science achievment scores relative to other similar nations and lagging numbers of Americans pursuing science degrees relative to industrial leaders such as China and India. At the very least, on the surface it seems that a rethinking of our systems of science education is in order.

Marshall (2010) suggested "our nation is once again focused on ensuring that all students acquire the knowledge, skills, and habits of mind essential for scientific research, creative exploration, complex problem-solving, and breakthrough innovation" (p. 49). To this end, the *America COMPETES Act* was passed in a bipartisan fashion in 2007. The goals of this legislation were increasing research investment, increasing opportunities in STEM education, and developing an infrastructure system aimed at creativity and innovation (Thomas & Williams, 2010). The intersection of the education system and a broader infrastructure is foundational in talent development.

The Who of Developing Science Talent

Who has science talent to develop? How do we find them? Important questions, to be sure. Identification procedures need to be targeted to specific skills or outcomes. In his 10 Commandments of Talent Development, Gagné (2007) argued, "The third commandment targets the identification procedure, whose goal, in the context of a talent development intervention, consists of pinpointing individuals who have the best chances of benefiting maximally from special enrichment services" (p. 98). I agree with Gagné that we should know our end goals and target accordingly. A critical issue here is avoiding the potential vagaries inherent in "special enrichment services." They need to actually develop both interest and capacity. Additionally, whatever our identification procedures, we should make efforts to find talented students of color, students of across the socioeconomic spectrum, and students with English language deficits (Roberts, 2010b). We must do so to fully encompass the "who" in our science talent development programs.

The second question of finding students is more taxing. Specific assessments for science should be used. They should always mirror the goals of the program as closely as possible. With potential content acceleration or curriculum compacting in mind for students with science talent, the use of off-level testing may provide unique information (Thomson & Olszewski-Kubilius, 2014). Most significantly, the testing can provide insights into how the student might fit into future steps of a talent development program. One might discover an aptitude for a specific science subject, allowing a preemptive strike of sorts via enrichment or outside-of-school activities.

Fiest (2006) reported that high performers in the Westinghouse Science Competition (now Intel Science Talent Search) showed more long-term promise in the science field. Importantly, they found the earlier age at which the talent was first recognized, the higher productivity and contribution to scientific fields as adults. In other words, the earlier they are found, the more passion and capacity can be instilled. Similar results have been obtained in longitudinal studies of Westinghouse winners (Subotnik, Duschl, & Selmon, 1993; Subotnik & Steiner, 1994). Taken together, these studies suggest talent search programs and science competitions ought to be part of a broad recruitment strategy in efforts to develop science talent. One might scoff that these "assessment" programs would be difficult to broadly implement in schools. I see this as the dismissive drivel of stakeholders not truly committed to developing science talent. I challenge those skeptical of such ideas to pinpoint the difficulties in fashioning such a program. I suspect the concerns would be largely the same as those often dealt with by others in the field of gifted education. That is, the concerns would be largely nebulous matters of disruption rather than substantive dealbreakers.

The What of Developing Science Talent

Olszewski-Kubilius (2010) provided a grounding for the "what" question in a description of common program options for advanced STEM students. These include dual-enrollment programs with local colleges and participation in Advanced Placement or International Baccalaureate programs. Rigorous curricula are seen as advantages, but a lack of explicit broader connections outside of school are viewed as problematic. Her advocacy seemed to lean toward a system of specialized high schools as do others in the same special STEM focused issue of *Roeper Review* (Roberts, 2010a; Subotnik, Tai, Rickoff, & Almarode, 2010; Thomas & Williams, 2010).

Specialized science (and/or math) schools seem to provide unique benefits both in terms of academic preparation and psychological well-being (Cross & Frazier, 2010). Although the work of these authors focused on residential programs, not typical public schools, breaking bonds of traditional schooling is a tenet of many programs and theorists in talent development. Now may be a pivotal time to reimagine what such schools would entail (Marshall, 2010).

Any talent development approach needs something beyond the status quo curriculum. One potential outlet for talented students is extracurricular participation in science activities. Stand-alone programs of this type have shown promise (Hausamann, 2012). In the Hausamann (2012) study, two-thirds (or more) of participants noted an increase in STEM interests, the importance of relating material to real life, and a likelihood they would want to visit again and participate in intellectually stimulating activities. Creating these sorts of opportunities via community partnerships is a likely pathway to meeting this need. Establishing partnerships or, at least, building awareness of these sorts of programs is critical to any school system fostering the development of science talent. However, alone these sorts of programs will not be sufficient, because they focus so heavily on sparking interest, rather than building foundational and extended capacity. Ironically, it seems intuitive that students gravitating toward such programs are probably the ones least likely to need support of their science affect in the first place.

Importantly, quality programs require recognition that many students in disadvantaged and/or rural areas lack opportunities for the advanced course-work or extracurricular options that would be foundational to a talent development approach (Kettler, Russell, & Puryear, 2015). In addition to the talent identification issues, making these connections will require unique solutions. Distance learning may help to bridge the gap by offering opportunities beyond geographic limitations while building capacity with technological tools. Hopefully such programs can spark further science interest and opportunity as well as support goals of technological literacy (Olszewski-Kubilius & Lee, 2004).

Clearly, special schools and outside time commitments for enrichment are not options for all students. I find myself partial to the work of Ngoi and Vondracek (2004), given its applicability to a broad range of settings. They reported the advanced science practices of Evanston Township High School in Illinois. Their description of "independent studies, extracurricular, academic competitions, and independent science research projects" echoes suggestions rooted in a talent development approach, but works within the present system (Ngoi & Vondracek, 2004, p 146). They found opening up the Advanced Placement science courses to everyone both increased enrollment numbers to support those programs and pushed more advanced students into even more advanced college-level work.

Although this work points us in the right direction, it is still (1) constrained by a vision of working within a system of standard curriculum requirements, and (2) does not take a holistic view regarding curriculum options or consider combinations that might best allow a budding scientist to thrive. In my opinion, the changing of course requirements is probably the easiest way to more rich talent-developing experiences, but the era of accountability and standards seems unlikely to allow this outcome. We are essentially forced to work within a system. Typically, in the literature of talent development, we see breaking the boundaries of traditional schools as advocacy (Dai & Chen, 2013). Pushing beyond those boundaries leads to recommendations for special schools and magnet programs and outside enrichment. Although those are great opportunities, the vast majority of gifted students seeking to develop elite science talent are in traditional school settings. Thus, educators and other advocates engaged in the work of gifted education learning design are seeking innovative ways to develop advanced science talent in school settings.

I recommend that science talent development begins with a questioning of the tacit assumptions of advanced academic students. We need to move beyond the rat race of taking every advanced academic class at a school while forsaking a specialization. For example, why should a student wanting to be a chemical engineer take Advanced Placement U.S. History? To be clear, this is *not* an advocacy against the significance of such coursework in a general intellectual sense. Having taught Advanced Placement (and International Baccalaureate) courses, I assure you I appreciate their value. My argument simply falls along these lines: Why wouldn't we have that budding engineer fulfill that history credit by some alternative means so he or she can take another advanced math course during the school day? Could we not do the same with other required courses outside the talent development curriculum such as government, geography, and language arts courses? Why not have accelerated English and literature programs for those students who could handle the heightened pace if it means freeing up room in the students' schedules for an advanced engineering design class? Perhaps one the gifted science and mathematics faculty designs itself? Perhaps the school could design other higher level courses in science, like a course in fluid dynamics where students would be able to synthesize content from previously taken AP Chemistry, AP Physics, and AP Calculus courses? I believe there is plenty of boundary breaking that can be done *within* traditional schooling, if only we commit to such genuine paths of science talent development.

The How of Science Talent Development

At the heart of developing science talent ought to lay a push toward developing a strong content base, adept scientific skills, and an appreciation of the principles of the discipline. We need tangible ways of assessing such outcomes. Assessing performance via student science competitions may be one sort of measure. Most states have subject-specific academic contests as part of a broader scheme of scholastic competition. Beyond these competitions, students can participate in regional, state, national, and international programs in three core areas: Biology Olympiad, Chemistry Olympiad, and Physics Olympiad. I myself have coached students in such competitions and they are worthy outcomes, but these sorts competitions primarily only focus on a base of content knowledge only, at least at the regional and state levels. National and international levels of Olympiad competition do often include specific science training and assessment types that require the application and synthesis of content in practical settings. The rigorous amount of studying for these competitions often nurtures the students' interest and motivation for the field, but, as I have argued previously, there is more to developing talent.

Teaching students to think, act, and communicate like scientists is paramount (Ericsson, Prietula, & Cokely, 2007), in my view. It is also the part of talent development programs in science that requires the most dedication and effort. An interview conducted with Dr. Robert Pavlica, director of the Authentic Science Program at Byram Hills High School in New York, provides an array of insights relevant to the *how* of developing science talent (Robinson, 2004). In each of the past 17 years, the school has had a student represented as, at least, a semifinalist in the Intel (Westinghouse) Science Talent Search competition. Only two schools in the nation can boast more finalists during that time.

The program is open to any student willing to put in the effort. It offers mentoring opportunities with professionals and educators outside the school that provide content in a meaningful context and the opportunities to do authentic research and build their skills as scientists. In the interview, Pavlica recalled the story of a student telling him he had taken every AP science option at the school and didn't know a "damn thing about science" (Robinson, 2004, p. 104). That was the epiphany for Pavlica. He realized there was something missing. The program features a curriculum in scientific research, writing, and presentation that spirals upward through the last 3 years of high school, culminating in a research symposium. Seniors are required to enter their research into the talent search competition. The program provides tangible, real-world goals beyond a science content curriculum. He aims to develop scientists. Pavlica's program embodies a spirit of science talent development at which I marvel.

Curriculum Design for Developing Science Talent

Up to this point in the chapter, I have outlined and extended upon research in the field of talent development in science. At times, the description of the vision is rapid-fire and stream-of-consciousness-like in nature. I hope that will make for rich discussion of the text and the underlying ideas. However, I also believe it is important that I explicitly lay out my advocacy for practical curriculum design issues to more fully address the needs of a talent development approach in science:

1. Nurture and sustain students' interest in science and their motivation to do science. I suggest pushing well beyond this, but this is a critical foundation.

2. Build opportunities for students to engage in the practice of science, actually doing science in the form of active inquiry and experimentation. Commitment to learning and implementing the skills and practices of a given discipline are critical, particularly for advanced students.

3. Maximize the amount of time gifted science students can spend in school working on a science or applied science curriculum. Stop thinking about what you cannot do, but what you can. Demonstrate willingness to engage in discussions aimed at breaking down implicit practices that stifle this sort of macrocurricular change.

4. Externally validate expertise through competitions and contests. Train for the content of science. Train for the practice of science. Make sure you have a solid grasp on how your programs function with regard to each.

Implications for Research

I have tried to articulate the case for developing talent in science in a number of ways. As adamant as I am regarding these issues, most importantly, as a researcher, educator, and advocate for gifted students, I strive to remember these roles are nearly always intertwined. Reading the reflections of others at these intersections (e.g., Roberts, 2010a) gives one guidance and wisdom about the roles we can play.

A wealth of research opportunities exist. Subotnik et al. (2010) suggested future research questions in their work. Given their particular interest in specialized schools, they wondered (1) how specialized schools would compare to other campuses with respect to college pursuits in STEM fields? and (2) what characteristics of STEM specialized schools are most effective? These are rich questions with surely nuanced answers. Even more nuanced, and I would argue richer, findings might come from seeking out schools doing things differently with regard to course options and at those developing their own courses as I suggested.

Along the lines of the "why" question, we will need to be focused in research on the underlying reasons for our talent development systems and interventions in gifted education more globally. We can go so far as to question the need for certain types of interventions. New reasons will also emerge with the rise in numbers of twice-exceptional students, for example.

The issue of twice-exceptionality bleeds into the "who" question and our need for effective, efficient, and equitable identification practices. We ought to further investigate the moderation effects on interventions of racial, gender, and socioeconomic differences. These might include stereotype threat issues related to competitions or advanced course taking that can be so successful in predicting the development of science talent.

One can devise a sea of new research ideas from the "what" question. New types of curriculum design and new extracurricular opportunities will be studied. Cost-benefit analyses will be performed to determine the relative benefit of these new programs versus those in the status quo. Ever-developing technology will push distance learning availability and new human interactions that will have to be considered to put talent development schemes into ever-changing contexts.

Lastly, the "how" issue is limited only by the will of researchers and practitioners. The inner working of interventions can be studied. The cognitive and affective effects of talent development need to be further studied, but Robinson (2012) hits at the bottom line:

> Engineers, scientists, artists, and activists are not frightened by talent development. They want access to human capital for their own purposes. So much the better for our field if we can share research from the psychological sciences to explain the development of talents to other professional fields whose leaders are moved by data, rationality, and the bottom line. (p. 203)

We have much work to do. Even within a framework of talent development, let us push ourselves forward, conceptually and practically, by stretching the limits of what can be done within and outside status quo educational systems to best meet the needs of those with science talent to be developed. Let us authentically develop our own scientific talents through our research, our practice, and our advocacy.

Discussion Questions

1. Consider your own experience in K–12 schools with respect to science. What aspects of talent development articulated in this chapter have you observed?
2. To what extent do programs focused on affect and building interest meet the needs of those with science talent to be developed?
3. What types of new identification methods would you suggest to better get at "who" should be involved in programs of science talent development?
4. Which "what" should be the goal of talent development in science: special schools or regular schools with additional, perhaps newly crafted, programs? Why?
5. "How" can we best foster science talent? What specific traits are most important?

References

Bloom, B. S. (1985). *Developing talent in young people*. New York, NY: Ballantine Books.

Committee on Prospering in the Global Economy of the 21st Century: An Agenda for American Science and Technology, National Academy of Sciences, National Academy of Engineering, Institute of Medicine. (2007). *Rising above the gathering storm: Energizing and employing America for a brighter economic future: Executive summary*. Washington, DC: National Academies Press.

Cross, T. L., & Frazier, A. D. (2010). Guiding the psychological development of gifted students attending specialized residential programs. *Roeper Review, 32*(1), 32–41.

Dai, D. Y., & Chen, F. (2013). Three paradigms in gifted education: In search of conceptual clarity in research and practice. *Gifted Child Quarterly, 57,* 151–168. doi:10.1177/0016986213490020

Dai, D. Y., & Chen, F. (2014). *Paradigms of gifted education: A guide to theory-based, practice-focused research.* Waco, TX: Prufrock Press.

Ericsson, K. A., Prietula, M. J., & Cokely, E. T. (2007). The making of an expert. *Harvard Business Review.* Retrieved from https://hbr.org/2007/07/the-making-of-an-expert

Fiest, G. J. (2006). The development of scientific talent in Westinghouse finalists and members of the National Academy of Sciences. *Journal of Adult Development, 13*(1), 23–35.

Gagné, F. (2007). Ten commandments for academic talent development. *Gifted Child Quarterly, 51,* 93–118.

Hausamann, D. (2012). Extracurricular science labs for STEM talent support. *Roeper Review, 34,* 170–182.

Kettler, T., Russell, J., & Puryear, J. S. (2015). Inequitable access to gifted education: An examination of variance in funding and staffing based on locale and contextual school variables. *Journal for the Education of the Gifted, 38,* 99–117.

Makel, M. C., & Plucker, J. A. (2014). Facts are more important than novelty: Replication in the educational sciences. *Educational Researcher, 43,* 304–316. doi:10.3102/0013189X14545513

Marshall, S. P. (2010). Re-imagining specialized STEM academies: Igniting and nurturing decidedly different minds, by design. *Roeper Review, 32,* 48–60.

Ngoi, M., & Vondracek, M. (2004). Working with gifted science students in a public high school environment: One school's approach. *Journal of Secondary Gifted Education, 25,* 141–147.

Olszewski-Kubilius, P. (2010). Special schools and other options for gifted STEM students. *Roeper Review, 32,* 61–70.

Olszewski-Kubilius, P., & Lee, S. Y. (2004). Gifted adolescents' talent development through distance learning. *Journal for the Education of the Gifted, 28,* 7–35.

Renzulli, J. S. (1986). The three-ring conception of giftedness: A developmental model for creative productivity. In R. J. Sternberg & J. E. Davidson (Eds.), *Conceptions of giftedness* (pp. 53–92). Cambridge, England: Cambridge University Press.

Renzulli, J. S. (1994). *Schools for talent development: A practical plan for total school improvement.* Mansfield Center, CT: Creative Learning Press.

Roberts, J. L. (2010a). Lessons learned: Advocating for a specialized school of mathematics and science. *Roeper Review, 32,* 42–47.

Roberts, J. L. (2010b). Talent development in STEM disciplines: Diversity—Cast a wide net. *NCSSSMST Journal, 16*(1), 10–12.

Robinson, A. (2012). Psychological science, talent development, and education advocacy: Lost in translation. *Gifted Child Quarterly, 56,* 202–205.

Robinson, G. (2004). Replicating a successul Authentic Science Research program: An interview with Dr. Robert Pavlica. *Journal of Secondary Gifted Education, 25,* 148–154.

Subotnik, R. F., Duschl, R. A., & Selmon, E. H. (1993). Retention and attrition of science talent: A longitudinal study of Westinghouse Science Talent winners. *International Journal of Science Education, 15*(1), 61–72.

Subotnik, R. F., & Steiner, C. L. (1994). Adult manifestations of adolescent talent in science: A longitudinal study of 1983 Westinghouse Science Talent Search winners. In R. F. Subotnik & K. D. Arnold (Eds.), *Beyond Terman: Contemporary longitudinal studies of giftedness and talent* (pp. 52–76). Norwood, NJ: Ablex Publishing.

Subotnik, R. F., Tai, R. H., Rickoff, R., & Almarode, J. (2010). Specialized public high schools of science, mathematics, and technology and the STEM pipeline: What do we know now and what will we know in 5 years? *Roeper Review, 32,* 7–16.

Thomas, J., & Williams, C. (2010). The history of specialized STEM schools and the formation and role of the NCSSSMST. *Roeper Review, 32,* 17–24.

Thomson, D., & Olszewski-Kubilius, P. (2014). The increasingly important role of off-level testing in the context of a talent development perspective. *Gifted Child Today, 37*(1), 33–40.

CHAPTER 19

LEARNING DESIGN AND SOCIAL STUDIES FOR GIFTED AND ADVANCED STUDENTS

JOSEPH RUSSELL

Most people can probably recount a tale or two of their high school history or civics classes. They might remember some details of the American Revolution or how a bill becomes a law. They might remember one of their teachers as particularly nice, or they might even remember how they got their first voter registration card as a senior in high school. Although some of the people in this hypothetical exercise might have even called a social studies course their favorite class, how many of them, if pressed, could really say how what they learned truly mattered?

Social studies faces a unique problem of relevance among the four areas generally accepted as core content in American public schools. Language arts is obviously important and relevant; even if one is not a fan of literature, the ability to read and write is essential for other learning and for the completion of most tasks in life. Math and science can be challenging, but for those with an aptitude or determination in those areas it is easy to see how the effort translates into lucrative career options in adulthood. But the social studies may seem difficult to justify as a content area, because it is often difficult to demonstrate their importance. History, for example, is interesting, but is it really important to people and how they live their day-to-day lives?

DOI: 10.4324/9781003236696-22

Social Studies and the Gifted Learner

The problem of relevance in the social studies may be compounded for gifted learners. Jones and Hébert (2012) pointed out that the advanced development of gifted learners compared to their age-group peers often leads to the gifted student being the one to challenge a classroom lesson as boring or not engaging because he or she does not see the relevance of the curriculum. Furthermore, social studies curricula may be structured in a way that is full of unchallenged cultural assumptions that only increase this seeming lack of relevance for gifted learners from diverse backgrounds (Clinkenbeard, 2012). Additionally, because social studies is a discipline that by definition deals with ambiguity and differences of interpretation, it can be very frustrating for highly motivated gifted learners who want to be able to deliver the "right" answer (Graham, 2013).

Teachers and curriculum designers for gifted and advanced learners in the social studies often find themselves in a maddening balance act between low-level objectivity (names and dates) and high-level subjective analysis in the design of learning tasks and assessments. They spend time making sure lessons are culturally balanced and factually accurate, and they approach a given block of material from a variety of historical viewpoints and interpretations. Still, even when all of this work is done, there is no guarantee that the gifted students in the course will be engaged or motivated to learn the material because the question of why it even matters in the first place has still not been addressed.

As high-quality Common Core State Standards for language arts and mathematics and the Next Generation Science Standards have gained national appeal, it may appear the social studies have been left behind. State standards for the social studies are often characterized as having greater breadth than depth, focusing on knowledge acquisition at the lower level of the cognitive taxonomy. It is easy to see how these courses could become a confusing mix of rote memorization and unconnected analytical writing. For social studies to remain a relevant and engaging discipline for gifted learners, the design of courses and curricula should focus on purpose, meaning, and authentic engagement with questions and problems that are both timeless and immediate.

Rethinking the Approach to Pedagogy in Social Studies

The contemporary understanding of pedagogy is generally considered to be the art or the craft of teaching. In the modern usage, it refers to all of the tricks of the trade that teachers learn either through professional preparation, through observation of other teachers, or from experience in the classroom. Most states have a requirement that pedagogy be included in the training and certification assessment of teachers, and beyond this initial training and testing, professional educators improve the practice of their craft through experience and ongoing professional training.

One cannot help but wonder if there might not be a better way. Perhaps the field of gifted education could benefit from considering the original definition of pedagogy: *to lead a child*. That is very different than the focus of professional development or a college course. Pedagogy is not a classroom management strategy or some tips on how to get essays graded more efficiently. For the social studies teacher, it is the purposeful restructuring of the classroom to create an environment whose purpose is the training of free-thinking, well-reasoned citizens of a republic capable of self-governance (Hooks, 1994).

In his seminal work, *Pedagogy of the Oppressed*, Paulo Freire (1970) made the assertion that the process of education and the process of liberation are essentially the same thing; a truly free person must be intellectually self-aware and it is the job of the teacher to guide students toward that objective. Note the use of the term *guide* here. For this process to be effective for gifted learners, the motivation for it must be intrinsic (Clinkenbeard, 2012). Self-awareness, after all, cannot be extrinsic. Although *Pedagogy of the Oppressed* is widely read and its philosophy is highly influential in the design of gifted programs in many countries (Gyarmathy, 2013; O'Reilly, 2013; Sieglinde, 2013; Tirri & Kuusisto, 2013), it has yet to be widely read in American education settings, either by teachers or students. In a later book, *Pedagogy of Freedom*, Freire (1998) focused on why this type of education matters in American society. Echoing Washington and Jefferson, he argued that for any type of self-ruled society to function as it is intended, its citizens must constantly question the wisdom, ethics, morality, and judgment of its leadership.

For gifted education in the social studies, this call for a liberating education is compelling. Where else will our gifted students, many of whom will be leaders in some capacity or another in the future, learn to critically examine our society and their role in it if not in a social studies classroom? Null

(2011) argued that "Liberal education is the opposite of indoctrination" (p 15). Students educated in this tradition consider issues from multiple perspectives, base their judgments on reason, and avoid blindly following the thoughts and dictates of others (Null, 2011). If we are to answer that challenge, then we must think carefully about the design of our social studies programs and the purposes that they serve. What follows is an attempt to do just that in a way that is aligned with accepted standards of gifted education and with thought given to program design in the social studies that provides some practical guidance to curriculum designers and classroom instructors alike.

Components of Instructional Design

The field of gifted education includes competing paradigmatic approaches, curriculum models, and instructional methodologies that are beyond the scope of this chapter. However, for purposes of developing an engaging, thoughtful curriculum approach for the social studies, several of the most popular and widely used of these models, paradigms, and methodologies were analyzed for agreed upon best practices (Assouline & Lupkowski-Shoplik, 2012; Charap, 2013; Dai & Chen, 2013; Eckstein, 2009; Johnsen, Haensly, Ryser, & Ford, 2002; Jones & Hébert, 2012; Rollins, Mursky, Shah-Coltrane, & Johnsen, 2009; VanTassel-Baska & Brown, 2007; VanTassel-Baska & Wood, 2010). A modern approach to curriculum in gifted education must engage the following: critical-thinking, independent learning, effective research practice, meaningful collaboration, and production of quality, advanced-level products.

The social studies as a discipline are replete with opportunities to push students in those areas, but those opportunities are not always fully realized. State standards often do not push students to higher order thinking and contain little or no requirements for advanced-level products. Even Advanced Placement (AP) standards for courses like U.S. History and World History have not adequately addressed critical thinking, independent learning, authentic research, collaboration, and advanced-level products (Russell, 2014). They, too, have focused heavily on knowledge acquisition without critical engagement; however, recent changes in AP course designs suggest promise for those courses engaging gifted learners in the future.

Critical thinking, independent learning, effective research practice, meaningful collaboration, and production of quality, advanced-level products have been advocated in the broad guidelines for historical education set forth by the American Historical Association (n.d.) and in the standards set forth by the UCLA Center for History Education, which maintains one of the most comprehensive, research-based, continuously updated set of standards for history education in the United States (National Center for History in the Schools, n.d.). Learning designs focusing on chronological thinking, historical comprehension, historical analysis and interpretation, and historical research capabilities characterize critical engagement and a thoughtful approach to social studies curriculum, and these approaches could be adapted across the social studies given the similarity of disciplines from history to civics to the social sciences. This curriculum framework for gifted and advanced learners in the social studies focuses heavily on questioning assumptions about history, politics, economics, culture, and how we receive information and use knowledge to formulate our own interpretations of truth. Thus, each design component is accompanied by a description of what the students are most obviously encouraged to question in the attempt to produce more critical learning and engagement in the social studies classroom.

Lecture 2.0

Who the strategy questions: The expert (in this case, the teacher himself).
What the strategy questions: The reliability of a narrative.

At some point, there is no getting around three learning activities in the social studies: reading, writing, and the lecture. The first two are obvious, but it is the lecture that may be the bane of gifted student and gifted teacher alike. Lectures may not seem very engaging or exciting. In history, for example, we have a frustrating tendency to take material that should instantly engage intellectual students and make it the most boring thing they do all day.

It does not have to be this way (Baer, 2010; Milgram & Davidovich, 2010). A teacher has information that students might need, but they are not the only source. Nor are they or their source materials always correct. Instead of the lecture following the "sage on a stage" model, it should be restructured as an interactive learning experience. Using as an example a lesson on The Declaration of Independence, some forethought could turn the class into a dynamic teaching environment. For example, the day before the lecture the teacher could assign several students to read biographical studies on important founders and their lives. Others could be assigned the task of justifying the American claims in the Declaration of Independence. Still others could be assigned the task of countering the points of the Americans with the points of the British. In this way, all students have some of the information and the teacher comes to the lecture as a storyteller pausing frequently to ask questions of the new experts in the room: the students.

Of course, such a lesson is easy to theorize, but the realities of a classroom are sometimes a bit more chaotic and the lecture often becomes the last-minute solution to unforeseen problems that wreck carefully designed learning events. In this situation, the teacher can still engage the students in meaningful and critical ways. Modern technology provides instant access to information for most people through computers, tablets, and phone devices. In the course of a lecture, an effective instructor of the gifted in this new model should embrace this technology for what it can provide (Eckstein, 2009). The teacher could break from the narrative for a few minutes and challenge the students to address why what is being taught might be biased. Information accepted as fact could be challenged with the requirement that any challenge be supported with sources. Then, the students could be pushed to defend the source of the material with which they are challenging the initial assertions. This will be challenging at first because so many students are afraid to be wrong and many educators fear admitting that they do not know everything, but the effort will be rewarded with far more engaging lecture days.

The Counterfactual: The Critical Thinker's Friend

What the strategy questions: The cause and effect relationship between events.

All historians play the "what-if" game at some point. If we change X, how does that alter event Y? In the gifted history classroom (or other social studies with some modification), play away. Students will be engaged by the chance to create an alternate scenario and will have to learn the actual details of the historical events being discussed to justify their assertions about how things might have been different. For those teachers in a mixed-abilities classroom, this is also a useful strategy. Students could be assigned to ability groups and given pieces of a broader lesson to work on. On-level students could be assigned to do a detailed timeline of Revolutionary War events while slightly more advanced students might be assigned to analyze historical speeches of the period for rhetoric and bias and gifted students assigned to create a counterfactual narrative that speaks to a what-if scenario in which George Washington chooses not to take command of the Continental Army. In this way, all students are engaged with something meaningful and worthwhile that engages them at their ability level and that produces an end result that is beneficial to the whole group when the pieces are drawn back together.

Current Events and Public Policy: Contemporary Critical Engagement

What the strategy questions: The ethics and integrity of forces like political leadership and the media.

Current events are a commonly used tool in many social studies classrooms, but often their use is of limited benefit. Students might be asked to discuss current events, but the bias of how those events are portrayed is often neglected. Similarly, public policy is often uncritically discussed in civics courses, but how often is the public policy of the past looked at in a history class or how a particular policy might impact something like mental health as it is studied in a psychology class? Further, how often do these lessons involve real-world documents or the creation of real-world products?

For gifted students in the social studies, to be given this information is not enough. Nor is just discussing it in a classroom setting. Gifted students must be pushed to produce new ideas on their own. Instead of a lesson on how a bill becomes a law, they should write one. Instead of presenting it just to their class, they should be encouraged to send it to their local, state, or federal elected officials with a written request to support it in the legislature. A similar approach could be taken with historical writing. Instead of being asked to write a paper for their history class that they will probably never read or use again, gifted students at the secondary level should be pushed to write for publication in an academic journal. *The Concord Review* (http://www.tcr.org/tcr/current.htm) is a great example of advanced high school students' social studies papers. The quality of this level of work should define the standard for writing projects in the gifted social studies learning design.

Local and Oral History: Ordinary People and Places Matter

What the strategy questions: The importance of micro-history and understanding historical events beyond battles and major events.

One of the biggest challenges to teaching history is overcoming the idea that history is only created by great people long ago in faraway places, and that it only matters if somebody took the time to write it down in a book. It can be much more. Gifted and advanced learners are capable of designing authentic research projects and producing advanced, even professional-level products as a result of this work.

As an assignment, students might be tasked with going out and talking to people about events in their lifetime and recording that for posterity. In this way, gifted learners come to see how historical events are shaped by real people (Ritchie, 1995). A lesson on the Vietnam War or the Civil Rights Movement becomes a much more meaningful lesson when students have a real person and his or her experiences to associate with it.

Further, this type of lesson does not have to be about large-scale events. Every community has its own history, and it is common knowledge in the field of historical studies that much of that local history, which often provides invaluable insight into how people actually lived in the past, is being lost in the modern world because no one writes it down or takes it out of small local libraries and museums and does anything with it (Kyvig & Marty, 2000).

Gifted students tasked with either of these types of assignments should be given the end goal of a real-world product. A class report is fine, but how much better would it be for the student's work to find publication in a historical journal, a respectable online history forum, or even the local newspaper? Gifted students often struggle with the fact that they are developmentally ahead of others their own age, but that their ideas and efforts are often dismissed as amateurish by adults around them. What better way to see to the social-emotional needs of a bright learner than to have his or her work legitimized beyond the classroom? And, frankly, this type of assignment, when done correctly, illustrates for students that there can be a career in this type of work if they are interested in it and that they do not have to bow to the pressure of "learning something that gets you a real job."

Historiography: The Tools of the Trade

What the strategy questions: The validity of the texts, course materials, and other sources of information.

It is vital to teach kids to do careful, systematic research and analysis of evidence. In history, this is called *historiography*, but the principles are basically the same as in any of the social sciences. What is called for is a healthy dose of skepticism when analyzing source material. Students, even gifted ones, often accept as fact something they read or that their teachers tell them. They often need help in learning to distinguish reliable material from unreliable.

Information cited on a reputable website and corroborated by several different sources and primary documents is probably more trustworthy than, say, a claim about some historical event in a work of historical fiction with no proof of research behind it.

Technology: Our History Doesn't Have to be in the Past

What the strategy questions: Overreliance on traditional texts, methods, and sources of information.

All too often it seems that there is a perception that the social studies are the purview of the Luddite. However, the stereotype of the lovably absent-minded history teacher with his or her head constantly in a book or pontificating on trivia and complaining about modern technology is not how serious historians operate; furthermore, neither can it represent an acceptable model for a gifted social studies classroom. As teachers of the gifted, we must be open to changes in technology and the mediums by which information can be presented both by the teacher and by the students.

Imagine an artistically gifted young person bored and disengaged from his text suddenly stimulated to learn by the use of a good historical graphic novel. Or better yet, imagine that same young man tasked with creating a graphic novel of those historical events to be used by other students as a text. You could take it one step further and partner that student with others who excel at historical research and computer design and produce a historically themed video game that could help others to learn history without even realizing it (Gee, 2007).

Philosophy: What Ever Happened to Critical Thinking?

What the strategy questions: That there is only one way to think.

Some might have read the introduction to this chapter and asserted that what was being proposed was really nothing new. It is an absolutely fascinating phenomenon that every time someone comes along with some new approach or idea in education that really catches peoples' attention in the field it often boils down to something to do with engaging students as better critical thinkers. Perhaps it is a testament to how far out of our awareness and education classical philosophy has fallen, but no one ever points out that most of these *new* ideas in education are really just retreads of Aristotle. Is this because we as teachers and researchers have forgotten or never been taught our classics?

Many teachers claim to use the Socratic method, but have they ever read the works of Plato from which it comes?

Western philosophy is essentially the history of rationality and thinking critically. Ideas and approaches that stand up to reasoned analysis and criticism over time are superior to ideas and approaches that do not. The Aristotelian methodology is at the heart of critical thinking in most academic fields, so why have we abandoned it in the social studies? Gifted learners, especially those taught to question everything, will benefit from instructional design that includes the study of philosophy. Gifted social studies curricula should require students to struggle to make sense of historical and current events using the tools of critical analysis set down two millennia ago.

Talent Development and the New Social Studies Paradigm

In the field of gifted education, there are those who favor a talent development approach to the identification and service of gifted young people. In this model, a wide number of students are assessed for giftedness and then reassessed for talent in a specific discipline or field. Those identified through this process are intensely schooled in the area of their talent and interest, with the end result being students who finish the program as the absolute best in their field (Assouline & Lupkowski-Shoplik, 2012). This model has been applied to those talented in many different fields of human endeavor from music to athletics to science and mathematics, but what would a talent development approach look like to develop gifted social studies students?

Imagine a specialized program whose goal is to develop the best public policy thinkers and researchers that could possibly be produced; elite students ready to take on the challenges of the 21st century armed with an eye for critical thinking, a keen insight into how historical events have shaped the modern world, and a deep knowledge of how social and political forces affect people and how they live. Such a program would have the potential to turn out the next generation of leaders; young people willing to question assumptions and provide the best-informed, most well-reasoned solutions to problems facing the world. That is a bold vision for gifted social studies education, and it's time for a bold vision.

Implications for Research

This chapter has sought to reimagine the social studies for gifted students in a way that creates relevance and meaning not only in the lessons themselves, but in the minds of those bright young people for whom they are designed. There are several implications for research on advanced social studies curriculum and the development of elite talent in social studies domains.

First, there is a dearth of research in the area of social studies as it pertains to giftedness. Jolly and Kettler (2008) reviewed research published in gifted education over a 10-year period from 1994 to 2003 and found a combined 48 published studies in science, mathematics, and language arts, but not a single study in social studies curriculum. More research needs to be done on the cognitive and motivational benefits of gifted and advanced students engaging in critical thinking, authentic research, purposeful collaboration, and advanced product development in social studies. To this end, we need studies to propose and investigate outcomes and benchmarks of advanced or elite performance in the social studies domains.

Second, the development of the Common Core State Standards (CCSS) for Language Arts includes standards for literacy in grades 6–12 social studies. Curriculum design specialists in gifted education have advocated for systematic differentiation of the CCSS language arts for gifted and advanced learners (Hughes, Kettler, Shaunessy-Dedrick, & VanTassel-Baska, 2014; VanTassel-Baska, 2013). To this point, little advocacy and no research has addressed the implementation for these CCSS social studies literacy standards for gifted students. What process or learning design models are used to integrate those literacy standards in social studies? How do curriculum designers differentiate the literacy expectations and cognitive demands of the learning tasks for gifted and advanced learners? In what ways are advanced outcomes measured to document advanced literacy development in social studies? These are good questions that are timely and important to understanding the impact of CCSS literacy in social studies.

Third, there are more AP courses in the social studies than in any other domain (e.g., U.S. History, World History, European History, Human Geography, U.S. Government, Comparative Government, Macroeconomics, and Microeconomics). There seem to be assumptions that these courses are appropriate curriculum models for gifted students in social studies; however, little or no research has documented advanced performance outcomes associated with gifted students traversing these curricula. Furthermore, some studies (e.g., Russell, 2014) suggest that some AP social studies courses include curriculum with little opportunities for critical thinking, independent research, or advanced-level products. Perhaps as we recommend teaching our students to question assumptions, it may be a good idea to question some assumptions about the adequacy of AP courses for the development of elite levels of social studies talent.

Finally, there needs to be a larger body of research about the preparedness of teachers of the social studies in general and for those instructing the gifted specifically. Some studies suggest that large percentages of American students learn the social studies from a teacher not properly grounded in how to teach them (National Center for Education Statistics, 2006). More data is needed to determine what could be done to improve the preparation of social studies teachers to teach gifted students for the development of domain specific talents.

Conclusion

Thought-provoking and engaging social studies learning design cannot be grounded in the memorization of names and dates. Advanced social studies learning design for gifted students ought to be founded in critical-thinking, independent learning, effective research practice, meaningful collaboration, and production of quality, advanced-level products. The potential to reimagine social studies as the foundation for developing 21st-century leaders, thinkers, and intellectual innovators is vast, open, and compelling. Such is the purview of modern gifted education and curriculum design.

Discussion Questions

1. In what ways might unlimited information, global connections, and ubiquitous technology influence social studies learning design?
2. What are evidences of advanced talent or elite performances associated with the various social studies domains?
3. How can curriculum designers emphasize intellect, problem solving, and imagination in advanced social studies?

4. What are the possibilities for integrating philosophy and other humanities disciplines into advanced social studies curriculum?
5. What are advanced-level products and performances that could be articulated in a viable scope and sequence of social studies curricula from elementary through high school?

References

American Historical Association. (n.d.). *AHA history tuning project: History discipline core.* Retrieved from http://www.historians.org/teaching-and-learning/current-projects/tuning/history-discipline-core

Assouline, S. G., & Lupkowski-Shoplik, A. (2012). The talent search model of gifted identification. *Journal of Psychoeducational Assessment, 30*(1), 45–59. doi:10.1177/0734282911433946

Baer, J. (2010). Lectures may be more effective than you think: The learning pyramid unmasked. *The International Journal of Creativity and Problem Solving, 20,* 15–28.

Charap, L. (2013). Redesigning advanced placement U.S. history. *Magazine of History, 27*(3), 31.

Clinkenbeard, P. R. (2012). Motivation and gifted students: Implications of theory and research. *Psychology in the Schools, 49,* 622–630. doi:10.1002/pits.21628

Dai, D. Y., & Chen, F. (2013). Three paradigms of gifted education: In search of conceptual clarity in research and practice. *Gifted Child Quarterly, 57,* 151–168. doi:10.1177/0016986213490020

Eckstein, M. (2009). Enrichment 2.0 gifted and talented education for the 21st century. *Gifted Child Today, 32*(1), 59.

Freire, P. (1970). *Pedagogy of the oppressed.* New York, NY: Bloomsbury.

Freire, P. (1998). *Pedagogy of freedom: Ethics, democracy, and civic courage.* Lanham, MD: Rowman & Littlefield Publishers, Inc.

Gee, J. P. (2007). *What video games have to teach us about learning and literacy.* New York, NY: Palgrave MacMillan.

Graham, O. (2013). A gifted education. *Harvard Educational Review, 83*(2), 295.

Gyarmathy, E. (2013). The gifted and gifted education in Hungary. *Journal for the Education of the Gifted, 36,* 19–43. doi:10.1177/0162353212471587

Hooks, B. (1994). *Teaching to transgress: Education as the practice of freedom.* New York, New York: Routledge.

Hughes, C. E., Kettler, T., Shaunessy-Dedrick, E., & VanTassel-Baska, J. (2014). *A teacher's guide to using the Common Core State Standards with gifted and advanced learners in English/language arts.* Waco, TX: Prufrock Press.

Johnsen, S. K., Haensly, P. A., Ryser, G. R., & Ford, R. F. (2002). Changing general education classroom practices to adapt for gifted students. *Gifted Child Quarterly, 46,* 45–63. doi:10.1177/001698620204600105

Jolly, J. L., & Kettler, T. (2008). Gifted education research 1994–2003: A disconnect between priorities and practice. *Journal for the Education of the Gifted, 31,* 427–446.

Jones, J. K., & Hébert, T. P. (2012). Engaging diverse gifted learners in U.S. history classrooms. *Gifted Child Today, 35*(4), 252–261.

Kyvig, D. E., & Marty, M. A. (2000). *Nearby history: Exploring the past around you* (2nd ed.). Walnut Creek, CA: AltaMira Press.

Milgram, R. M., & Davidovich, N. (2010). Creative thiking and lecturer effectiveness in higher education. *The International Journal of Creativity and Problem Solving, 20,* 7–14.

National Center for Education Statistics. (2006). *Qualifications of public secondary school history teachers, 1999–2000.* Retrieved from http://nces.ed.gov/pubs2006/2006004.pdf

National Center for History in the Schools. (n.d.). *History standards.* Retrieved from http://www.nchs.ucla.edu/history-standards

Null, W. (2011). *Curriculum: From theory to practice.* Lanham, MD: Rowman & Littlefield.

O'Reilly, C. (2013). Gifted education in Ireland. *Journal for the Education of the Gifted, 36*(1), 97–118. doi:10.1177/0162353212470039

Ritchie, D. A. (1995). *Doing oral history.* New York, NY: Twayne Publishers.

Rollins, K., Mursky, C. V., Shah-Coltrane, S., & Johnsen, S. K. (2009). RtI models for gifted children. *Gifted Child Today, 32*(3), 20–30.

Russell, J. (2014). *Advanced placement United States history and its effectiveness for the gifted learner.* Manuscript submitted for publication.

Sieglinde, W. (2013). Gifted education in Austria. *Journal for the Education of the Gifted, 36,* 365–383.

Tirri, K., & Kuusisto, E. (2013). How Finland serves gifted and talented pupils. *Journal for the Education of the Gifted, 36*(1), 84–96. doi:10.1177/0162353212468066

VanTassel-Baska, J. (Ed.). (2013). *Using the Common Core State Standards for English language arts with gifted and advanced learners.* Waco, TX: Prufrock Press.

VanTassel-Baska, J., & Brown, E. F. (2007). Toward best practice: An analysis of the efficacy of curriculum models in gifted education. *Gifted Child Quarterly, 51,* 342–358. doi:10.1177/0016986207306323

VanTassel-Baska, J., & Wood, S. (2010). The integrated curriculum model (ICM). *Learning and Individual Differences, 20,* 345–357. doi:10.1016/j.lindif.2009.12.006

CHAPTER 20

CURRICULUM TO CHALLENGE GIFTED LEARNERS IN THE SOCIAL STUDIES

DANIEL L. WINKLER, ROBYN ANDERMANN, JAMES MOORE, AND DAVID BACKER

Empirical research on social studies instruction for the gifted is scant (Hockett, 2008; Troxclair, 2000). Because of this lack of empirically validated practices, a number of curricular modifications and instructional methods are presented in this chapter. Although not all of these learning designs have been validated with gifted students, each shows promise. Discerning educators should consider these different techniques, which include inquiry-based instruction, Advanced Placement courses and related methods, discussion techniques, acceleration strategies, and service learning, as potential curriculum design elements for their own settings. We will present introductions and guidelines for each technique, so that educators can determine for themselves which of these options is best for their educational setting. This will hopefully help educators experiment in their social studies curriculum, helping to academically challenge gifted students.

DOI: 10.4324/9781003236696-23

Social Studies and Gifted Education

Social studies is a complex and even controversial construct. The National Council for the Social Studies (NCSS, n.d.) has defined social studies as the interconnected study of the social sciences. However, exactly which social sciences and which humanities are to be integrated, as well as what constitutes civic competence are topics which have been hotly debated since the field's inception in the early 20th century (Evans, 2004). Additionally, many have questioned if civic competence ought to be the end goal of social studies, with scholars, policy makers, teachers, and others offering a variety of opinions on what social studies is and how it should be taught. Should social studies courses be approached as a way to transmit cultural knowledge and a common civic heritage (Cheney, 1987; Schlesinger, 1991)? Should course content focus on the rudiments of various humanities and social sciences, helping students to become junior historians and social scientists (Bruner, 1960; Fenton, 1991)? Should social studies be approached as a framework to help students engage in reflective inquiry (Evans, 2004)? Or should social studies embody elements of all of these, as well as other approaches (Evans & Passe, 2007)? Current scholarship suggests that these questions have long been asked by social studies leaders and policymakers and will continue to be asked.

In addition to these issues, educators of the gifted must also concern themselves with the underserved learning needs of gifted students. In 2001, Congress updated the Javits Gifted and Talented Students Education Act (originally passed in 1988) to fund research on gifted and talented students and provide effective strategies to assist schools and teachers in meeting the needs of this student population (Gollnick & Chinn, 2013). Unfortunately, funding for gifted education remains far below that which is provided by the 2004 Individuals with Disabilities Act (Public Law 108-446), even though gifted and talented students have different needs that justify appropriate education services (Zevin, 2007).

With or without funding, social studies teachers can still academically challenge their gifted students. To teach gifted students, educators should move beyond traditional teaching methods—lectures, worksheets, reading from the textbook, and answering questions—that are viewed as boring, irrelevant, and a reason why some gifted students remain unchallenged (Martorella, Beal, & Bolick, 2005). Negative student attitudes are a logical consequence of reducing social studies to rote memorization of facts and ignoring the critical importance of controversy, passions, competing values, attitudes, and beliefs in all human affairs. This is unfortunate, especially in light of the importance of social studies in producing American citizens capable of meaningful participation in a dynamic and pluralistic democracy, one of the proffered purposes of social studies described above. It is vital that teachers create activities that generate critical thought and passion in gifted students and allow them to be actively engaged in all of their educational experiences. To do this, educators can create curricular changes or introduce new classroom practices. These approaches offer a variety of opportunities that can help students in different settings. No one approach is a surefire solution for social studies teachers, but each could be considered an option despite their limitations.

The Common Core and C3 Framework

Standards, like the Common Core State Standards (CCSS; National Governors Association Center for Best Practices [NGA] & Council of Chief State School Officers [CCSSO], 2010a, 2010b), are a ubiquitous feature of contemporary educators' lives. The CCSS, created by state governors in conjunction with content experts in English and mathematics, are a set of standards that prepare students for college or the workplace in a modern high-tech economy. The CCSS describe the literacy skills that social studies students are expected to know, but do not mandate any social studies content. The NCSS (2013) created the College, Career, and Civic Life Framework (C3) in response to state requests for clarity on what college and career preparation would look like in social studies courses. Thus, the C3 Framework in social studies supports CCSS goals by focusing on the knowledge and skills that students will need for civic life and successful economic participation in a knowledge- and skills-based economy.

The C3 Framework focuses on developing knowledge and skills via an *inquiry arc* that requires developing compelling questions, research, evidence-based claims, disciplined thinking, communication, and assessment (NCSS, 2013). The C3 Framework focuses on history, geography, economics, and civics, although the NCSS does have 10 social studies themes (see Figure 20.1, which lists these within the structure of a sample project). Indeed, improving preparation for civic life—more informed and active citizens committed to democracy and civic participation—is a major goal of the new inquiry-based program. The C3 Framework (NCSS, 2013) has four dimensions:

1. *Developing Questions and Planning Investigations*: Students will develop questions as they investigate societal issues, trends, and events.
2. *Applying Disciplinary Concepts and Tools*: Students will analyze societal issues, trends, and events by applying concepts and tools from civics, economics, geography, and history.
3. *Gathering, Evaluating, and Using Evidence*: Students will work toward conclusions about societal issues, trends, and events by collecting evidence and evaluating its usefulness in developing causal explanations.
4. *Working Collaboratively and Communicating Conclusions*: Students will draw on knowledge and skills to work individually and collaboratively to conclude their investigations into societal issues, trends, and events. (p. 12)

For example, the inquiry project begins with the formulation of a compelling question such as, "What policies and programs should society create to reduce poverty?" The next step requires students to employ the disciplinary tools of the social sciences to describe and analyze the trends, causes, consequences, and solutions to poverty. In order to achieve these objectives, students must gather and evaluate data—Census Bureau facts and statistics, political and economic articles and books that discuss poverty, evidence on the impact of poverty on individuals and society, viable solutions, and historical trends—that leads them to make informed decisions and policy recommendations. Finally, students present their research in an authentic setting (ideally, the audience will include business and community members, political leaders, parents, and other stakeholders) in the form of presentations, reports, published essays, mock trials, simulations, debates, and other forums. The C3 Framework is challenging because it requires active student behaviors, critical thinking, research, collaboration, and communication, which is precisely the type of challenge that gifted and talented students need in order to reach their academic potential and eventual successful civic and economic participation (Chapin, 2015). Figure 20.1 offers another illustration of how this can be done by integrating inquiry techniques with the NCSS themes, other subject areas, and the C3 principles into an inquiry project about the Black Plague.

Black Death Project

How-to-Steps
1. Define the problem. Create a compelling question that guides the students.
2. Students drive the project by researching the problem, collecting and analyzing data, and doing other authentic tasks.
3. Remember, the teacher is the guide who facilitates the students' inquiries.

Example Topic:
The Black Death (bubonic plague in Europe, ca. 1348–1352)

Compelling Question
   How did the Black Death impact Europe socially, economically, and politically in the 14th century (causes, consequences, and possible solutions to the Black Death)?

Questions Associated With the 10 NCSS Themes
   Each group could take one NCSS theme for their project:
1. *Culture:* How did the Black Death change family structure in Europe? How did certain religious groups respond to the plague?
2. *History:* Research primary sources to determine the number of people who died and were afflicted with the plague. Compare and contrast the Black Death with the AIDS epidemic circa 1980–2014. How does the mortality of the plague compare with other infectious diseases, such as smallpox and malaria? What can we learn from the history of the plague that could help us prepare for a similar crisis today?
3. *Geography:* Trace the diffusion of the plague from Asia to Europe. Explain how and why the plague spread geographically.
4. *Psychology:* Describe the psychological impact of the plague on families and church officials.
5. *Sociology:* What social classes had the highest rates of mortality and morbidity? How were the Jews treated during the plague?
6. *Political Science:* What role did the Catholic Church play during the plague? Describe the official policies and positions of the Church. How did local rulers deal with the plague as a public health disaster?
7. *Economics:* Analyze the economic impact of the plague on feudalism and manorialism. How did the plague impact serfs and peasants?
8. *Science, Technology, and Society:* Describe what the plague is in medical terms and explain how it affects humans (conditions, symptoms, overall health, prognosis, etc.). Identify some of the "cures and treatments" for the disease. How would the plague be treated today?

FIGURE 20.1. Example of an interdisciplinary inquiry project that addresses the 10 NCSS themes.

9. *Global Connections:* How did the plague impact European trade with other regions? How did the plague impact China and India?

10. *Civic Ideals:* Describe how some individuals reacted with courage and compassion during the horrors brought by death and suffering. Create a public policy plan to effectively deal with a public health crisis today.

Example Activities/Assessments

Products produced by students could include: videos, debates, posters, essays, PowerPoint presentations, art, music, literature, models, portfolios, interviews, photographs, and so forth.

Other possible interdisciplinary, inquiry projects could include:

Drug legalization	Environmental issues
School dress codes (workplace)	War and terrorism
Capital punishment	Health issues
Immigration	Welfare
Employment	Racism
First Amendment	Homelessness
Sexuality and the law	Gender issues

FIGURE 20.1. Continued.

Advanced Placement Courses and Techniques

Another common element of some educators' lives is the College Board's Advanced Placement (AP) program. Although the AP social studies courses are not gifted education programs per se, the programs are, nevertheless, intended to offer rigorous, college-level curricula and assessment. Some studies have found that gifted students prefer the rigor of AP curricula over boredom associated with many typical high school courses (Hertberg-Davis & Callahan; 2008; Kyburg, Hertberg-Davis, & Callahan, 2007). The College Board's curriculum framework for each of its AP social studies courses notes specific skills and habits of mind necessary to succeed on the AP examinations, as well as recommendations for instruction to cultivate those skills, both at the AP and pre-AP level. In addition, a number of AP social studies courses, particularly in history, are undergoing revision for the purpose of allowing teachers more flexibility to focus on state and local priorities, especially as they relate to the CCSS (College Board, n.d.). The result is a framework that emphasizes critical thinking rather than content coverage. It is possible for educators to adapt some of the AP program's recommendations to create challenging learning opportunities for all gifted social studies students, including those who might enroll in pre-AP and AP courses.

One aspect of AP courses educators of the gifted could adapt/emphasize would be reflective and critical inquiry of the past. The curriculum framework for AP U.S. History states that developing students' ability to reason chronologically and to compare and contextualize historical events are skills that support this goal (College Board, 2014). This means that students should push beyond merely identifying and describing the sequence of both long- and short-term causes and effects of a particular event to analyzing and evaluating the relationship among those causes and effects. Often the short-term causes of an event are relatively easy to identify and describe. However, when students are given primary and secondary readings that speak to the overarching social, political, and economic forces at play over a given timeframe, they have a chance to discern the complex system of causes and effects of historical events that interact over time. For example, a rigorous analysis of America's entry into World War I might examine the relationship between short-term and long-term causes and effects. Students' readings and discussions about the long-term divergence of democratic and autocratic societies could be weighed against the short-term incidents of U.S. publication of anti-German propaganda and Germany's policy of unrestricted submarine warfare.

A critical view of the past also requires that students understand that history itself is a product of human thinking. Thus, the AP program's suggestion to engage students in analyses of historical periodization is a sound one to promote rigorous instruction and thoughtful learning. Students should be provided with opportunities to reflect on how the tool of periodization, that is, the organization of history into discrete periods or eras, represents the perspectives of certain historians. How a historian defines historical periods depends on what political, economic, social, and cultural factors the historian considers most significant (College Board, 2014). These choices serve to highlight certain events, people, and places and to de-emphasize others. Students could be given the opportunity to compare two or more different periodization schemes—perhaps one in a textbook and that of the AP framework or a syllabus for a college course—and to justify or critique the historians' choices in light of circumstances in which the historians lived and worked. This exercise also serves to reinforce their skills of chronological reasoning and contextualization. Students might investigate how periodization has changed over time. They might experiment with creating their own examples of periodization and consider how any changes they make might influence the historical narrative.

Perhaps the most effective teaching strategies in AP classrooms are frequent writing assignments connected to the analysis of primary documents (Gross, 2004). Gross (2004) found that successful AP teachers used brief interpretive essay questions at least once per week, and required students to interpret the meaning of both a piece of text and a visual document, such as a cartoon, a map, a chart, or a graph. These activities are typically done in preparation for Document-Based Questions, which are key components of the writing portions of AP history examinations, which contain both textual and visual documents. Students proficient in the interpretation and synthesis of documents are able to craft nuanced and thoughtful historical arguments that are supported by ample evidence (Wineburg, 2001). In choosing documents to analyze, it is important that educators provide students with evidence that illuminates multiple sides of an issue. Exposure to a variety of sources reflecting a wide range of points of view can help students to draw their own conclusions and inferences and help them understand that history is as much a matter of interpretation as it is fact.

Drake and Drake-Brown (2003) devised a three-tier approach to analyzing point of view using primary documents. In the first stage, the teacher presents a "core document" to illustrate a central concept (Drake & Drake-Brown, 2003, p. 467). In the second stage, students are given other documents that support or conflict with the original source and are encouraged to discuss the contrasting evidence. For example, by contrasting a photo of a sharecropper with that of a landowner, students can learn about differing perspectives and experiences within the same time and place. In the third stage, students are taught research skills necessary to locate their own sources. Sources should either relate to the overall historical picture, reflect the point of view of one of the prescribed documents, or offer an altogether new interpretation. These stages, as well as some of the other features of AP courses, could be adapted for gifted and advanced learners across multiple grade levels.

Acceleration and Online Learning

Acceleration is one of the most useful methods to academically challenge gifted students (Colangelo, Assouline, & Gross, 2004). There are multiple types of acceleration, but it typically involves moving "students through an educational program at rates faster, or at younger ages than typical" (Colangelo et al., 2004, p. xi). This could include grade skipping, early entry to college, earning college credit in high school through dual enrollment or AP examinations, grade telescoping, and several other techniques (Rogers, 2004). Many forms of acceleration have yielded great success (Culross, Jolly, & Winkler, 2013). However, success is easier to attain in some subjects than others. In mathematics, for instance, the content is linear, requiring consecutive mastery. The same could be said in language arts curriculum with regard to mastering increasingly complex elements of grammar and syntax. Linear curriculum more easily accommodates acceleration.

However, social studies is not linear in this sense. Instead, each year, or even semester, students are presented with an entirely different subject, such as civics, economics, American history, psychology, etc. These topics are certainly related and can be interconnected, but students could conceivably be content experts in American history and know nothing about economics. Because of this, acceleration in the social studies should be done in a more measured manner. AP courses are one example of this. They are yearlong, self-contained courses that can provide the student with college credit.

Another way to accelerate effectively in the social studies would be through pretesting and differentiation (Reis & Renzulli, 1992). Students could be given the end-of-unit or even end-of-semester/year test. If they scored highly, they could be exposed to new, more challenging content. Such content could be derived from many universities that post free online lectures, occasionally referred to as *open courseware* or *open content*. In many cases, hour-long videos, podcasts, and other content can be freely streamed or downloaded on the iTunes store. In other cases, transcripts of the lectures are provided, as are outlines, course syllabi, and additional notes/information. Content in open courseware is provided by university professors around the world including prestigious universities in the United States, such as Yale, Stanford, and MIT.

Students could enroll also in a free Massive Open Online Course, or MOOC. Many MOOCs pertain to social studies, and some offer certificates for completion. A MOOC, unlike most open courseware, is actually going on in real time. MOOCs have teachers and graders with whom students can correspond. There are also other students in the course who live all over the world, and while this provides opportunities for collaboration, it can also introduce privacy concerns. The website http://www.coursera.org is a useful aggregator that can help interested teachers, coordinators, and interventionists find appropriate courses. Students could cite their completion certificate on college applications, demonstrating experience with online, college-level courses.

While presenting vast opportunities such as worldwide collaboration and college-level experience, these methods of acceleration can also present logistical challenges for educators. In pull-out settings, interventionists could more easily offer gifted students access to necessary technology, but in whole class settings, the number of devices available may be limited. Additionally, teachers may have to explain why a few students are doing independent study work, as is often the case with differentiation strategies (Goree, 1996). Teachers could, however, use a sampling of the online video content in the course of their regular instruction. This technology integration enriches the curriculum by providing more diverse and challenging content for gifted students.

And although such accelerative experiences might not progress students toward a higher level of social studies mastery, as would be in the case in math, mastering several social studies does make future eminence in some of the social sciences more possible. For instance, historians who study the economy must know a great deal of history, economics, and mathematics. Those gifted at sociology would need to not only understand much of sociology, but also have at the very least a passing grasp of psychology, history (of that particular society), economics, and potentially even geography. As time is limited, students who master social studies content at earlier ages would probably increase their likelihood of becoming an adult social scientist.

Service Learning

Service learning programs encourage students to engage their surrounding community and address a real need or problem. The highest level of service learning recommended for gifted students is community action (Terry, 2008; Terry & Bohnenberger, 2003). Community action programs encourage students to explore issues in their communities, identify a problem, and develop and implement a solution. Examples of such projects may include environmental and economic activism. Community action service learning offers gifted students the opportunity to engage in authentic tasks and develop important skills. In several case study examples, students met with politicians, studied law, and developed novel and appropriate solutions to complex social problems (Terry, 2008). These projects engaged students in their society and in the social studies, and the students also developed a sense of citizenship and service as a result, one of C3's stated goals.

One complication with such activities is the amount of time, effort, and coordination that they would require from students, teachers, and outside parties. In order to reduce this burden, educators could engage their students in service learning for their own community, the school. Renzulli (2002) illustrated this, detailing how one girl, Melanie, helped another who was partially sighted. Due to his exceptionality, the student could not read any of the books in the library and was bullied. But after some time and effort, Melanie helped end the bullying and had the library acquire appropriately readable books. This kind of smaller-scale, action service project can help students learn how to navigate and improve their own communities, key skills for their eventual lives as adult citizens.

Harkness Teaching

Another more easily implemented, though difficult to master, method is Harkness discussion. Dillon's (1990) research on questioning has demonstrated that higher level student thinking occurs when students ask questions. Given that gifted students may already be thinking at higher levels, the discussion pedagogy one chooses for gifted students should create the conditions for students to ask their own questions. In a social studies context, the Harkness discussion method provides a useful tool to facilitate such discussions.

Inspired by a large grant given to Phillips Exeter Academy in New Hampshire by Edward Harkness, the son of oil magnate Stephen Harkness, Harkness teaching attempts to lead

> student-centered discussions in class, finding ways to get students to make the discoveries for themselves, to get them to draw their own conclusions, to teach them how to consider all sides of an argument, and to make up their own minds based on analysis of the material at hand. (Smith & Foley, 2009, p. 490)

Harkness teachers, in their attempts to get the students to make discoveries for themselves, tend to reject a *sage on the stage* view of pedagogy by using conversational tactics that shift student focus away from the teacher and toward student interactions.

For example, a history teacher is interested in teaching the abolition of slavery in the United States after the Civil War. The Harkness teacher might choose two primary source texts: an abolitionist editorial written in the North and an editorial written by a slaveowner in the South. The students then read these documents, set themselves in a circle, and get ready to discuss. The teacher begins by saying, "Who would like to begin?" The students begin to respond, but the teacher does not respond to their initial responses. Rather, the teacher writes down what they say and serves as more of a guide or facilitator in the discussion.

Harkness teachers do a number of different things to modulate their authority, including not speaking to the content of the lesson, but only to the process of the student interaction, recording the frequency and kind of comments during that interaction, and encouraging students to make their own transitions during discussion. Although there is no clear agreement about exactly how to facilitate a Harkness discussion, three provisional principles of Harkness teaching are as follows:

1. *Let it go and leave it up to them*: A Harkness teacher must, to some degree, relinquish control of classroom events, allowing the group as a whole to share in the administration of the educational outcome.
2. *Track*: A Harkness teacher must produce some account (or trace) of what occurred during class like notes on the kind, frequency, and quality/substance of comments.
3. *Learn through discussion*: A Harkness teacher's goal is to create discussion, which is when a group addresses a question in common through an equal and various sequence of turns taken. The aim is for all participants to learn in this distinct way.

Harkness teaching takes time. Focusing on process rather than product of learning requires a counterintuitive focus on not speaking, listening, and creatively avoiding putting oneself in the expert position, all for the sake of putting the gifted student in that expert position, from which will follow powerful constructivist learning.

Implications for Research

There is less research on social studies curriculum for gifted students than any of the other three core curriculum areas. Our goal was to offer options that can inform the development of curriculum and teaching approaches focused on developing advanced talent in the social studies disciplines. Curriculum designers and teachers should consider how to best address their students' unique needs, and discern from these techniques which ones would be most beneficial for their students.

Moving forward, we need to solidify understandings of advanced social studies as an inquiry-based curriculum that includes critical thinking, creative productivity, and action-oriented outcomes. In addition to conceptual work to guide curriculum design, curriculum experts need to articulate measurable advanced social studies outcomes that can inform research designs on curriculum effectiveness. Revision of the AP U.S. History course and additional AP social studies revisions seem to be moving in a more inquiry-based approach focusing on critical thinking. How might we design studies to capture successful implementations of those programs in a way that develops advanced talent in social studies?

Technology can bring world-class faculty from around the world into our social studies classrooms. At this point, little research exists on the potential effects of open courseware and MOOC courses for social studies. We find ourselves at a time ripe for innovation in curriculum design in the social studies disciplines. How might we use open and available courses to help students engage in deep studies on topics of interest leading to advanced, authentic products and performances? Additionally, inquiry approaches to student-centered learning, like the Harkness model may be beneficial to focus the discipline on critical thinking, argumentation, and intellectual curiosity. We need field-based research designs capable of capturing the value of these approaches to learning in social studies; furthermore, this model for instruction has implications for curriculum design and professional development. We also need to study the types of staff training needed to move to more open-ended inquiry models of social studies.

Discussion Questions

1. What are advanced student outcomes in the social studies disciplines?
2. Advanced Placement courses are widely used in social studies in high schools. In what ways are AP courses appropriate for gifted and advanced learners, and in what ways might they fall short of the ideal curriculum in social studies?
3. What types of professional learning are needed to prepare social studies teachers to implement advanced curriculum including inquiry and student-centered instruction?

References

Bruner, J. (1960). *The process of education.* Cambridge, MA: Harvard University Press.

Chapin, J. R. (2015). *A practical guide to middle and secondary social studies* (4th ed.). New York, NY: Pearson.

Cheney, L. (1987). *American memory: A report on the humanities in the nation's public schools.* Washington, DC: National Council for the Social Studies.

Colangelo, N., Assouline, S., & Gross, M. U. M. (Eds.). (2004). *A nation deceived: How schools hold back America's brightest students* (Vol. 2). Iowa City: The University of Iowa, The Connie Belin and Jacqueline N. Blank International Center for Gifted Education and Talent Development.

College Board. (n.d.). *Get the facts about the advanced placement U.S. history redesign.* Retrieved from https://secure-media.collegeboard.org/digitalServices/pdf/ap/ap-us-history-fact-sheet.pdf

College Board. (2014). *AP United States history: Course and exam description.* Retrieved from http://media.collegeboard.com/digitalServices/pdf/ap/ap-us-history-course-and-exam-description.pdf

Culross, R. R., Jolly, J. L., & Winkler, D. L. (2013). Facilitating grade acceleration: Revisiting the wisdom of John Feldhusen. *Roeper Review, 35,* 36–46.

Dillon, J. T. (1990). *The practice of questioning.* London, England: Routledge.

Drake, F. D., & Drake-Brown, S. (2003). A systematic approach to improve students' historical thinking. *The History Teacher, 36,* 466–489.

Evans, R. W. (2004). *The social studies wars: What should we teach the children?* New York, NY: Teacher College Press.

Evans, R. W., & Passe, J. (2007). Dare we make peace: A dialogue on the social studies wars. *Social Studies, 98*, 251–256.

Fenton, E. (1991). Reflections on the "new social studies." *The Social Studies, 82*, 84–90.

Gollnick, D. M., & Chinn, P. C. (2013). *Multicultural education in a pluralistic society* (9th ed.). Upper Saddle River, NJ: Merrill Prentice Hall.

Goree, K. (1996). Accepting the challenge: Making the most out of inclusive settings. *Gifted Child Today, 19*(2), 22–23, 43.

Gross, R. M. (2004). Strategies for improving the Advanced Placement examination scores of AP social studies students. *The History Teacher, 1*, 115–117.

Hertberg-Davis, H., & Callahan, C. M. (2008). A narrow escape: Gifted students' perceptions of Advanced Placement and International Baccalaureate programs. *Gifted Child Quarterly, 52*, 199–216.

Hockett, J. A. (2008). Social studies. In J. A. Plucker & C. M. Callahan (Eds.), *Critical issues and practices in gifted education: What the research says* (pp. 603–616). Waco, TX: Prufrock Press.

Individuals with Disabilities Education Improvement Act, Pub. Law 108-446 (December 3, 2004).

Kyburg, R. M., Hertberg-Davis, H., & Callahan, C. M. (2007). Advanced Placement and International Baccalaureate programs: Optimal learning experiences for talented minorities? *Journal of Advanced Academics, 18*, 172–215,

Martorella, P. H., Beal, C. M., & Bolick, C. M. (2005). *Teaching social studies in middle and secondary schools* (4th ed.). Upper Saddle River, NJ: Merrill Prentice Hall.

National Council for the Social Studies. (n.d.). *National curriculum standards for social studies: Executive summary*. Retrieved from http://www.socials-tudies.org/standards/execsummary

National Council for the Social Studies. (2013). *The college, career, and civic life (C3) framework for social studies state standards: Guidance for enhancing the rigor of K–12 civics, economics, geography, and history*. Silver Spring, MD: Author.

National Governors Association Center for Best Practices, & Council of Chief State School Officers. (2010a). *Common Core State Standards for English language arts*. Washington, DC: Authors.

National Governors Association Center for Best Practices, & Council of Chief State School Officers. (2010b). *Common Core State Standards for mathematics*. Washington, DC: Authors.

Reis, S. M., & Renzulli, J. S. (1992). Using curriculum compacting to challenge the above-average. *Educational Leadership, 50*(2), 51–57.

Renzulli, J. S. (2002). Expanding the conception of giftedness to include cognitive traits and to promote social capital. *Phi Delta Kappan, 84,* 33–58.

Rogers, K. B. (2004). The academic effects of acceleration. In N. Colangelo, S. Assouline, M. U. M. Gross (Eds.), *A nation deceived: How schools hold back America's brightest students* (Vol. 2, pp. 47–57). Iowa City: The University of Iowa, The Connie Belin and Jacqueline N. Blank International Center for Gifted Education and Talent Development.

Schlesinger, A. M., Jr. (1991). *The disuniting of America: Reflections on a multicultural society.* New York, NY: W. W. Norton.

Smith, L. A., & Foley, M. (2009). Partners in a human enterprise: Harkness teaching in the history classroom. *History Teacher, 42,* 477–496.

Terry, A. W. (2008). Student voices, global echoes: Service-learning and the gifted. *Roeper Review, 30,* 45–51.

Terry, A. W., & Bohnenberger, J. E. (2003). Service-learning: Fostering a cycle of caring in our gifted youth. *The Journal of Secondary Gifted Education, 15,* 23–32.

Troxclair, D. A. (2000). Differentiating instruction for gifted students in regular education social studies classes. *Roeper Review, 22,* 195–200.

Wineburg, S. (2001). *Historical thinking and other unnatural acts: Charting the future of teaching the past.* Philadelphia, PA: Temple University Press.

Zevin, J. (2007). *Social studies for the twenty-first century: Methods and materials for teaching in middle and secondary schools* (3rd ed.). Mahwah, NJ: Lawrence Erlbaum.

ABOUT THE EDITOR

Todd Kettler, Ph.D., is an assistant professor in the Department of Educational Psychology in the College of Education at the University of North Texas, where he teaches courses in gifted education, creativity, and child development. He was a contributing author on *Using the Common Core State Standards for English Language Arts With Gifted and Advanced Learners* (Prufrock Press, 2013), and a co-author on *A Teacher's Guide to Using the Common Core State Standards with Gifted and Advanced Learners in English/Language Arts* (Prufrock Press, 2014). He earned his Ph.D. in Educational Psychology from Baylor University, and he was recently honored with the Advocate of the Year award by the Texas Association for the Gifted/Talented. Dr. Kettler currently serves on the Texas Commissioner of Education's Advisory Council for Gifted Education in Texas, and he serves on the Texas Association for the Gifted/Talented Advocacy Committee. His work has appeared *in Gifted Child Quarterly, Gifted Child Today, Journal for the Education of the Gifted,* and *Journal of Advanced Academics.* In addition to his work as a teacher and researcher at the University of North Texas, he spent 17 years as an English teacher and gifted and talented program administrator.

ABOUT THE AUTHORS

Robyn Andermann is a doctoral student of education at Louisiana State University. She has a B.A. in history from Vanderbilt University and a M.Ed. in social studies education from Loyola University Chicago. Ms. Andermann was a high school social studies teacher for 17 years and has taught in a variety of learning environments, including public and private educational settings, as well as schools in the international community. She currently teaches undergraduate courses in social studies methods at LSU.

David Backer, Ph.D., is the Visiting Assistant Professor of Social Foundations of Education at Cleveland State University. He is an expert on various classroom discussion methods, and he studies whether learning to speak differently can create social change. He has taught in both the United States and South America.

Ronald A. Beghetto, Ph.D., is an international expert on creativity in educational settings. He serves as Associate Professor of Educational Psychology in the Neag School of Education at the University of Connecticut. Prior to joining the faculty at UConn, Dr. Beghetto served as the College of Education's Associate Dean for Academic Affairs and Associate Professor of Education Studies at the University of Oregon. His research focuses on infusing creativity in teaching and learning, and he has extensive experience providing professional development to teachers and instructional leaders in an effort to help them develop new and transformative possibilities for classroom teaching, learning, and assessment. He has published numerous books, scholarly articles, and book chapters on creativity and education. Dr. Beghetto is the editor in chief for the *Journal of Creative Behavior* and serves on the editorial board for several creativity and education journals. He is a Fellow of the American Psychological Association and the Society for the Psychology of Aesthetics, Creativity and the Arts (Div. 10, APA). Dr. Beghetto has received numerous awards for excellence in research and teaching. He is the 2015 UConn ALD Faculty Member of the Year and the 2006 Ersted Crystal Apple Award (University of Oregon's highest teaching award for early career faculty). More information about his work can be found on his website, http://www.ronaldbeghetto.com

Shannon Buerk is founder and Chief Executive Officer of Engage Learning, Inc. (Engage). Engage works with educators and communities nationwide to strategically design and implement innovative learning solutions grounded in best practices with a special emphasis on systems thinking and coaching educators through the change process. Shannon has been an educator for more than 20 years starting as a high school teacher, and later serving as a curriculum director, assistant superintendent for curriculum and instruction, associate superintendent for strategic initiatives, community college instructor, graduate assistant, and consultant. Her entire career has been focused on transformation in education including innovative program development for career education, gifted education, special education, and general education. Her research interests include integration and development of career readiness skills with relevant content and effective collaborative learning frameworks for youth and adult learners. Shannon is a regular speaker at national conferences including AASA, ASCD, NSPRA, ISTE, and their regional counterparts on topics related to the transformation of public education and innovative learning platforms.

Eric Calvert, Ed.D., is an associate director at the Center for Talent Development at Northwestern University, where he oversees the Gifted LearningLinks online program, teaches graduate courses in gifted education, and facilitates professional development on gifted education topics for K–12 educators. Prior to coming to Northwestern, he served as Assistant Director for Gifted Education at the Ohio Department of Education and taught in the Learning Design program at Bowling Green State University. He also previously served as Director of Youth Programs at the Gifted Education Resource Institute at Purdue University. He is actively involved in gifted education and educational technology organizations, and currently serves on the governing board of the Ohio Association for Gifted Children.

Alicia Cotabish, Ed.D., is the Gifted Education Program Coordinator at the University of Central Arkansas. Previously, she served as one of two principal investigators of STEM Starters and the program coordinator of the Arkansas Evaluation Initiative in Gifted Education (AEI), both federally-funded Jacob K. Javits projects housed at the University of Arkansas at Little Rock. She is the current president of the Arkansas Association of Gifted Education Administrators and serves on the board of the Council for Exceptional Children–The Association of the Gifted (CEC-TAG). She has authored and coauthored four books and more than 50 journal articles, book chapters, and products focused on K–20 STEM and gifted education, and serves as the Associate Editor of the *Journal of Advanced Academics*. Her recent research has focused on STEM and gifted education, and examining the effects of virtual coaching on the quality of gifted and teacher candidates using Skype and Bluetooth Bug-in-the-Ear (BIE) technology.

Debbie Dailey, Ed.D., is an assistant professor of teaching and learning at the University of Central Arkansas where she is an instructor in the master of arts in teaching program and the gifted and talented education program. Formerly, Debbie was the Associate Director for the Jodie Mahony Center for Gifted Education and Advanced Placement at the University of Arkansas at Little Rock. Debbie also served as the Curriculum Coordinator and Peer Coach of a federally funded program, STEM Starters, which focused on improving science instruction in the elementary grades. Prior to moving to higher education, Debbie was a high school science teacher and gifted education teacher for 20 years.

Tamara Fisher is the K–12 Gifted Education Specialist (both teacher and coordinator) for the Polson School District on the Flathead Indian Reservation in Montana. She has 20 years of experience teaching gifted youth; served for 10 years on the Executive Board of the Montana Association for Gifted and Talented Education, including a term as president; blogged for 6 years about gifted education and gifted students for the national online magazine *Education Week Teacher*; earned a master's degree in gifted education in 2004 (University of Connecticut); and is co-author (together with Karen Isaacson) of *Intelligent Life in the Classroom: Smart Kids and Their Teachers* (winner of the 2007 TAGT Legacy Book Award and a 2008 *Learning Magazine* Teacher's Choice Award). She has presented numerous times on various gifted-related topics for local, county, tribal, state, regional, national, and international audiences, including teachers, parents, students, administrators, pre-service teachers, and the general public. She was selected as the 2001 Polson Teacher of the Year and the 2013 Montana AGATE Educator of the Year. While earning her B.S. in elementary education from Montana State University-Bozeman, where she was an Honors Scholar, Tamara co-created a volunteer mentor program matching college honors students with gifted kids in the local schools. Over 20 years later, the Mentor GATE program is still running today, and some of the recent volunteers have been Tamara's former students! Most recently, Tamara has struck out on her own as a blogger, continuing her Unwrapping the Gifted blog on her own website. Beyond gifted education, Tamara's other interests include hiking, construction, four-wheeling, and photography.

Claire E. Hughes, Ph.D., is an associate professor at the College of Coastal Georgia in an integrated Elementary/Special Education teacher preparation program. She received her doctorate in gifted education and special education from the College of William & Mary, has been a Visiting Fellow at Oxford, and was recently a State of Georgia Teaching Fellow. She is the Past-Chair of the Special Populations Network for the National Association for Gifted Children and the co-editor of *Excellence and Diversity in Gifted Education* (EDGE), a journal for CEC-TAG. Author of two books on high-functioning autism, her research areas include twice-exceptional children, positivistic views of exceptionality, and Response to Intervention. She lives on St. Simons Island in Georgia.

Tracy Ford Inman, Ed.D., has devoted her career to meeting the needs of young people, especially those who are gifted and talented. She has taught on both the high school and collegiate levels, as well as in summer programs for gifted and talented youth. This Who's Who Among American Educators teacher was a Kentucky Teacher of the Year semifinalist in 1992. Dr. Inman now serves as associate director of the Center for Gifted Studies at Western Kentucky University in Bowling Green, KY.

Susan K. Johnsen, Ph.D., is a professor in the Department of Educational Psychology at Baylor University where she directs the Ph.D. program and programs related to gifted and talented education. She is editor-in-chief of *Gifted Child Today* and coauthor of *A Teacher's Guide for Using the Common Core State Standards With Mathematically Gifted and Advanced Learners, Using the Common Core State Standards for Mathematics With Gifted and Advanced Learners, Using the NAGC Pre-K–Grade 12 Gifted Programming Standards, Math Education for Gifted Students,* and more than 250 articles, monographs, technical reports, chapters, and other books related to gifted education. She has written three tests used in identifying gifted students: *Test of Mathematical Abilities for Gifted Students* (TOMAGS), *Test of Nonverbal Intelligence* (TONI-

4), and *Screening Assessment Gifted Students* (SAGES-2). She is a reviewer and auditor of programs in gifted education for the Council for the Accreditation of Educator Preparation, and is past chair of the Knowledge and Skills Subcommittee of the Council for Exceptional Children and past chair of the NAGC Professional Standards Committee. She is past president of The Association for the Gifted (TAG) and past president of the Texas Association for Gifted and Talented (TAGT). She has received awards for her work in the field of education, including NAGC's President's Award, CEC's Leadership Award, TAG's Leadership Award, TAGT's President's Award, TAGT's Advocacy Award, and Baylor University's Investigator Award, Teaching Award, and Contributions to the Academic Community.

Jennifer L. Jolly, Ph.D., is a senior lecturer in gifted education at the University of New South Wales. Her research interests include the history of gifted education and parents of gifted children. Her work has been published in *Gifted Child Quarterly, Journal for the Education for the Gifted, Roeper Review*, and *Gifted Child Today*. Jennifer has written and edited several books, including *A Century of Contributions to Gifted Education: Illuminating Lives* (Routledge) with Ann Robinson. Jennifer and Claire Hughes also guest edited the March/April 2015 special issue of *Teaching Exceptional Children* on gifted educaiton. She also served as editor of *Parenting for High Potential* from 2007–2012. Currently, she serves on the editorial advisory boards of the *Journal for the Education of the Gifted, Journal of Advanced Academics*, and *Gifted Child Today*. Her classroom experience includes 8 years in the U.S. public school system working with both gifted and regular education students.

Michael S. Matthews, Ph.D., is associate professor and Director of the Academically & Intellectually Gifted graduate programs at the University of North Carolina at Charlotte. He is coeditor of the *Journal of Advanced Academics*, and serves on the Board of Directors of the National Association for Gifted Children (NAGC). Dr. Matthews also is incoming Chair of the Special Interest Group—Research on Giftedness, Creativity, and Talent of the American Educational Research Association. His professional interests in advanced academics and gifted education include research methods, policy, science learning, motivation and underachievement, parenting, and issues in the education of gifted and academically advanced learners from diverse backgrounds, specifically those who are English language learners. Dr. Matthews is the author or editor of five books, more than 30 peer reviewed journal articles, and numerous book chapters in gifted education. His work has been recognized with the Early Scholar Award (2010) from NAGC, and the Michael

Pyryt Collaboration Award from the AERA SIG—Research on Giftedness, Creativity, and Talent (2012).

James Moore, Ed.D., is associate professor of social studies education at Cleveland State University with research interests in teaching about the First Amendment, religion, Islam, ethnicity and nationality, global issues, and incorporating the arts into social studies courses. He teaches social studies methods, world geography, and diversity in educational settings. Dr. Moore taught world history and government in the Miami-Dade County Public Schools for 22 years.

Paula Olszewski-Kubilius, Ph.D., is currently the director of the Center for Talent Development at Northwestern University and a professor in the School of Education and Social Policy. Over the past 30 years, she has created programs for all kinds of gifted learners and written extensively on issues of talent development, particularly on programming for underrepresented gifted students and accelerative models of gifted education. Her most recent work is a monograph written with Rena Subotnik and Frank Worrell, "Rethinking Giftedness and Gifted Education: A Proposed Direction Forward Based on Psychological Science," published by the Association for Psychological Science, which received the Award for Excellence in Research in 2013 from the Mensa Education and Research Foundation of Mensa International, Limited. She has served as editor of *Gifted Child Quarterly*, coeditor of the *Journal of Secondary Gifted Education*, and on the editorial review boards *of Gifted and Talented International, Roeper Review,* and *Gifted Child Today*. She currently is on the board of trustees of the Illinois Mathematics and Science Academy and the Illinois Association for the Gifted. She also serves on advisory boards for the Center for Gifted Education at the College of William & Mary and the Robinson Center for Young Scholars at the University of Washington. She is past-president of the National Association for Gifted Children from whom she received the Distinguished Scholar Award in 2009 and the GCQ Paper of the Year Award in 2011.

Scott J. Peters, Ph.D., is an associate professor of educational foundations at the University of Wisconsin–Whitewater where he teaches courses related to measurement and assessment, research methodology, and gifted education. He received his Ph.D. from Purdue University specializing in gifted and talented education with secondary areas in applied research methodology and English education. His research work focuses on educational assessment with regard to policy and practice and identification of student exceptionalities—particularly those from low-income or underrepresented groups, and gifted and talented programming outcomes. He has published in *Teaching for High*

Potential, Gifted Child Quarterly, Journal of Advanced Academics, Gifted and Talented International, Gifted Children, Journal of Career and Technical Education Research, Ed Leadership, Education Week, and *Pedagogies.* He is the past recipient of the Fedlhusen Doctoral Fellowship in Gifted Education, the NAGC Research an Evaluation Network Dissertation Award, the NAGC Doctoral Student of the Year Award, and the UW-Whitewater College of Education Innovation Award and Outstanding Research Award. He has served as the Program Chair of the AERA Research on Giftedness, Creativity, and Talent SIG, on the Board of Directors of the Wisconsin Association for Talented and Gifted, and as the National Association for Gifted Children Research and Evaluation Secretary.

Jeb Puryear is a doctoral candidate in gifted and talented education at the University of North Texas. His practical experiences include 13 years as a secondary chemistry teacher and 5 years as the coordinator of an International Baccalaureate Diploma Program. He is an active member of numerous organizations related to gifted education and educational research. His research interests include systems of beliefs in gifted education, cognitive aspects of creativity, underrepresentation in advanced academic pathways for secondary students, and the practical applications of STEM research to gifted education.

Karen E. Rambo-Hernandez, Ph.D., is an assistant professor of Educational Psychology at West Virginia University in the College of Education and Human Services in the department of Learning Sciences and Human Development. She received her Ph.D. from the University of Connecticut in Educational Psychology in Measurement, Evaluation, and Assessment. Prior to her becoming an academic, she was a classroom teacher in Texas for 10 years, where she worked with mathematically talented students, which still provides much inspiration for her work. In her research, she is interested in assessing student learning and academic growth, especially for gifted students, and the evaluating of the impact of curricular change. Specifically, her substantive research interests include academic acceleration, STEM education—particularly diversity in engineering, mathematics education, gifted education, and assessment. She uses advanced quantitative methods, such as multilevel modeling and structural equation modeling, to assess the impact of curricular changes and track student growth. Her research has been supported by grants from the American Psychological Foundation and the National Science Foundation.

Julia Link Roberts, Ed.D., Mahurin Professor of Gifted Studies at Western Kentucky University (WKU), is Executive Director of the Carol Martin Gatton Academy of Mathematics and Science in Kentucky and The Center for Gifted Studies at WKU. Dr. Roberts is a member of the Executive

Committee of the World Council for Gifted and Talented Children, president of The Association for the Gifted, Co-Chair of Advocacy and Legislation for the National Association for Gifted Children, and the Legislative Chair of the Kentucky Association for Gifted Education.

Joseph Russell is a researcher and doctoral student at the University of North Texas. More importantly, he is a full-time teacher of secondary gifted students in English and the social studies. He holds a bachelor's degree in history and a master's degree in the humanities from the University of Texas at Dallas. In addition to helping improve the quality of social studies education for the gifted, Joseph's other areas of research interest are effective gifted preparation for classroom teachers (because he is one) and the issues of gifted children in rural school systems (because he was one). He lives in McKinney, TX, with his very lovely, very patient wife, Jill, who indulges his obsession with public education as long as he remembers to tell her stories about the all of the crazy stuff his G/T kids do every day.

Gail R. Ryser, Ph.D., is the Director of the Testing, Research-Support, and Evaluation Center (TREC) and a Research Fellow of the Initiative for Interdisciplinary Research Design & Analysis (IIRDA) at Texas State University. In these roles, she provides support to faculty at Texas State who have research questions about a variety of quantitative methodology topics, including those related to survey research, structural equation modeling, and the general linear model. She is the Associate Editor of *Gifted Child Quarterly* and recently coauthored *A Teacher's Guide to Using the Common Core State Standards With Mathematically Gifted and Advanced Learners*. Her research interests include talent development in mathematics and assessment of students with talent.

Laila Y. Sanguras has been an English language arts teacher for 15 years. Her experiences led her to an opportunity to develop and teach blended English I courses for gifted and honors students. She saw great value in the ability to offer different learning environments to meet individual needs and witnessed the power of the online environment in education. From there, she became a teacher in a blended learning community for eighth graders. She personally developed the language arts curriculum and, while working on her Ph.D., is gathering data on the effectiveness of the blended learning environment. As an advocate for all students and quality curriculum, she remains deeply committed to sharing her vision with other educators.

Elizabeth Shaunessy-Dedrick, Ph.D., is an associate professor of gifted education at the University of South Florida where she teaches graduate courses in gifted education. She coauthored a recent text focused on differentiating instruction, *A Teacher's Guide to Using the Common Core State Standards With Gifted and Advanced Learners in the English/Language Arts*. Her other research efforts include the social-emotional needs and development of high school students pursuing Advanced Placement and International Baccalaureate Diploma coursework, preparation of teachers of the gifted, and supporting schools in their efforts to identify and serve gifted students who are English learners and children from low-socioeconomic backgrounds.

Joyce VanTassel-Baska, Ed.D., is the Smith Professor Emerita at The College of William & Mary in Virginia where she developed a graduate program and a research and development center in gifted education. Formerly, she initiated and directed the Center for Talent Development at Northwestern University. She has also served as the state director of gifted programs for Illinois, as a regional director of a gifted service center in the Chicago area, as coordinator of gifted programs for the Toledo, OH, public school system, and as a teacher of gifted high school students in English and Latin. Dr. VanTassel-Baska has published widely including 29 books and more than 550 refereed journal articles, book chapters, and scholarly reports. Her major research interests are on the talent development process and effective curricular interventions with the gifted.

Daniel L. Winkler, Ph.D., is the Visiting Assistant Professor and Coordinator of Gifted and Talented Education at Cleveland State University. There, he teaches and develops online graduate courses in gifted education. His research interests include resistance to acceleration, the relationship between evolutionary psychology and giftedness, and online education.